SLOW TRAVEL

Northumberland

including Newcastle, Hadrian's Wall & the Coast

Local, characterful guides to Britain's special places

Gemma Hall

EDITION 3

Bradt Guides Ltd, UK
The Globe Pequot Press Inc, USA

Third edition published March 2025
First published March 2015
Bradt Travel Guides Ltd
31a High Street, Chesham, Buckinghamshire, HP5 1BW, England
www.bradtguides.com
Print edition published in the USA by The Globe Pequot Press Inc,
PO Box 480, Guilford, Connecticut 06437-0480

Text copyright © Gemma Hall 2025
Maps copyright © Bradt Travel Guides Ltd 2025 includes map data © OpenStreetMap
contributors & contains OS data © Crown copyright and database right 2025
Photographs copyright © Individual photographers, 2025 (see below)
Project Manager: Emma Gibbs
Cover research: Pepi Bluck, Perfect Picture
Picture research: Faeze Shad

ISBN: 9781804692530

British Library Cataloguing in Publication Data
A catalogue record for this book is available from the British Library

Photographs © individual photographers credited beside images & also those from picture
libraries credited as follows: Alamy.com (A); Dreamstime.com (DT); Shutterstock.com (S);
Superstock.com (SS)

Front cover Lindisfarne Castle at dawn (Superstock.com)
Back cover The Cheviot Hills from Lordenshaws hillfort (Dave Head/S)
Title page Hadrian's Wall (Robert Harding Video/S)

Maps David McCutcheon FBCart.S. FRGS

Typeset by Ian Spick, Bradt Guides
Production managed by Gutenberg Press Ltd; printed in Malta
Digital conversion by www.dataworks.co.in

Paper used for this product comes from sustainably managed forests, and recycled and
controlled sources.

AUTHOR

Gemma Hall (⌀ gemmahall.co.uk) is a freelance travel writer from the North East who began her career in journalism writing for BBC magazines, then as deputy editor for the National Trust. She has written widely on the region and is also the author of the Bradt Slow Travel Guide to Durham. Alongside writing, she spent ten years co-ordinating environmental projects abroad with  The Conservation Volunteers (TCV) and, in the North East, for the RSPB. Her hobbies include birdwatching, camping, hiking, cycle touring and photography. She has walked and cycled many long-distance, hill and coastal routes in Northumberland. Gemma is a fellow of the Royal Geographical Society.

AUTHOR'S STORY

I grew up in Newcastle and spent many weekends as a child around Rothbury getting lost on the heather slopes of the Simonside Hills and paddling in burns. The Northumberland coast also figures heavily in my early memories, and when I recall summer days at Newton-by-the-Sea, sailing with Dad and messing about with my siblings on the beach, I am always barefoot, free to explore as far as I dared to venture, and poorly dressed for the weather. This unbound contact with nature must have sparked an appreciation of the outdoors, Northumberland's landscapes — and the importance of good outdoor clothing. I now have a base on the same coastline where my own children spend their holidays knee-high in rock pools, catching toads in the dunes and being dragged to Dunstanburgh Castle on another 'it will be fun!' walk.

I've hiked a number of the long-distance routes in the region including the Hadrian's Wall Path, St Cuthbert's Way and the Northumberland Coast Path, all of which I've summarised within these pages alongside a selection of my favourite short day walks around Northumberland. While out exploring on foot, I met many fascinating Northumbrians with knowledge of music, heritage, wildlife and folklore who influenced the pages of this book. Indeed, much of the first edition of this guide was completed while hiking, camping out or taking off with binoculars for the day. Now with three young children, I'm rather more familiar with steam trains, waterfalls, country shows, ice-cream parlours and family-friendly trails, though I still manage to escape to the hills now and then.

ACKNOWLEDGEMENTS

The team at Bradt did a superb job of pulling this guide together but particular gratitude must be paid to Anna Moores for everything she did behind the scenes to make *Slow Northumberland* publication ready; Emma Gibbs for her diligence, patience and meticulous edits; David McCutcheon for the maps; and Ian Spick for making this book look gorgeous. Also to Hugh Brune for making sure it hits shelves, and of course huge thanks to Claire Strange and Adrian Phillips for commissioning me to write this guide and their commitment to reaching the northern corners of England for the Slow series.

Many people provided insight on Northumberland's heritage and its natural history which I must acknowledge. They include Katrina Porteous, Geoff Heslop, Ian Tait and Martin Kitching, the Newton-by-the-Sea crew, experts at English Heritage, the National Trust, and rangers at Northumberland National Park and the North Pennines National Landscape office.

My thanks also to my family, and friends in the north for their tips, corrections and nuggets of information.

FEEDBACK REQUEST

At Bradt Guides we're aware that guidebooks start to go out of date on the day they're published – and that you, our readers, are out there in the field doing research of your own. You'll find out before us when a fine new family-run hotel opens or a favourite restaurant changes hands and goes downhill. So why not tell us about your experiences? Contact us on ℘ 01753 893444 or ✉ info@bradtguides.com. We will forward emails to the author who may post updates on the Bradt website at ⬧ bradtguides.com/updates. Alternatively, you can add a review of the book to Amazon, or share your adventures with us on Facebook, 𝕏 or Instagram (@BradtGuides).

DEDICATION
For Farne, Cheviot and Harthope
Gemma Hall

SUGGESTED PLACES TO BASE YOURSELF

These places make ideal starting points for exploring localities the Slow way.

EMBLETON page 108
Quiet coastal village set back from the sea; popular with families, with plenty of self-catering options.

ALNWICK page 78
Medieval castle and renowned gardens in a prosperous market town between the coast and national park.

ALNMOUTH page 96
Highly picturesque coastal town nestled behind soft sands and with direct access by train from London, Newcastle and Edinburgh.

BAMBURGH page 125
Popular village on the coast with an arresting castle, superb beaches and good quality B&Bs close to the historic centre.

WOOLER page 190
Market town and popular gateway to the Cheviot Hills.

CHATTON page 174
Countryside setting with excellent B&Bs clustered close to the village centre; a springboard for exploring the national park and coast.

ROTHBURY page 213
Handsome town in the national park and a popular base for trips into the Cheviot Hills and Coquetdale.

N

0   5 miles
0   10 km

NORTH SEA

Northumberland Heritage Coast

Lindisfarne (Holy Island)

Farne Islands

Berwick-upon-Tweed

Seahouses

Bamburgh

Embleton

Craster

CHAPTER 2
page 64

Chatton

Breamish

Wooler

A1

College Valley

Harthope Valley

Breamish Valley

Ingram

Cheviot Hills

Upper Coquetdale

Alwinton

CHAPTER 4
page 184

CHAPTER 3
page 144

SCOTLAND

Till

Tweed

Alnwick

B6341

A697

Alnmouth

Warkworth

A1

Amble

Coquet Island

Rothbury

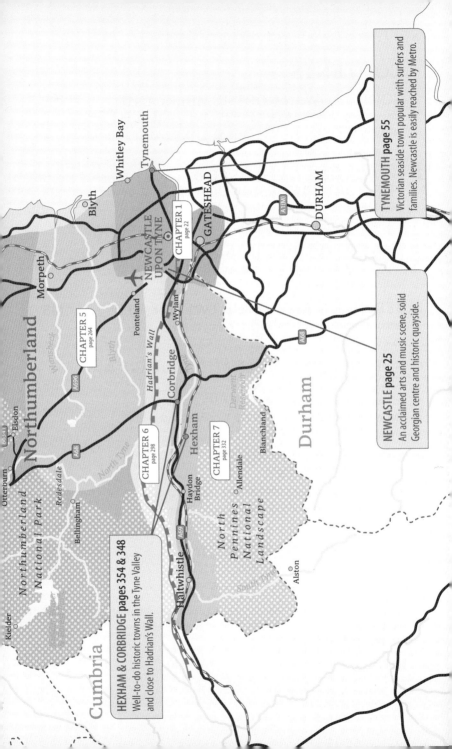

Cumbria

Kielder

Northumberland
National
Park

Otterburn

Elsdon

Bellingham

Redesdale

HEXHAM & CORBRIDGE pages 354 & 348
Well-to-do historic towns in the Tyne Valley and close to Hadrian's Wall.

Haltwhistle

Alston

South Tyne

North
Pennines
National
Landscape

Allendale

Haydon
Bridge

Blanchland

Hexham

CHAPTER 7
page 332

CHAPTER 6
page 298

Corbridge

North Tyne

Hadrian's Wall

Wylam

Ponteland

CHAPTER 5
page 264

Blyth

Wansbeck

Morpeth

Northumberland

Derwent
Reservoir

Durham

Whitley Bay

Tynemouth

Blyth

NEWCASTLE
UPON TYNE

CHAPTER 1
page 22

GATESHEAD

DURHAM

TYNEMOUTH page 55
Victorian seaside town popular with surfers and families. Newcastle is easily reached by Metro.

NEWCASTLE page 25
An acclaimed arts and music scene, solid Georgian centre and historic quayside.

CONTENTS

NORTHUMBERLAND

> We walk all day on long ridges, high enough to give far views of moor
> and valley, and the sense of solitude above the world below… It is the
> land of the far horizons…
> G M Trevelyan *The Middle Marches,* 1914

A glance at a night sky map of England shows that the northeastern shank of the country is sparsely inhabited and supremely bleak in places. From the Cheviot Hills to the Pennine moors; through England's largest forest and across the empty beaches of Ross Back Sands and Druridge Bay; over the humped hills of the Cheviots and the wild Whin Sill escarpment where the Roman emperor Hadrian built his wall – miles and miles of open upland and coastal scenery beneath the most star-filled skies you will see anywhere.

Here you can hunker down in the dunes or walk all day through the heather and see only a handful of people; pitch a tent undisturbed on the fells; experience a private viewing of a hen harrier skydancing; take the plunge butt-naked in a Cheviot waterfall; and get up early and see Hadrian's Wall ribboned across the hills without another rambler in sight.

The poet W H Auden, who loved the North East's isolation, bygone industries and climate, wrote in an article for *House and Garden* in 1947: 'the North of England was the Never-Never Land of my dreams . . . the wildly exciting frontier where the alien south ends and the north, my world, begins.' That sense of escape and wildness is undoubtedly one of the region's greatest draws.

I spent a year researching and writing the first edition of this guide and many months on this update, which involved revisiting my favourite spots and picking through the hills and coastline in search of the hidden and unsung corners of Northumberland. Friends, relatives and heritage experts provided tips and suggestions, but many of the curious and

more unusual places peppered in these pages were gleaned by cycling the back roads, chatting to locals, driving along unclassified lanes, going for a wander and, most of all, having a nosey around.

Some places may be too obscure, unconventional or out of the way to tempt many visitors but, even if you don't seek them out, I hope you enjoy reading about them. Sometimes it's enough just to know that as you read these words Rapper sword dancers are practising in Byker's Cumberland Arms, wild goats with a lineage to the primitive herds of Neolithic Britain are roaming the Cheviot Hills, the Edwardian wind 'clock' at Lindisfarne Castle is telling the weather, a Northumbrian piper is playing a centuries-old ballad in Morpeth Chantry, and the primeval stone faces of the Green Man in Old Bewick's church are gnashing their teeth at worshippers as they have done for hundreds of years.

EMPERORS, KINGS, VIKINGS & INDUSTRIALISTS

A frontier land spanning almost the entire Scottish–English border, Northumberland's history from the end of **Roman occupation** in the late 4th century is one of almost continuous conflict. Invaders from across the North Sea made their move on England following the retreat of the Romans, making Bamburgh their main seat of power in the north of England in AD547. The **Kingdom of Northumbria**, as it eventually became known, extended from the Tweed to the Humber and was one of the most powerful **Anglo-Saxon kingdoms** in England. Ruling the border lands inevitably led to clashes with the Scots and Picts, in addition to all the tussles between other Anglo-Saxon kings, the Viking raids in the 9th century and the Normans a few hundred years later.

Despite all the turmoil through the Dark Ages, this was a rich period of artistic and religious development, particularly around the time Lindisfarne became an important centre for **Christianity** in Britain, with the founding of Lindisfarne Priory in AD634.

◀ **1** The pretty village of Craster – home to the famous smokehouse (page 104).
2 The heather-clad hills above Rothbury offer expansive views of the Simonsides (page 218).

Repeated attacks from the Scots and between rival **Border Reiver clans** raged throughout the late medieval period until more peaceful times prevailed following the union of the Scottish and English crowns in 1603. There's a reason why Northumberland is famous for its castles, shall we say. Indeed, despite being the most sparsely populated county, Northumberland is the most fortified corner of England, with more embattled manors, defensive farms, churches, walls, battlefields and medieval fortresses than anywhere else.

The English Civil Wars aside, from the 17th century relative political stability gave rise to the expansion of **industries** – iron foundries, lead and coal mines, glass works and shipbuilding. With industrial growth came the need to transport large quantities of raw materials (and workers into the expanding villages and towns) which was made possible by the development of rail transport, first with horses pulling wagons. By the early 19th century, steam locomotives operating on the earliest railways in the world were driving the Industrial Revolution across the North East. Much of the region's history of the last few hundred years is a rich tapestry of innovation, mineral extraction, production and community, the evidence of which is visible all around, from coal staithes and Pennine lead-mining villages to the first buildings in the world to be lit by electricity.

HILLS, COAST & WILDLIFE

Northumberland is renowned for its wild coastal and hill scenery. Yes, there are stunning wooded valleys, riverscapes and meadowlands too, but it's the expansive and sparsely populated uplands of the **Cheviots**, **Simonsides** and the **North Pennine moors** that seal Northumberland's reputation as the 'land of the far horizons'.

Wildlife spectacles peak in a few key places. **The Farne Islands** archipelago is an outstanding reserve for breeding seabirds, and the hunting grounds of grey seals, dolphins and the odd whale. Further north, **Lindisfarne** island's saltmarshes and tidal mudflats are a supreme

---

1 The spectacular site of nesting seabirds on the Farne Islands (page 122). **2** Bamburgh Castle under the Milky Way (page 125). **3** Look for fishing osprey at Kielder Water and Forest (page 253). **4** Fly fishing on the River Coquet. **5** Descending from Wyndy Gyle in the Cheviots. **6** Fossil hunting on the Whin Sill at Cullernose Point. ▶

ION MES/S

SEBASTIAN RUTKOWSKI/S

CHENG-WEI/S

GEMMA HALL

DUNCAN ANDISON/S

DR IAN KILLE/NORTHUMBRIAN EARTH

THE SLOW MINDSET

Hilary Bradt, Founder, Bradt Guides

> **We shall not cease from exploration**
> **And the end of all our exploring**
> **Will be to arrive where we started**
> **And know the place for the first time.**
> T S Eliot, 'Little Gidding', *Four Quartets*

This series evolved, slowly, from a Bradt editorial meeting when we started to explore ideas for guides to our favourite part of the world – Great Britain. We wanted to get away from the usual 'top sights' formula and encourage our authors to bring out the nuances and local differences that make up a sense of place – such things as food, building styles, nature, geology, or local people and what makes them tick. Our aim was to create a series that celebrates the present, focusing on sustainable tourism, rather than taking a nostalgic wallow in the past.

So without our realising it at the time, we had defined 'Slow Travel', or at least our concept of it. For the beauty of the Slow movement is that there is no fixed definition; we adapt the philosophy to fit our individual needs and aspirations. Thus Carl Honoré, author of *In Praise of Slow*, writes: 'The Slow Movement is a cultural revolution against the notion that faster is always better. It's not about doing everything at a snail's pace, it's about seeking to do everything at the right speed. Savouring the hours and minutes rather than just counting them. Doing everything as well as possible, instead of as fast as possible. It's about quality over quantity in everything from work to food to parenting.' And travel.

So take time to explore. Don't rush it, get to know an area – and the people who live there – and you'll be as delighted as the authors by what you find.

birdwatching destination in autumn and winter for its internationally important populations of migrant geese, ducks and wading birds.

Northumberland is home to England's largest forest, **Kielder**, where ospreys fish from the trout-filled depths of the forest's central lake. This is also one of the last refuges for red squirrels in the country. But what makes this upland landscape truly special are the extensive peat moors of the surrounding Cheviot range, with their covering of dwarf shrubs and mosses and A-lister birds: black grouse, merlin and hen harrier.

Between the hills and coast, Northumberland is a patchwork of lowland fields supporting sheep and cattle farming, interrupted only by a scattering of old farmhouses, stone villages and meandering **waterways**. The Tweed, Till, Coquet and Tyne rivers with their wooded banks, waterbirds, otters and strong populations of trout and salmon offer much to the walker, nature watcher and angler.

A HISTORY OF NORTHUMBERLAND IN 20 OBJECTS (& PLACES)

Beyond Northumberland's famous castles, Roman ruins and manor houses are many more lesser-known places that add depth to the story of the region: its history, people, industries and changing landscapes. I have cherry-picked 20 architectural jewels, archaeological sites and curious objects that illuminate some aspect of the North East's heritage, from the Bronze Age to recent times.

1 Lordenshaws cup-and-ring marked stones (page 218) One of the largest clusters of Neolithic decorated stones in the country, on a hillside near Rothbury.

2 Yeavering Bell hillfort (page 193) Iron Age ramparts crown many peaks in the Cheviot range, including this hill near Wooler, which is also noted for its wild goats and nearby Anglo-Saxon royal palace at Ad Gefrin.

3 Roman writing tablets (page 317) Some of the most important Roman finds ever discovered, these small scraps of wood scrawled with messages lay intact in the anaerobic soil at Vindolanda Roman Fort for nearly 2,000 years until their discovery in the 1970s.

4 Anglo-Saxon throne (page 126) Bamburgh's magnificent fortress was once the seat of King Oswald, who ruled the Kingdom of Northumbria from AD634 and fostered the development of Christianity in northern England. A section of a stone throne dating to this period is housed in the castle's Archaeology Room.

5 Lindisfarne Gospels (page 139) Representing the 'Golden Age of Northumbria' is this decorated manuscript and one of the most treasured Anglo-Saxon objects in Britain, produced during a period of intense cultural, artistic and religious development in the 7th and 8th centuries. A facsimile is on display at Lindisfarne Priory's Museum.

6 Viking Domesday stone (page 136) The Danish raids along the east coast of England in the 8th and 9th centuries had a lasting impact on the North. Lindisfarne Priory's museum houses a lively stone depiction of the marauding Danes invading Lindisfarne in AD793.

7 Norham Castle (page 161) Repeated attacks by the Danes and Scots prompted the Normans to shore up their northern strongholds, including this crumbling fortress on the Scottish border.

8 Aydon Castle (page 353) Not a true castle but a fortified manor – a Northumbrian speciality – near Corbridge, embattled during a period of almost continuous warfare in the late medieval period.

9 Twizel Bridge (page 164) In the days leading to the momentous Battle of Flodden in 1513, tens of thousands of Scottish and English soldiers marched to war across this then newly constructed bridge over the River Till.

10 Black Middens bastle (page 245) Wealthy landowners took refuge in fortified 'pele' towers during raids by Border Reivers; those further down the social ladder built defensive farmhouses known as 'bastles', a number of which remain in remote areas, including this one near Greenhaugh.

11 Dukesfield Arches (page 380) Two huge stone arches by the banks of Devil's Water in Hexhamshire once connected to a lead-smelting mill, and today stand as a monument to an industry that defined the North Pennines from the mid-1700s until the early 1900s.

12 Lion Bridge (page 82) The Dukes of Northumberland have historically exerted huge influence over the region since Norman times. This striking medieval crossing, which bears the family's emblem, offers an outstanding view of the current 12th Duke's stonking fortress at Alnwick.

13 Wylam Waggonway (page 338) Coal was transported on wooden tracks powered by horses along this historic tramway before metal rails and early steam engines were trialled here. Now a dual-use path tracing the River Tyne, the old wagonway makes for a rewarding cycle ride from Newcastle passing a quaint 19th-century cottage, the childhood home of the railway pioneer George Stephenson.

14 Coble boats (page 90) Clinker-built wooden boats peculiar to the North East are still worked out of Amble, Boulmer, Newbiggin and Craster – villages with a long tradition of fishing.

15 The Lit & Phil (page 37) Newcastle's historic 1825 purpose-built public library was a meeting place for some of the engineering giants of the Victorian era, including Joseph Swan who demonstrated his electric lightbulb here in 1881, making this the first public building in the world to be lit by electricity.

16 Haltwhistle station (page 334) An architectural highlight on the historic Newcastle–Carlisle line, Haltwhistle is one of the most unchanged Victorian stations anywhere and a reminder of the great railway heritage of the North East.

17 Spanish City (page 60) Whitley Bay's landmark 1920s pleasure hall evokes the heyday of Edwardian trips to the seaside by rail.

18 Pitmen Painters (page 74) Coal mines featured throughout the North East at the height of mining in the mid-19th century. At Ashington, a group of miners turned to art in their free time, capturing their lives on canvas to great acclaim. A permanent exhibition of their works hangs at Woodhorn Museum on the site of the old mine.

19 Featherstone POW Camp (page 372) A complex of World War II buildings by the River South Tyne once housed German prisoners of war who ran a theatre, orchestra and newspaper from this isolated spot.

20 *Angel of the North* prototype (page 49) The 1990s marked a pivotal moment for the North East as the region turned to the arts and culture to redefine its economy in the post-industrial era. Antony Gormley's *Angel of the North* was the most high-profile arts project of its time and offered symbolic hope to a region looking to reinvent itself. Gateshead's Victorian Shipley Art Gallery houses Gormley's original *Angel* prototype a mile away from the iconic sculpture (page 49) above the A1.

SAVOURING THE TASTES OF NORTHUMBERLAND

In updating this guide I was struck by the proliferation of restaurants, pubs, delis, farm shops and roadside food vans genuinely committed to sourcing food from the bounty on their doorstep, and foraging and growing ingredients to bring authentic local tastes to dishes. Pubs serving regional ales are now too numerous to list and micro-breweries with tap rooms are popping up in the most unexpected corners of the countryside and city.

Northumberland boasts many of the best salmon and trout rivers in England, extensive game moors and working fishing communities, so it makes sense. Famous names include Craster Kippers, Lindisfarne Oysters, Pumphrey's and Pilgrim's coffees, Chain Bridge Honey, Doddington Dairy, the Northumberland Cheese Company, and Allendale and Cheviot breweries. Find their products for sale in farmers' markets, farm shops and some of the superb independent food stores around the region, including the Corbridge Larder, Wooler's Good Life Shop, Fenwick's Food Hall in Newcastle, The Morpeth Larder, Embleton's Village Farm Shop and Tully's of Rothbury. And that's before I mention all the local butchers, bakeries, fishmongers and cheese shops on high streets and the famous smokeries at Craster and Seahouses.

Dishes unique to the North East include **Pan Haggerty** (a hearty potato and onion side dish) and **Singin' Hinny** (a very filling kind of scone that 'sings' as it hits the bubbling butter on a griddle pan). Also look out for sandwiches made with **stottie bread** (flat, spongy and slightly sweet), best filled with **pease pudding** (spiced split yellow peas blended into a spread).

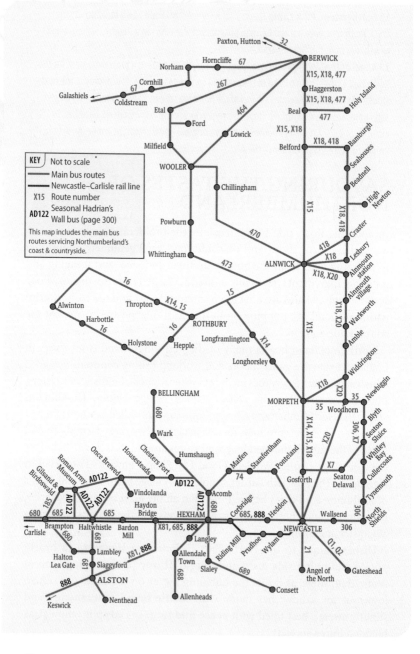

KEY Not to scale

― Main bus routes
━ Newcastle–Carlisle rail line
X15 Route number
AD122 Seasonal Hadrian's Wall bus (page 300)

This map includes the main bus routes servicing Northumberland's coast & countryside.

HOW THIS BOOK IS ARRANGED

PUBLIC TRANSPORT

I've provided an overview of **public transport** options at the beginning of each chapter. Also refer to the public transport map on page 18.

MAPS

The **numbered points** on the map at the beginning of each chapter correspond to the numbered headings in the text. They are mostly larger settlements with attractions and smaller places nearby listed under their own (unnumbered) headings.

A ❋ symbol on these maps indicates a walk in that area. I've also included sketch maps for some routes, but they are not a substitute for an Ordnance Survey map.

SPECIAL STAYS

The places to stay included within this guide are a personal selection of independent bed and breakfasts, glamping huts, self-catering cottages and one or two very special hotels – places that struck me for their location, green ethos, commitment to local food or character, or a mixture of all four. While only the truly outstanding places I visited receive a detailed review, I've peppered the text with additional accommodation options worth considering.

The hotels, bed and breakfasts and hostels are indicated by the symbol 🛖 under the heading for the nearest town or village in which they are located; self-catering options by 🏠.

ACCESSIBILITY

Where you see a ♿ symbol, the place listed has step-free access, an entrance wide enough for a wheelchair and, if it's a place to eat, a disabled toilet. Where there is no loo but the building is step-free, or there is partial access to a public building, I've indicated that with a ♿ symbol.

IMPARTIALITY

Reviews in this guide are totally independent. The attractions, museums, restaurants and tour companies were selected on the quality of their services, and no business paid to receive a mention in this guide.

DOGS

Dogs are welcome at attractions and places to eat and drink where you see a 🐾 symbol.

OPENING TIMES

Under listings, I've detailed contact information where it seemed useful and included non-standard opening times. 'Daily' means Monday to Sunday from around 09.00/10.00 to 16.00/17.00. Opening times change from year to year so it's always best to call and check.

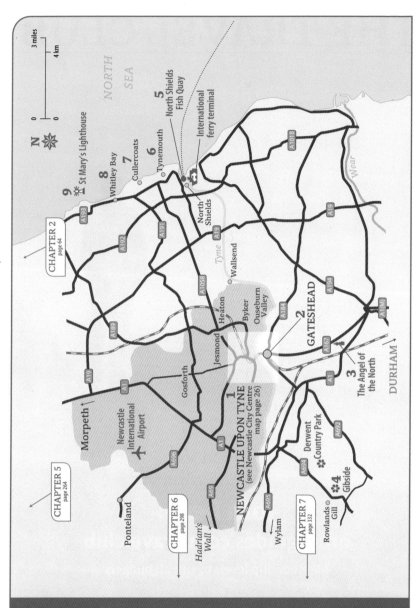

NEWCASTLE, GATESHEAD & THE
NORTH TYNESIDE COAST

NORTH SEA

3 miles
4 km

N

9 St Mary's Lighthouse
8 Whitley Bay
7 Cullercoats
6 Tynemouth
5 North Shields
   Fish Quay
4 International
   ferry terminal

CHAPTER 2
page 64

A193

A192

A191

A1058

North
Shields

A19

Wallsend

Tyne

Heaton
Byker
Ouseburn
Valley

Jesmond

A189

A19

A1

Gosforth

Morpeth

Newcastle
International
Airport

A696

A69

A1

Ponteland

CHAPTER 5
page 264

CHAPTER 6
page 398

Hadrian's
Wall

A695

Wylam

CHAPTER 7
page 332

Rowlands
Gill

A694

Gibside

Derwent
Country Park

A692

A1

3 The Angel of
   the North

DURHAM

A167

GATESHEAD

2

A184

A194

A1(M)

A19

A1018

Wear

NEWCASTLE UPON TYNE
(see Newcastle City Centre
map page 26)

1

22

1
NEWCASTLE, GATESHEAD & THE NORTH TYNESIDE COAST

Before the 1990s and *The Angel of the North,* Tyneside was famed for coal, shipbuilding, football, Bigg Market bar crawls and scantily dressed revellers. As the economy pivoted at the turn of the century away from heavy industry, the region looked more to the arts and architecture to reinvent itself. High-profile music and arts venues now front **Gateshead's waterfront** (page 48) and Newcastle's edgy hub of young artists, writers and musicians at the **Ouseburn** (page 41) has become a cultural force in the city, with more former industrial spaces being converted into galleries, studios and imaginative restaurants than ever. Football remains sacred, however, and drinkers have not taken to wearing coats in winter. The last two things are unlikely to change.

Newcastle's famous Georgian avenues define the city architecturally, with some of the finest Neoclassical buildings in England radiating from its centre at **Grey's Monument** (page 25). On the **quayside** (page 29), 300-year-old merchant houses sit alongside modern, glass-clad architecture, creating a striking waterfront where people wander and *consume* the city. Throngs of Tynesiders do just that on their Sunday morning cycle rides tracing the River Tyne, and on outings to the famous **Quayside Market** (page 31) and **Baltic Centre for Contemporary Art** (page 48). Here, crowds gather around the **Millennium Bridge** when the crossing tilts open, for the sheer spectacle of it. This is a playful city on show and wanting to be seen.

In the 19th century, seaside resorts developed around the mouth of the Tyne at places like **Cullercoats** (page 59) and **Tynemouth** (page 55), providing a recreational space for Tynesiders to escape the city smoke. It's all surfboards, monkfish-tail wraps and 'artisan' this and that these days, but locals and visitors still mainly come to enjoy simple pleasures:

a walk along the promenade, fish and chips, an ice cream and a dip in the sea. **Whitley Bay's** (page 60) restored promenade, Victorian terraces and Edwardian centrepiece building, Spanish City, have transformed the seafront into an exciting recreational space once more.

GETTING AROUND

The **Metro** system links Newcastle, Gateshead, Sunderland, the south and north Tyneside coasts (with stations at Tynemouth and Cullercoats), **Central Station, Newcastle International Airport** (25 minutes from Newcastle city centre) and North Shields international **ferry** terminal (Percy Main station is a 20-minute walk from the port). In Newcastle, the most useful stop for the city centre is **Monument**, with **Haymarket** and Central Station (for direct trains to London and Edinburgh) close by.

A good **bus** network connects Newcastle and Gateshead with the coast and Northumberland. Eldon Square (buses to *The Angel of the North* for example) and Haymarket bus stations are the main hubs. If travelling to the ferry terminal at North Shields, DFDS buses stop opposite Central Station on Bewick Street and take around half an hour.

QuayCity Q3 (⊘ gonortheast.co.uk) buses connect north Newcastle (Gosforth and Jesmond) with the city centre, the quayside and the Ouseburn. A useful stop by the Theatre Royal in the Monument area makes for a swift downhill journey to the quayside.

A hop-on, hop-off **sightseeing bus**, Toon Tour (⊘ gonortheast.co.uk ⊙ late May–early Sep daily; mid-Sep–early Oct w/ends), departs from Central Station every half hour from 10.00–17.00 and stops at various locations in the city centre and along the quayside.

A recommended, cheap **taxi** company in Newcastle is Blueline Taxis (⊘ 0191 262 6666).

WALKING & CYCLING

Newcastle's centre is compact and a number of principal streets are closed to motor traffic so it is best explored on foot. **Walking tours** (book online at ⊘ newcastlegateshead.com or just show up ⊙ May–Oct 10.30 daily) led by knowledgeable volunteer guides depart from outside the music shop in the Central Arcade (near Monument) and last 1½ hours.

Along Newcastle and Gateshead's quaysides (and at the coast) are paved promenades, perfect for strollers – and cyclists – who make good use of the **Hadrian's Wall Path** & **Hadrian's Cycleway/Coast to Coast** route, which connects with Tynemouth on an almost completely car-free dedicated cycle lane (page 300). The Cycle Hub, a handy bike shop, **hire** and café (see below) sits right on this cycle path on Newcastle's quayside. Continuing upriver on Hadrian's Cycleway from Newcastle's quayside to Wylam, the landscape becomes increasingly green and makes for a lovely afternoon's ride (page 345) that ends in a great pub by the train station (from where you can return by train with your bike).

 CYCLE HIRE & REPAIRS

The Cycle Hub Quayside, Newcastle (located on Hadrian's Cycleway/Coast to Coast) ✆ 0191 276 7250 ○ daily ♿ bicycle workshop including café. Bike hire operated by Cycle Centre Express ✆ 0191 524 1781 (also with a shop on Shields Rd, Byker).
Edinburgh Bicycle Cooperative 5–7 Union Rd (top of Shields Rd), Byker ✆ 0191 265 8619 ○ daily.
Start Cycles 33–35 Market St, Newcastle ✆ 0191 917 3803 ○ daily. Large shop and repairs.

1 NEWCASTLE UPON TYNE

For numbered points within Newcastle, see map, page 26.

1 GRAINGER TOWN

> **As for the curve of Grey Street, I shall never forget seeing it to perfection, traffic-less on a misty Sunday morning. Not even Regent Street, even old Regent Street London, can compare with that descending subtle curve.**
> Poet and architectural historian John Betjeman speaking at the Literary and Philosophical Society in Newcastle, 1948

Grey's Monument marks the retail centre of Newcastle – and the heart of the city's celebrated Grainger Town where there are more Georgian buildings than anywhere outside London and Bath. The most distinguished 400yds of beautifully dressed sandstone in Newcastle is found on **Grey Street** – a wide Neoclassical boulevard that falls steeply away from Lord Grey's fluted column towards the River Tyne.

Clustered around Grey's Monument (which you can climb, incidentally, on the first Saturday of the month ○ Apr–Sep 10.00–

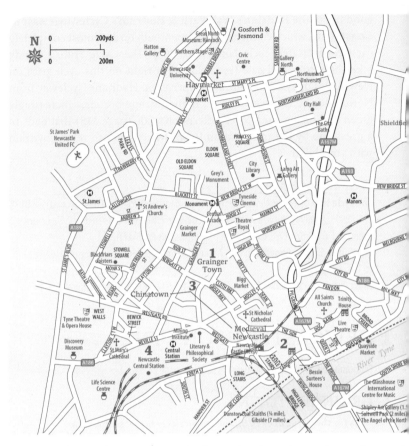

16.00; book in advance ⌀ newcastlegateshead.com) are the main shopping centres and streets. A short stroll from Monument is the **Theatre Royal** (Grey St ⌀ 0191 232 7010 ♿), a Classical jewel on Grey Street and one of only nine Grade I listed theatres in the country. The regional home of the Royal Shakespeare Company, the theatre also puts on a full programme of family shows, ballet, opera and comedy throughout the year.

Also close by is the wonderfully restored Art-Deco **Tyneside Cinema** (Pilgrim St ⌀ 0191 227 5500 ♿) still with its original mosaic floor. The cinema began life as a news theatre in 1937 and it's now hugely popular with art-house cinema buffs and a youthful crowd packing out the downstairs bar.

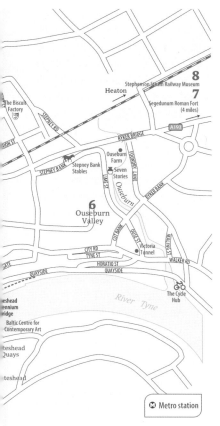

With an interior dating to the early 1900s, the **Central Arcade** (50yds downhill from Monument on the right-hand side) is an exquisite Edwardian shopping centre decorated with floor-to-ceiling period tiles and mosaics – an absolute must-see while touring Newcastle. Folk musicians often play outside J G Windows; the largest music shop in the North East, it's been in business since 1908 and is the start point for walking tours (page 24).

Grainger Market (page 28) is somewhat hidden but well known in the city and considered one of the country's standout Victorian covered markets. Once specialising in cut-price clothes, secondhand records, groceries and greasy spoon cafés, many of today's visitors shop for regional delicacies from the excellent **Matthew's Cheese Shop**, **Pumphrey's Coffee**, a Newcastle institution since 1750, and excellent **fishmongers** showcasing today's catch, much of it landed a few miles away at the mouth of the Tyne. Those with a keen eye for vintage shopfronts will appreciate an original **Marks & Spencer's Penny Bazaar** with its unchanged 1895 decorative glass windows, the 19th-century signage on the **Northern Optical Co.** (an optician still in business) and the **Weigh House** – a wonderful relic from the days when retailers weighed goods (now, for 50p, an assistant records the weight of people).

The Laing Art Gallery (New Bridge St ☏ 0191 278 1611 ☉ Mon–Sat; free admission; café ♿), a short walk from Monument, houses a good number of pre-Raphaelite and Impressionist paintings, as well as a couple of excellent exhibitions showcasing works by 20th-century coastal artists' colonies (Newlyn and Cullercoats) and 19th-century regional artists, many depicting local scenes. *The Women* by John Charlton is one of the most stirring. The large, dark canvas tells the story of a famous ship rescue near Whitley Bay in 1861 (page 59). Also here are Thomas Bewick's most famous natural history books, opened to reveal his detailed woodblock prints of birds, animals and landscapes; and an excellent gallery devoted to photographer Chris Killip, who documented working-class lives on Tyneside in the 1970s and 80s.

¶¶ FOOD & DRINK

There's no shortage of cafés and bars in the Monument area. The standout traditional pub selling craft beers is **Lady Greys** (20 Shakespeare St), but for the ultimate Geordie experience, take yourself (but not your southern accent) to the **Black Garter** (25 Clayton St) and order a Newcastle Brown Ale. It is, shall we say, a lively venue on a Friday night.

Blakes 53 Grey St ✐ 0191 261 5463 ☉ from 07.00 daily ⅋. When I was a teenager in the 1990s, Blakes was dead posh and you'd have to queue for ages for a table on Saturday lunchtimes. Today they serve delightfully unstuffy, inexpensive cooked breakfasts, sandwiches and jacket potatoes for lunch from a menu that actually hasn't changed that much in the last 30 years.

Dabbawal 69–75 High Bridge ✐ 0191 232 5133 ☉ 12.00–14.30 Mon–Fri ⅋. 'In Mumbai, the dabbawala is more than a simple delivery man. Inside his tiffin boxes he carries authentic dishes made from recipes stretching back generations.' Here at this vibrant, well-regarded Indian restaurant a short walk from Monument, the same traditional Indian street-food recipes (samosas, wraps, butter chicken, vegetable curry, lamb kebab) are plated for a lunchtime crowd who are happy to pay a little extra for superb food. Sister restaurant to the branch in Jesmond (page 40).

Grainger Market Grainger St ✐ 0191 211 5541 ☉ Mon–Sat. For great street food, head to this Victorian market hall (page 27). Authentic Chinese dumplings, quality sausage rolls from Geordie Bangers, serrano ham carved off the bone at the Spanish deli, vegan Indian street food, and superb cakes and traybakes from Pet Lamb Patisserie. Also here is the Firebrick Brewery taproom, with beers produced by the banks of the Tyne. Among all the new, somewhat upmarket places, you can still buy beans on toast at the good value café under the glass-roofed atrium. **Pumphrey's Coffee** has been trading in the Grainger Market since 1750 and every local knows this is the place to buy bagged coffee beans or a superb take-away coffee.

Magic Hat 3–5 Higham House, Higham Pl ☉ Thu–Sun ⅋. Tucked away round the back of the Laing Art Gallery. Long communal tables, green foliage, industrial lighting, plywood cladding and an ethical outlook with all food and drinks produced from ingredients destined for landfill. But don't let that put you off – this is a fab spot for brunch/lunch with small, imaginative dishes. On the menu last time I visited were mac and cheese with roast leeks and green beans; a steak sandwich; and an aubergine, tomato and mushroom dish with quinoa. Even the drinks (no cans or bottles) are homemade with surplus produce: pineapple and fennel fizz for example. Excellent coffees, too.

Panis 61–65 High Bridge ✐ 0191 232 4366 ☉ Mon–Sat ⚹. Guests for lunch or evening meals are greeted with a friendly 'buongiorno' at this great, long-established Italian close to Monument. No pizzas; just authentic chicken, fish, filled pasta, Sardinian tapas and favourites like lasagne – all homemade.

2 HISTORIC QUAYSIDE: THE CLOSE, SANDGATE & SIDE

There is something surprising in the sight of the Tyne, with its busy traffic, its fleet of keels and steam-tugs, coal-ships, and merchant vessels from the north of Europe . . . The banks are for the most part high and steep, rough and bare, or patched with ragged grass; pantiled cottages dot the slopes, or crowd the levels and hollows, and here and there dormer windows appear that look as if imported ready made from Holland.

Victorian view of the quayside from Walter White's *Northumberland, and the Border*, 1859

A wander along Newcastle's medieval roads and alleys reveals the city of past centuries when wealthy merchants lived by the Tyne and the riverside was a wall of masts and rigging.

Below the towering legs of the High Level Bridge are some of the oldest buildings on Tyneside, dating from the 16th to 18th centuries when the city was rapidly expanding and this was the commercial centre. The architecture of **Sandgate** and the **Close** evokes days when sailing ships and wherries lined the quayside, merchants occupied the now crooked timber and brick houses set back from the river, and boatmen called 'keelmen' transported coal along the Tyne to waiting ships. (Incidentally, the catchy 18th-century Tyneside folk song, *The Keel Row*, recalls the job of keelmen in verse and remains a popular North East tune.) The timber-framed **Cooperage** (where barrels were made), upriver from the Swing Bridge, is one of the oldest and dates to the mid 16th century; but the most striking is the Tudor-looking building on the corner of the Side, **Bessie Surtees's House** (✐ 0191 403 1635 ☉ Heritage Open Days in September and special events at other times).

KANCHANAWAT SOMPOMTIP/S

HAZEL PLATER/S

MARC VENEMA/S

GRAEME PEACOCK

Now housing the regional offices of Historic England, the impressive Jacobean interior with extensive wood panelling and ornate plasterwork is well worth seeing if you get the chance at an open day.

A stroll along the **quayside** from the Swing Bridge to the Millennium Bridge is recommended for the views of the city's **bridges** and Gateshead's acclaimed music centre and art gallery on the banks of the Tyne opposite. On Sundays, the quay walls are thronged with locals and visitors, many of whom come for the historic **Quayside Market**, a tradition that began in 1736. Pick up original crafts, secondhand books, jewellery, handmade beauty products, chocolates and locally produced food, from cupcakes to posh hot dogs.

Set back from the quayside, occupying a former bonded warehouse, is the well-regarded **Live Theatre** (✆ 0191 232 1232; plays, music, comedy & workshops; café & bar ♿).

Hidden quayside: back streets & alleys

Narrow passageways and streets called 'chares' (possible Anglo-Saxon origins from 'cerre' meaning a bend or turning) connect the waterfront with the medieval markets near the cathedral and castle. They are full of surprises: the sudden appearance of the medieval town walls, a concealed Georgian church, and an archway through the castle wall. **Hanover Street** – a long lane linking the Close with Forth Street – still has its smooth granite tracks on the uphill side of the road from the days when horses pulled carts around these parts.

Dog Leap Steps off the Side, **Long Stairs** next to the Cooperage and **Castle Steps** opposite the Swing Bridge are still used by pedestrians. The latter passageway climbs steeply to the Castle Keep in 107 steps, passing the crumbling masonry of the castle, a well and continuing under an archway through the old castle wall. Once there were small shops selling old clothes and clogs here.

At the top of **Broad Chare**, beyond the Live Theatre (see above), a medieval passageway leads to one of the most fascinating historic buildings on the quayside: **Trinity House** (✆ 0191 232 8226; ☉ by appointment). It was originally a charitable guild formed by seafarers

◀ NEWCASTLE: **1** The city skyline at night. **2** The entranceway to the Edwardian Central Arcade. **3** The sumptuous interior of the Tyne Theatre & Opera House. **4** Pumphrey's coffee roasters have been operating out of the historic Grainger Market since 1750.

BRIDGES OVER THE TYNE

Seven bridges span Newcastle and Gateshead's quaysides. **Gateshead Millennium Bridge** (2001) connects the Baltic Arts Centre to Newcastle's quayside and was the first bridge in the world to tilt, allowing boats to pass underneath. See the spectacle every day at noon between May and early September.

Defining Newcastle more than any other piece of architecture is the green **Tyne Bridge** (1928). At the time of opening, it was the largest single-span crossing in Britain, designed by architects in Middlesbrough (the same company that built the Sydney Harbour Bridge that opened a few years later but was, incidentally, designed prior to the Tyne Bridge).

Joining the quayside promenades either side of the Tyne is the **Swing Bridge** (1876) – an eye-catching red and white wrought-iron bridge that pivots on a central point to allow ships to pass. It's driven by hydraulic engines and was engineered by Victorian industrialist William Armstrong.

Once known as 'Lang Legs', the **High Level Bridge** (1849), Robert Stephenson's combined road and rail crossing, marches across the Tyne at 120ft above the water. Its cream, wrought-iron frame is best appreciated from the pedestrian walkways, which are encased by arches across its entire 450yd length.

Next upriver is the **Queen Elizabeth II Metro Bridge** (1981), painted brilliant blue, then the **King Edward VII Rail Bridge** (1906) and finally, concrete **Redheugh Bridge** (1983).

to support mariners in the city. Highlights inside include a wooden chapel dating to 1505 and an 18th-century Banqueting Hall. On the hill above Broad Chare, reached by climbing Dog Bank, is the unusual oval-shaped **All Saints Church** (page 35) dating to the late 18th century. Its fine interior with curved pews and decorative ceiling is really worth seeing (only really open to Sunday worshippers though).

¶¶ FOOD & DRINK

There's a cluster of top-end restaurants rubbing shoulders with boozy bars right along the quayside. The city's Michelin-starred restaurants are both headed by the same chef, Kenny Atkinson. **Solstice** (5–7 Side ✆ 0191 222 1722 ◷ lunch Fri & Sat; dinner Wed–Sat), with only six tables, has a curated lunch and dinner tasting menu of up to 18 exquisite courses, for which you should expect to pay a few hundred pounds per head. Kenny's flagship restaurant is round the corner: **House of Tides** (28–30 The Close ✆ 0191 230 3720 ◷ lunch Thu–Sun & dinner Wed–Sat ♿) occupies an old merchant's building on the quayside and has been plating French classics for years. It offers exceptional dining with a fairly straightforward menu of roast meats and fish dishes.

In a similar league is **21** (see below) led by another of Newcastle's famous chefs, Terry Laybourne; **Dobson & Purnell** (see below) and **Six** (page 52), over the river at the Baltic Centre for Contemporary Art.

The Bridge Tavern 7 Akenside Hill ✐ 0191 261 9966 ☺ noon–late daily ♿. Microbrewery and restaurant with sought-after roof-top tables directly under the Tyne Bridge attracting a lively crowd. The food (modern British with a local twist) is seasonal, with a good mix of meat and fish options including haddock and chips, steak, and lamb curry. Good Sunday roasts, too. Bar snacks are rather special and there are some great sharing platters including a bountiful mound of langoustines and mixed meat and fish plates. Food stops at 18.00 on weekend evenings (20.00 Mon–Thu) and the Bridge takes to the night with an excellent choice of drinks – it is known for its ten cask handpulls – all local lines.

The Broad Chare 25 Broad Chare ✐ 0191 211 2144 ☺ lunch daily & dinner Mon–Sat ♿. Michelin-rated restaurant in an old warehouse, The Broad Chare delivers both as a good craft pub (downstairs) and as a restaurant (upstairs). Expect British comfort food alongside an interesting range of smaller dishes (crispy blood pudding, haggis on toast, crispy pig's ears) and prices a bit above average for the area.

Dobson & Purnell 21 Queen St ✐ 0191 221 0904 ☺ lunch Thu–Sun & dinner Wed–Sun. Elegant period building set back from the riverside, right under the Tyne Bridge. Inside, there are plenty of nods to the building's 19th-century heritage with exposed brick walls and metro tiling, but the furnishings are modern and chic. The British/continental kitchen delivers on its promise as a casual, upmarket restaurant. Roast wood pigeon, trout, fish stew, steak and chips, barbequed monkfish tail – just a selection from the small, considered menu, which changes monthly to accommodate seasonal shifts in the availability of fish and vegetables. The set menu is great value at around £30 for three courses. Also serves Sunday roasts.

21 Trinity Gardens ✐ 0191 222 0755 ☺ lunch & dinner Tue–Sat & afternoons Sun ♿. Over several decades, this contemporary restaurant has earned a reputation as one of the premier places to dine in Newcastle. The décor – clean lines and all red and black – is reminiscent of a top-end Asian restaurant but the food is a delectable array of classic French and British dishes: roast Kielder deer, a monkfish masala, steak frites, Sunday roasts. Attentive service, as you'd expect. Prices are not obscene but obviously above average. Look out for special set menus.

Crown Posada 31 The Side ✐ 0191 232 1269 ☺ daily. A wonderful step-back-in-time real ale pub with bags of character: wood-panelled interior, stained glass and gramophone tunes. What you might call an old-man's pub.

The Cycle Hub Quayside (near the Ouseburn) ✐ 0191 276 7250 ☺ daily ♿ 🐾. Modern café and bicycle shop/workshop/hire welcoming anyone out for a wander or cycle along the

Tyne. Simple food, nothing special, served until 15.00 (bacon butties, bagels, sandwiches, traybakes and cakes). Great river views, outdoor seating, local beers, a relaxed atmosphere.

PureKneed Bakery & Café 38 Dean St ℘ 0191 230 5857 ☉ 10.00–14.00 Tue–Sat 🐾. Incredible cakes, pastries and filling sandwiches made with homemade sourdough bread in this cute artisan café on the way down to the waterfront. Sister café to the one in Whitley Bay.

Simla 39 Side ℘ 07917 391319 ☉ Tue–Sun ♿. Indian restaurant and one of the best curry houses in Newcastle.

3 MEDIEVAL NEWCASTLE & CHINATOWN

In four things Newcastle excels: walls, gates, towers, and turrets.
William Gray, historian, 1649

Within bowshot of the Castle Keep is Newcastle's medieval quarter, characterised by winding streets and alleys connecting the markets around the cathedral to the quayside. Cloth Market, Flesh Market, Groat Market and the Bigg Market (bigg was a type of barley) evoke a sense of what this area must have once looked (and smelled) like.

Newcastle gets its name from a 'new' timber castle built in 1080 by the son of William the Conqueror on the site of the old Roman fort, Pons Aelius. The wooden fortress was replaced a century later in stone and it is this later Norman building (well, its keep, mid 13th-century gateway and barbican at least) that still stand to this day.

"Newcastle was enclosed by a stonking town wall that formed a protective two-mile loop around its perimeter."

Newcastle Castle (formally the 'Castle Keep' in case you're asking a local for directions; Castle Garth & St Nicholas's St ℘ 0191 230 6300 ☉ daily), the oldest building in Newcastle and one of the most intact 12th-century keeps in the country, is a labyrinth of stone staircases that lead into many chambers including the Great Hall and up to the roof where you gain a stupendous view of Newcastle's bridges. A small museum houses curious objects discovered during excavations including cannonballs and other weaponry. The castle's barbican, the **Black Gate** (♿) served as the fortified entranceway into the castle. Its stones have been tampered with over the centuries and you'll notice that the upper parts look younger (well, Victorian at least) than the worn sandstones at the bottom, but it is still a formidable structure in its own right.

FOUR CHURCHES

All Saints Church (Pilgrim St – best reached by climbing the King St stairs from the end of Queen St; ☉ 10.30 & 17.00 for Sunday worship) is one of Newcastle's great Georgian treasures. A tremendously tall steeple and Grecian-styled portico hide its unusual elliptical body, a characteristic shared by just a handful of other churches in England.

Compared with many of England's other cathedrals, **St Nicholas's** (St Nicholas's St ☎ 0191 232 1939 ☉ daily ♿) is neither stupendously impressive nor particularly elegant (with the exception of the steeple) mainly because it originated as a 15th-century parish church. However, it bears some curious features, including a small square of medieval coloured glass depicting the Virgin Mary breastfeeding Jesus (fittingly above a children's play area) and a lantern tower, the first of its kind in Britain, which was lit as a navigational aid for mariners.

The other cathedral in Newcastle is the Catholic **Cathedral Church of St Mary** (Clayton St West ☎ 0191 232 6953 ☉ daily ♿) opposite Central Station, a Grade I listed building dating to the mid 19th century and designed by Pugin. It is known for its magnificent organ, mosaic floor tiles and East Window – the work of one of the great stained-glass manufacturers of the day and Newcastle local, William Wailes. Lovely, quiet café here too.

St Andrew's Church near Chinatown (Newgate St ☎ 0191 232 7935 ☉ 11.00–15.00 Mon–Fri & for Sunday worship ♿) is clearly very ancient (some parts were constructed in the 12th century) and even contains a stretch of the old town wall running through the churchyard, and stone slab roofing. Here lies Charles Avison (sometimes known as 'England's Mozart') who lived in Newcastle and died in 1770, as well as 15 women executed in 1650 for witchcraft (graves are unmarked).

By the mid 14th century, Newcastle was enclosed by a stonking **town wall** that formed a protective two-mile loop around its perimeter with towers, gateways and turrets along its length. It was 25ft high and 7ft thick and was said to 'far passith all the waulls of the cities of England and most of the cities of Europe'. The **West Walls** near Stowell Street in Chinatown is the most substantial length of the barricade remaining, with four towers and standing to full height.

Just within the protective boundary of the West Walls is the restored 13th-century **Blackfriars cloisters** (now workshops and a restaurant; page 36) on Monk Street. The cloisters' walkway is no longer covered but the building as a whole is worth seeking out and you can still see the outline of where the church once stood.

HOWAY THE LADS

Strawberry Pl, NE1 4ST ✆ 0191 201 8704 🖥 newcastleunited.com ♿

Geordies, if you haven't noticed, are mad keen on football. For fans not at the St James' Park stadium on a Saturday afternoon, there's no sound quite as joyous as the roar when Newcastle score.

At no time are passions stirred more than when the players – known as the 'Magpies', on account of their black-and-white shirts – are playing Sunderland. Rivalry between the two teams goes back a long time and you'll quite often hear Geordies using the pejorative term 'Mackem' to describe not just Sunderland supporters, but anyone from Wearside. The word's origins perhaps only date to the 1980s and are thought to stem from the closing years of the region's shipbuilding industry when Sunderland shipbuilders would make the boats and the Geordies would fit them out, hence mack'em and tack'em (make them and take them).

Book tours of St James' Park online to walk through the famous tunnel to the dressing room and see the pitch.

With a sumptuous auditorium dating from 1867 and housing its original wooden stage machinery (tours several times a year) is the **Tyne Theatre & Opera House** (117 Westgate Rd ✆ 0191 243 1171 ♿), which puts on family shows, comedy nights, operas and events with well-known personalities.

🍴 FOOD & DRINK

Stowell Street in Newcastle's **Chinatown** is lined with East Asian restaurants. A couple that come highly recommended are **Dojo** (26–28 Stowell St ✆ 0191 903 8582) for great Japanese food, and **Mennaza** (1 Monk St ✆ 0191 232 7950), a traditional Korean BBQ restaurant where you grill your own marinated meat at your table.

Blackfriars Restaurant Friars St ✆ 0191 261 5945 ⊙ 11.00–midnight daily ♿ ground restaurant & cloister garden 🐾 cloister garden only. Creative British/French dishes served in the 13th-century surroundings of a Dominican monastery (low ceilings, stone walls, dark wood furnishings) or outside in the cloister gardens, which remain wonderfully tranquil. Blackfriars is well known in Newcastle and has a loyal following especially for its Sunday roasts and evening meals – one for a special night out. Expect to pay top-end prices for fillet of salt-aged beef with a blue cheese pomme purée, rare-breed pork with apricot stuffing, and roast halibut, glazed ox cheek and oyster pie, though you can also come here just for coffees and snacks during the day or for drinks (beers made in the on-site micro-brewery). Barbecue nights are held in the cloister gardens on Fridays from May through the summer.

Bridge Hotel Castle Sq ℘ 0191 232 6400 ⊙ daily 🐾. A short stroll from the train station and right opposite Newcastle Castle is this great traditional British pub with a fine range of cask ales and a wonderful interior – all dark wood panelling and screens and period stained glass. Lovely terrace out the back too.

4 CENTRAL STATION & AROUND

Newcastle's much-admired Victorian railway station is not an area many visitors spend much time around, but there are a couple of fascinating buildings open to the public, and a great museum, all within a short walk of the station, should you find yourself with an hour or two before your train.

The **Literary & Philosophical Society** library (23 Westgate Rd ℘ 0191 232 0192 ⊙ 09.30–19.00 Mon, Wed & Thu, until 20.00 Tue, until 17.00 Fri & until 13.00 Sat) – or the 'Lit and Phil' as it is known to locals – is a little-known gem a short stroll from Central Station. Bookshelves extend almost to the dome glass skylights, and oak chairs and tables, wooden coat stands and antique clocks evoke a bygone era. Politics and religion were the only topics banned when this society was founded in 1793 as a 'conversation club'.

"The Neville Hall Library has an outstanding interior with tiers of stained-glass windows."

Over the years, many distinguished engineers, historians and writers have lectured here including Joseph Swan on 20 October 1880, during which he demonstrated the electric light – making this the first public building to be lit by electricity in the world. The tradition of public lectures continues today (see the society's website for upcoming talks).

Next door to the Lit and Phil is the **Mining Institute** (Westgate Rd ℘ 0191 233 2459 ⊙ Mon–Fri ♿ possible but phone in advance to arrange), which was founded when mines operated all over the North East in the 19th century. The **Neville Hall Library** has an outstanding interior with tiers of stained-glass windows, a lofty central atrium and superb wood panelling and fittings, and contains journals, geological surveys and books on engineering, geology and mining.

Within a few minutes' walk of Central Station is the **Life Science Centre** (Times Sq ℘ 0191 243 8210 ⊙ daily ♿), a research centre and large visitor attraction with interactive exhibitions aimed at families:

robots, the solar system, dinosaurs and so on. Displays change throughout the year, but the planetarium is a permanent feature. Arts and crafts workshops with hands-on tuition help keep the very young occupied.

The **Discovery Museum** (Blandford Sq ✆ 0191 232 6789 ⊙ daily; free admission except some special exhibitions ♿) is one of the most engaging and well-visited museums on Tyneside, devoted mainly to the region's industrial and maritime heritage. Dominating the interior is the 115-foot-long *Turbinia* – the first ship to be powered by steam in the world – which was launched into the Tyne at Wallsend in 1894. Displays are not just related to science, however, and you'll find rooms devoted to various aspects of Newcastle's social and cultural history. For children, the Science Maze, with its hands-on activities and craft and model-making corner, will occupy youngsters for an hour or longer.

🍽 FOOD & DRINK

Central Station stands close to a clutch of pubs and cafés, the best of which are squeezed into the city's infamous **Pink Lane,** including **The Forth Hotel** (✆ 0191 232 6478 ⊙ daily ♿ 🐾), a popular, trendy pub and restaurant with a young-ish crowd, and **The Town Wall** (✆ 0191 232 3000 ⊙ daily ♿ 🐾), a wonderful Georgian building with high ceilings, exposed walls and a lot of stripped wooden furnishings, serving Wylam beers and good gastro-pub nosh. **Pink Lane Bakery** (✆ 0191 261 0606 ⊙ Mon–Sat) is well known in Newcastle, not just for its bread, but its fabulous pastries (some vegan), tarts and sausage rolls. For a caffeine kick, head to **Pink Lane Coffee** (✆ 07841 383085 ⊙ daily), a little modern café in the street's elbow, right opposite Central Station and serving fab coffees, pastries, sandwiches and 'things on toast'.

Centurion Bar ✆ 0191 261 6611 ⊙ daily ♿. The tiled interior of this bar-cum-bistro within Central Station is every bit as sumptuous as you'd hope of a Victorian first-class passenger lounge. It's worth having a coffee or a drink here just to savour the surroundings (though it gets a bit rowdy in the evenings).

Kafeneon 8 Bigg Market ✆ 0191 260 2577 ⊙ daily ♿. Authentic Greek food bistro equidistant between Monument and Central Station serving moussakas, meat stews, meze platters and lighter pita toasties stuffed with veg. Sunny outdoor tables.

My Delhi 87 Clayton St ✆ 0191 230 2302 ⊙ daily. Multi award-winning Indian roadside food transported to central Newcastle by Delhi chefs and voted the BBC's Britain's best take-away a few years ago. Inside it's vibrant, youthful and the dishes are wonderfully authentic: lamb curry, railway-station style, Punjab 'highway' chicken and Tandoori street plates:

from chicken tikkas to Afghani kebabs. Indian cocktails crown the drinks menu, including a Rangpur Bramble (Rangpur gin and blackberry) and Himalayan Sour (Indian spiced rum with a squeeze of citrus).

Prohibition Cabaret Bar 25–27 Pink Ln ⊙ Wed–Sun ♿ 🐾. Bringing 1920s glamour to Newcastle in the intimate surroundings of the city's legendary old jazz bar, with table seating and a lot of red velvet. Live blues, swing or jazz every Friday and Saturday evenings and burlesque nights every third Friday of the month.

5 HAYMARKET, THE CIVIC CENTRE & THE UNIVERSITIES

🏠 **Jesmond Dene House Hotel**

Haymarket Metro station at the top of Northumberland Street marks the end of the main shopping area. You have left the classical streets of Grainger Town and are now in a more modern space by the Civic Centre and Newcastle and Northumbria universities.

Both universities have art galleries worth visiting. Exhibitions change regularly at Newcastle's **Hatton Gallery** (Kings Rd ✆ 0191 277 8877 ⊙ Mon–Sat ♿ entrance on King's Walk) with contemporary solo artists and university students showcasing their work. Northumbria's long-established **The University Gallery** (Sandyford Rd ✆ 0191 349 5382 ⊙ Thu–Sat ♿) puts on contemporary exhibitions by national and international artists.

Northern Stage (✆ 0191 230 5151 ⊙ Tue–Sat ♿), in the grounds of Newcastle University, is a well-known production theatre. Nearby is Newcastle's premier natural history and archaeological museum, the **Great North Museum: Hancock** (Barras Bridge ✆ 0191 208 6765 ⊙ daily; free admission ♿), a wonderfully engaging museum that caters well for families with its replica tyrannosaurus, stuffed animals, planetarium and children's events but also houses an impressive collection of Roman finds, Egyptian mummies and traditional ceremonial costumes. The Hadrian's Wall and Natural Northumbria galleries are particularly notable.

Standing between the two universities is the Scandinavian-influenced **Civic Centre** (Barras Bridge ✆ 0191 277 7222; tours by appointment & for Heritage Open Days ♿), a much underappreciated modern building. The fantastically well-preserved interior will make Danish design aficionados weep. The architect travelled all over Europe sourcing the finest marbles for the corridors, landings and staircases;

woods for the ceilings, screens and banisters; and slates for the walls. Upstairs in the committee rooms, walls are decorated in red silk and orange leather; the rosewood chairs, tables and sideboards are the work of Danish furniture maker, Arne Vodder. The Council Chamber is superbly unchanged, still with its original 149 green leather chairs.

SPECIAL STAYS

Jesmond Dene House Hotel Jesmond NE2 2EY ✆ 0191 212 3000 ⌖ jesmonddenehouse. co.uk ♿. There may be fancier places to spend the night in the city, but you won't find a more tranquil setting than the wooded valley of Jesmond Dene, which was landscaped into a woodland 'garden' in the 19th century. The setting feels a world away from Newcastle city centre but it's actually only a 15-minute walk to the nearest Metro (Ilford Rd) and, from there, the same time direct to the centre of Newcastle and Central Station. This independent boutique hotel, and very good upmarket restaurant, retains plenty of original Arts and Crafts features in guest areas downstairs: decorative tilework, wood panelling, opulent fireplaces and stained-glass windows; upstairs rooms are modern and sleek with weighted fabrics and luxury touches. Craster Kippers for breakfast on the outside terrace are a treat on a sunny morning.

FOOD & DRINK

Plenty of inexpensive cafés cater for the student market in the area around Haymarket, including the youthful bistro and bar at Northern Stage (page 39), but for something a little more special, hop on the Metro to West Jesmond (one stop from Haymarket). Brentwood Avenue, just by the Metro station, is a single street of side-to-side independent cafés and shops. My favourite place for an evening meal is **Dabbawal** (1 Brentwood Mews ✆ 0191 281 3434 ☉ daily ♿ 🐾 outside tables only), which competes with My Delhi (page 38) as one of the best Indian street-food restaurants in the North East.

Fenwick's Food Hall 39 Northumberland St ☉ until 19.00 daily (closes earlier on w/ ends) ♿. Navigate through the perfume counters in one of the city's oldest department stores to this fabulous gastronomic hub showcasing the very best food and drink from Tyneside, the North Sea and Northumberland's hills to eat in or take-away (from the excellent fishmonger's, butchery, cheese and deli counters). There's so much here with three great restaurants and the **Ouseburn Coffee Company** for an unbeatable morning cuppa. **Fuego** (✆ 0191 232 5100) is a Mediterranean restaurant serving up a feast of tapas and classic Spanish dishes; **Porterhouse Grill** (✆ 0191 239 6612) is one for carnivores; while **Saltwater** (✆ 0191 239 6613) offers the freshest seafood going from their fish counter to take-away or eat in (fish stew, ceviche, pâtés, fish cakes, seafood platters or simply a plate of Lindisfarne oysters with a glass of wine).

The Little Dumpling House 25 Ridley Pl ✆ 07588 682028 ⊙ daily. Great Chinese street food: inexpensive steamed dumplings and bao buns to enjoy inside or pavement side.

Mascalzone 238 Helmsley Rd, Sandyford ✆ 0191 261 6661 ⊙ from 18.00 Tue–Sat ♿. A bit of a walk from Haymarket (or 5 minutes or so by bus) is this wonderful laid-back Italian on the street corner of a residential neighbourhood serving Sardinian plates as good as any in Italy (pasta, authentic pizza, risotto, seafood and meat). Their seafood risotto comes highly recommended.

Trent House 1–2 Leazes Ln ✆ 0191 261 2154 🐾. There are few places for an evening drink in the Haymarket area if you're not 19 years old and/or don't like rowdy boozers, but The Trent is an exception. It's a traditional Geordie pub a short walk from St James' Park (so busy on match days) and is a well-loved, somewhat tatty drinking hole in the city selling good beers. A 'talky talky' pub, as my brother puts it.

Wylam Brewery Exhibition Park ✆ 0191 650 0651 ⊙ Thu–Sun ♿ but phone ahead for assistance 🐾. A pleasant 10-minute walk from the RVI hospital through Exhibition Park leads to this cool brewery, bistro and music venue of factory proportions overlooking the park's lake and housed in a landmark domed building (built for the North East Exhibition in 1929). Limited menu of small British dishes (Thu–Sat) and sit-down Sunday roasts (popular so book ahead). Check online for upcoming events.

6 THE OUSEBURN VALLEY

Stepney Bank/Lime St, Quayside East, NE1 2NP ✆ 0191 261 6596 ⌖ ouseburntrust.org.uk

Newcastle's creative quarter extends along a concealed tributary of the River Tyne east of the city centre where there were once lead works, lime kilns, flour mills, iron foundries, glassworks and potteries at different times over the last 500 years. The area remained a ramshackle sort of a place with scrapyards, garages and workshops until the late 1990s. One by one these have been converted into cultural venues, recording studios, artist workshops, micro-breweries with taprooms, cafés, restaurants and bakeries. Despite what some see as gentrification, the Ouseburn remains a laid-back, unpretentious place that is still agreeably scruffy round the edges. Regulars like it that way.

On sunny weekends, families, aging rockers, lefties and students lounge outside on the 'village' green between the Cluny pub and the delightfully higgledy-piggledy **Ouseburn Farm** (Ouseburn Rd, off Lime St ✆ 0191 232 3698 ⊙ Tue–Sun ♿) with a small number of animals you can stroke, a welcoming café and free-range hens clucking about the farmyard and kitchen garden. Horses from nearby **Stepney Bank Stables** trot by, and young'uns wander in and out of the **Seven Stories** exhibition centre (30 Lime St ℘ 0300 330 1095 ☉ Thu–Tue; free admission 👍), a special museum devoted to children's literature and with an excellent bookshop.

Unbeknown to casual visitors is a subterranean tunnel that runs right across Newcastle. **The Victoria Tunnel** (℘ 0191 261 6596; book tours online 👍 ouseburntrust.org.uk/events/tunnel-tours 👍) was opened in 1835 and designed for wagons to carry coal underground from a colliery near the Town Moor to the quayside, rather than through the streets. During World War II it served as an air-raid shelter. A 700yd length of the narrow tunnel, which has an entrance on Lime Street, is open to the public via one- or two-hour guided tours – which are highly recommended.

"On sunny weekends, families, aging rockers, lefties and students lounge outside on the 'village' green."

A ten-minute walk from the main Ouseburn Valley hub is **The Biscuit Factory** (Stoddart St ℘ 0191 261 1103 ☉ daily 👍) – which claims to be the UK's largest independent commercial art gallery. It has a deservedly excellent reputation for quality, range and affordability, and sells jewellery, sculptures and paintings, as well as large works by international and local artists. On the top floor is a good café with indoor and conservatory seating.

The Ouseburn buzz is catching on in neighbouring **Byker**, a poor suburb of Newcastle famous for its pioneering 1960s social housing estate, Byker Wall, and hit 1990s kids TV show, *Byker Grove* (which wasn't actually filmed in Byker at all, but I digress…). Decent places to eat and drink are popping up here and there, and artists are finding new, affordable spaces in which to showcase their works.

🍴 FOOD & DRINK

It's hard to know where to start with the Ouseburn – there are just so many alternative little places to lunch, drink, buy bread, enjoy ice cream (praise be, **Di Meo's**) and be cheerful. A few of the pubs detailed in the box on page 44 offer decent grub, notably **The Cluny** and **Brinkburn St Brewery**. And then there's nearby Byker and Heaton (more

---

NEWCASTLE: **1** Wood Hall, the Common Room of the Great North. **2** The Stephenson Railway Museum. **3** Interactive exhibits at the Life Science Centre. **4** You can take a tour of the Victoria Tunnel which was used to carry coal beneath the streets of the city. **5** Literary & Philosophical Society library. ▶

TAPROOMS, BOOZERS & BARS: THE OUSEBURN VALLEY

New, edgy little taprooms and pop-up bars are opening all the time — or so it seems. There are now five **micro-breweries** operating in the area, including **The Old Coal Yard** (12 Elizabeth St ☉ Fri & Sat for drinks and live music), home of Northern Alchemy beers; and **Brinkburn St Brewery** (page 45). You can visit all these venues on special afternoon walking **brewery tours** on the first Friday of every month (book at ✆ 0191 261 6596 ♂ ouseburntrust.co.uk).

Five long-standing pubs with a lively independent and folk music scene centre around the Ouseburn. **The Cluny** (36 Lime St ✆ 0191 230 4474 ♿ 🐾) pub and club is well known for hosting bands and up-and-coming artists, and attracts a mix of young indie music followers and older drinkers who come for the beers. On the other side of the green is the **Ship Inn** (Stepney Bank ✆ 0191 222 0878 🐾), a veteran snug pub — all stripped floors and mismatched vintage furniture, with outdoor seating.

A steep bank rising from the Ouseburn leads into the beer garden of **The Cumberland Arms** (James Place St ✆ 0191 265 6151 🐾), another cracking pub with wooden furniture, open fires and an extensive range of regional ales and ciders. The Cumberland is best visited on a balmy summer's evening when you can sit outside in the sun with a pint of cider, or on cold nights in winter when the fires are roaring, the windows are steamed up and the fiddle players are really going for it. Enjoy ukulele, folk and acoustic sessions every night except Friday, Saturday and some Mondays. On Wednesday evenings, Rapper sword dancers (a North East tradition) practise in the upstairs room and will allow you to watch if you ask.

Downriver and close to Newcastle's quayside is **The Tyne Bar** (Maling St ✆ 0191 265 2550 ♿ outdoor seating only 🐾), a youthful, laid-back and unpretentious pub with a vibrant live music scene at the weekend. It's a favourite of many hip kids in the city who come here swinging a retro '90s look, which amuses me because I remember when the pub rose to prominence 30 years ago. During the week, it's something of a community hub with local groups (a young crochet club last time I visited) and pub-goers from many walks of life.

The Free Trade Inn (St Lawrence Rd, off Walker Rd ✆ 0191 265 5764 🐾) is a scruffy drinking spot above the River Tyne popular with students, artists and university lecturers with a fondness for Van Morrison tunes. The cask ales are good, everyone is in a cheery mood day and night, and it is customary to talk nonsense to the old geezers (and their dogs) at the bar. The beer garden is soaked in sunshine on summer evenings and offers an unbeatable view of the river.

or less walking distance), which is well known for its independent restaurants along Heaton Road and Chillingham Road ('Chilli Road' if you're asking a local). They include the fantastic traditional Spanish tapas restaurant, **Boquerones** (194 Heaton Rd ✆ 0191

209 2359 ☺ Tue–Sat (&) which you ought to book in advance; and **wonderful Chucho's** (271A Shields Rd ✆ 07716 562684), an authentic and inexpensive Mexican taco bar/take-away at the top of Byker's high street.

Brinkburn St Brewery Ford St ✆ 0191 338 9039 ☺ daily &. 🐾. Laid back, cheerful taproom and restaurant stuffed with curios and mismatched furniture, serving drinks, lunches and evening meals. You may have to wait a while on a Friday evening for your steak burger (the homemade Brinkburger is one of the best you will find in Newcastle), pizza or sharing nachos, but when you are surrounded by joyful souls, from the waiting staff to the students on the table next to you, are you really going to complain? Just order another pint of craft beer (brewed on site – choose cask or tap) and roll with it.

Cook House Foundry Ln ✆ 0191 276 1093 ☺ Tue–Sun & downstairs only. Michelin rated and easily the most upmarket place to eat in the Ouseburn for breakfast, lunch or dinner. This is one for foodies, who will appreciate all the seasonal, regional and doorstep produce (veg and bread from the Ouseburn), and anyone celebrating something special who wants impeccable service and a choice of truly imaginative British/continental dishes big on flavour and provenance.

Ernest 1 Boyd St ✆ 0191 260 5216 ☺ 10.00–late daily (until 21.00 for food) &. 🐾. Colourful corner café and bar with gig posters on the walls and known for its music, trendy clientele and good food (breakfasts, veggie and meat burgers, flatbreads and wraps). Superb coffees (made with beans roasted in the Ouseburn).

Northern Rye 4 Riverside Walk ✆ 0191 250 9716 ☺ from 09.00 Mon–Sat (closes 13.00 on Sat). Aside from fresh loaves of sourdough, this cool bakery and sit-out café (heaving at the weekend) sells a great coffee and delicious take-away toasties and sandwiches made with their homemade bread and stuffed with cheeses and ham. Best enjoyed perched on a bench by the river in the morning sun.

The Tanners Arms 1 Byker Bridge ✆ 0191 245 3477 ☺ daily 🐾. Hands-down one of the best places on Tyneside for a roast, hence why you won't get a table if you don't book at least a few days in advance. From the 'scranner's arms' menu to the lively ambience inside, this is a young person's pub with an excellent posh burger and hot dog menu in addition to the Sunday roasts. Veggies and vegans exceptionally well catered for.

7 SEGEDUNUM

Buddle St, Wallsend ✆ 0191 278 4217 ☺ call before visiting as opening times change yearly &

A tall viewing platform like an airport control tower rises over this ruined Roman fort (pronounced as 'Segg-e-doo-num'), providing an arresting bird's-eye view of the garrison buildings that lie at the end (or beginning) of Hadrian's Wall. A branch line of the wall ran into the Tyne from the southeast corner of the fort, forming the 'wall's end' – hence the name of the suburb. From this high vantage point, cast your eye to the banks of the Tyne and the historic Swan Hunter shipyards, where some of the most famous ocean liners of the early 20th century were built.

On the ground, the outlines of the fort buildings are marked by cobbles where no original stones remain. Most striking are the cavalry barracks identified by the sunken pits in the front partition of each room where the horses' urine would collect. In the rear lived the horsemen – three to a room.

The main attraction for many visitors, however, is a full-scale reconstruction of Europe's only fully working **Roman bathhouse** (closed at the time of writing until further notice), where part of the hot-room floor has been removed to show how the Romans engineered under-floor heating.

An indoor **museum** contains more recreated fort buildings, including the aforementioned cavalry digs, and displays of Roman finds (look out for the rare stone toilet seat).

8 STEPHENSON STEAM RAILWAY MUSEUM

Middle Engine Ln, North Shields (nr Silverlink) ✆ 0191 277 7135 ⊙ weekends; trains run on Sun (& Thu in school holidays) ♿ 🐾

Before shipbuilding, it was coal that defined the banks of the Tyne at Wallsend, the people and the local economy, as it did throughout Tyneside. And where there was coal, there were railways. Celebrating this heritage is a modern museum between Newcastle and the coast operating **heritage train rides** along a track a couple of miles long.

Inside, the star attraction is George Stephenson's 'Billy' steam engine, the forerunner to the famous 'Rocket' and the third-oldest locomotive in the world, built in 1816 to haul coal waggons. Also on display is the wonderful Edwardian Tyneside Electric Parcel Van, the only surviving vehicle that ran on the forerunner of Newcastle's Metro railway.

During the summer of 2013, archaeologists working a few miles away close to the roman fort at Segedunum made an unexpected discovery during a dig. Instead of Roman finds, they unearthed wooden rails and sleepers thought to be the earliest standard-gauge railway ever discovered. The significance of the find is hard to overstate. Constructed in 1785, the **Willington Waggonway** (page 312) transported coal from

ROMAN NEWCASTLE

Walkers and cyclists following the 84-mile Hadrian's Wall Path (page 304) from Wallsend (four miles east of Newcastle city centre) to the west coast usually follow the National Trail through Newcastle along the River Tyne. Roman history enthusiasts will know, however, that the true line of Hadrian's Wall is a little further north, running underneath some of the city's most prominent streets.

Of the 15 forts along Hadrian's Wall, three are in Tyneside: at Wallsend (Segedunum), Newcastle (Newcastle Castle) and Benwell (Condercum). They're all now in fragments of course, and there are very few fort or wall stones visible above ground in the city centre, except at a couple of locations including remnants of milecastle 4 in the courtyard of the **Newcastle Arts Centre** near Central Station and at **Newcastle Castle** (page 34) where you can see the outline of several Roman buildings belonging to the garrison fort on which the castle was constructed.

Gone is Pons Aelius – or 'Hadrian's Bridge' – that once spanned the Tyne where the Swing Bridge crosses the water today, and almost all signs of Hadrian's Wall.

It is fascinating, nonetheless, to see where Newcastle's streetscape is influenced by the line of the wall. This is particularly true of the strikingly long, straight avenue, **Shield's Road**, in Byker (check out a short run of Hadrian's Wall in the pedestrianised square in front of East End Pool) and **Westgate Road** (A186) and its continuation, the **West Road**, that shoots past Central Station on a straight trajectory out of the city.

In truth, the few pieces of Roman masonry in situ here and there in Newcastle are unlikely to excite most visitors (the very best pieces are now housed in Newcastle's excellent **Great North Museum: Hancock**; page 39) but venturing a little way out of the city are two exceptions: **Segedunum** roman fort museum (page 45) at Wallsend and the fascinating **Benwell Roman Temple** (page 306).

nearby collieries to the Tyne in carts pulled along the wooden rails by horses. A length of the railway has been extracted and it is hoped a replica will go on display at the museum in coming years.

2 GATESHEAD

Traditionally the smaller, less glamorous cousin of Newcastle on the south side of the River Tyne, Gateshead has attracted national attention in recent decades for its daring contemporary architecture and arts venues – and made Newcastle sit up and take notice. Rejuvenating **Gateshead's quayside** began with the success of *The Angel of the North* on a hill outside of the town. Following Gormley's 1998 masterpiece, the forward-thinking council embarked on a major redevelopment of the riverfront that put Gateshead on the arts map of Britain, though Newcastle often gets the credit.

Gateshead's centre and urban fringes lack the Victorian architecture and stately streets of Newcastle, but the town does have some historic buildings and attractions worth seeking out, including those described in these pages, as well as the wonderfully restored 19th-century public parkland and garden, **Saltwell Park** (Saltwell Rd South, NE9 5AX).

GATESHEAD QUAYS

South Shore Rd; Access on foot or bicycle from Newcastle's quayside by crossing the Millennium Bridge

Gateshead's quayside is now a major culture and leisure attraction sharing similarities with cities like Bilbao in Spain that also underwent arts-led regeneration works in the 1990s. Our Guggenheim equivalent is **The Glasshouse International Centre for Music**, formerly known as the 'Sage', (✐ 0191 443 4661 ♿), a bulbous building wrapped in steel on a bank above the Tyne and the home of the Royal Northern Sinfonia. Inside, it's airy, bright and voluminous and there's a well-placed café and bar with views of the Tyne Bridge and Newcastle's waterfront (and an upmarket brasserie for evening dinners). If you come to a concert here (mainly classical, folk, indie and world music), you'll be able to appreciate the much-praised acoustics in the timber halls.

The **Baltic Centre for Contemporary Art** (✐ 0191 478 1810 ☉ daily; free admission ♿) started life in the mid 20th century as a flour mill before it was gutted and transformed into one of the premier modern art galleries in the UK. Over the years the Baltic has staged some superb exhibitions, including the Turner Prize and a couple of shows by the North's favourite contemporary artists, Antony Gormley and Anish Kapoor, but for the most part it's known for experimental art, photography exhibitions and large-scale installations. Even if you find such works inaccessible, it's worth visiting for the views of the Tyne alone.

Just over a mile upriver from the Baltic, **Dunston Coal Staiths** (Staiths Rd, Dunston, Gateshead) is another precious relic from Tyneside's industrial era. The late 19th-century pier-like structure, said to be the largest wooden construction in Europe, once enabled wagons loaded with Durham coal to transport their contents directly on to ships moored along its side. The staiths ceased operating in the 1980s but it remains largely intact. It is easily viewed from the promenade or railway bridge (when crossing the river by train, look upriver, away from the Tyne Bridge). Note the wading birds at low tide. Since the water quality in the Tyne has improved in recent decades, a saltmarsh 'garden' is flourishing, and otters occasionally delight onlookers.

SHIPLEY ART GALLERY
Prince Consort Rd, NE8 4JB ✆ 0191 477 1495 ◷ Tue–Sat; free admission ♿

Opened in 1917 in a grand stone building, the Shipley originally housed paintings but changed focus in the 1970s to embrace contemporary arts and crafts. Today visitors will find a mixture of both with oils by leading early 20th-century regional artists such as Ralph Hedley, as well as some intriguing collections: teapots to chairs, pottery and glassware. Some rare single pieces that caught my eye: a penny farthing bicycle from 1868; Antony Gormley's *Angel of the North* prototype made of plaster and balsa wood; and the cherished North East painting, *The Blaydon Races* – a lively depiction of the popular 19th-century event (still enjoyed today). The song of the same name is a well-loved Geordie anthem.

3 THE ANGEL OF THE NORTH
Signposted off the A1 south of Gateshead, also reached from the Durham Rd through Gateshead; parking on site; the **Angel Bus** (Go North East service 21 ⟁ gonortheast.co.uk) runs daily at least every 10mins from Eldon Square Bus Station in Newcastle (& a few other stops in the city centre) and Gateshead Interchange (Metro)

Boasting a wingspan the breadth of a jumbo jet was something of a PR disaster when the then-largest sculpture in Britain was unveiled in 1998. *The Angel of the North* was much criticised by locals who thought the 65ft sculpture did indeed look like a plane and not the feminine form perhaps some had hoped for. Many residents hated the sculpture – really hated it – and wanted it taken down; but locals have come to love Antony Gormley's rusty red masterpiece.

The prominent hillock on which it stands was once a colliery and the mining history of the site – and the region – is very much reflected in the colour, steel fabric and form (undeniably masculine). It's said to be one of the most viewed pieces of public art in Britain, situated as it is by the A1 and in sight of the London to Edinburgh railway line. Other memorable sculptures around Gateshead include Sally Matthews's

life-size metal goats below the blue Metro Bridge and *Cone* by Andy Goldsworthy (west of the High Level Bridge).

4 GIBSIDE

Near Rowlands Gill, Gateshead NE16 6BG (signed off the A1) ℘ 01207 541820 ☉ daily; chapel open weekends only in winter ♿ some paths bumpy; all-terrain electric wheelchairs for hire (book ahead by phone) 🐾; National Trust

> [The Hall] stands in the midst of a great wood of about 400 acres, through which there are a great many noble walks and rides interspers'd with fine lawns, with a rough river running thro' it, on each side of which are very high rocks, which gives it a very romantick [sic] look.
> Local colliery owner, Edward Montagu, in correspondence with his wife in the mid 1800s

Once you set foot in this Georgian parkland on the outskirts of Gateshead, you will feel as cut off from the 21st century as you would on any remote National Trust estate. The grounds have all the grandeur you would expect of an 18th-century landscaped garden with eye-catching monuments, wooded walkways, classical architecture and open vistas. A stroll from the **Palladian chapel** (see below) along a half-mile tree-lined avenue to the 140ft **Column to Liberty** is wonderfully romantic, especially in autumn when the intensity of light and colour is spectacular. The ruins of an **orangery** and **Jacobean hall** lie halfway between the two.

Work began on **Gibside Chapel** (☉ May–Sep daily; Oct–Apr Sat & Sun; Sunday services at 15.00; choral evensong & prayer at 15.00 on the first Sunday of the month ♿ using a side ramp), a treasured centrepiece in the parkland, in 1760 to a plan by renowned architect of the day, James Paine. George Bowes, the estate owner (a local coal baron), didn't live to see the completion of the exterior of his mausoleum which was later converted into a church in 1809. Constructed using a cream sandstone, the swags on the dome, row of urns on the balustrade and fine carvings on the portico columns are much admired. Many decades would pass before the interior of Bowes' classical masterpiece would be unveiled to reveal its exquisite, intricately carved plasterwork, unusual three-tiered pulpit and curved pews made of bright cherry wood.

◀ **1** The Angel of the North. **2** The Glasshouse International Centre for Music. **3** The Baltic Centre for Contemporary Art. **4** The Georgian parkland of Gibside.

Much of the focus for a day out is centred around the two extreme ends of the estate: the area around the chapel where there's a café, walled garden, secondhand bookstore, shop, vegetable stall and, a short walk away, a large adventure playground known as **Strawberry Castle**; at the other end of the Avenue is the unusually grand **Stables**, more offerings of cakes, artist studios and trails into the surrounding conifer woodland.

The wider Gibside estate offers several miles of woodland **walks**.

FOOD & DRINK

Both the **Baltic Centre for Contemporary Art** (page 48) and the **Glasshouse music centre** (page 48) have cafés, bars and restaurants with fabulous views of the river and Newcastle's quayside. Above the quayside, between the High Level Bridge and Tyne Bridge, the newly renovated Wellington Street area (also known as the **Railway Quarter**) has a great reputation for its independent drinking scene and includes **Microbus** (see opposite) and **Axis** (Wellington Street ☉ Wed–Sun 🐾), the latter specialising in wines and craft beer. Round the corner, and a great choice for pre-concert drinks if visiting the music centre, is **The Central Bar** (Half Moon Ln ✆ 0191 478 2543 🐾), a traditional pub with a rooftop terrace (watch trains passing by) housed in one of Gateshead's most striking 19th-century buildings. It's very well-known for its large selection of beers and whiskys and now serves food too.

Gateshead's somewhat tired town centre lacks decent places to eat and drink, with a few exceptions including **Sapori** (208 High St ✆ 0191 432 9432 ☉ Tue–Sat ♿), a really good Italian.

In and around the Derwent Valley countryside, a few gems I'd recommend include **The Land of Oak & Iron Heritage Centre** (Winlaton Mill NE21 6RU ✆ 01207 524898 ☉ breakfast and lunch daily ♿), a gorgeous modern café and community hub by the River Derwent; the National Trust's café at **Gibside** (page 51); and the very well-regarded **Feathers Inn** at Hedley-on-the-Hill (page 344).

Baltic Centre for Contemporary Art Gateshead ✆ 0191 478 1810. With outdoor seating on the quayside and views of the Millennium Bridge is the **Baltic Kitchen** (☉ daily ♿), a modern and casual ground-floor café serving coffees, breakfasts, pastries and a small selection of sandwiches, toasties and sausage rolls for lunch.

Zip to the top floor of the art gallery in a glass lift (a thrill in itself for the views) for an altogether more refined dining experience at **Six Restaurant** (✆ 07922 427019 ☉ Tue–Sun ♿). The light-filled dining room boasts one of the finest views on Tyneside: a striking panorama of Newcastle's historic quayside and the Tyne's bridges. Attentive waiting staff, cocktails with a regional twist, and a curated six and nine-course tasting menu (modern British/European food and plenty of local delicacies) as well as Sunday lunches.

Microbus Wellington St 🖉 0191 477 3001 ⊙ daily 🐾. Hop on pretty much any bus from Newcastle to Gateshead and you'll stop right outside this cracking drinking hole (hence the name) which overflows with cheerful locals on weekend nights. Awarded CAMRA regional pub of the year a few times for its array of craft beers, this is a great find under a railway arch in the renovated Railway Quarter area of Gateshead. Regular live music sessions.

Prism Coffee top end of Saltwell Park, access from East Park Rd ⊙ Tue–Sun 🦽 🐾. I was intrigued about the coffee roasted in Blaydon and the sign which says 'oat milk as standard' and so the friendly owner scooped up a handful of beans for me to smell and mentioned something about notes of cherries and chocolate (as if we were talking about wines). As for the oat milk, 'it pairs best with our coffees but you can also go cow if you'd rather'. Clearly connoisseurs of their trade, Prism, a little take-away hut (with outdoor seating) in Gateshead's wonderful Victorian Park know how to make a superb coffee – you won't find a better brew anywhere on Tyneside.

The Staiths Café 1 Autumn Drive, Staiths Southbank, NE8 2BZ 🖉 07733 335313 ⊙ Mon–Thu & Sun; also Fri & Sat evenings 🦽 🐾. Modern café opposite the end of Dunston Staiths with a terrace overlooking the Tyne (blankets supplied in chilly weather). This is a quiet spot for morning coffee or breakfast and is easily found by walking or cycling 20 minutes upriver from the Baltic on the promenade. Filling sandwiches for lunch and a dedicated vegan menu, too. There's also a good selection of flapjacks and cakes and a small evening menu.

THE NORTH TYNESIDE COAST: NORTH SHIELDS TO WHITLEY BAY

Pleasure beaches at **Tynemouth**, **Cullercoats** and **Whitley Bay** became hugely popular during the 19th century when train travel made the seaside resorts accessible to ordinary folk. Tyneside's coast is still easily reached by public transport, with Metro stations at all the beaches and **North Shields** (a journey that takes just 20 minutes from Newcastle). You can also cycle from Newcastle, largely road free (page 25).

5 NORTH SHIELDS FISH QUAY

It's a lively scene when the fishermen are landing their catch: buckets of haddock, monkfish, plaice and shellfish are passed from the boats to the harbour, engines throbbing, seabirds swarming behind the trawlers as they travel up the Tyne, and the incessant cry of herring gulls announcing the start of another fishing day.

Even at quiet times, the Fish Quay evokes nostalgia for the fishing industry of bygone centuries with its old Victorian Customs House, Shipping Office buildings, warehouses and open yards where rows of girls once stood over barrels filleting herring. The area's fishing heritage goes back some 800 years since the monastery at Tynemouth developed fishermen's huts (shielings, hence North Shields) on the banks of the river. **High Lights** and **Low Lights** are the two navigational white towers built in 1802 to warn mariners of the dangerous Black Middens Rocks at Tynemouth, scene of numerous shipwrecks (page 56). Climb up the bank to High Lights for an expansive view of the Tyne or walk along the promenade (&) to Tynemouth in about 15–20 minutes.

FOOD & DRINK

Close to Low Lights, a couple of excellent **fishmongers** (try **Lindisfarne Seafoods** or **Phil's Plaice**, both at Cliffords Fort Moat), open from 7am until early afternoon, sell the freshest of seafood landed at Shields that morning. And what doesn't get sold locally is sent to the continent. One of the fishmongers told me that North Shields is the biggest supplier of langoustines in Europe. Think about that next time you order *langostinos* on your Tenerife holiday.

Opposite the fishing boats and the River Tyne is a long curved avenue (Union Street becoming Bell Street) with a number of mid-range and inexpensive restaurants, bars and a couple of fish and chip shops including **The Waterfront** (22–26 Union Quay ✆ 0191 296 1721 ☺ daily & ✿) for a decent fish supper (take-away or sit in). There's a lively scene on a Friday night and the streets are thronged with groups spilling out of the river-facing pubs and restaurants; during the day, it's very different with folk out for a stroll along the river and families buying ice creams.

Low Lights Tavern Brewhouse Bank ✆ 0191 257 6038 ☺ daily ✿. Set back from the Fish Quay is this very old pub dating to 1657, and one-time drinking hole of fishermen. Today it's known more for its food – well, its pies at least: corned beef, chicken, ham and leek, peppered steak and a veggie option.

The Ship's Cat Tanners' Banks ✆ 0191 257 7507 ☺ daily ✿. Lovely spot with a terrace bathed in evening light. A young person's place, you'd think by the styling, but actually it's full of all sorts. The food menu is clearly designed with drinkers in mind, with quality kebabs, pizzas, tacos, burgers and fish and chips.

Three Tanners Bank 3 Tanners' Bank ☺ Wed–Sun ✿. Artsy, young crowd stolen from Newcastle's Ouseburn and dropped in Shields. A cocktail and pizza on a summer's evening is the thing here (there's an outdoor pizza oven by the beer garden).

6 TYNEMOUTH

The striking ruins of an 11th-century priory stand on a commanding rocky cape at the mouth of the River Tyne, looking across three sandy bays. Tynemouth's vibrant, well-kept town centre with its cafés, bars, craft and antiques shops kneels behind, and stretched along the seafront are the grand Victorian houses for which the historic resort is celebrated. Heading north on the seafront, you'll come to a Victorian model boating lake, aquarium and a surf shop.

All three beaches are minutes away from the town centre. **Longsands** is the largest expanse of sand and is popular with families and surfers, who can hire surf boards and take lessons at the **Tynemouth Surf Company** (Grand Parade (promenade above Longsands) ✆ 0191 258 2496 ◌ tynemouthsurf.co.uk). Tynemouth's 1920s **outdoor swimming pool** at the south end of Longsands will hopefully reopen in years to come thanks to the heroic efforts of a community-driven scheme to revive the decaying gem.

Tynemouth Market

Station Tce ☺ Sat & Sun ♿ 🐾. Travel by Metro direct to the market from Newcastle city centre in half an hour

Housed in Tynemouth's sumptuous Victorian train station (now the Metro station) is this well-known flea market held every weekend. It's worth coming here even on non-market days to admire the station architecture, this being one of the most ornamental stations of its era anywhere in England with a huge amount of decorative ironwork in the canopies and pillars.

The original covered timber bridge arches steeply over the railway, from where you gain a near bird's-eye view of the market stalls – over 150 – selling bric-a-brac, vintage clothes, vinyl records, books, jewellery, cakes, crafts, antiques and regional foods. On the third Saturday of the month, the station also hosts a farmers' market.

Tynemouth priory, castle & battery

Pier Rd ✆ 0191 257 1090 ☺ Apr–early Nov & school holidays daily, winter w/ends only; ♿ except the gun battery 🐾 English Heritage

Built in 1090 on the site of an earlier Anglo-Saxon monastery that had been destroyed by invading Danes, the current **priory** survives remarkably well considering its exposed position and age. Up close, the sandstone has been heavily worn away by the sea air, and the faces of headstones have formed wind-sculpted patterns. Though gaunt, the priory is still impressive, displaying soaring lancet window arches, a wealth of stone carvings and a 15th-century chapel with a rib vaulted ceiling and 33 roof bosses.

Tynemouth Castle, a ruined medieval gatehouse, stands at the entrance to the priory. You can wander inside, climb spiral staircases and enter the Great Chamber and Kitchen with its 10ft open fire.

Beyond the priory and looking across the North Sea is a **World War II battery**, complete with gun emplacements, storerooms containing the original mechanisms for transporting ammunition to the guns above, and a small changing room entered by a copper door (to prevent any friction sparks igniting the battery when the men were changing from their outdoor clothes to battery clothes).

Tynemouth Volunteer Life Brigade Watch House Museum

Spanish Battery, between Tynemouth & North Shields; easily walked from Tynemouth Priory ✐ 07464 327603 ☉ Easter–Sep 10.00–15.00 weekends & bank holidays; Oct–Easter by appointment; free admission (but donations appreciated) ♿

> **Thus it was that the lifeboat and rocket failed and the spectators were left to idly and helplessly see their fellow-men drowning before their eyes, and in the sight of land… A few minutes after ten o'clock, the schooner, which had drifted a good way to the westward, was plainly seen going down, and the cries of those on board were heard as she sank.**
> *Newcastle Guardian and Tyne Mercury*, Saturday 26 November 1864

This is a really special museum that deserves to be better known. Packed inside the striking 1887 blue, white and yellow wooden building is a huge hoard of artefacts amassed over the years that it has operated as a volunteer-manned station: bells, clocks, old black-and-white photographs, a breeches buoy and several ship's figureheads. From the south tower you can peer along the Tyne at fishing boats chugging up the river. Immediately below are the once feared Black Midden rocks where a steamship carrying 30 passengers sank on 24 November 1864 –

---

1 Pristine sands at Tynemouth. **2** St Mary's Lighthouse at Whitley Bay. **3** North Shields Fish Quay. **4** Tynemouth Priory and Castle. ▶

PETE STUART/S

PAUL JACKSON/DT

JIMMONKPHOTOGRAPHY/S

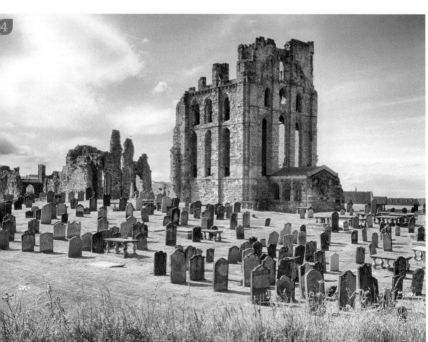

RW JEMMETT/S

an event that sparked the creation of the volunteer life brigade – the first of its kind – 11 days later.

Though still operational with well over a hundred calls a year, the brigade undertakes land-based coastal rescues these days. A stone garage houses a professional search-and-rescue vehicle where once a cart, pulled by horses and loaded with breeches buoys and ropes, waited for call-outs.

"The timber-clad cottage behind the museum used to be home to the Duke of Northumberland's salmon bailiff."

'We're one of only three independent volunteer life brigade units left in the country; the others are in South Shields and Sunderland,' a member of the Tynemouth brigade told me. Volunteers come from many walks of life and enjoy the camaraderie that comes with the position. Traditions at the Watch House persist, including a competition held every November to see which brigade member can keep a clay tobacco pipe smoking the longest. It stems from when free tobacco was offered as an incentive to new volunteers.

Incidentally, the timber-clad cottage behind the museum (now in private ownership) used to be home to the Duke of Northumberland's salmon bailiff, whose job it was to apprehend poachers on the Tyne.

¶¶ FOOD & DRINK

Tynemouth's **Front Street** is packed with cafés, seafood restaurants and bars. Side street eateries are also worth checking out, including the popular **Priory Café** (Percy Park Rd ✆ 0191 259 0627 ☺ daily), which does breakfasts and lunches and is a hit with tea lovers. For picnics or a take-away sandwich, the **Deli Around the Corner** (61 Hotspur St ✆ 0191 259 0086 ☺ Tue–Sat), just off Front Street, sells very tempting homemade quiches, sausage rolls, regional cheeses and meats, and quality bread.

Crusoe's Longsands beach (south end) ✆ 0191 296 4152 ☺ daily ♿ 🐾. It's located right on the beach so Crusoe's is an immediate winner with dog walkers, runners and parents with kids (they drink coffee on the outside terrace; their kids play at their feet in the sand). Crusoe's trades mainly in breakfasts and light lunches (paninis, burgers, jackets, battered cod) and you can also pick up take-away fish and chips from a hatch round the side of the restaurant. **Longsands Fish Kitchen** 27 Front St ✆ 0191 272 8552 ☺ Wed–Mon ♿. Considered one of the best fish and chip take-away in town, hence the queues coiled inside. Many ingredients come direct off the boats at Shields' Fish Quay so you won't find a fresher fish platter. Also on the menu is grilled hake, Whitby scampi, seafood curry and fish pie.

Riley's Fish Shack King Edward's Bay (below the north side of the Priory) ✆ 0191 257 1371 ⊙ daily until late. Right on the beach is this super (and super pricey) seafood restaurant that everyone talks about. Smoke billows out of the kitchen (housed in one of two shipping containers) on to the veranda where trendy 30-somethings on bar stools devour chargrilled squid and monkfish tail wraps. On the sand, customers recline on deckchairs watching families playing rounders and kids running into the sea.

The View Longsands Beach (north end) ✆ 0191 253 5459 ⊙ daily ♿ 🐾. At the north end of Longsands is a modern, glass-walled restaurant raised above the sand serving crowd-pleasing breakfasts and hot lunches (burgers, fish and chips etc).

7 CULLERCOATS

> **Very familiar indeed is the figure of the Cullercoats fishwife, as, clad in blue serge jacket, short petticoats with ample skirts, large apron and black straw bonnet she trudges along with a heavy creel of fish on her shoulders, calling, in shrill and not unmusical tones of voice 'Buy fee-s-ch.'**
> W W Tomlinson, *Comprehensive Guide to Northumberland,* 1888

A mile north along the seafront from Tynemouth, this small former fishing village faces the sea above a quiet sandy cove where Sunday strollers take in the salty air from the clifftop promenade and braver children – their legs and arms pink with the cold – jump off the little pier. The adventurous may like to hire a kayak (or a stand-up paddleboard) from the friendly **CBK Adventures** (1A Norma Crescent ✆ 0191 251 9412 ⌂ cbkadventures.co.uk ⊙ summer daily; autumn & winter variable) and cross the waves to St Mary's Lighthouse. You'll see plenty of birdlife and perhaps bottlenose dolphins.

The beach here formed the backdrop to many paintings by the **Cullercoats Colony** of artists who captured the lives of local people from around 1870 to 1920: men returning from sea in their wooden boats, women mending nets, collecting seaweed and carrying baskets of fish, and scenes similar to those observed by the Victorian travel writer Tomlinson in the excerpt above. A small number of these atmospheric paintings hang in the Laing Art Gallery in Newcastle (page 27) including John Charlton's well-known 1910 masterpiece, *The Women*, depicting the rescue of the *Lovely Nellie* ship that ran aground on New Year's Day in 1861 near St Mary's Lighthouse. A storm prevented the Cullercoats lifeboat reaching the stricken vessel so it was pulled overland for two miles to where it could be launched. Everyone was saved except for the cabin boy. The focus in the painting is on the strong local women, shirtsleeves rolled up, heaving the boat in lashing rain alongside men and boys.

The old **lifeboat station** is still operational, but much has changed in the village: many buildings were razed in the latter half of the 20th century, and where Tomlinson counted some 40 fishing boats in his 1888 guide, today just a few cobles are moored in the bay.

¶¶ FOOD & DRINK

Cullercoats is becoming a popular alternative to busy Tynemouth. A lot of folk head straight for **Beaches & Cream** (1 Victoria Crescent ☎ 0191 251 4718 ♿) for its sea-facing location, sundaes and afternoon teas, but there are some good places round the corner worth considering for coffee, breakfasts and lunches. **Cullercoats Coffee** (22 John St) is one: chatty staff, a laid-back Sunday morning vibe (even on weekdays), decent coffees and breakfasts. Across the road is **The Boatyard** (1 John St ☎ 0191 280 1077 ♿ 🐾), known for its really good brunch menu: avocado on toast with a kick of chilli, haggis on sourdough, eggs cooked many ways, fry ups, pancakes.

8 WHITLEY BAY

> The sharp bite of the saline waters at Whitley Bay is of the utmost value in all cases of debility, and especially to the jaded business man.
> Guidebook to Whitley Bay, 1909

Once the Blackpool of the North East, Whitley Bay's popularity began to wane in the latter half of the 20th century when the coastal resort had an air of 'faded grandeur' about its old sea-facing hotels and promenade. But things are really looking up for Whitley since an injection of funds has transformed the area around the landmark **Spanish City** pleasure hall – an eye-catching Edwardian building with a huge white dome and two towers – reopened in 2018 following extensive restoration. Works included new replica copper casts of the two dancing girls on either tower (the originals are displayed inside for safekeeping) and a complete overhaul of the interior, with new restaurants and a couple of shops on the promenade selling regional gifts and local beers (page 61). When built in 1910 with a theatre and roof gardens, the Spanish City had the largest dome in the UK after St Paul's Cathedral in London.

One building in the vicinity of Spanish City that was saved from the bulldozer is the **Amusement Centre** with its dazzling red frontage. In previous decades, it might have been considered an eyesore, but the building's unchanged interior (check out the 1980s patterned carpet), lighting and delightfully unsophisticated arcade machines seem wonderfully retro today. One day Historic England will pay a visit. A couple of doors up, incidentally, is **Di Meo's** (see below), probably the best ice cream parlour in the whole of the North East.

More retro fun can be had at the **Whitley Bay Playhouse** (Marine Avenue ℰ 0191 2515484 𝄞 playhousewhitleybay.co.uk) – a magnet for tribute music acts and community shows.

A wide beach-side **promenade** (♿) connects Spanish City with St Mary's Lighthouse, around a mile north. You can also walk on the beach of course – a long expanse of beige sand that meets the black reefs of St Mary's Island (great for rockpooling and birdwatching) at its northern end (page 62). If you happen to be visiting during stormy conditions when there's a high tide, the waves surge over the promenade to the delight of

"An injection of funds has transformed the area around the landmark Spanish City pleasure hall."

onlookers. To actually surf the waves, you'll need some kit: **Northern Swell** (Watts Slope ℰ 07869 270702 ☉ daily; winter weekends only) on the promenade below Spanish City will sort you out with paddleboards, surf boards and kayaks. Bikes for hire too.

🍴 FOOD & DRINK

Fish and chip shops, cafés and Italian restaurants are plentiful in Whitley Bay's town centre and along the seafront. With a couple of standout options around Spanish City, Whitley is a rival to Tynemouth these days for a decent meal or take-away. If you're walking south on the promenade or beach towards Cullercoats, pick up hot drinks, light lunches and cakes at the **Links Art Gallery** (Dukes Walk ℰ 0191 447 5534 ☉ daily ♿ to the rear, accessed from the promenade). Next door, with more space and a fetching blue and red vintage interior (kitsch or simply old fashioned, I don't know) is the **Rendezvous Café** (ℰ 0191 252 5548 ☉ daily 🐾), which has the advantage of sea views but not a great food menu. One for a tea after a blustery beach walk perhaps. Note too, the **Hazy Daze Bottle Shop & tap room** (☉ from noon daily) on the Spanish City terrace which has an excellent selection of local beers to take-away (and enjoy with your fish supper perhaps).

Di Meo's 9 Marine Av ℰ 0191 252 3814 ☉ 10.00–20.00 daily. Famous regionally for making the most outlandish and delicious ice creams in the North East. All the standard favourites (heavenly Belgian chocolate and raspberry pavlova) but unusual ices too (battenberg made with marzipan for example) and a few vegan options. The downside is the queues, which line the pavement whatever the season and weather.

Fisherman's Bay 6 East Pde ✐ 0191 447 4774 ☉ daily ♿. Rivals to Trenchers at Spanish City (see below) for great fish and chips to eat in the pleasant modern restaurant or take-away. This is where I come for a fish supper when in the area: the batter is crispy, the twice-cooked chips dark gold and soft, and there are plenty of benches outside to enjoy your food with a sea view. Also note a few surprises on the menu: squid, haggis and chips, extensive vegan and gluten-free options, pea fritters and posh cod finger sandwiches. The downside: the queues and the price for dining inside, unless you are a kid or qualify for the good-value 'Pensioner's Special'. Take-away prices are average for the area.

Spanish City ✐ 0191 691 7090 ☉ daily ♿. Landmark Art Deco domed pleasure hall with stunning sea views from the top floor where there's a **champagne bar** (also serving very special afternoon teas). Downstairs, **Trenchers Restaurant** (great fish and chips to eat in or take-away, but with plenty of other options including fish pie, burgers and sharing boards) occupies a beautiful, airy dining space under the dome where a pianist plays a few days a week. **Valerie's Tearoom** is a friendly terrace-side café with views across the landscaped open spaces outside Spanish City. All-day breakfasts and brunch (full English, pancakes, bacon buns, eggs on toast many ways), sandwiches, toasties, quiches and scones. Fancy cakes and afternoon teas for those who have booked.

9 ST MARY'S LIGHTHOUSE

Whitley Bay ✐ 0191 643 4777 ☉ May–Sep, subject to the tides so check the council website (⊘ northtyneside.gov.uk) or call; Oct–Apr: w/ends & school holidays (again, subject to tides) ♿ shop 🐾

St Mary's Lighthouse first shone her beam across the North Sea on 31 August 1898 and for the next 86 years the white beacon helped keep mariners away from the dangerous rocks off the coast of Whitley Bay until it was decommissioned in 1984. A short causeway links the mainland with the lighthouse isle. Visitors can climb to the top of St Mary's by way of 137 steps up a dizzying spiral staircase and enjoy the expansive view at the top: from Blyth to the mouth of the Tyne. Below, grey seals haul themselves up onto the rocks at low tide. They are spotted quite easily from the top of the lighthouse.

Rockpooling around the causeway is a favourite pastime of many who visit and you might want to join one of the family **events** during school holidays, organised by the lighthouse rangers. They also run fossil-hunting forays (but you can also do your own search on the little bay just north of the causeway) and rockpooling events in the dark for the over 12s. 'At night, the wildlife comes alive,' one ranger told me.

St Mary's Island wetland nature reserve hosts large numbers of ducks and wading birds, especially from October and through the winter months but it's a nice place to visit in any season to see, from the viewing hide, the Exmoor ponies doing their bit for the conservation of the grassland site. It's easily reached from the lighthouse car park.

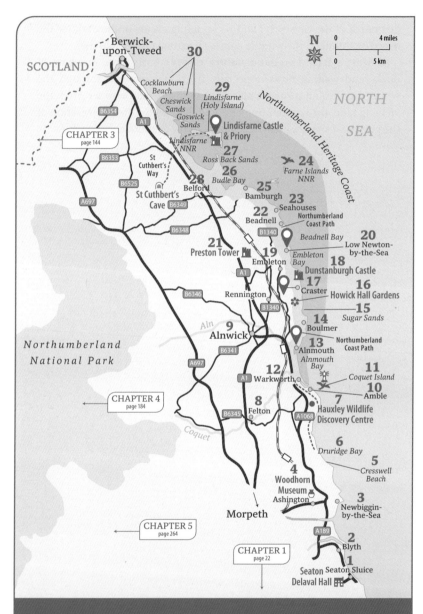

THE NORTHUMBERLAND COAST

2
THE NORTHUMBERLAND COAST

Northumberland's 70-mile coastline is a desolate sweep of sea, soft sands, dunes, offshore islands and rocky promontories, interrupted only by medieval castles and the odd fishing village and town. It's one of the finest and most unspoilt coasts in England, popular with families, hikers, birdwatchers and watersports enthusiasts, but, for the most part, wonderfully crowd free.

Nowhere is this more apparent than between Amble and Berwick-upon-Tweed, the **Northumberland Heritage Coast** (page 89). Here you'll find most of the best bathing beaches, the **Farne Islands National Nature Reserve** (page 122), **Lindisfarne Priory** (page 134) and all the famous **castles** – four within 20 miles. Most striking is mighty **Bamburgh** (page 125), which rises spectacularly from the dunes, dominating its namesake village and the silky sands below.

Many visitors – and particularly families – tend to head for the **beaches** close to Embleton, Beadnell, Seahouses and Bamburgh, leaving the likes of Sugar Sands, Rumbling Kern, Football Hole, Ross Back Sands, Lindisfarne's bays and Cheswick Sands to those solitude seekers in the know.

Don't overlook the **south Northumberland coast** (page 68), either. Some of the longest and most appealing sands are at Cresswell and Druridge Bay, which also have much to lure the birder, particularly in autumn. North Tyneside's coastal strip between North Shields and Whitley Bay is described in *Chapter 1,* and Berwick-upon-Tweed's in *Chapter 3.*

GETTING AROUND

If using public transport to access the Heritage Coast, you'll have to be well organised as buses (page 66) are not particularly frequent (except

> **TOURIST INFORMATION**
>
> **Alnwick** Alnwick Playhouse, Bondgate Without ✆ 01665 511333 ◷ Mon–Sat ♿
> **Berwick-upon-Tweed** (page 147)

for services to Alnwick), and the train stations (Berwick, Alnmouth and Chathill) are set back at least a mile from the shore. That said, the two coast buses (see below) shuttle between all the popular villages on the Heritage Coast and can come in very handy. A bicycle is your friend in some parts but even the main coast trail (NCN Route 1) re-routes away from a number of popular destinations, making it tricky to access the seafront without using the road network.

BUS

Getting to the **south Northumberland coast** is relatively easy, with several buses an hour from Newcastle to Blyth, Whitley Bay and Seaton Sluice (308) and Seaton Delaval Hall (X7). The 306 is the more useful service for coast visitors, passing the likes of Tynemouth and North Shields.

The **Northumberland Heritage Coast** is surprisingly well serviced, though buses are not as frequent. Two Arriva buses connect Newcastle with Berwick via Alnwick: the X15 is fast and fairly direct; the X18 is useful for reaching the beaches and smaller villages. See map on page 18 or ⌨ arrivabus.co.uk/north-east.

Buses X18 and 418 connect all the sea-facing villages and towns between Morpeth and Berwick, including Alnwick. They are also helpful with return journeys on linear walks.

CYCLING

The popular **Coast and Castles** route, National Cycle Network (NCN) Route 1, from Newcastle to Edinburgh (some 200 miles) and part of the North Sea Cycle Route, runs the length of Northumberland's coast to Berwick though it turns inland between one of the most beautiful stretches of coastal scenery between Craster and Lindisfarne. At the border you turn inland and trace the Tweed for the final leg to Edinburgh. The whole route is manageable on a touring bike and you can stay by the sea from Berwick to Edinburgh by transferring to NCN Route 76.

The Bike Shop (Willowburn Trading Estate, Alnwick ℰ 07599 350000 ⊙ Tue–Sat) is your go-to for anything bike related on the Heritage Coast, including repairs. Hire bikes from the shop in Alnwick, including electric bikes, and pick the brains of the knowledgeable owner, Adam, who can answer any technical question and provide info on the best routes, including an almost entirely off-road circuit direct from the shop to Druridge Bay via Alnmouth. He also runs **Coquet Cycles** (ℰ 07599 350000) a very useful mobile emergency service for all biking disasters, wherever you are in Northumberland.

For bike hire in the Amble area, cycle holidays, pick-up and drop-off services, and bike and baggage transfers, contact **Pedal Power** (page 301).

WALKING

Linear beach walks are unbeatable and well marked thanks to the 64-mile **Northumberland Coast Path** from Cresswell to Berwick-upon-Tweed, sometimes signed as the **England Coast Path**. It's walkable in six days.

Generally, the scenery behind the dunes is flat and not in the same league as the coastal strip, so mostly you're confined to the seafront itself. Walkers therefore make good use of the X18 bus (page 66) for return journeys. **Newton-by-the-Sea to Alnmouth**, for example, is a fabulous 11-mile linear route taking in many of Northumberland's best beaches and is easily completed in four to five hours, but you could walk a shorter section such as **Newton-by-the-Sea to Craster** (page 114), **Beadnell** (page 119) or **Seahouses**; or **Bamburgh to Budle Bay** (page 125).

A couple of circular walks worth highlighting are the **Craster to Howick** route (page 105) and the **Lindisfarne round-island** walk (page 140). Cresswell Beach, Druridge Bay, Alnmouth Bay, Ross Back Sands and Cheswick Sands are the ultimate beaches for a lonesome windswept walk.

St Cuthbert's Way takes in the best of Northumberland's hill and coastal scenery on its 62½-mile journey from Melrose in Scotland across the Cheviot Hills to Lindisfarne. It's a stunning route and there is a tremendous view of the coast once you reach the Kyloe Hills; the final nine-mile leg from Holborn (parking at Holborn Grange) to Lindisfarne makes for a superb linear day hike (book a taxi for the return).

TAXIS

Alnwick Taxis Alnwick, Alnmouth, Seahouses & around ✆ 01665 606060 / 07976 606060 &

Knights Taxis Alnmouth, Amble & Alnwick ✆ 01665 714555/07760 751667

RSM Taxis Alnmouth & Alnwick areas ✆ 07308 953929. Always friendly, helpful and have a large six-seater.

Sovereign Taxis Alnwick & surrounds ✆ 07553 360662

Woody's Taxis Berwick ✆ 01289 547009 &

THE SOUTH NORTHUMBERLAND COAST

Between Seaton Sluice and Amble, the coastline offers glimpses of what makes Northumberland's shores so renowned: vast stretches of soft sands, high dunes and old seaside towns. Though the sands are interrupted now and then by places that hold little appeal to tourists, beaches like those at **Cresswell** and **Druridge Bay** are some of the very best in the region.

The industrial past of these shores reveals itself at **Blyth** and **Newbiggin**, and even well-known beauty spots such as **Hauxley nature reserve** were once industrial sites. To learn more about the mining history in these parts, a tour of the engaging **Woodhorn Museum** (page 73) near Ashington is highly recommended.

1 SEATON SLUICE

The main draw to this unassuming village is **Seaton Delaval Hall** (see below), a Baroque mansion that has far outlived the coal and glass industries on its doorstep. The settlement gets its name from the sluice gates in the harbour designed by one of the Delavals to keep the inlet clear of silt on each tide. This improved the export of salt, coal and glass – as did enlarging the harbour by blasting through the cliff. The colliery and the six 18th-century glassworks cones that used to frame the skyline, however, are long gone. In 1862, 204 men and boys died at the nearby Hartley coal pit when the mine shaft caved in, imprisoning them underground.

Seaton Delaval Hall

The Avenue, NE26 4QR ✆ 0191 237 9100 ☉ Wed–Sun; school holidays daily; bus X7 from Seaton Sluice stops outside the Hall & grounds & café 🐾 grounds only; National Trust

Awesome in its scale, lavish in design and incongruous to the unremarkable surroundings, Seaton Delaval Hall comes as a fabulous surprise to visitors in the area. Since the National Trust opened the doors in 2010, it has become one of the region's most visited historic attractions, celebrated for its formal gardens and exterior by Sir John Vanbrugh (the most eminent country house architect in England during the early 1700s), who died a few years before the mansion – one of his greatest – was completed in 1730.

Before a fire destroyed the interior of the central block in 1822, Seaton Delaval was infamous as a place of spectacle, drama and mischief. Costume balls, parades and parties were notorious – as were the elaborate tricks: disappearing walls and furniture being fixed to the ceiling. The National Trust have brought to life the flamboyant side of the Delaval family with a series of contemporary, playful exhibits – a huge shiny sphere suspended with ropes, and more mirrored installations in the outdoor play areas among the trees, continuing the theme of surprise and trickery.

"Seaton Delaval was infamous as a place of spectacle, drama and mischief."

As for the **Great Hall** and **Saloon** that remain gutted, restoration works are ongoing but, even today, you gain a strong sense of how extravagant the marble-floored entrance must have been before the fire. Armless stucco statues line the walls and a wrought-iron balcony frames the first-floor landing. Either side of the portico are the impressive **Stables** (east wing) and **Kitchen** (west wing). To the rear of the central block, the south portico opens with a view of countryside where families make use of the open space to play ball games. Walk around the side to reach the **gardens**: formal hedging, roses, herbaceous borders and a magnificent weeping ash planted at the time the manor was built.

The only furnished part of the house today is the **West Wing**. One of the highlights is an 'upside down' room with furniture fixed to the ceiling. Portraits on a nearby wall include that of the only male heir of Sir John Delaval, who died before his father. Apparently the young man was already a sickly creature when he was kicked in the genitals by a maid whom he had assaulted. He never recovered from his injuries.

A very short stroll from the Hall (or reached via the A190) is the Norman **Church of Our Lady** (✆ 0191 2371136 ☉ generally 13.00–

16.30 when the hall is open & for Sun services) which is well worth visiting. It dates to 1102 and was for 700 years the private chapel of the Delaval family. It's unusual in having two Norman arches spanning the interior.

You can **walk** from the coast to Seaton Delaval Hall in 15 minutes on pavement along the A190, but if you have the time I recommend the longer 2½-mile riverside route from Seaton Sluice (start from below the Melton Constable pub). You'll need ❈ OS Explorer map 316. Follow the river through Holywell Dene then cross fields with Seaton Delaval's obelisk coming into view through a parting in the trees. Access the Hall via the aforementioned church.

2 BLYTH

From Seaton Sluice, a thick belt of dunes criss-crossed by sandy trails and a paved path leads to Blyth. Though its town centre holds little appeal to casual visitors, look for the house on Bath Terrace with a prominent stone porch and the word 'BATHS' inscribed above that dates to the early 19th century. Curiously, in the back lane stands a **lighthouse** that once caught the eye of painter L S Lowry, who sketched the 60ft-tall beacon. The lower half dates to 1788; the tiers above were added in the Victorian era.

Close by is **Ridley Park** (Wensleydale Ter), an Edwardian family park with a water play area and lots of green space. To the north is Blyth's **South Beach**, a popular bay with local dog walkers and families. Here, colourful beach huts face the sea and a World War I and II **battery**, complete with a replica naval gun and observation post, stands prominently in the dunes, providing good hiding places for children playing on the grassy slopes (if they're not already occupied in the playground). Beyond Blyth is **Cambois Bay** – another desolate expanse of sand.

¶¶ FOOD & DRINK

Coastline Fish and Chips South Beach, Links Rd, Blyth ✆ 01670 797428 ☺ daily &. Fish and chips and ice-cream parlour just behind the beach. Always busy.

3 NEWBIGGIN-BY-THE-SEA

When I last visited this old fishing town, a wicked northeasterly was blasting the bay where I watched a woman and her dog both walking sideways to the wind. In poor weather, it wouldn't be unfair to describe Newbiggin as a rather pinched-looking place, but the sun brings families onto the promenade where sands drift over the walkway, and Newbiggin suddenly seems altogether much more agreeable – a place with a fascinating maritime history and bucketloads of community pride set around a perfect horseshoe bay.

A clutch of heritage attractions below the 14th-century **St Bartholomew Church** dominate the northern curve of the bay by the wonderful **Maritime Centre** (see below). Offshore, the eye is drawn to a modern sculpture, *Couple*, of a man and a woman poised on a platform above the waves.

A short stroll along the promenade from the Maritime Centre, past a play area, takes you to a boatpark with many fine traditional cobles and old tractors on display. Note the historic **rocket house** and **RNLI** (Royal National Lifeboat Institution) building (☉ Fri–Tue), the oldest working station in the UK, established in 1851. Today's modern lifeboat is housed inside under wooden boards detailing rescue missions over the last 170-odd years, but the modern tractor steals the show for many young visitors.

Before tractors pulled the lifeboat to the sea from the mid-20th century onwards, women volunteers did the job using ropes and brute strength. The services of the women lifeboat launchers of Newbiggin are legendary and were called on not that long ago when the historic *Mary Joicey* **lifeboat** returned to Newbiggin in 2011. Elderly ladies, children, mums and teenagers came out to haul the boat to its final resting place.

Newbiggin Maritime Centre

Church Point ✆ 01670 811951 ☉ summer daily; winter Tue–Sun ♿

Visitors and locals fill the bright café and exhibition spaces housed within this modern, purpose-built heritage centre that celebrates the fishing traditions of the town – and the wider Northumberland coast.

Engaging displays include one of herring tools and another showcasing a hand-crafted example of a Newbiggin 'Gansey' jumper traditionally worn by fishermen. The cable patterns of individual jumpers were altered slightly to help identify the wearer should disaster strike at sea. Some fascinating early photos show the beach scene over a hundred years ago with traditional coble boats on the sands and the upturned

MILOSZ MASLANKA/S

DAVE HEAD/S

GAIL JOHNSON/S

GEMMA HALL

hulls of herring boats repurposed into boathouses. Fisherwomen pose for the camera in their customary way, with fists on hips.

Old video footage captures Newbiggin when fishing was at the heart of many sea-facing towns and villages in the region – a story that is as much about the hard-working women of the town. Newbiggin women were famous for pulling in the boats up the sands every morning. Centre stage in the museum is the beautiful *Girl Anne* **coble** that used to work out of the bay, and the famous 1966 *Mary Joicey* **lifeboat** (page 71).

4 WOODHORN MUSEUM

Ashington NE63 9YF ⌀ 01670 528080 ☉ Wed–Sun & bank holidays; school holidays daily ♿

A few miles inland near Ashington, once known as 'the biggest pit village in the world' is the best surviving example of a late 19th-century northern colliery, complete with winding houses, yards and pit-pony stables. Even without the miners, horses, smoke and clatter of machinery and waggons, you gain a good sense of what it was like here before the colliery closed in the 1980s, and the excellent visitor centre and approachable stewards, some of whom are former miners, bring that side of the colliery to life.

"Visitors can stand inside an original pit 'cage', once used for transporting miners underground."

An indoor **exhibition** takes you forward in time from the height of coal mining through to the strikes and closures in the late 20th century (plenty of 1980s memorabilia will trigger the memories of visitors of a certain age). Visitors can stand inside an original pit 'cage', once used for transporting miners underground, but perhaps the most stirring exhibit is a wooden 'tally board' with metal numbered discs the size of a coin hanging from hooks. Each belonged to a miner and recorded who was down the mine in case of an accident.

Woodhorn also provides insight into the domestic life of miners and their pastimes. Nowhere is this more vividly represented than in the **Ashington Group gallery** with its famous collection of artworks by the

---

◄ **1** Seaton Delaval Hall. **2** Newbiggin-by-the-Sea is home to a number of historic fishing boats including these cobles in a boatyard near the RNLI. **3** The Woodhorn Museum is the best surviving example of a late 19th-century northern colliery. **4** Cresswell Beach.

THE PITMEN PAINTERS

Here I found an outlet for other things than earning my living. There is a feeling of being my own boss for a change and with it comes a sense of freedom.

Harry Wilson, founder member of the Ashington Group, quoted at the Woodhorn Museum

The story of how a group of coal miners from Ashington became painters is an unlikely one. In 1934, a group of miners hired a lecturer from Durham University to teach art appreciation. As part of their tuition, they learned to paint and were encouraged to capture their surroundings on canvas, which they did for 50 years to much acclaim while continuing to work in the colliery.

Their unsentimental paintings depict men working underground, domestic routines and their leisure activities (growing leeks, dog racing, bowling, pigeon-keeping and so on). In the early noughties, a Lee Hall play based on the Ashington Group opened in London's West End. A compelling collection of their paintings is on permanent display in the Woodhorn Museum (page 73).

Pitmen Painters (see opposite), which provides the inspiration for a changing contemporary arts programme across the museum. A **pop-up art studio** for children is open every day during the school holidays (☺ noon–15.00).

The other artworks really worth your time over at the museum are the old **colliery banners** with their rousing socialist slogans and images of a better future.

Close to the museum is the **QEII Country Park** – a large scenic lake with picnic tables, a lakeside trail and pub.

5 CRESSWELL BEACH

Cresswell's soft sands are easily accessible from the coast road. Picture a pristine bay, high dunes and a great ice-cream shop that also sells buckets and spades. The beach is reached via some steps to the side of Cresswell Ices (see opposite), but to find your very own stretch of sand, head north out of the village for half a mile or so where a few paths snake through the dunes and on to the bay. Nearby is a **nature reserve** – a brackish lagoon fringed by reeds and a known stopping-off point for migrant birds (pink-footed geese and snow buntings in autumn/winter are the star visitors). The last time I was here, a barn owl was quartering over the grasslands.

Cresswell **village** shelters the ruins of a 14th-century **pele tower** (facing the ice-cream shop across the large green).

¶¶ FOOD & DRINK

Cresswell Ices ⊙ Apr–Oct & Feb school holidays. This fetching vintage-looking corner shop has been making children happy since 1933 and stocks most things you could need for a day out at the beach, as well as a load of plastic tat (parents beware). The owner makes her own ice cream, with 15 flavours on offer.

Drift Café Cresswell ✆ 01670 861599 ⊙ from 09.00 daily ♿ 🐾. North of Cresswell, on the outskirts of the village, is this extremely busy café and popular rest point for cyclists, serving light lunches, soups, scones, cakes and coffees outside in the sun or in the modern café. On the downside, it is pricey for casual dining, with wraps, jackets, quiche, omelettes and hot stottie sandwiches coming in at around £10.

6 DRURIDGE BAY

One of Northumberland's most deserted beaches is a sweeping expanse of sand backed by high dunes that extends for six wind-whipped miles from Cresswell to just south of Amble. Popular with walkers and birdwatchers, Druridge Bay is also known for its **wetland nature reserve** – a series of lagoons created from old coal mines. Sheltered behind the dunes, the pools attract large numbers of birds in winter, notably pink-footed geese, short-eared owls and whooper swans. I once saw a bittern clamber out of the reedbeds in a rare burst of extroversion. The pools are linked by the **coast path**, which takes a varied route along the beach, tracks and grassy dunes.

"Druridge Bay is also known for its wetland nature reserve – a series of lagoons created from old coal mines."

Within the **Druridge Bay Country Park** (access from Red Row) is **Ladyburn Lake**, where there's a **visitor centre** (NE61 5BX ⊙ w/ends & school holidays daily ♿), modern **café** (⊙ 10.00–16.30 daily, winter till 15.00) for breakfast sandwiches, toasties, baked potatoes, cakes, pastries and scones etc, and large picnic area and playground. If you have your own canoe, windsurfing board or sailing boat, purchase a permit from the visitor centre to use the lake (⊙ Apr–Oct); otherwise you can **hire watercrafts** (kayaks, stand-up paddleboards, windsurfers and accessible sailing dinghies) from the Coquet Shorebase Trust by calling ✆ 01665 710367 the day before. From the parking area you can also access the beach or walk around its perimeter (♿ south shore).

7 HAUXLEY WILDLIFE DISCOVERY CENTRE

Near Low Hauxley village, Druridge Bay NE65 0JR 🕿 0191 284 6884 ⊙ daily; free admission
♿ accessible trail, visitor centre & café

At the northern end of Druridge Bay is this wonderfully secluded Northumberland Wildlife Trust reserve, visitor centre and café. Viewing hides overlook a secluded lagoon, once an open-cast coal mine but now inhabited by otters, wildfowl and gulls (four species of terns visit in summer). A couple of short trails take you through the main habitats.

The surrounding meadows come alive during the summer with many species of butterfly and wildflowers. Red squirrels and tree sparrows (like a house sparrow but with dark patches on either cheek) frequently visit the feeders close to the car park. Autumn sees the arrival of wading birds and ducks in large numbers.

Quite randomly by the side of the road is a **milk vending machine** supplied by Hauxley Farm with a variety of flavoured milkshakes for sale as well as standard plain milk – all in glass pint bottles. They also sell handmade butter.

Hauxley Haven & Amble Links

The dune-backed sands between Low Hauxley and Amble tend to be overlooked by those travelling along the coast, but not by birdwatchers and locals who appreciate a lonesome stroll with a view of Coquet Island and the promise of excellent fish and chips and ice cream on reaching Amble. Children may also enjoy the rock pools along the way. From the vantage point of the dunes, you might see puffins, eider ducks and gannets out at sea, and wading birds and terns along the shore.

8 FELTON

Moments from the A1 (but not within sight or sound of the road), is this highly picturesque stone village arranged along a wooded stretch of the River Coquet. Spanning the waterway is a 15th-century stone **bridge** worthy of a few photographs. Two very good places to eat face each other either side of the Coquet (page 78), making Felton popular with weekend day-trippers. On the south side, a walkway leads to the **river,**

◄ **1** Golden light on the marram grasses at Druridge Bay. **2** Winter sees migrant birds gather at Druridge Bay wetland nature reserve. **3** From the dune-backed sands along the coast, look for eider ducks out at sea. **4** View towards Coquet Island.

which flows slowly under the boughs of mature trees. Children may like to while away some time throwing stones from the wide shingle bank here.

St Oswald's Way (page 301) long-distance path enters the village on the north side of the river, crosses the bridge and then continues to the coast on the south side. The path is well trodden, wooded and makes for a very pleasant riverside wander.

¶| FOOD & DRINK

Northumberland Arms The Peth ℘ 01670 787370 ☺ daily ♿ 🐾. An old coaching inn dating to 1820 with a double-barrelled frontage, the Northumbrian Arms overlooks a dreamy stretch of river and is a very fine place to eat – one of the very best rural pubs in Northumberland, for its food, service and surroundings. It's also a great place to stay, with immaculate, upmarket rooms. Needless to say, you'll need to book ahead at peak times. Outside tables across the road take in the scenery to the full.

A lot of care and thought has gone into the menus (lunches, evening dinners, children's, light lunches) which are peppered with local produce. Start your meal with a langoustine raviolo with shellfish landed at North Shields, or sea trout, orange and fennel salad; and follow with a classic: fish and chips, steak frites, pie or something a bit special like the truffle-stuffed chicken. For a simple al fresco lunch by the river, a posh fish finger sandwich, soup or a hot roast beef stottie sandwich is just the thing on a sunny day. Prices are above average.

The Running Fox Café 2–4 Riverside ℘ 01670 787090 ☺ daily. So good are the breakfasts, lunches and especially the cakes that new Running Fox cafés have popped up in a number of unexpected places in recent years, but this is the original bistro. And what a lovely spot to enjoy your hearty soup with Running Fox bread, quiche or an enormous slice of cake than from the sunny terrace above the Coquet. Also doubles as a shop selling newspapers and a small selection of Northumbrian goodies (honey, chutneys and jams etc).

9 ALNWICK

🏠 The Cookie Jar

'Alnwick is ever under the spell of the dreamy past', a late 19th-century visitor to the town observed. Today, you might also say it is under the spell of *Harry Potter*, whose fans flock to the town's famous medieval **castle**, better known to some as Hogwarts. For others, even without its fortress and celebrated **gardens**, Alnwick (pronounced 'Annick') is one of the most vibrant and historically interesting market towns in Northumberland, and easily reached from the coast by car in 20 minutes.

ALNWICK'S TOWN CENTRE

In or out? That is the question in Alnwick. Are you *within* the old town walls or outside (*without*) them? One long road passes through the centre of Alnwick, divided by a mighty medieval gateway: Bondgate Without becomes Bondgate Within once under **Bondgate Tower**, which has served as a main entry point into the once-walled town since its construction in 1450. The marketplace, castle and many places to eat are within; Barter Books, The Alnwick Gardens and the tourist information office at the Playhouse are without.

To explore all the popular attractions, a free hop-on hop-off **sightseeing bus** (☉ end May–Sep daily) makes a circular route of the town, stopping at marked Alnwick Attractions bus stops.

Bondgate Within, the Market Place & around

Enter Alnwick from the north on the B6341 for a highly picturesque view of the castle as you cross the River Aln over the 18th-century **Lion Bridge** (page 82). From the south or east, it's still a memorable arrival as you pass under **Bondgate Tower** and enter Bondgate Within, a wide thoroughfare of Georgian and Victorian buildings.

Market Place marks the heart of this lively town where three venerable streets wrap around a piazza (still with its medieval market cross) and boasts a regular Thursday, Friday and Saturday **market** (mainly crafts and clothes but with some local food stalls) and several outdoor cafés.

Behind the Market Place is **Fenkle Street** – a long run of old merchants' houses. The street curves to meet **Narrowgate** where there's a scattering of tea rooms, interiors shops, an antiques emporium, art gallery and deli. The dusty bottles in the window of **The Dirty Bottles** restaurant and bar (page 88) and restaurant, at the junction with Pottergate, are said to be cursed and have not been touched in 200 years.

By continuing uphill and away from the Market Place you will reach the entrance to the **castle** (page 80), which blocks one end of Bailiffgate, Alnwick's most elegant street of sandstone houses. At the other end is **St Michael's Church** (page 83) and halfway along, the **Bailiffgate Museum** (page 84). The entrance to **Hulne Park** (page 84) is close by and recommended for an extended country walk.

Those with an interest in fishing will know the world-renowned **Hardy** (30 Bondgate Within ✆ 01665 510027 ☉ Tues–Sat ♿ shop only), manufacturers of rods and reels (the 'Rolls Royce of fishing reels'), is based in Alnwick. Traditional bamboo rods cost thousands but are still sold to those with a fondness for the craftsmanship of yesteryear, the likes of King Charles III, for example. A small museum chronicles the 150-year-old business.

Heritage seekers should also look out for the **White Swan Hotel** ($\mathscr{O}$ 01665 602109). In the 1930s, the then owner of the hotel bought all the fittings and artworks from the decommissioned *Olympic* cruise liner (the *Titanic*'s sister ship) and reconstructed them to make an opulent dining room. You don't need to stay at the hotel to dine in the sumptuous oak-panelled restaurant that transports you back to the era of transatlantic cruises, Edwardian style.

Bondgate Without & further afield

Outside the medieval gateway is **Alnwick Playhouse** ($\mathscr{O}$ 01665 660550 $\odot$ Tue–Sat &), a family-focused theatre with cinema screenings, drama, dance and music events for all ages, and now also housing the **tourist information office** (page 66).

Many folk make straight for the acclaimed secondhand bookshop, **Barter Books** (page 86), housed in Alnwick's old railway station. Raised on a grassy mound opposite is the **Percy Tenantry Column**, a fluted pillar surmounted with a lion and guarded at its base by four other feline beasts. It was erected in 1816 by the tenants of the 2nd Duke of Northumberland after he reduced rents during tough economic times. The lion is the emblem of the Percy family of Alnwick Castle and crops up in many places about town. Turning down the road here (B1340) the entranceway to **The Alnwick Garden** (page 82) is reached in a few hundred yards.

ALNWICK CASTLE

Where Bailiffgate meets Narrowgate $\mathscr{O}$ 01665 510777 $\odot$ end Mar–Oct & grounds only

Known as the 'Windsor Castle of the North' in tourism literature on account of its size and imposing buildings, Alnwick is the second largest inhabited castle in the UK. Like Windsor, it's home to royalty; well, Geordie royalty at least: the Duke and Duchess of Northumberland. Historically one of the most powerful aristocratic families in England, with a lineage dating to the Norman Conquest, Alnwick has been their principal seat for 700 years, since Henry de Percy bought the stronghold from the Bishop of Durham in 1309. Stonework from the earlier

Norman building is seen in the archway into the keep, but the castle was extensively rebuilt in the 14th century and again in the latter half of the 18th century.

The present buildings are largely medieval and the castle roughly retains its original layout with a circular **keep** about a courtyard and an **inner and outer bailey**. Miniature stone warriors guard the parapets. From a distance, they look life-size and may have originally been intended to give the impression of a well-armed castle. Indeed, Alnwick was very much built with military use in mind, and its strength has been tested several times by the Scots. The formidable **barbican** (next to the visitor entrance) is said to be one of the best examples of its kind in the country.

Within the castle **grounds**, families (and *Harry Potter* fans) are well catered for with broomstick-riding lessons, falconry displays and a medieval-styled courtyard with crafting activities and a dressing up area with handmade costumes and reproduction armoury. The Dragon's Quest is a walk-through dark labyrinth with roaring dragons and mirrored walkways designed for older kids.

"From the northern ramparts the broad tree-studded grassland rolls away from the castle walls to the river."

A taste of the duke's riches are revealed in the **State Rooms**, which house a distinguished collection of **Renaissance art**, including eight Canalettos and three Titians. The **dining room**, **library** and **drawing room** are sumptuously furnished with highly decorative ceilings, fireplaces, paintings and furniture. The two ornately carved and painted Italian Cucci cabinets either side of the Drawing Room fireplace, originally made in the late 17th century for Louis XIV's palace at Versailles, are thought to be some of the most valuable pieces of furniture in the world. The **China Gallery** holds an extensive collection of Meissen porcelain.

One of the Canaletto oils depicts the ruinous castle as it was in 1750 before the Georgian restoration under the first Duke of Northumberland. He directed the transformation of the fortress into a stately home, and landscaped the surrounding **parkland** to a design by local landscape architect, Lancelot 'Capability' Brown. The glorious 18th-century vista is best viewed from the northern ramparts where the broad tree-studded grassland rolls away from the castle walls to the River Aln. It is one of the most beautifully designed landscapes in Northumberland. To enjoy

HARRY 'HOTSPUR'

I'll empty all these veins, And shed my dear blood drop by drop in the dust.

William Shakespeare *Henry IV, Part One*

Of all the Percy men through the centuries, the most legendary is Harry 'Hotspur', a fearless and impulsive knight who fought in several conflicts during the 1300s, including the midnight Battle of Otterburn in 1388. Hotspur went on to lead the rebellion against Henry IV in the Battle of Shrewsbury in 1403 and like all infamous knights he died in combat when, it is said, an arrow pierced his skull. Shakespeare immortalised Hotspur in *Henry IV, Part One*.

Today, Hotspur is remembered in many place and building names in the North East and in the London football club, Tottenham Hotspur, so called because the Percy family owned the land where the club originated.

the scenery on foot, you'll need to exit the castle and cross the 1773 **Lion Bridge** (all castellated parapets, faux arrow slits and guarded by an arresting statue of a lion) on the B6341 and pick up a public footpath north of the river. The view of Alnwick Castle rearing above the River Aln is highly memorable.

THE ALNWICK GARDEN

Denwick Ln, Alnwick ✆ 01665 511350 ☺ Feb–Oct daily; free entry for children ♿

The gardens at Alnwick are unashamedly bold and contemporary and designed to thrill. You can easily spend a whole afternoon – or day – here and you'll find children are entertained as much as garden lovers are absorbed by the plant collections.

In 1997, Jane Percy, the 12th and current Duchess of Northumberland began steering the development of the overgrown gardens into this eye-catching pleasure ground. The centrepiece is the **Grand Cascade**, a huge modern waterfall that plunges over many tiers. Below, children drive toy dumper trucks under the spray of water (parents in the know come prepared with a change of clothes). If children do manage to escape getting wet here, they probably won't at the nearby **Serpent Garden**, where a series of interactive contemporary installations use water to creative effect.

"If children do manage to escape getting wet here, they probably won't at the nearby Serpent Garden."

The **Ornamental Garden** crowns the top of the cascade where a profusion of flowering plants bring colour and scent to structured spaces set within a walled enclosure. Several thousand rose shrubs and climbers grow here and in the **Rose Garden**, including the Alnwick Rose, a beautifully scented old English rose for sale in the **plant shop**.

Elsewhere, you'll find a **maze** within a thicket of bamboo (close to the main café), a **Cherry Orchard** (boasting the largest collection of Japanese cherry trees in the world) and the **Poison Garden** where visitors on guided tours can get up close to some of the world's most toxic plants.

Lilidorei
The Alnwick Garden ✆ 01665 511350 ⊙ daily ♿

Much fun to be had in this fairy- and goblin-themed playground aimed at children under 11, with the huts of elves and sprites reached on a walkway winding round a central castle described as the largest play structure in the world. Children of all ages (and even, ahem, some adults) will enjoy the tunnel slides and lookouts. Glance through the windows to see what potions are brewing in the fairy houses or ask one of the play stewards to teach you how to juggle.

Located near the treehouse restaurant and within the grounds of The Alnwick Garden, a trip to Lilidorei makes for an enjoyable extension of a visit to the gardens, but you'll need a separate ticket.

ST MICHAEL'S CHURCH
Opposite end of Bailiffgate from the castle ⊙ May–Sep most afternoons ♿

'Don't tell me the Victorians were good engineers,' said the warden pointing to a bowed wall that began to tilt in the years following a 19th-century reconfiguration of the medieval church. Despite this, St Michael's certainly gives the appearance of strength and steadfastness with its short, castellated tower supported by wide buttresses, and retains much of its earlier structure built under King Henry VI in 1464. The unusual turret on the southeastern corner of the church served as a lookout point during the centuries of Border fighting.

Inside, note the crescent moons stamped about the stonework, which should tell you something about the close relationship between the church and the Percy family of Alnwick Castle, this being their motif.

Stone effigies include a depiction of King Henry VI and a serene-looking martyr whose body is pierced with many arrows.

BAILIFFGATE MUSEUM
Bailiffgate 🕾 01665 605847 ⊙ daily

Northumbrian pipe music draws visitors into this small museum housed in the former Catholic church, which provides a good introduction to the history of Alnwick district – its buildings, industries and people – across three floors. Many of the exhibits have been donated by locals and include a recreated print workshop with a Victorian printing press, and an Edwardian schoolroom. Changing exhibitions feature on the top floor – often with young people in mind – and have in recent times included a wonderful Penguin children's book cover art display.

HULNE PARK
Ratten Row 🕾 01665 510777 ⊙ generally all year from 11.00–16.00; free admission; no dogs, no cyclists; download trail maps from 🖗 northumberlandestates.co.uk ♿

Not far from St Michael's Church is the imposing gateway to Hulne Park – a huge area of woods and open parkland (formally the hunting grounds of the Percy family of Alnwick Castle) enclosed by walls and owned by the Duke of Northumberland. Several miles of permissive footpaths and paved tracks wind through the trees, over stone bridges, past dells and across open grasslands.

The red route (just under five miles) is a popular **walk** that loops round Hulne Priory before returning to the town along the River Aln – a picturesque waterway that meanders through Capability Brown parkland under the gaze of Alnwick Castle.

If Alnwick wasn't already stuffed with so many old buildings, perhaps more would be said of the romantic ruins of **Hulne Priory**, founded by Carmelite friars in 1265. Also in the park is one of the most outlandish Gothic follies in England, **Brizlee Tower** (reached by following the yellow route) and the imposing 14th-century gatehouse of **Alnwick**

ALNWICK: **1** The River Aln and view towards the castle. **2** Bondgate Tower has served as a main entry point into the town since its construction in 1450. **3** The interior of Alnwick Castle. **4** Barter Books in the old railway station. **5** Entranceway to the Poison Garden – home of some of the world's most toxic plants. ▶

DAVE HEAD/S

NIGEL JARVIS/S

ALNWICK CASTLE

BARTER BOOKS

THE ALNWICK GARDEN

Abbey, a striking turreted tower that stands alone in open ground by the River Aln. Once you're past the working sawmill, you'll find the parkland a wonderfully tranquil place to visit for an extended walk or morning jog.

BARTER BOOKS

Alnwick Station, Bondgate Without ✆ 01665 604888 ◷ 09.00–19.00 daily ♿

You have to wonder how many customers to this characterful secondhand bookshop in a former Victorian railway station are here to buy books. Children sit on the floor picking through the shelves as if in a library, visitors wander in for lunch in the old waiting rooms and to admire the station architecture, and locals sip coffee by the open fire in the entrance reading the papers. 'I wanted it to be a place people could just go and be left alone and stay all day if they want,' says the founder of Barter Books, Mary Manley, who began converting the station rooms into a bookshop with her husband in 1991.

Barter Books oozes old-world charm with its decorative ironwork, working station clocks, wonderful waiting room café (page 88), open fires and model trains that trundle along on a track above the rickety bookcases. Between two bookshelves is a stone water basin (still with its brass cups attached to chains) once used by railway passengers.

On the books front, 'it's a bit of luck what you'll find,' says Mary. There's something for everyone with most shelves stocked with non-fiction according to theme. You'll find antique books for upwards of £10,000 and those costing just a few pounds.

Barter Books is also the home of one of the original 'Keep Calm and Carry On' World War II posters, which was found among a stash of books bought at auction. The crinkled poster is displayed in a frame.

A word of warning: Barter Books gets very crowded, especially at weekends and on rainy days during school holidays when half the tourist population of Alnwick are looking for indoor activities. Best times are therefore the reverse conditions: a sunny day, mid-week and especially early mornings and late afternoon.

ALN VALLEY RAILWAY

Lionheart Enterprise Park (southeast of Alnwick town centre), NE66 2HT ⌗ alnvalleyrailway. co.uk ◷ Easter–Sep w/ends & bank holidays (steam or diesel engines) and Wed ('Pacer' 1980s engine) in summer; Santa Specials on w/ends during Dec ♿ 🐾

From the 1850s a four-mile branch train line operated from Alnwick town to the coast at Alnmouth for 110 years. Restoration of the heritage line by a dedicated team of volunteers began in the 1990s with the first shuttle ride opening in 2013. The heritage line is being opened in stages and is now at the half way point between Alnwick and Alnmouth where eventually it will connect with Edinburgh–London trains on the East Coast Main Line.

At the time of writing, trains travelled for a few miles to Greenrigg Halt over the recently restored Cawledge Viaduct designed by the great Victorian engineer, Robert Stephenson. Passengers can alight here and watch the engine moving tracks and recoupling for the return journey. Steam and diesel locomotives on weekends (and a 1980s 'Pacer' engine on Wednesdays) complete the journey in a round trip of half an hour and run five times daily from the newly constructed **Lionheart Station** (Alnwick's original Victorian station now houses Barter Books) where there's also a shop, café, playground, museum and miniature 'ride on' railway for youngsters.

Cheerful crew make much of the experience with a guard dressed in old-fashioned British Rail uniform stamping tickets, and plenty of toots from the engine whistle as the train trundles alongside farmland. After alighting, you could take a stroll to the engine shed or admire the model railways on display.

Special Events are held throughout the year, including Afternoon Tea Trains with all the sweet trimmings and the popular Santa Specials at Christmas (book ahead).

A dual **cycleway** and **footpath** runs along the side of the line and connects with a number of quiet lanes, tracks and paths for onward travel to Alnmouth station (one mile), the coast path and cycleway, NCN Route 1 (1½ miles) and Alnmouth village (two miles).

SPECIAL STAYS

The Cookie Jar 12 Bailiffgate ✆ 01665 510465 ⌕ cookiejaralnwick.com ♿ A short stroll from the entrance to Alnwick Castle is this luxury small hotel converted from an old convent on one of Alnwick's most handsome sandstone streets. Elegant furnishings and deep-blue walls and fabrics throughout place The Cookie Jar firmly in the category of boutique hotel; clearly every armchair, cushion and wall decoration has been expertly placed by the hand of an interior designer. High prices for doubles reflect the superior standard of comfort and extras. As for the **restaurant**, which has earned a very good local reputation, all the dishes are crafted using many local ingredients. Lunch (sandwiches, soup, fish and chips, burgers, salads), evening meals (choose from a handful of meat and fish dishes like pork with a black pudding mash or poached trout with potatoes, crab and samphire) and afternoon teas. Expect a hefty bill.

¶¶ FOOD & DRINK

Alnwick is not short of tempting cafés and mid-range pubs and restaurants. They include **The Dirty Bottles** (32 Narrowgate ✆ 01665 606193 ⊙ daily ✧ 🐾), trading mainly in slow-cooked BBQ food with pulled pork and various steaks alongside a choice of 11 burgers. A self-service beer wall allows you to pull your own pint.

There are really only a couple of choices for a very special evening meal in Alnwick (see **The Cookie Jar**, page 87, and **The Treehouse**, see below) but also consider the exquisite 14-course tasting menu at **Sonnet** (41 Bondgate Without ✆ 01665 517628 🐾) – undoubtedly the finest dining experience in town.

For good fish and chips, **Carlo's** (Market St ✆ 01665 602787) is a reliable choice.

For those self-catering, pick up meats and a wide range of regional deli produce from **Turnbull's** (Willowburn Retail Park ✆ 01665 602186 ⊙ daily ✧), a well-respected Alnwick butcher for over a century.

The Alnwick Garden ✆ 01665 511852 ⊙ daily ✧. The most widely visited place to eat in the gardens (ticket required) is the **Pavilion Café** opposite the cascade, where you'll find a fairly limited choice of sandwiches, cakes and scones alongside pizzas, freshly made to order and cooked in a pizza oven. Outside tables are in a suntrap and sought after. **The Treehouse restaurant** (⊙ variable), reached via a roped walkway, is a rather special dining experience with mains a cut above your average Alnwick restaurant: roast duck with a rhubarb and ginger gel for example. Nice to see pan haggerty on the menu (a potato-based pie peculiar to the North East). Start your evening with a cocktail made with Poison Gin inspired by the toxic plants in Alnwick's Poison Garden and take in the canopy views.

Barter Books Station Buffet Alnwick Station, Bondgate Without ✆ 01665 604888 ⊙ daily ✧ 🐾. Wonderful café in Alnwick's historic former train station. Lunches are hearty: hot roast beef sandwich, Northumbrian rarebit and macaroni cheese with bacon bits (a sinful dish you will need time to recover from); but what makes lunch here really special is dining in the original Victorian waiting rooms, complete with tiled walls and cast-iron fireplaces (almost always roaring).

The problem on weekend lunchtimes is trying to get a table (and before that, parking). Early risers for breakfast (French toast with syrup, bacon and eggs, avocado on toast) and those arriving after 14.00 shouldn't need to hover for a table, however. The old stationmaster's office next door is now the **Paradise** ice-cream parlour (sit in or take-away ices made along the coast), also offering a variety of other sweet treats, sandwiches and pricey hot food (chip butties, toasties, soup, hot dogs, jacket potatoes).

Grannies Tearoom 18 Narrowgate 🕾 01665 602394 ⊙ daily. The smell of fresh bread and tea wafts up the stairs of this tiny café hunkered down in the cellar of a 400-year-old building (upstairs there's a deli). It looks out of the pages of a nursery book with copper kettles hanging from the ceiling and a range among its furnishings. Homemade cakes, scones, pies, quiche, soups and simple sandwiches. Nothing fancy.

The Old Stables Broomhouse NE66 2LB 🕾 07594 044904 ⊙ 10.00–15.00 (last food orders 14.00) Wed–Sat ♿ 🐾 outside only. This wee coffee shop on the outskirts of Alnwick is a pleasant find, with a sunny courtyard backing on to farmland. Good homemade breakfasts and lunches: soups, quiche, sandwiches made with locally baked sourdough; fresh cakes and traybakes. Afternoon teas served Wed only (with 48 hours' notice).

THE HERITAGE COAST

Northumberland's beaches don't get creamier or softer than those between Warkworth and Berwick-upon-Tweed – known as the Northumberland 'Heritage Coast'. The likes of **Sugar Sands**, **Embleton Bay** and **Beadnell Bay** are popular with families and walkers but despite this they are surprisingly crowd-free, even in high summer. Family-friendly seaside villages include **Alnmouth**, **Seahouses** and **Bamburgh**. Heritage hunters and nature watchers are spoiled with the renowned **Farne archipelago**, **Lindisfarne National Nature Reserve**, and a string of fantastically arresting castles punctuating the coastline.

10 AMBLE

With its ice-cream parlours, fish and chip shops, boat tours to nearby Coquet Island (page 91) and gift stores, Amble attracts plenty of holidaymakers these days, but its roots are in fishing. A scattering of very good seafood restaurants face the mouth of the River Coquet where fishing nets are strewn along the harbour wall, lobster pots are stacked four high and lads in yellow wellies make for their boats. A number of traditional wooden cobles continue to work out of the town.

At low tide, below the old timber staithes on the north side of the Coquet, the rib cages of wrecked ships poke through the mud flats. Beyond them rises Warkworth Castle (page 93), appearing impressively – and deceptively – intact. You can actually **walk** to Warkworth from Amble in a couple of miles along the coast path, which follows a fairly

COBLE BOATS

The traditional wooden fishing boat peculiar to the North East was for a long time a familiar sight all the way along the Northumbrian and Yorkshire coasts. Painted bright colours and with broad sides, a high bow, horseshoe-shaped stern and a characteristic flat bottom (easy for hauling up the North East's sandy beaches), cobles have operated out of Northumberland's harbours for many hundreds of years. Some say the design originates from Viking boats.

A scattering of cobles work out of Cullercoats, Newbiggin-by-the-Sea, Amble, Boulmer, Craster and North Shields, but most were abandoned or scrapped during the collapse of the North Sea fishing industry in the latter half of the 20th century. There are probably only around 40 left, a very small number of which are the original sailing type. The most famous coble belonged to Grace Darling and is now housed in her namesake museum in Bamburgh (page 127).

busy road for half the way, although the path itself hugs the Coquet and is really quite pleasant, particularly where the riverbanks become leafier on entering Warkworth.

The rest of Amble, including the marina, is somewhat spread out and there's not much to entice visitors away from the immediate harbour area except for the rocky cove below the pier (access by car from Harbour Road) which is an enjoyable spot to while away a few hours crabbing with the kids. You could also pick up the coast path here for a **walk** of a few miles south across the sands and dunes between Amble and Low Hauxley, perhaps as far as the wetland nature reserve (page 77).

⍾⍿ FOOD & DRINK

Amble has some very good places to eat. Of the fish and chip shops, **Harbour Fish Bar** (corner of Leazes St & Broomhill St ✆ 01665 710442 ⊙ 11.30–20.00/21.00 Mon–Sat & lunch Sun) is a favourite with locals, hence the queues.

The Fish Shack 29 Harbour Rd ✆ 07426 277158 ⊙ daily ♿. Watch boats motoring out to sea from this laid-back little seafood bistro in Amble's harbour, decked out with fishing nets and nautical objects. Blankets on the backs of chairs come in useful – even inside. The food is straightforward and good: smoked haddock, mussels, sardines, kippers from Seahouses and crab from North Shields. Lobsters come straight off the boats within eyeshot of your table.
Jaspers 8 Bridge St ✆ 07853 449465 ⊙ daily. Seriously good laid-back seafood restaurant with a handful of tables (so you must book), set back from the harbour. Start your evening with a cocktail and then move on to crab soup or North Sea langoustines cooked fresh to

order, followed by a seafood platter, pan-seared squid, battered monkfish and chips, fish pie or one of the meat or veggie options grazing the menu: steak, pork belly or a mushroom risotto. Puddings are that bit special too: a Northumbrian vanilla ice cream with Alnwick gin and crushed meringue, as well as others with a local twist.

The Old Boathouse Leazes St ✆ 01665 711232 ◷ noon–21.00 daily ♿. The best seafood restaurant on the waterfront, popular with couples; more upmarket than its sister venue, The Fish Shack, with inflated prices to match (for similar dishes) though still what you might consider casual dining. The chalkboard specials include a tempting array of delicacies: roast scallops, Korean fried monkfish, smoked kippers from Seahouses and whole Amble-landed lobster. The seafood sharing platter is incredible: local and Scottish shellfish piled around a whole lobster, accompanied by smoked and pickled fish, goujons, samphire, chips and homemade bread.

Spurreli Ice Cream Coquet St ✆ 01665 710890 ♿. The queues say it all: this award-winning parlour makes superb ices, sundaes and sorbets dribbled with syrup and infused with fruit, sprinkles and chunks of toffee and chocolate.

11 COQUET ISLAND

Near Amble ✆ 0300 777 2676; RSPB

From mid-April, thousands of seabirds descend on this grassy 16-acre lighthouse isle a mile off the coast of Amble and begin squabbling over the best nest site. **Boat tours** from Amble in spring and summer sail to the RSPB-managed reserve where 40,000 puffins, eider ducks, kittiwakes and fulmars nest. Landing is not permitted because of the sensitivity of the site, but you'll get excellent views of the birds, as well as spy-hopping grey seals. **Puffin Cruises** (✆ 01665 711975, 07752 861914 ♂ puffincruises.co.uk ◷ East–Sep three daily Mon–Sat) operate out of Amble harbour, by the restaurants (not the marina). The trips last around an hour; call a couple of days in advance to check sailing times and book tours. The seabirds depart the island in July and August but it's still possible to see various other birds and seals for the rest of the summer.

Coquet Island is home to the only colony of Britain's rarest breeding seabird, the **roseate tern**, which nests on this tiny isle and almost nowhere else in Britain. Each pair is provided with a ground nest box that the birds 'decorate' with shells, shingle and objects washed up on the shore. The island's long-serving former manager, Paul Morrison (aka 'Captain Coquet'), told me that one year he found a nest adorned with daffodils and another with fragments of paint.

The **lighthouse** was built in 1841 on top of a Benedictine monastery (the stone base of which is still visible). You will also see restored stone cottages (built in 1840 in the ruins of a 15th-century monastic chapel).

12 WARKWORTH

🏠 **Fairfield House**

Warkworth's 14th-century fortress rears over the rooftops of a long row of sandstone houses that step down to the River Coquet, linking the parish church at the bottom with the castle at the top. This medieval layout is one of the most intact and celebrated in the whole of England.

At the foot of the picturesque village, the Coquet flows around **St Lawrence Church**, making coastal Warkworth feel much more like a riverside settlement. Despite its protective loop, the river was not enough of a barrier to keep the Scots out in 1174 when they raided Warkworth and massacred the men, women and children sheltering inside St Lawrence's. A church has stood here since Saxon times, but the present building dates to 1130 with medieval and Victorian modifications. Its Norman origins are immediately apparent in the chancel with its, now slightly crooked, arch and impressive stone vaulted ceiling. The only medieval stained glass to survive is in the top of the east window.

Opposite the church is the **market cross** where, on 9 October 1715, Warkworth became the first public place in England to proclaim James III as king, during the ill-fated **Jacobite Rebellion**. The night before, the legendary Earl of Derwentwater (page 377) and 40 rebels dined at the nearby Masons Arms. The event is recorded on a beam inside the pub and described on a plaque outside.

On the **main street** leading away from the church and market cross, you'll find a few pubs and cafés, a village store, contemporary art gallery selling pottery, jewellery and paintings, and a chocolaterie.

The **river** is crowded with trees and is a pleasant place for a stroll. Half a mile or so upriver from the church is the crossing point for the medieval **hermitage** (𝒹 01665 711423 ⊙ closed at the time of writing but check online at 𝒹 english-heritage.org.uk), a 15th-century rock-cut chapel concealed by trees on the north side of the river. To get there, you must take the rowing boat operated by English Heritage. A walkway connects the castle with the riverside, enabling a combined visit to the castle and hermitage.

Walking downriver, you'll come to Warkworth's 14th-century **bridge** featuring cutwaters between its two arches and a fortified tower (once used as a toll house). It's a cobbled pedestrian bridge these days and worthy of some photos. On the north side, a road on your right leads to Warkworth **beach** (page 95) in half a mile, a dreamy stretch of coastline.

Warkworth Castle

Castle Tce, NE65 0UJ ✆ 01665 711423 ⊙ Easter–Oct & school holidays daily; autumn & winter w/ends only; ♿ 🐾 grounds; English Heritage

> worm-eaten hold of ragged stone
> William Shakespeare, Henry IV, Part One

Warkworth is a fortress to be reckoned with. Though much ruined internally, its 14th-century keep still maintains a heavy presence at the head of the village and is considered one of the greatest surviving medieval circular buildings in England. The perimeter walls and restored gatehouse date from around 1200 and have resisted the ravages of time better than many of the buildings inside.

Percy is a name you will have heard on your travels along the coast, especially if you've already visited Alnwick Castle, currently the Duke of Northumberland's main seat (page 80). Several centuries ago, Warkworth was the family's principal residence, hence the lion motif stamped about the place. Nowhere else is the beast more strikingly carved than above the doorway to the **Lion Tower** at Warkworth.

"Though much ruined internally, its 14th-century keep still maintains a heavy presence at the head of the village."

The impressive **Keep** is formed of four polygonal wings arranged around a central square. Its roof, battlements and turrets are long gone, exposing the building's ribcage to the sea air, but you still gain a good sense of the layout of rooms and can imagine the Duke's medieval banquets in the Great Hall. From his private chamber, he could look over the village and, as today, see all the way to Coquet Island.

The three doorways in the **Great Hall** are interesting: two are a similar size (leading to the buttery and pantry) but the third is wider to allow servants to easily come and go with roasts from the kitchen for a feast. Facing them on the other side of the Great Hall is a minstrels gallery, where entertainers would delight guests. Mentally fill in the gaps with

tapestries, painted ceilings and stained glass in the windows and you are looking at a complete medieval banquet.

Service buildings including a bakery, stables, brewery, kitchens, larders and wells, lie ruined in the **bailey** – the open grassy areas below the keep.

Warkworth's beach (Alnmouth Bay)

From Warkworth, a glorious long stretch of pale sand backed by thick dunes shoots north to Alnmouth. To reach the beach, take the paved lane heading east from the north side of Warkworth's medieval bridge. In half a mile there's a parking area with toilets.

In the dunes, a fingerpost directs you to Alnmouth (4½ miles) along the **coast path**. If there were a footbridge crossing the estuary at Alnmouth, this would be one of the most popular **beach walks** in Northumberland. Unfortunately, however, you get within a hop, skip and a jump (almost) of Alnmouth and have to turn back or pick up the coast path that heads inland and follows the road into the village. It's a long slog of a few miles, albeit through a field on the other side of a hedgerow from the road. The return journey from Alnmouth can be made in ten minutes on the coast bus (X18 operates hourly).

 SPECIAL STAYS

Fairfield House 16 Station Rd, Warkworth ✆ 01665 714455 ⌂ fairfield-guesthouse.com. This grand Victorian guesthouse on the edge of one of the most historically alluring villages in Northumberland is a short stroll from the village centre and one mile from a pristine sandy bay. Garden lovers will enjoy the well-kept grounds, framed by mature trees, and the delightful conservatory and terrace soaked in sunshine. Inside, the corridors and four traditionally styled rooms are spotless, and all have period details, solid furniture and luxury extras. For breakfast, you'll find Craster Kippers and Turnbull's sausages of Bamburgh on the menu. For a long stay, you may want to consider the self-catering garden apartment.

 FOOD & DRINK

A couple of fair pubs and cafés dot Warkworth's main street, but there's really only one place that everyone raves about – Bertram's (page 96). For reasonable pub grub, try the **Mason**

◄ **1 & 2** Coquet Island is the only place in the UK where one of our rarest seabirds, the roseate term, breeds. **3** Warkworth Castle above the River Coquet. **4** An iconic view of Alnmouth from Church Hill.

Arms (✆ 01665 711398) and for a good evening meal, either Bertram's again or head to **Amble** for its seafood restaurants (page 90).

Bertram's 19 Bridge St ✆ 01665 798070 ⊙ daily 🐾. There's rarely a vacant table at this modern bistro (and B&B). All-day breakfasts include Craster kippers on toast; for lunch, it's crab sandwiches, chunky sourdough toasties, quiche, soups and a whole lot more; then, from 5pm, the evening menu delights with dishes like North Sea squid in a fennel pollen batter, and roe deer with roasties and whisky apples. For food this good, you're going to pay above average prices despite the decidedly casual surroundings. There's a sheltered rear courtyard where a glass of wine with a sharing plate of Amble langoustines hits the spot late in the afternoon. Only evening meals can be booked.

Morwick Dairy NE65 9DG ✆ 01665 711210 ⊙ Tue–Sun ♿ 🐾. Delicious ice cream made right on the farm, a couple of miles west of Warkworth, from Holstein, Ayrshire and Jersey cows milked less than 60yds away by Pete, Michael, Frazer, Kaz and Chris. The ice creams are then churned in small batches and decanted by hand. With 16 flavours (and more tubbed varieties in the freezer), the only issue is the dilemma: strawberry, chocolate or something completely different? Let me tempt you with the rose and pistachio or the mango yoghurt (it's out of this world, since you asked). There's a small play area and picnic benches.

13 ALNMOUTH

⛪ **St Valery**

Some London to Edinburgh trains stop at Alnmouth station (one mile inland from the village)

Alnmouth's pastel-coloured cottages crowded above butter-coloured sands and the Aln Estuary make this old village one of the most distinctive (and photographed) places on the Northumberland coast. An unbeatable vantage point is **Church Hill**, a grassy knoll with a cross and ruined Victorian chapel, on the coast path. A much older church once stood on this hillock but it was destroyed during a storm in 1806 that was so violent it changed the course of the river, cutting off Church Hill from the village.

"The sharp-eyed visitor will notice that a few buildings have irregular-shaped windows."

Alnmouth's main road, **Northumberland Street**, opens generously to sand dunes at its southern end. Along its length are a few gift shops, a basic convenience store and sweet shop, a church and a number of pubs and cafés. The sharp-eyed visitor will notice that a few buildings have irregular-shaped windows (the row leading away from the post office for example). They were built as granaries during the 18th century when Alnmouth was a busy port and exported large amounts of corn.

At the sand dune end of the main street in the side of a stone house is a small window displaying an old barometer that was given to the Alnmouth coastguards in 1860 by the Duke of Northumberland. It is a pleasing object, as is the description of its history.

Out of sight at the far north end of the village is the wonderful **Old School Gallery** (Foxton Rd ℘ 01665 830554 ☉ daily), one of the best affordable art galleries in Northumberland. Original paintings hang on walls above crafts and pottery items. Gifts and coffees too.

🧳 SPECIAL STAYS

St Valery 27 Northumberland St ℘ 01665 833123 ⌂ stvaleryalnmouth.com. Much emphasis is placed on comfort at this sophisticated yet homely adults-only B&B on Alnmouth's main street. The rooms are absolutely spotless, the beds are king-sized and the breakfasts top notch, with plenty of local produce including coffee roasted on Lindisfarne. With just three rooms, guests are given first-class treatment by the owners. Original fireplaces and patterned rugs over wooden floors offset the modern furnishings beautifully.

🍴 FOOD & DRINK

For **fish and chips**, I like the **Hope & Anchor** (42–44 Northumberland St ℘ 01665 830363 ☉ daily ♿ 🐾), which also offers a take-away service. Order a pint of local beer while you wait.

Bistro 23 23 Northumberland St ℘ 01665 830393 ☉ usually breakfast & lunch daily; seasonal evening meals on select days. A great choice – one of the best – for food in Alnmouth. It's a fairly simple eatery: tea room in the daytime serving all-morning breakfasts & lunches (local stottie sandwiches, pan haggerty and seafood platters); come dusk, the linen tablecloths come out and, with them, a small, considered menu of dishes prepared from scratch using local ingredients such as wild sea trout from Alnmouth Bay, Cheviot lamb and Boulmer lobster. Northumberland beef always makes an appearance. Friendly owners and consistently outstanding food. Book ahead.

Old School Gallery Foxton Rd ℘ 01665 830554. Traybakes and coffees to take-away and enjoy in the old playground. From April to October, a weekend pizza van (☉ noon–17.00) freshly cooks to order.

Red Lion 22 Northumberland St ℘ 01665 830584 ☉ daily ♿ 🐾. Traditional old inn with a low-beamed ceiling, open fire and laid-back atmosphere. There's a large beer garden overlooking the estuary. Good local ales and wood-fired pizzas April–October.

Scotts of Alnmouth 15–16 Northumberland St ✆ 07590 564963 ⊙ daily ♿. Scotts wouldn't be out of place on a chi-chi street in London with its basket of sourdough loaves and regional artisan deli products. Order hot and cold breakfasts, and lunch food to take-away, as well as really good pies and sausage rolls from the deli counter. In short, everything you need for a posh picnic. And don't forget your take-away coffee (beans roasted on Lindisfarne). Holidaymakers can order quality homemade frozen ready meals.

The Whittling House 24–25 Northumberland St ✆ 01665 463001 ⊙ 08.00–21.00 daily ♿ 🐾. When it's blowing a hooley on Alnmouth Bay, this sophisticated restaurant (upholstered chairs, wood panelling, tables set with glassware, log burner roaring) is where I want to take refuge. Friendly staff and the promise of a beautifully cooked cut of meat or plate of local seafood: monkfish curry, homemade venison pie, asparagus risotto, steaks. You'll pay above-average prices in the evening and for Sunday lunches, but the breakfast and lunch menus (homemade burgers, salads, hearty sandwiches) are average for the area.

* * *

🚶 SEA VIEWS & ROCK POOLS: A CIRCULAR WALK FROM ALNMOUTH

❄ OS Explorer map 332; start: The Wynd, Alnmouth, 📍 NU246106; 2 miles; easy

A n easy family route with expansive sea views, beach walking and rockpools.
At the top end of Alnmouth's Northumberland Street, turn downhill by the 19th-century fountain and wander along **The Wynd** towards the sea. At the England Coast Path fingerpost, turn left and climb up through trees to reach the top of the hill. Turn right and continue on the footpath for 500 yds to a **battery** and well-known look-out point with a fabulous view.

Continue on the coast path, skirting the edge of a **golf green** and then pass some holiday cabins on a rough track. (You can take the short route back to Alnmouth via the beach by following this track downhill and bearing right at the bottom.) Strike off left, continuing north, on the coast footpath (signed).

On reaching a fork in the grassy path, bear right towards some houses (marked Foxton Hall on maps). You'll see an unofficial sign for the beach ahead and will soon be able to pick your way down the grassy dunes and on to the beach at **Marden Rocks** (good for beachcombing). Alternatively keep on the coast path to the golf club house for bar drinks and lunches.

Turn right and walk back to Alnmouth along the beach, passing two mid 19th-century **lifeboat houses** by some well-placed picnic benches. Press on, with Alnmouth Links on your right, and re-enter the village at its southern end.

* * *

14 BOULMER

This straggling old fishing village with a rocky shore and RAF base was once legendary for its smugglers. 'As many as twenty or thirty of them, mounted on horseback, would come to Boulmer for gin, and carry it to the centre of the county and the wilds of Coquetdale, not without many hair-breath escapes and lively encounters with the excisemen,' says Tomlinson in his *Comprehensive Guide to Northumberland*. The centre of the illicit activities was the Fishing Boat Inn, which is still in business today (see below). Tomlinson said that casks of liquor were sometimes still dug up on the coast, but he was writing in 1888, so there's little chance of contraband finds today.

While Boulmer lacks tourist infrastructure and places to visit, it's nice to see a few traditional coble boats and lobster pots pointing to the enduring fishing traditions in this low-rise and unassuming old village.

By the side of the main road through Boulmer, look out for a corrugated **World War I Memorial Hall**, a former army hut, opened 1920, restored in 2015, and now a much-appreciated community hall open for craft and music events. Next door, artist Jenny Allan displays her original artworks and crafts in a shepherd's hut, **Gallery St Andrews**.

¶¶ FOOD & DRINK

Fishing Boat Inn Boulmer ✐ 01665 577 750 ◷ lunch & evening meals Tue–Sat, lunch Sun. Spectacular coastal views from the rear restaurant and beer garden in this revamped old inn now serving seafood lunches and dinners (including a Smugglers Fish Pie) with a couple of meat and veggie dishes too. It's pricey, mind.

15 SUGAR SANDS & AROUND

Whin Sill outcrops and limestone between the villages of Boulmer and Craster come together to create a striking and unusual shoreline, particularly between Howick and Craster where horizontal sheets of rock heave in great shelves on to the beach. Hidden along this coastline (just south of Howick) are three sandy bays perfect for families. The middle beach is **Sugar Sands** – one of Northumberland's finest secluded coves.

The bays are reached in quick succession from the coast path. If driving or cycling to Sugar Sands, take the paved lane east from Longhoughton where there's a rough ticketed parking area at the end of

HOWICK SHIPWRECK

South of Rumbling Kern and viewed from the coast path lies an old ship's boiler (it looks like a large square of concrete) once belonging to a French steam trawler which hit nearby rocks in March 1913 on its way to Icelandic fishing grounds.

According to a newspaper report at the time, the lifeboat from Boulmer and many local people came to the aid of the fishermen. They rescued 25 men, but five sailors (one just 16 years old) drowned. A few of the deceased had tied themselves to the rigging and mast to avoid being washed away in the storm and had to be cut down. The newspaper described the scene as so harrowing that the coastguard ordered all local children away from the shore. The Frenchmen are buried in the church on the Howick Hall estate and the event is summarised on the memorial stone.

Howdiemont Sands (another glorious dune-backed beach which can become crowded owing to the car park) but note that Low Steads Farm halfway along the track charges £1 to pass through the gate, which is locked at 18.00. The other parking area (where there is no charge and is always open) is on the lane east of Howick Hall for **Rumbling Kern** (see below).

Rumbling Kern

Such an evocative name for a beach (just north of Sugar Sands) piled with rocks and with plenty of holes and channels for the sea to roar through. At low tide this is a great bay for bouldering and coasteering, and, when the tide comes in, there's much fun to be had sitting in a rock plunge pool splashed with wave water.

Rumbling Kern's secluded location makes it fairly private, although it's right on the coast path and walkers increasingly stop here to picnic.

The Victorian house on the headland (now a holiday cottage; *&* originalcottages.co.uk) is known as the **Bathing House**, built by the 2nd Earl Grey of nearby Howick Hall for his 15 children to stay in while enjoying a dip in the sea below.

For organised **coasteering** fun here, I recommend Adventure Northumberland (*&* 01665 252073 *&* adventurenorthumberland.co.uk).

16 HOWICK HALL GARDENS

Howick NE66 3LB *&* 01665 577191/285 ☉ early Feb & Mar Wed–Sun, Apr–mid-Nov daily ♿

Set back from the sea and surrounding an 18th-century manor is one of Northumberland's finest gardens open to the public. Howick's flowering season starts with a dazzling display of snowdrops followed by daffodils, then rhododendrons, camellias and magnolia blossom. In high summer, the **Bog Garden** is a visual treat: a water garden with a lake surrounded by bushy lupins, roses, delphiniums and poppies spilling over into grassy paths. Some 11,000 trees and shrubs were planted in the arboretum by the current Lord Howick, who is an ardent collector of exotics. Many specimens were grown from seeds gathered on expeditions to China.

"Howick's flowering season starts with a dazzling display of snowdrops followed by daffodils."

The **Woodland Garden** is one of the highlights, especially for its eye-catching stone bridge, spring-flowering shrubs and the way it merges naturally into the woods beyond the road. Here, a path called the **Long Walk** takes a meandering route to the sea, roughly following the bubbling Howick Burn that comes in and out of view for the 1½-mile stroll to Sugar Sands (page 99), a beautiful bay for bathing.

You can **walk** to the coast under certain conditions, enforced by a couple of gates. When the gardens are closed in winter, the gates are always open and you can walk in either direction. When the gardens are open (early February to mid-November), the gates permit one-way travel (from the estate to the coast) for those who have paid to see the gardens. I've described a circular route from Craster on page 105.

Howick Hall was built in 1782 and rebuilt following a fire in 1926. It has been a home, first to the Grey family and later inherited by the Howicks, for over 700 years. Only a few rooms are open to the public (unusually, visitors are permitted to sit and relax in the refined surroundings). A display in the entrance provides detailed information

EARL GREY TEA

Howick is home to the famous Earl Grey tea, which became popular among London's political elite when Lady Grey served her delicate brew blended with bergamot (to offset the taste of the lime-rich spring water on the Howick estate) at social events. Twinings marketed the tea but the trademark was not registered and no royalties have, therefore, ever been received.

Leaf Earl Grey tea is served in the old ballroom at Howick Hall (page 103).

about the gardens and arboretum. A pianist sometimes plays in the **Chinese Room**, a sumptuous space and one-time breakfast room. The exquisite Chinese wallpaper, featuring cranes and fruit trees, was reproduced from the hand-painted design in the upstairs hallway.

The most illustrious of the Greys was **Charles, second Earl Grey**, who served as prime minister from 1830 to 1834, and is best known for the Great Reform Bill of 1832 that influenced the development of our modern democracy. He loved the family home at Howick and stayed in Northumberland as much as he could, to the frustration of colleagues in London. Described by Howick Hall as 'one of Britain's greatest Prime Ministers, and one of the century's greatest truants', he is buried in the estate's **church**. Incidentally, he had a thoroughly blue-blooded way of preventing his children from developing a fear of the dark. On the first full moon in the July following their tenth birthday, they had to follow the Long Walk to the sea at midnight and return with a stem of grass of Parnassus, a white flower that grew (and indeed grows to this day, albeit in an inaccessible location) on rocks at the coast.

¶¶ FOOD & DRINK

Earl Grey Tea House Howick Hall ✆ 01665 572232 ☺ lunches served noon–14.45 ♿. A cup of leaf Earl Grey tea served in the home of the famous brew (page 101) is a real treat – as are the sumptuous surroundings of the old ballroom with its floor-to-ceiling windows, though the dining is very casual with sandwiches, scones, cakes and afternoon tea on the menu. Howick Hall's cream tea is one of the best I've tried along the coast (the fruit scones are particularly good as is the Earl Grey tea loaf), but to eat here you must purchase a ticket for the gardens.

17 CRASTER

The smell of burning firewood wafts through the streets of stone cottages gathered around a snug harbour in the old fishing village of Craster. There's no mistaking where the famous **smokehouse** is situated: white plumes curling out of wooden vents in the roof of the building opposite the Jolly Fisherman is a dead giveaway. Herring has been smoked here by the Robsons for over 150 years.

◀ **1** The picturesque village of Craster. **2** Sugar Sands beach. **3** Rumbling Kern beach with the Bathing House in the distance. **4** Howick Hall Gardens.

CRASTER KIPPERS

L. Robson & Sons Smokehouse Haven Hill, Craster (✆ 01665 576223 ⊙ from 09.00 Mon–Sat, from 11.00 Sun; autumn & winter closed early afternoon Sat & Sun ♿

More famous than its namesake village, kippers have been smoked in the same sheds at Craster by the Robson family for over 150 years. When built in 1856, in the days when smoking fish was as much about preserving as it was about the flavour, the smokehouse was one of many along the Northumberland coast.

Until the late 20th century, herring were landed by local fishermen and cut by 'herring girls' who did the unenviable job by hand. Today the fish come from Norway's waters ('only the plumpest herring with a high oil content' is good enough) and machines split the fish, but other than that the process is exactly the same as in the 19th century: after being cut, the fish are washed, brined then hung on tenterhooks in the smokehouse above a mixture of white wood shavings and oak sawdust for around 16 hours. Salmon takes 40 hours to smoke.

Visitors will find Craster Kippers in many farm shops, including the Village Farm Shop up the road in Embleton, and breakfast and restaurant menus in most villages and towns around here (including the Jolly Fisherman opposite the smokehouse, and in a bun from Pipers Pitch in Craster's public car park) – but you can also purchase kippers and other local seafood from the smokehouse fish counter.

In addition to the pub, a few paces from the smokery is also a tempting café and the **Mick Oxley Gallery** (✆ 01665 571082 ⊙ daily) whose moody landscapes capture the Northumberland coast in all lights and conditions.

With this appealing cluster of places to eat and visit, combined with the stonking ruins of Dunstanburgh Castle (page 107) a short walk away, its plain to see why Craster is so popular. With that in mind, do book your table at the pub.

One last mention: there's almost no mobile-phone signal in the village so if you need a taxi, for example, you'll need to do this in advance – or join the gaggle of walkers by the bus stand waiting for the useful coast service (page 66).

¶¶ FOOD & DRINK

Bearing in mind there is only one restaurant in Craster, finding a weekend table at the Jolly Fisherman can be a challenge. That said, turnover at the pub is high (especially in summer when a take-away van boosts capacity for those in the beer garden) and there's always the wonderful Pipers Pitch (see opposite).

Jolly Fisherman Haven Hill ✆ 01665 576461 ⊙ lunch & evening meals daily ♿ bar area only, where you can also eat 🐾 bar only. Craster's only pub is a good place to eat throughout the day where seafood platters, fish pie, sea trout, crab sandwiches, burgers and Sunday roasts are served to a lively crowd of holidaymakers and walkers (for inflated prices, I might add). On sunny weekend days, the Jolly can become extremely busy and you might have to make do with a picnic table outside which you can't book (views of the sea and Dunstanburgh Castle though). Their crab soup has long been a favourite of many regulars. And if there's no table in the beer garden, a (seasonal) food van in the car park will sort you out with fish and chips and crab sandwiches to take-away (grab a bench by the harbour).

L Robson & Sons Smokehouse see opposite. Kippers are the obvious choice, but the nationally famous smokehouse run by the same family for four generations also sells smoked haddock, cod and salmon; fishcakes, kipper pâté, mussels and scallops among other seafood delights from their on-site shop.

Pipers Pitch Craster quarry car park ✆ 07585 605607 ⊙ Feb–Oct daily, winter w/ends. Locally famous food shack run by a friendly Scottish man serving fantastically tasty lunch bites at low prices: Craster kipper in a bun for under £5, bacon baps, burgers. His speciality is Auchtermuchty (haggis and bacon in a roll). Excellent coffee too.

The Stable Yard 1 mile inland from Craster, NE66 3SS ✆ 01665 571240 ⊙ Tue–Sat 🐾. This small café-cum-garden shop with outdoor tables in a sheltered courtyard is known for its cakes and is a wonderful find for anyone escaping the lunchtime queues in Craster. Soups and sandwiches for the not so sweet-toothed.

✳ ✳ ✳

🚶 COAST & COUNTRY TRAIL: CRASTER TO HOWICK HALL

❆ OS Explorer map 332; start: Whin Hill, Craster, 📍 NU258198; 6 miles; easy

This is one of my favourite coastal walks because of the variety of scenery: woodlands, coastal flower meadows, historic gardens, sandy beaches, bird cliffs and castle views – and a great pub at the end.

Owing to the one-way gates on the Howick Hall estate (page 101) from March to November, you must walk in the direction I've described here. In winter, you can walk either way.

1 Set foot from **Whin Hill** (opposite the Jolly Fisherman). At the top of the lane, take the (signed) path south for Howick Scar. Once through the kissing gate, turn right skirting gorse-covered **Howick Scar** before descending on a track through **Howick Scar Farm**.

2 Cross the road and take the signed footpath to Howick Hall along the edge of a field. Go through the gate at the field end, bearing left by the fingerpost and skirting the rocky gorse-covered **Hips Heugh** (look out for birds of prey here).

3 Cross the dry-stone wall just beyond two prominent trees, using the ladder stile (or gate), and walk diagonally through the field ahead, aiming for the corner where there's a gate by trees. A clear track, fringed by woodland on your right, runs along the side of a wheat field. Ahead, enter woodland on a wide farm track that emerges on to a lane by the visitor car park for **Howick Hall**. If you don't want to visit the hall, you can walk the mile or so along the country lane to the coast just north of Rumbling Kern. Otherwise, pay your entrance money and wander through the gardens or head to the tea rooms (page 103).

4 After lunch, pick up the wooded **Long Walk**, which is reached by crossing a bridge over the road. There's a one-way turnstile here and another as you near the sea. You have to use

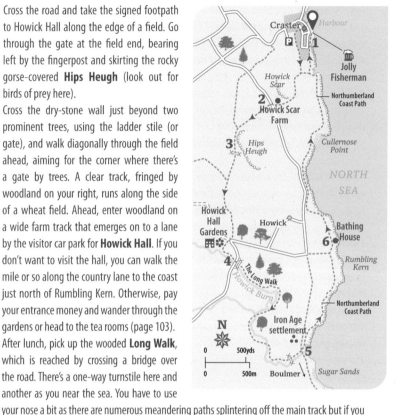

your nose a bit as there are numerous meandering paths splintering off the main track but if you keep close to the burn, following the waterway downriver, you'll eventually come out at the coast.

5 For **Sugar Sands**, turn right; for Craster, turn left, heading north on the coast path (feasting on blackberries in late summer as you go). An **Iron Age settlement** on the hill behind you is accessed via a gate just north of the footbridge, but most visitors may find the low stone and earthen ramparts not worth the uphill climb.

6 Halfway to Craster the coast path skirts the Bathing House at **Rumbling Kern** (page 100) – a fine spot for a picnic. Continue on the coast path for one mile to the **Cullernose Point** bird cliffs where fulmars and kittiwakes nest in summer. Distant views of Dunstanburgh Castle will enrich the rest of your amble into **Craster**. In late spring and through much of summer, the flower meadows on the outskirts of the village are stuffed with buttercups, clovers, knapweed and orchids. Follow the coast path directly into the beer garden of the Jolly Fisherman.

* * *

18 DUNSTANBURGH CASTLE

Craster; no road access, 1¼-mile walk north from Craster across grassland ✆ 01665 576231
🕐 Apr–Oct & Feb school holidays daily; winter mainly w/ends but check online 🐾; English
Heritage but free admission for National Trust members

Viewed from the north, Dunstanburgh is a shattered ruin clinging to the edge of a Whin Sill cliff. Through sun haze or haar, the medieval edifice rarely looks anything but rough and moody: its crumbling turrets and curtain walls almost always seen in silhouette form. But from the south, Dunstanburgh bares its formidable chest, appearing more brutish – and terrifically romantic. It doesn't matter that most of the fortress has succumbed to the wind and sea and is now under the ownership of fulmars and kittiwakes.

But for all its might, the 14th-century stronghold of Thomas, Earl of Lancaster, the richest man in England after the king, was more a show of power than an important military base. After the execution of Lancaster for treason, the castle was inherited by John of Gaunt, son of Edward III, who built a gateway bearing his name in the west curtain wall (still visible today). Dunstanburgh never came under attack by the Scots (though plenty of local inhabitants and their livestock were driven within its protective walls by Scottish raiders); but it was besieged during the Wars of the Roses in 1462. On one of two attacks, the garrison, which had taken to eating their horses, only really surrendered to the Yorkists out of starvation. By the mid 1500s, Dunstanburgh was a ruin, and, in any case, after the Union of England and Scotland in 1603 it had become militarily redundant.

"From the south, Dunstanburgh bares its formidable chest, appearing more brutish – and terrifically romantic."

For a castle of which little remains, Dunstanburgh still holds its own in the line of Northumberland's great coastal fortresses. But, unlike Alnwick, Bamburgh or Lindisfarne, it has not been patched up or altered much over the centuries by its owners and most of what you see today dates from its original construction in 1313. From the ruined rooms and staircases, enjoy the view of the coast from **Liburn Tower** and seek out the medieval **garderobes** in the sea-facing perimeter wall (English Heritage rate them as some of the best examples in England). Beyond this wall, incidentally, the sea ferociously pounds the rocks, especially when there's a strong onshore wind. Sit here and enjoy the spectacle.

THE GREAT WHIN SILL

Three hundred million years ago, hot, molten rock from the Earth's core surged through to the surface and solidified, forming hard basaltic outcrops rising sporadically – and dramatically – throughout Northumbria. These ridges caught the eye of emperors, Saxon settlers, dukes – and seabirds. It is what Hadrian's Wall teeters along, Bamburgh Castle rises from and what makes the Farne Islands such a special sanctuary for wildlife. On the coast near Craster, the combination of the hard dolerite outcrops and softer limestone has created many contorted, serpent-like formations on the shoreline. For more information and guided walks by expert local geologist, Dr Ian Kille, see Northumbrian Earth ⊘ northumbrianearth.co.uk.

The legend of **Sir Guy the Seeker** – and his ghost, which is said to haunt Dunstanburgh – is immortalised in a ballard that begins:

> **Sir Knight! Sir Knight! If your heart be right,**
> **And your nerves be firm and true,**
> **Sir Knight! Sir Knight! A beauty bright**
> **In durance waits for you.**

Searching for shelter one stormy night, the knight met with a wizard who ushered him through Dunstanburgh Castle to the bedside of a maiden lying asleep under a spell. She was guarded by two skeletons: one holding a sword and the other a horn. The fate of the maiden rested on the knight choosing the sword or the horn. He wrongly opted for the latter and spent the rest of his life being taunted by the wizard's words:

> **Now shame on the coward who sounded a horn**
> **When he might have unsheathed a sword.**

19 EMBLETON

Set back half a mile from one of the most popular sandy beaches in Northumberland, the picturesque village of Embleton draws in visitors to its pleasing nest of stone cottages, pubs, church and farm shop.

Holy Trinity stands opposite the village green. Its arcades date from the 13th century, and the lower sections of the tower from even earlier. Viewed from across the churchyard is the old vicarage, which was built in the 19th century on to the side of a 14th-century **vicar's pele tower**, once used to defend the clergy from attack.

Reaching **Embleton Bay** is easy on foot or by car (a pavement runs the length of the lane connecting Embleton with the

Dunstanburgh Castle Golf Club at the bottom). From the golf club, cross the green to the estuary. At the plank bridge, go straight ahead and pick your way through the dunes to the softest of sands (and popular surfing spot). This is also the **beach walk** to **Dunstanburgh Castle** (page 107). Alternatively, turn left before the bridge and skirt the estuary to the beach for **Newton-by-the-Sea** (half a mile north).

¶¶ FOOD & DRINK

Dunstanburgh Castle Golf Club Sea Ln ✆ 01665 576562 ⊙ daily ♿. Behind the dunes between Embleton and the sea is this casual clubhouse restaurant popular with walkers on the coast path. Inexpensive, simple menu of sandwiches, toasties and jackets and usually no wait for a table. Also sells lollies to take-away.

Dunstanburgh Castle Hotel Embleton ✆ 01665 576111 ⊙ daily ♿ 🐾. Dine inside the hotel restaurant or in a pretty enclosed garden over the road. For lunch: crab sandwiches or a more substantial plate of Northumberland meat or local seafood.

Eleanor's Byre Spitalford NE66 3DW ✆ 01665 571371 ⊙ Tue–Sat 🐾. An unexpected **café** (and gift room) with a sunny courtyard by the roadside south out of Embleton serving great coffees and cakes. A wood-fired **pizza kitchen** (♂ emberswoodfired.co.uk ⊙ 16.00– 20.00 Tue–Fri) in a repurposed shipping container in the café car park serves great take-aways. Order online for collection.

The Village Farm Shop Embleton ✆ 01665 576215 ⊙ 08.00–17.00 Mon–Sat, till 15.00 Sun in winter ♿. Fantastic farm shop stocked with everything you need for a picnic or holiday-cottage stay. So much regional produce here: cheeses, honey, jams, oils, chutney, coffee, sourdough bread, biscuits, fruit, veg, Bamburgh Bangers sausages, local kippers and, best of all, pork joints and various other cuts of meat direct from the farm up the road. And then there's the counter tempting you with scones (the cheese ones are gorgeous and made with wild garlic in spring) and hefty sausage rolls, pies, quiches and cakes. Excellent selection of Northumbrian bottled beers too. It's impossible to leave with only the paper, cornflakes

SCARECROW FESTIVAL

This is a wonderfully eccentric and popular family event held on the late August bank holiday weekend in Rennington village (between Alnwick and Embleton). Garden owners go all out to amuse with creations that will appeal to all ages. In previous years, a flying E.T. on a bicycle, Stick Man, Donald Trump and Monty Don all made appearances. A genuinely fun family trail and quiz will keep children occupied for a good few hours. Finish with a slice of cake in the village hall.

and milk you came in for. The shop is also home to the village **Post Office** (☉ Mon–Sat) where you can withdraw cash.

The Pack Horse Inn Ellingham ✆ 01665 589292 ☉ evening meals Mon–Thu, lunch & dinner Fri & Sat, lunch Sun 🐾. Old pub in a sleepy village several miles inland serving decent homemade food (steak and ale pie, scampi, burgers, hot baguettes).

Rocking Horse Café Midstead Farm, Rock ✆ 01665 579041 ☉ daily 🐾. Great roadside café, set back from the coast in an old farm dairy, which is also a photographic gallery with prints for sale by former jockey, Richard Dunwoody. Stop here for filling breakfasts (and all-day filled breakfast rolls), stottie sandwiches for lunch plus cakes, scones and ices (from Morwick Dairy at Warkworth). Coffee from Pilgrim's on Lindisfarne and plenty of other local produce. Super dog friendly and great for kids too, who are welcome to run around in the rear garden.

20 LOW NEWTON-BY-THE-SEA

Low Newton holds instant appeal with its sheltered sandy bay, sea-facing square of whitewashed stone cottages, and popular **pub** (page 113) serving beers brewed on site to a cheerful crowd of walkers and families.

Today, visitors lounge around the green barefoot, eat lobster caught fresh in the bay, and attend folk music concerts in both the pub and the corrugated iron **church** on the road as you enter the hamlet (bought in kit form over 100 years ago). Back in the mid 19th century, when the square was built, the scene was quite different. The travel writer Walter White in his 1859 *Northumberland, and the Border* observed boys coming and going from herring boats and the cottages where 'women fling their household slops and fish offal' and 'are content to live within sight thereof.' White was not impressed. 'Newton is not pretty or pleasing,' he wrote.

Walking between Newton and Embleton on the popular coast path to Dunstanburgh Castle (page 114), you'll pass around 40 wooden **shacks** in the dunes. They belong to a community of holidaymakers who help care for the National Trust dune landscape; some have been in the same family for three generations. Originally built for golfers, the oldest huts date to the 1920s and were used by the army during World War II. Note, too, the war-era **pillboxes** on the beach and another on the coastal path as you near the castle.

---

1 Dunstanburgh Castle. 2 Look for turnstones on the rocks at Newton.
3 Faulted sedimentary rocks near Howick. 4 Beautiful Embleton Bay. ▶

BIRDLIFE AROUND EMBLETON BAY & NEWTON

In summer, watch gannets plunging into the sea in open water and terns cruising along the shoreline (all five British breeding species could show up). Fulmars and kittiwakes nest on the cliffs under **Dunstanburgh Castle** and at **Cullernose Point** (south of Craster). In winter, the wave-washed rocks at **Newton Point** are reliable for eider ducks, turnstones and red-breasted mergansers.

Behind the dunes and south of the boatpark at Newton is a freshwater lake, **Newton Pool**, overlooked by a National Trust **bird hide** (&). All the usual suspects are found here: coots, swans, geese and gulls. I've seen marsh harriers quartering over the reedbeds in spring, and not infrequently a barn owl hunting over the wildflower grasslands behind the hides.

The track between Newton and the bird hide skirts the side of a damp field – the **scrape** – which is usually more exciting and has become a well-known birding destination on the coast, especially in winter when wading birds and migrating geese gather, and in summer for the nesting avocets (the most northerly breeding avocets in England). Also look out for stonechats and linnets on the bramble bushes hereabouts. Migrant passerines rest in the wet **scrubland** as you walk to the bird hides in autumn; in spring, the thicket is full of chiffchaffs and other warblers.

A grassland **nature reserve** and a large lagoon behind the dunes form an important refuge for migrating and nesting birds. To walk to the National Trust's **Newton Pool**, follow the lane behind the pub (by the public toilets) that becomes a wide gravel path from the boatpark. The field on your right, known to birders as the 'scrape', is the first stopping point to pull out your binoculars. See above for more on the birdlife.

Embleton Bay & Newton Haven

Between Newton-by-the-Sea and Dunstanburgh Castle is a glorious stretch of buttery-coloured sand (technically two bays) and one of the most popular family beaches in Northumberland. That said, even on hot days in summer, kite-boarders can still find an empty run of sand, and children can be lord of their own dune.

The most accessible rock pools are at the northern end opposite Newton square but the **Emblestones** (halfway along the bay) are also full of anemones, starfish, hermit crabs and so on. At low tide, **grey seals** haul themselves on to the south-facing rocks and particularly the outermost isle, but you are just as likely to see them spy-hopping in the bay. Pods of bottlenose and white-beaked **dolphins** frequently patrol the waters between the castle and the Farne Islands. Look out for them in the early morning on dead-flat days.

To escape the throng of visitors at Newton, wander north on the coast path (accessed via a gate opposite the post box on the main road into Newton) over the headland to **Football Hole** – a small, secluded bay – and hunker down in the dunes.

¶¶ FOOD & DRINK

Carnaby's Café Brownieside, Chathill NE67 5HW ☉ daily from 09.30 (kitchen closes at 15.00) ♿. Just off the A1 (northbound) is this fantastic independent café and smart gift shop with a small outdoor children's play area. Inside, it's bright, spacious and modern and the food is all freshly made. In other words, not your usual British roadside café. Behind the counter sit large bowls of some very nourishing-looking Ottolenghi-inspired salads piled high with pulses, nuts, beetroot, cheese, leaves and fruit; above them three or four varieties of inventive frittatas and rolls. Hot meals include burgers, hearty sandwiches (pulled pork, chunky fish finger) and top-notch breakfasts (with homemade baked beans and field mushrooms). Cakes are unusual and delish.

Joiners Arms High Newton-by-the-Sea ☏ 01665 376112 ☉ daily ♿ 🐾. Always-heaving gastro pub (book ahead at weekends), largely on account of wedding parties. All the usual pub staples (burgers, steaks, posh fish fingers, scampi and so on) in a lovely village set back from the sea. Fish and chips to take-away (but sit-in prices). Also has boutique-style B&B rooms upstairs.

The Ship Inn Low Newton-by-the-Sea ☏ 01665 576262 ☉ daily; food 11.00–15.00 daily & evening dinners usually only Wed–Sat in summer, but phone to check 🐾. Tucked into the corner of a stone square of old fishermen's cottages and facing one of the most glorious bays in Northumberland, The Ship is surely one of the best-placed pubs on England's coast. Inside the 18th-century building, the windows are steamed up and the smell of kippers and fruit crumble wafts through the two dining rooms, which usually overflow with Gortex on a Saturday afternoon.

BEACH ACCESS FOR ALL

Beach Access North East (☏ 0300 999 4444 ☝ beachaccessnortheast.org) is a brilliant charity run by volunteers working to make the coastline accessible to everyone through the loan of specialist equipment. A variety of beach wheelchairs with wheels able to roll on soft sand are available to hire for free to members (simple online joining form).

Access storage units are located at popular beaches: Tynemouth, Whitley Bay, Blyth, Newbiggin, Newton-by-the-Sea, Beadnell and Bamburgh.

Northumbrian produce from the sea and local farms dots the lunch menu: stottie baps filled with Doddington's cheese, crab sandwiches, kippers on toast, and pies people will travel for. The beer is brewed on site. What's not to like? Fighting for a table when the kitchen opens (you can't book and queues start forming soon after 11.00).

✳ ✳ ✳

🚶 BEACH, CASTLE & SMOKEHOUSE WALK: NEWTON TO CRASTER

❄ OS Explorer maps 332 & 340; start: Newton-by-the-Sea, 📍 NU241245; 4 miles one way; easy

The return linear walk to Dunstanburgh Castle and Craster from Newton-by-the-Sea is one of the most popular on the Northumberland coast and has all the ingredients of a perfect coastal trail: a sandy bay, castle and a great pub at either end. It's also straightforward to navigate and you can do away with your map – just head for the ruined fortress on the headland.

From Newton, walk for 1½ miles south along the beach until Embleton Bay comes to an abrupt end by a mass of boulders. Note that an estuary runs across the sands at the midway point and can be crossed when the tide is low (you might have to go barefoot); otherwise head inland along the edge of the golf course and over a plank bridge.

At the end of Embleton Bay, climb on to the headland, skirting the golf course on your right and a World War II pillbox before making your way under **Dunstanburgh Castle's** walls to its mighty south entrance. **Craster** is visible just over a mile to the south and reached on a well-worn grassy track across farmland.

Buses X18 & 418 from Craster make the return journey to High Newton via Embleton in 15 minutes but make sure you catch the 418 that stops in High Newton village, otherwise it's a slog of around half a mile on a dangerous road with no pavement and you'd be better off alighting in Embleton and walking to Low Newton through the dunes (which takes half an hour or so).

To vary the return on foot, from the castle, you could follow the official **Northumberland Coast Path**, which heads inland and skirts the western edge of the golf green.

✳ ✳ ✳

21 PRESTON TOWER

Preston, near Chathill NE67 5DH ⊙ until dusk or 18.00, whichever is earlier, daily

As far as young children are concerned, this is a 'proper' castle with turrets, old stonework and slit windows. In fact, it is a medieval pele tower dating back to 1392. It stands in landscaped parkland a couple of miles southwest of Beadnell. Very few fortified towers quite as well preserved and special as this are open to the public and provide such a vivid sense of the border clashes that were so frequent in Northumberland until the 17th century. Rooms are partially furnished with items typical of the period. I like the way you are free to visit on any day and enjoy the tower at leisure; just remember to pop your entrance fee into the honesty box (£4 at the time of writing and 50p for kids) – and switch off the light when you leave.

Though Preston Tower looks like a complete building, it is in fact one half of a four-turreted 'castle', part of which was pulled down when the threat of violence from marauding clans waned. At one time the entrance would have been on the first floor (accessed by way of ladders, which were then lifted off the ground). Livestock was housed on the ground floor. The slit windows and 7ft-thick walls would have been very difficult to penetrate.

A clear highlight is the 1864 **clock** which, the information panel tells you, has a similar mechanism to Big Ben. On the hour, cogs start spinning

COASTAL FLOWERS

In summer, **bloody crane's-bill** puts on a deep pink-purple display among the **marram grass**, **sea campion** and **burnet roses** in dunes along the Northumberland coast. **Orchids** flower in localised places including the damp grasslands behind Beadnell Bay, which are covered in pyramidal orchids from June to August. You'll also see marsh orchids scattered throughout buttercup meadows on the southern fringes of Craster, and in the grasslands behind Newton's bird hides.

The most special orchid is the **Lindisfarne helleborine** (lime-green flowers with a white 'lip' coloured brown inside), an endemic species that flowers on the island and nowhere else, along with ten other orchids including the **dune helleborine**, **frog orchid** and a profusion of **marsh** and **common spotted orchids**. They grow in such dense numbers on the island's northern dune slacks that they are hard to avoid stepping on in places. By the flats either side of Lindisfarne's causeway, **sea thrift** puts on a stunning pink display over the saltmarshes.

Whin grassland is an important habitat in Northumberland appearing around outcrops of the dark-grey Whin Sill (around Dunstanburgh Castle, Craster and Lindisfarne's castle, for example). Associated plants include common rock rose, maiden pink, chives, purple milk-vetch and field garlic.

Above the high tide line, **sea rocket** brings a pale-pink hue to the sands along many dune-backed bays in Northumberland.

and a metal arm is depressed, triggering another lever that pulls a cord that moves the hammer which strikes the deafening half-tonne bell at the top of the tower – to the excitement of both children and adults. The dilemma is whether to watch the whirring mechanism or experience the powerful, bone-vibrating gong of the bell. Fortunately, you can do both if you are quick enough up the stairs (be careful – there's no hand rail at the top). From the turrets, you can see all the way to the sea.

Three short **trails** lead around the estate gardens, providing a view of the mansion house, built in 1802, and the mature ornamental trees including redwoods and a beautiful copper beech. Look out for red squirrels.

Quite wonderfully, you can **camp** in the grounds. Call ✆ 07966 150216 to book.

22 BEADNELL

Beadnell has two pleasant historic areas, the harbour and village, connected by a number of residential roads. This one-time fishing village is now mainly a holiday area boasting one of the most unspoilt sandy beaches in the region and plenty of holiday cottages.

Beadnell is full of quirks. It's a difficult layout for starters and its 18th-century **harbour** faces the wrong way (the only west-facing harbour on the east coast of England). It's backed by a knot of curious buildings including **lime kilns** dating to the same period (nothing odd with that, they are quite common along the Northumberland coast) and a turreted stone guesthouse. Close by is a ramshackle hut in fenced-off grassland by the side of the Harbour Road. It's the only traditional **fishing hut** remaining in Beadnell. There are more fishing relics on the seafront if you're up for a heritage hunt (page 121).

"At its core is the church, dedicated to St Ebba, the wise sister of Anglo-Saxon King Oswald."

The old **village centre** is set back from the seafront. At its core is the **church**, dedicated to St Ebba, the wise sister of Anglo-Saxon King Oswald. St Ebba is thought to have founded a monastic site on a

---

1 Nesting birds on the Farne Islands. **2** Preston Tower. **3** Among the marram grass, look for burnet rose in the dunes on the Northumberland coastline. **4** Boat trips to the Farne Islands allow for good sightings of grey seal. **5** Working boats in the harbour at Seahouses. ▶

DAVE CLAYTON/S

DARKINGS.PHOTOGRAPHY/S

SIBGHAT DOTANI/S

COLIN SEDDON/S

GEMMA HALL

rocky promontory east of the harbour, Ebb's Nook, in the 7th century. Unsurprisingly on this storm-battered outpost, almost nothing remains of the ruins or the later **medieval chapel** built on the same site, except for some turfed-over stones.

The present church is rather better protected and dates to the 1740s, though it was Gothicised in the 19th century. The spire with its crown of pinnacles is striking but the rest of the building, particularly the interior, is a rather plain Victorian renovation. Take a close look at the **churchyard** memorial stones, a number of which record the death at sea of fishermen in centuries gone by, including Andrew Fawgus and his three sons who 'were accidentally drowned within sight of their own home' on 31 January 1885. 'Their grave is in the mighty deep', reads the inscription.

On your way out of Beadnell, if heading south, look out for the rare **Automobile Association telephone kiosk** ('the AA' to British motorists) by the side of the B1340. It stands in a wooded area roughly opposite the turning for the caravan park. The fetching Tardis-like cabin, number 817, made of wood and painted black and yellow, is one of only 19 still standing in the whole of the UK out of the 862 constructed in the mid 20th century to provide assistance to motorists.

Beadnell Bay

A pristine sandy beach padded with dunes and lapped by blue water is not easily found anywhere in England, but to come across one as crowd-free as Beadnell is rare indeed.

Halfway along is **Long Nanny** – an inlet by a timber hut known for its breeding arctic terns, little terns and ringed plovers that nest in the dune grasses. This is the largest breeding colony of arctic terns on mainland Britain, though their success has been severely knocked in recent years due to outbreaks of bird flu. The hut is manned by National Trust wardens around the clock during the breeding season in summer and it is the best place to watch the birds at close range without disturbing them.

"A pristine sandy beach padded with dunes and lapped by blue water is not easily found anywhere in England."

Watersports enthusiasts (from beginners up) can book surfing, paddleboarding, wing foiling and kitesurfing lessons from **KA Adventure Sports** (☏ 07766 303876 ♂ kaadventuresports.co.uk) based in Beadnell's car park (by Beadnell Bay Caravan Park).

* * *

☘ BEACH, DUNE & ARCTIC TERNS: A WALK FROM BEADNELL TO NEWTON

❄ OS Explorer map 340; start: Beadnell, ♀ NU235288; 4 miles one way; easy

W alkers on the **Northumberland Coast Path** will find this four-mile route south to Newton-by-the-Sea an enjoyable amble with birdlife and beautiful beach scenery in abundance the whole way.

Set foot from the **Beadnell Bay Caravan Park** above Beadnell harbour, walking through the site on the well-signed England Coast Path (also known as the Northumberland Coast Path). Ahead, the path crosses the **Tughall Links** grasslands managed by the National Trust.

A narrow wooden **footbridge** carries the national trail over an estuary to the dune-backed sands of **Beadnell Bay** and **Long Nanny** with its arctic tern colony (see opposite). Walk the length of the beach (around 1½ miles) then climb back up onto the dunes and over grasslands to the sheltered cove of **Football Hole** – a nice spot for beachcombing and watching the turnstones pick through the seaweed.

Cross the horseshoe bay and up on to a promontory with the rocks of **Newton Point** below you (keep an eye out for dolphins when the sea is flat). The final run to **Newton-by-the-Sea** and its popular pub in the square is along the well-worn grassy coastal path that skirts a delightful meadow thronged with buttercups and clovers in summer.

The **coastal bus** (the 418) will shuttle you back to Beadnell in a matter of minutes from High Newton but you'll need to allow a good 20 minutes to walk from Low Newton to the bus stop in High Newton. Check times in advance (page 66).

* * *

▮▮ FOOD & DRINK

Courtyard Café Gardeners Cottage, The Haven ✆ 07951 405584 ⊙ 08.00–20.00 Tue–Sat, till 17.00 Sun & Mon ♿ ☸. Tucked down a driveway a few paces from Beadnell's churchyard is this secluded café with outdoor seating. A lovely choice for breakfast, a quiet, simple lunch (paninis, quiche, filling sandwiches, jackets, soup) and also evening meals (quality fish finger sandwiches, bubble and squeak with bacon and egg, omelettes, burgers and a few other dishes). Or simply for a cup of tea and slice of really good cake. A take-away bacon roll might be the perfect tummy filler if passing through on the coast path.

The Craster Arms The Wynding ✆ 01665 720272 ⊙ daily ♿ ☸. Old inn close to Beadnell's parish church with B&B rooms, a modern gastro-pub restaurant and large, sunny enclosed beer garden. A few regular items on the menu grabbed me: pies from Turnbull's in

Alnwick and the Beadnell sizzler, a sausage ring on mashed potato with gravy especially made for the pub by the famous sausage maker in Bamburgh. The specials board when I visited offered smoked duck with dauphinoise potatoes, a seared tuna niçoise salad and baked plaice. Also Sunday roasts.

The Landing By Beadnell Bay Caravan Park & behind Beadnell Bay car park ✆ 01665 524005 ⊙ 08.30–23.00 daily ♿ 🐾. The first bistro coast-path walkers come to on entering Beadnell from the south – and what a great place to shelter from the wilds, with heaters and a log burner. Mercifully, it's always open. Menus cover every base: breakfast to dinner. Great to see so much regional meat and fish: Northumbrian steaks and lamb, monkfish landed at North Shields, Seahouses kippers and sausages from Bamburgh, as well as crowd-pleasers like pizza and burgers. There's a bar too and sheltered outdoor seating under a tepee.

The Salt Water Café The Wynding ✆ 01665 720333 ⊙ 08.30–21.00 Tue–Sat, until 16.00 Sun ♿. Very pleasant modern bistro near the church with indoor and pavement seating, serving breakfasts, lunches and evening meals (book in advance). Menus are peppered with local specialities: Craster Kippers, Bamburgh's famous sausages, Northumberland lamb, lobster from Seahouses. Evening plates are a feast of seafood. It's not cheap for casual dining, however, with mains costing around £25 come dusk.

23 SEAHOUSES

Seahouses is a bustling fishing town, now busier with tourists popping into gift shops than with fishermen, but its **harbour** is still a working port. Eight fishing vessels were docked when I last visited and, as always, the lobster pots were stacked along the harbour wall. A couple of fishermen with caps and waterproofs stood around chatting: a timeless scene.

In the **town centre**, there are plenty of knick-knack shops selling all the usual seaside tat, buckets and spades, body boards and so on, as well as a soft play and crazy golf centre, an amusement arcade or two, and fish and chip shops aplenty (page 122), In other words, a good old-fashioned British seaside resort, complete with chip-stealing herring gulls.

The town grew as a holiday resort in the 1920s. Then, as now, the **Farne Islands** were the reason many people came here and today you'll find a number of **boat-tour** companies with kiosks at the harbour. Also here is the **RNLI Lifeboat Station**, a modern building housing working vessels. Historical boards list call-outs dating back 200 years to Grace Darling's time (though the lifeboat arrived after the famous rescue; page 127). Opposite the harbour are Seahouses' well-preserved **lime kilns**, dating to 1841. As at Beadnell and Lindisfarne they were ideally situated for the easy transportation of lime by boat.

FISHING HERITAGE

Katrina Porteous
Local historian, poet and editor of The Bonny Fisher Lad

Most of north Northumberland's coastal villages have been strongly shaped by fishing. Traditionally this was carried out from 'cobles', small open wooden boats launched from the beach. The fishing year was divided into the winter season, when long lines were used to catch cod and haddock, and summer, when herring were caught using drift nets. All the family was involved: women sold fish inland and, with their children, gathered mussels and limpets to bait the 1,400 hooks of each line.

Herring became a major industry from the early 19th century, and villages such as Seahouses prospered. In summer the men fished at night, and women worked in teams, gutting and packing herring into barrels for export, or smoking them as 'kippers'. Although herring are no longer caught locally, Craster and Seahouses still have active smokehouses. In **Seahouses** the remains of several 19th-century herring yards can be seen, now converted into cottages. Walk along South Street looking for blocked-off 'bowly-holes' in the walls, where cartloads of herring were shovelled into troughs for gutting. Nearby, the gateway of Chapel Row is marked by grooves made by generations of fisherwomen sharpening their limpet-picking tools on their way to the rocks.

On **Lindisfarne**, old upturned herring drifters are used as sheds, and on Harbour Road at **Beadnell** two tarry fishermen's huts, now disused, mark the Haven where cobles were launched. Near them, beside the footpath to the sea, stand the remains of a row of 18th-century 'bark-pots'. These square structures consisted of a hearth, chimney and large metal tank, and were used to boil nets, ropes and sails in a tannin-rich liquid to preserve them. This seashore is full of hidden clues to its past, such as mussel beds, lobster ponds and rectangular troughs called 'bratt holes', only visible at low tide, where fish were stored for live export in sailing sloops to London.

Today, fishing on this coast has greatly diminished. Where it still exists, it is mostly confined to catching crabs and lobsters. But look out for cobles still working traditional summer salmon nets in **Boulmer Haven**.

Seahouses' **bay**, just south of the harbour, is great for crabbing and rockpooling at low tide. Some well-placed benches by a couple of 200-year-old whale bones make a lovely spot to enjoy fish and chips, away from the busy town centre. From here, the Farne Islands, Bamburgh and Lindisfarne castles are all in view.

Anyone with a nose for old things will find a stroll around **South Street** interesting. Seahouses' 19th- and 20th-century fishing industry is much in evidence with herring yards, fishermen's stone cottages, 'bowly-holes' (page 121) and a very old **smokehouse** (see below).

FOOD & DRINK

One of the greatest pleasures at Seahouses is to sit on the terrace of benches facing the harbour eating some of the best fish and chips you will find anywhere in the UK. But, where's the best fish and chip shop? **Hook** (✆ 01665 720708 ⊙ daily) and **Neptune's** (✆ 01665 721310 ⊙ daily 🚻) face each other at the bottom of Main Street and have been serving great fish suppers for decades but **Lewis's Fish Restaurant** (✆ 01665 720475 ⊙ daily) further up Main Street seems to get the queues these days and is my usual go-to when in the area.

For everyday groceries, on Main Street there's a **Co-op** and the **Independent Food & Drink** store (✆ 01665 721057 ⊙ daily 🚻) selling cupboard staples and fresh produce, including fruit and veg and regional cheeses. For take-out sandwiches, sausage rolls and the like, the local butcher's, **Scotty's** (✆ 01665 720367 ⊙ Mon–Sat 07.30–16.00), just past the top roundabout on your left, will sort you out with picnic food – as well as everything you need for a barbecue.

Black Swan Inn 2 Union St ✆ 01665 720227 ⊙ daily 🚻 🐾. Pricey, old stone pub with a revamped interior serving good food: sharing platters, Lindisfarne oysters, whole lobster (make sure you pre-order – it comes straight off Seahouses' boats), a Thai seafood curry made with fish landed that day, North Sea haddock and chips, and a few delicacies from the nearby smokehouse (try their smoked fish pâté). Even the kids get fed quality Northumbrian fodder.

Olde Ship Inn Main St ✆ 01665 720200 ⊙ daily 🚻 🐾. A great seafarers' pub with bags of character (and nautical artefacts), overlooking the harbour. Come here for real ales, an open fire, a beer garden and convivial chatter. Also trading in breakfasts, lunches and dinners – all crowd-pleasing pub nosh as well as fish from the harbour.

Swallow Fish 2 South St ✆ 01665 721052 ⊙ Mon–Sat 🚻. Herring and salmon have been smoked here since 1843. It's worth visiting the smokehouse just to see the photos above an iron range, and old herring baskets and anchors. You can buy everything you need for a seafood barbecue: locally caught mackerel, whole crab and lobster. Their smoked salmon has a delicate flavour and is a superior, drier cut than the slippery supermarket stuff.

24 FARNE ISLANDS NATIONAL NATURE RESERVE

✆ 01665 720651 ⊙ Apr–Oct; boat prices exclude admission to the island, which is paid on landing; no refreshments; no dogs (not even assistance dogs) are permitted on Inner Farne but you can take dogs on Longstone Island (page 124); National Trust

'A boat may be secured for fifteen shillings. In addition to this charge, the boatmen expect to be provided with refreshments, solid and liquid.' Visitors to the Farne Islands no longer need to supply the tour-boat skippers with food and drink, as they did in the late 19th century, but little else has changed since Victorian tourists came to experience the famous chain of bird islands a couple of miles offshore from Seahouses.

The islands are divided into two main groups by Staple Sound. On **Inner Farne**, boardwalks guide visitors on a half-mile-long round-island walk. Thousands of puffins nest in burrows, while razorbills, kittiwakes and guillemots lay their eggs on the columnar sea-facing rocks (part of the Great Whin Sill that peaks in several places along the Northumberland coast).

Boat trips depart hourly depending on the weather and can be booked from the kiosks at Seahouses harbour or in advance online. They all offer similar excursions; operators include **Billy Shiel's Boat Trips** (✆ 01665 720308 ⌖ farne-islands.com) and **Serenity** catamarans (⌖ farneislandstours.co.uk). Tours of the islands offer close-up views of seals and cliff-nesting birds before landing on Inner Farne. Come mid-August, most birds depart for open waters, abandoning their empty nests to the wind and sea, but eider ducks, cormorants, shags and seals are seen throughout the year. Allow for a round trip of three hours.

Landing on Inner Farne is quite an experience and you'll soon be ducking and flinching from the dive-bombing **arctic terns**. A wave of the hands usually keeps the birds, which are ever so protective of their chicks running at your feet, from striking, but I strongly recommend wearing a hat just in case as strikes can be very painful.

And there's nothing quite like watching **puffins** crash-landing with beaks stuffed full of sand eels, cormorants sitting proud on their castles of dried seaweed, and **guillemots** guarding rock stacks painted white with guano. Young guillemots are known, rather wonderfully, as 'jumplings'

CUDDY'S DUCK

Several hundred eider ducks nest on the Farne Islands. Most of them inhabit Inner Farne, where they have received sanctuary for over 1,300 years, ever since St Cuthbert lived here in the 7th century. The saint afforded the ducks special protection and is sometimes referred to as the first bird conservationist. His love of eiders is the reason why Cuthbert is sometimes depicted with the bird at his feet, and the origins of the local name: Cuddy's Duck.

WHALES, PORPOISES & DOLPHINS AHOY!

Martin Kitching

The diminutive harbour porpoise can be seen along the Northumberland coast all year round, and minke whales peak in late August. Stunning white-beaked dolphins swim close to the shore in June and July, then they move offshore into deeper, cooler water and are often the highlight of trips to the Farne Deeps. Bottlenose dolphins, from the population around Fife and Tayside in eastern Scotland, seem to be taking a shine to Northumberland's coastline.

Above the waves, pelagic wildlife trips are often accompanied by fulmars, kittiwakes and squabbling gulls, while rarer sightings have included storm petrels, long-tailed skuas, sooty shearwaters, grey and red-necked phalaropes and, very occasionally, orcas. You just never know what you'll see …

Martin Kitching is a wildlife expert and director of Northern Experience Wildlife Tours (✆ 01670 827465 ⬧ northernexperiencewildlifetours.co.uk), which runs pelagic boat trips from Seahouses and North Shields near Newcastle to look for cetaceans and seabirds, as well as wildlife-watching trips elsewhere in the county.

and you may see them launching themselves off the Farne rocks on their maiden sea journey. There is no other wildlife experience quite like this anywhere else in Northumberland.

Inner Farne was inhabited by hermits and monks for 900 years; the most well known was **Cuthbert**, who lived twice on the island before and after he became Bishop of Lindisfarne. The second time, in AD687, he returned to his much-loved sanctuary to die. Nothing remains of Cuthbert's simple shelter and prayer room, but you will see a few old stone buildings, including a **chapel** built around 1300. The 17th-century wood stalls inside came from Durham Cathedral.

Two **lighthouses** still operate on the Farnes, both dating to the early 1800s. The red and white beacon on **Longstone** is the famous 'Grace Darling lighthouse' from where the lighthouse keeper and his daughter rowed through a storm in 1838 to aid survivors of a shipwreck. In the years following the rescue, Victorian tourists would visit the famous family at the lighthouse and delight in hearing of the extraordinary event firsthand. Today, one boat operator lands on Longstone (**Golden Gate Farne Islands Boat Trips** ✆ 07904 800590 ⬧ farneislandsboattrips. com 🐾) and permits a tour inside the lighthouse but otherwise you'll need to visit the Grace Darling Museum in Bamburgh (page 127).

25 BAMBURGH

One of the most bewitching coastal views in Northumberland bursts upon the traveller on reaching the brow of the B1340 between Waren Mill and Bamburgh. From here, Bamburgh's famous medieval **castle** comes into sight, spectacularly rising from the dunes – all rock, turrets and battlements. It is undoubtedly one of England's finest fortresses and this is one of the most unspoilt and dramatic coastal panoramas, with the Farne Islands to the south, Lindisfarne Castle silhouetted on its rocky perch to the north, and the wide, creamy sands of Bamburgh's three-mile **beach** below. The view is most expansive from the castle's Battery Terrace.

In the **village**, the castle maintains its heavy presence. My 19th-century travel guide describes Bamburgh as 'clean and cheerful' and a 'model village'. Nothing has changed in that respect and it's quite obvious why the village was named by Which? as the best seaside resort in the UK three years running. The centre is almost entirely made of stone and centred about a wooded green. **Front Street** has a pleasing run of 18th-century stone cottages, a number of which are now gift shops, bistros and B&Bs.

A **walk** (or cycle) along **The Wynding** – a quiet paved lane (opposite the Lord Crewe Hotel) provides easy access to Bamburgh's northerly **beaches** (where there is also parking). An excellent **surf school** is based in the car park. It's run by a friendly team (North East Surf Co. ✆ 07962 166486 ⬙ nesurf.co.uk) and offers small group lessons. Walkers can continue beyond the golf clubhouse to **Budle Point** and drop down on to the sandy shore or follow the coast path west for the bird-rich flats of **Budle Bay** (page 130).

Bamburgh Castle

Bamburgh ✆ 01668 214515 ⏲ mid-Feb–Oct daily, w/ends at other times ♿ grounds & some rooms including the Kings Hall 🐾 grounds only

Many writers and architectural historians have declared Bamburgh the most wondrous of all England's coastal castles. You may well agree when you see its stonking curtain walls and keep crowning a fist of basalt thrust 150ft through the dunes. Bamburgh is certainly the stuff of fairytales.

Its enviable situation proved a valuable vantage point for settlers from ancient times and almost certainly the Romans. From the Anglo-

SCENIC ROAD: BUDLE BAY TO BAMBURGH

An outstanding view of Bamburgh Castle awaits motorists and cyclists riding over the B1340 between Waren Mill and Bamburgh. As you reach the top of the hill, the sight of the fortress will make you want to pull over for photos. If you can time your journey for late in the afternoon on a clear day, you'll see the castle lit wondrously by the sun.

Saxon period to the present day, Vikings, kings, earls and dukes have seized, pounded and abandoned the castle in various states of ruin. Some of Bamburgh's Anglo-Saxon treasures are displayed inside the **Archaeology Room**, and include part of a stone throne.

After the Viking raids, the Normans rebuilt the castle in stone. The **Keep** standing today dates to the reign of Henry II. Bamburgh stood strong for several hundred years and survived invasions from north of the border until 1464 when its walls were razed by the Earl of Warwick during the Wars of the Roses. Connoisseurs of trivia will take pleasure in knowing that this was the first castle in England to fall to cannon fire.

Bamburgh was extensively rebuilt in the 18th century and contains later additions, such as the stables added by the Victorian industrialist Lord Armstrong, whose family has owned the castle ever since. As a rule of thumb, the pinkish outer walls are medieval, and those with a grey hue are Victorian. Much of the interior dates to this latter period, including the **King's Hall** (the former banqueting hall), a magnificent wood-panelled room of ballroom proportions with a false hammer-beam roof and stained glass. In addition to the King's Hall, don't miss the views from the **Court Room** and the intriguing bottle-shaped doorway at the bottom of the stairs which allowed knights on horseback to swiftly enter the building without having to dismount (how's that for style?). The **Billiard Room** and adjoining **Faire Chamber** evoke the era of high-society social events where aristocratic men played pool in one room and ladies conversed in the sumptuous surroundings of the chamber next door.

"Bamburgh stood strong for several hundred years and survived invasions from north of the border until 1464."

The **Armstrong and Aviation Artefacts Museum**, housed in the old castle laundry, gives visitors a glimpse into the life of the First Lord Armstrong and houses a collection of aviation artefacts donated and salvaged from the two world wars, including the wreckage of a Spitfire.

Grace Darling Museum

Radcliffe Rd, NE69 7AE ℘ 01668 214910 ☉ Mon–Fri & afternoons Sun; free entry ♿

Facing the sea to the northwest of the village is this enchanting museum that perpetuates the memory of the Victorian heroine who helped save shipwrecked passengers off the Farne Islands one stormy night in 1838.

The collection of memorabilia in the small museum – including the lifesaving coble rowing boat and some of Grace's clothes – is elegantly presented. You'll learn about events on that fateful night, the life of the lighthouse keeper and his family and Grace's rise to fame in the years following the rescue – an intriguing tale in itself (see below).

Above the staircase, note the atmospheric Carmichael oil depicting Grace and her father rowing across heaving waves to the sinking ship.

A couple of doors down from the museum at 3 Radcliffe Road is where Grace was born (a plaque above the doorway gives the date: 24 November 1815) and the churchyard opposite (page 129) is where she is buried, facing the sea, as is fitting.

GRACE DARLING

I had little thought of anything but to exert myself to the utmost, my spirit was worked up by the sight of such a dreadful affair that I can imagine I still see the sea flying over the vessel.
From a letter by Grace Darling in her namesake museum at Bamburgh

In the early hours of 7 September 1838, the paddle steamer SS *Forfarshire* hit the corner of Big Harcar off the Farne Islands. With his daughter Grace, William Darling, the lighthouse keeper on Longstone Island, launched his wooden coble, rowing through choppy waters to reach the nine shipwrecked survivors.

The story was widely printed in the papers and it seems the Victorian readership couldn't get enough of the romantic tale of the lighthouse keeper's daughter, who became famous in her lifetime. She sat for many portraits and received gifts, including £50 from Queen Victoria. Four years later, she died of tuberculosis aged 26 (in the building that is now the Pantry deli on Front Street). Her story endures, though the events and Grace's character have been much romanticised. Wordsworth penned the following verse, an extract of which appears on a memorial on the Farne Islands:

Pious and pure, modest and yet so brave,
Though young so wise, though meek so resolute –
Might carry to the clouds and to the stars,
Yea, to celestial Choirs, Grace Darling's name!

St Aidan's Church

Opposite the Grace Darling Museum on Radcliffe Road is this well-visited church, largely on account of its connection to Bamburgh's famous Victorian heroine, and its namesake saint and Bishop of Lindisfarne who was instrumental in establishing Christianity in Northumbria in the 7th century.

As you walk through the churchyard, **Grace Darling's resting place** is identified by following the trampled grassy trail to a large Gothic memorial (rebuilt in 1993 to the same design as the older, weather-beaten sandstone monument that now lies inside). She is also represented in a series of stained-glass windows in a small chapel to the left of the altar. In one she holds an oar, but note her blond locks (Darling had brown hair).

The **church** dates for the most part from the end of the 12th century and is notable for many reasons, including its long chancel and many arcades. It stands on the site of a much earlier church founded by **St Aidan** (page 138) in AD635. The only relic from that time is thought to be the wooden girder in the baptistry. According to legend, it was the same beam the saint died leaning against in AD651 and is said to have survived two fires. A modern shrine marks the spot.

¶¶ FOOD & DRINK

Average cafés and restaurants dot Front Street, including the **Copper Kettle** (✆ 01668 214315 ☉ daily), a snug, delightfully old-fashioned tea room with wood panelling depicting local scenes and best known for its cream teas. The **Lord Crewe Hotel** (✆ 01668 214243 ☉ breakfast to dinner daily ♿) has above-average B&B rooms and a fine restaurant with very tempting seafood mains including lobster and lighter lunch options – though with fish soup and crab sandwiches charged at £13 each, there are better-value seafood options locally. **Wyndenwell** (✆ 01668 214032 ☉ daily ♿) is a good choice for sandwiches, cakes and coffee but most of those in the queue have come for one thing: ice cream.

For picnic food, first head to the excellent **R Carter & Son** (Front St ✆ 01668 214344 ☉ Mon–Sat) – 'butcher, baker, sausage roll maker' – in business here since 1887, for their super sausage rolls (densely filled with Carter's famous and exceedingly good 'Bamburgh Banger') which are sold alongside cuts of regional pork, lamb and beef. **The Pantry**

◀ 1 Bamburgh's three-mile beach offers spectacular views towards the castle.
2 Grace Darling's memorial, St Aidan's Church, Bamburgh. 3 The King's Hall, Bamburgh Castle. 4 Escape the crowds at Ross Back Sands.

(🖉 01668 214455 🕒 09.00–14.00 daily), on the same street, sells local cheeses, pies and inexpensive filled rolls including hot kipper and crab sandwiches to take-away.

Creel & Reel Seafood Trailer Links Rd (carpark off the B1340 between Seahouses and Bamburgh) 🖉 07595 981399 🕒 usually afternoons Thu & Sat–Mon & evening Fri. Mobile food van on the coast road to Seahouses selling incredible seafood (as well as gourmet burgers) to take-away. Set behind the dunes in the Links car park, arrive early before they run out of lobster with crispy fries, monkfish and chorizo skewers, grilled squid, crab sandwiches or langoustines with garlic butter. Take your fish supper onto one of the most romantic beaches in all of Northumberland with a view of Bamburgh Castle. Sundowns don't get better than this.

The Potted Lobster 3 Lucker Rd 🖉 01668 214088 🕒 daily 🦽 🐾. A true feast of locally caught shellfish including crab, oysters (from Lindisfarne), langoustines and of course, lobster. A few non-seafood options to consider: lamb rump with mash, steak, and a squash and sweet potato curry. The restaurant itself is small, bright and all very Scandi-chic with its mid-century wooden chairs and minimalist décor. Ideally you'd want to dine here in the evening without kids but they do actually have a very good children's menu if the sprites have to join. Make sure you book.

26 BUDLE BAY

By road from Bamburgh to Belford or on the coastal footpath, enjoy far-reaching views of the swirling sand and mudflats sheltered in this deep, wide bay. Non-birdwatchers travelling with birders in autumn and winter beware: from here to Lindisfarne and beyond is serious binocular and field guide country. One of the best places to see some of the thousands of ducks, geese and waders that descend on the flats is from the roadside path and pull-in areas along the coast road east of Waren Mill. As the tide comes in, the birds are pushed closer to land.

27 ROSS BACK SANDS

The beach at Ross is a gloriously deserted sandy spit that extends for three breezy miles from Budle Bay almost to Lindisfarne. Access is via a mile-long footpath through Ross Farm and across the dunes, which puts off the few travellers who venture to this remote place. Your reward, however, is an unbeatable panorama: all sky, sea and white sands with Lindisfarne Castle at one end and Bamburgh Castle and the Farne Islands at the other. One Saturday afternoon in winter, I walked for over two hours without seeing another person.

OYSTER BAY

Oysters have been harvested for hundreds of years on the mudflats of Lindisfarne Bay. Past owners of the oyster beds include monks in the 14th century and a Victorian landowner. The industry died out in the early 1900s but was resurrected in 1989 by a local farmer who spotted oyster shells on the sand. Current owners, Christopher and Helen Sutherland, inherited the business in the early noughties and now supply many restaurants across the North East and further afield. You can buy their oysters at Swallow Fish smokehouse in Seahouses (page 122), online ⬦ lindisfarneoysters.co.uk, or direct from Ross Farm (between Budle Bay & Lindisfarne, NE70 7EN ⬦ 01668 213870) if ordered in advance.

For a truly authentic experience, pick up a dozen oysters at the farm and head over the dunes to enjoy them with a divine coastal view of Lindisfarne. Just remember to bring a glove and suitable knife for shucking. I did this some years ago but only had a penknife on me, which was a lethal tool for the job.

The secluded spot is appreciated by nudists, this being a **naturist beach**. I read somewhere that 'textiles walk south, naturists north'. I've only ever once seen a non-textile here and he was indeed walking according to the rule book.

A pair of binoculars will come in handy, both to check out the seals lazing on sand humps in Lindisfarne's bay (best viewed from Guile Point) and to scan the sea for divers, grebes and scoters in winter, and terns in summer. At the northern end of the spit on **Guile Point** (out of bounds from May to July because of nesting birds) are two triangular navigation towers. They help keep mariners on the right course through the dangerous waters that have claimed many boats, including the remains of two shipwrecks you see by walking the length of the beach. Keep in mind that from the main access point on to the sands (roughly the midway point of the spit) the towers look deceptively close but they take over an hour to reach.

A word of caution: make a mental picture of where the footpath enters the beach as it is difficult to find on your return.

28 BELFORD

A long row of grey stone houses curves away from the market cross (at least 200 years old) at the head of this quiet market town between the coast and the Cheviot Hills.

When Belford was a coaching stop on the old Edinburgh to London road, horses were fed and watered in stables (now somewhat changed) opposite the cross by the side of the Blue Bell Hotel.

Those interested in the history of the town should step round the corner to **Belford Hidden Histories** (adjacent to the inn on Church St ⊙ Mar–Nov daily). Among displays of war memorabilia and local artefacts is an intriguing photograph of suffragists standing outside the Blue Bell, which is thought to date to October 1912 when a group marched from Edinburgh to London with a Votes for Women petition.

Also close to the Blue Bell is the parish **church**, which was rebuilt in 1828 by John Dobson, the architect responsible for many churches and country houses in Northumberland. Note the Norman chancel arch.

¶¶ FOOD & DRINK

A couple of food-serving pubs, a fish and chip shop and places serving coffee are found on the main road running through Belford but the town centre is not known for its restaurants. **The Salmon Inn** (✆ 01668 213799 ⊙ Mon–Sat) specialises in burgers and pizzas. Families may prefer to travel to **Sunnyhills Farm Shop** (South Rd ✆ 01668 219662 ⊙ daily ♿ 🐾), in farmland on the southern outskirts of Belford, where there's a playground, bistro serving British breakfasts, lunches and evening meals as well as a farm shop with a pantry and deli counter.

St Cuthbert's Cave

St Cuthbert's Way long-distance path (page 187) from the Cheviot Hills to Lindisfarne passes a small wood near Holburn Grange (four miles west of Budle Bay and also accessible along a grassy track from the car park at Holburn Grange) where there's a cave set within a huge

GLASTONBURY (NORTHUMBERLAND STYLE)

Beal, nr Lindisfarne TD15 2PB ⊘ lindisfarnefestival.com

The annual, adults-only **Lindisfarne Festival** (⊘ lindisfarnefestival.com) grows year on year and sees increasingly well-known bands rock the coast over the August bank holiday weekend, with indie, rock, folk, jazz and dance DJs performing across nine stages. In previous years, headline acts included the Levellers, Orbital, Happy Mondays and Primal Scream. The site on the mainland at Beal Farm spectacularly overlooks Lindisfarne. Bring your tent or book a yurt.

sandstone outcrop. Monks carrying Cuthbert's body are said to have rested here (locally known as 'Cuddy's Cave') when they fled from Viking invaders on Lindisfarne at the end of the 9th century. If you continue on St Cuthbert's Way over the hills, you gain a spectacular panorama of Lindisfarne and Bamburgh castles.

Nearby (a mile north of St Cuthbert's Cave) is **Holburn Moss** – a wetland nature reserve with an artificial lake supporting overwintering ducks and geese.

29 LINDISFARNE (HOLY ISLAND)

🏠 **Hunting Hall**

Lindisfarne Castle seemingly rises out of the sea off the coast of north Northumberland; its namesake island a mere grey-green streak two miles wide, surrounded by saltmarshes mudflats and glistening waters. Even on overcast days, the reflected light is sharp and the sky perfectly mirrored in the silvery expanse. It's one of the most beautiful panoramas on the Northumberland coast, so slow down on reaching the mile-long paved causeway that connects the island to the mainland, and drink in the view.

Beyond the grasslands and dunes on the north side of the island are some of Northumberland's finest and whitest sandy **beaches**, which are often empty even in high summer. At low tide, the waters, mudflats and saltmarshes between the island and the mainland, part of the **Lindisfarne National Nature Reserve**, become a giant bird table supporting tens of thousands of ducks, geese and wading birds. Their numbers swell from early autumn until spring when **migrant birds** from the continent join in the banquet, including light-bellied Brent geese from Greenland and Svalbard, which forage on the vast eel-grass beds across the reserve. Good vantage points include the pull-in areas on the causeway (using your car as a hide) and the damp grasslands between the village and castle. The reserve is also known for its **grey seals**, usually spotted resting on sandbanks between the island and mainland, and flowering plants. Damp grassy areas behind the dunes on the northwest side of Lindisfarne Island blossom with 11 varieties of **orchids** in summer, including the Lindisfarne helleborine (page 115).

Lindisfarne, however, is best known as a place of **Christian pilgrimage** and is considered by many to be the birthplace of Christianity in northern England (page 138). For over 1,000 years, worshippers have travelled on foot across the mud and sands to the island to pay homage to St Cuthbert who was Bishop of Lindisfarne and died on the island in AD687. This pilgrimage is a tradition that continues today (page 135) to **Lindisfarne Priory** (see below), a glorious shattered post-Conquest ruin established by monks from Durham Cathedral. Beyond the priory and its **church** with a lineage dating to the first Christian community on the isle in the 7th century, is **Lindisfarne Castle** (page 136), a small Tudor stronghold and one of the great romantic fortresses on the Northumberland coast.

Lindisfarne village

Most visitors arrive by car and some take the infrequent 477 bus from Berwick to the village centre where there's a post office, a few places to eat, pubs, holiday cottages and a couple of B&Bs. Opposite the village green is **St Aidan's Winery** (✆ 01289 389230 ☉ daily ♿), distillers of the famous **Lindisfarne Mead**, a fortified wine made with honey, but which also trades in many other regional drinks and produce as well as gifts. **The Lindisfarne Centre** (Marygate ✆ 01289 389004 ☉ Mar–Oct daily, depending on the tides ♿) serves as a **tourist information centre** and has a very good bookshop selling local guides, as well as three exhibition spaces, one of which is devoted to the story of the **Lindisfarne Gospels** (page 139) and includes a facsimile of the AD698 illuminated manuscript.

Lindisfarne Priory & church

Church Ln ✆ 01289 389200 ☉ Mar–Oct, Feb school holidays, Easter & Christmas period daily; Nov–Mar w/ends only; check opening times before visiting due to the tides ♿ 🐾 English Heritage

The ruins of the early 12th-century priory and 13th-century parish church face each other on the southwestern tip of Lindisfarne, just a few steps away from the village green. Nearly 900 years of wind and rain, as well as damage during the Reformation, have badly worn the stones of the arcades and arches of the **priory**, which was founded by Benedictine monks from Durham Cathedral. Enough structures and geometric patterns remain – including the much-photographed **Rainbow Arch** that survived the collapse of a tower above it 200 years ago – to appreciate the layout of the building and recognise its architecture as Norman (and even to notice similarities with the

CAUSEWAY & PILGRIMAGE

A good service of horse-drawn traps, and a car, runs during low-tide, the charge being 6s. per conveyance, each holding three passengers.

Robert Hugill *Road Guide to Northumberland and the Border*, 1931

When the tide rolls in across the mudflats and over the mile-long paved causeway connecting Lindisfarne to the mainland, it can do so frighteningly quickly, so be sure to pay close attention to the safe crossing times listed on boards at either side of the causeway and found at & holyislandcrossingtimes. northumberland.gov.uk. If you get caught out (a couple of dozen cars are usually abandoned every year), there's a refuge on stilts. The RNLI will take care of you, but your car may be written off or washed away.

Walkers following the **Pilgrims' Way** across the tidal mudflats should be very cautious. It takes around an hour to walk the three miles from the mainland to the island. This should only be attempted if you can reach the other side by the midpoint of the safe crossing period. There is a refuge for walkers accessed by ladders halfway across.

nave at Durham). At dusk, the naturally blushed sandstones deepen in colour to that of a red night sky. The view from the churchyard with the priory to the left and the castle and boats in the bay to the right, is exceptionally picturesque.

To mark the location of St Cuthbert's original resting place, a new **commemorative stone** made of basalt rock, which outcrops along the Northumberland coast, and Frosterley Marble (the same stone featured extensively at Cuthbert's final resting place in Durham Cathedral), is now on display at the priory.

The oldest parts of **St Mary's Church** date from the time of St Aidan in the 7th century, but mostly it is 13th century. Notice the different style of the facing arcades: the arches on the south side are pointed and date from the 13th century while those on the north aisle are Romanesque. There's an eye-catching stained-glass window above the north altar of fishermen, and 20th-century glass in the west wall depicting St Aidan and St Cuthbert. The wood **sculpture** of monks carrying Cuthbert's coffin is identical to the bronze version in Durham city. They mark the start and end points of the monks' journey.

The churchyard provides a view of a tiny grassy offshore isle known as **St Cuthbert's Island**, marked with a wooden cross and remains of a medieval chapel. Cuthbert is thought to have lived as a hermit here before becoming bishop. Crossing the seabed on foot is possible at low tide but make sure you set off at the lowest point in the tide or an hour before the lowest point (as the tide is retreating).

The English Heritage **museum** (☉ see priory hours ♿ 🐾), housed by the entrance to the priory, provides an overview of the story of St Cuthbert and the monastic community's significance during a period of intense artistic and cultural activity that lasted for around 100 years from the mid 7th century. Among the collection of stones is the famous 9th-century '**Viking Domesday**' depicting the warrior invaders wielding axes. Its date is significant for it reveals that a Christian community endured at Lindisfarne after the ransacking by Danes. Other fascinating treasures include a rosary bead necklace, the earliest known prayer beads in Britain, and a knitted garment thought to be one of the oldest surviving knitted textiles in Europe.

Lindisfarne Castle

Near the harbour ✆ 01289 389244 ☉ mid-Feb–Oct daily, alternate w/ends in winter, check website or call ahead for times due to the tides; National Trust

Lindisfarne's Tudor fortress crowns a conical-shaped mound of Whin Sill rock and seems to naturally emerge from the dolerite, rather than be built upon it – a visual treat for visitors wandering from the village to the harbour. The castle dates from 1542 and was fortified in Elizabeth I's reign but the strength of the impenetrable-looking walls has never been fully tested.

Under the instruction of Edward Hudson, editor of *Country Life* magazine, who took on the lease in 1901, the castle interior evolved into an Edwardian house designed by architect **Edwin Lutyens**. Hudson created domestic rooms in every chamber, connected by way of passages. 'I want to amuse myself with the place,' he said. He certainly did that – not just in transforming the castle, but by holding summer parties.

Simple furnishings include items designed by Lutyens as well as arcades, spiral staircases and vaulted ceilings, which all have the Lutyens stamp, particularly the patterned flooring made with bricks arranged in herringbone formation (a Lutyens trademark). Also look out for the

---

LINDISFARNE: **1** The spectacular castle. **2** The Lindisfarne helleborine is an endemic species that flowers on the island and nowhere else. **3 & 4** The ruins of the priory and the statue of St Cuthbert. ▶

KINGS, BISHOPS, SAINTS & VIKINGS: THE STORY OF LINDISFARNE

In the centuries following Roman rule, Britain was divided into seven kingdoms, of which Northumbria, ruled in the early 7th century by **King Oswald** from his seat at Bamburgh, was one of the most powerful of all.

Oswald had previously been educated on the Scottish isle of Iona before he became king and he called upon **Aidan**, an Irish monk at Iona, to develop a monastic centre at Lindisfarne, six miles from Bamburgh and visible with the naked eye from his fortress. A priory was founded on the remote isle in AD634 which set the stage for a new era in political rule with king – and now bishop – at its core.

Cuthbert enters the story some 40 years later when he became part of the monastic community at Lindisfarne, but he gave up living with the monks, preferring to exist as a hermit on a nearby isle and then on the Farne archipelago. That didn't last long and he was summoned back to Lindisfarne to become bishop in AD685, though he died within two years.

Eleven years later, Cuthbert's coffin lid was removed by monks who found his body intact. Sainthood followed – and a cult following, owing to miracles reported at Cuthbert's shrine – and Lindisfarne became an important **pilgrimage** destination. The Kingdom of Northumbria and the monastery increased in strength, power and wealth and it was during this period that Lindisfarne developed as a centre of Christian learning and art, a cultural environment under which the astonishing decorated text of the Gospels of Matthew, Mark, Luke and John – known as the **Lindisfarne Gospels** – was created.

Remarkably, the book survived the deadly Viking raids of AD793 but eventually, the monks, carrying Cuthbert's coffin and the Gospels, fled Lindisfarne in AD875, abandoning their monastery and settling in Durham in AD995 after travelling about in the north of England. The new shrine in the city was later replaced with the magnificent Norman Durham Cathedral.

Monks at Durham returned to Lindisfarne to found a new priory in the 12th century – the wondrous **Lindisfarne Priory** standing, albeit in ruins, on the isle today.

Wind Indicator – a clock-like brass hand on a painted panel depicting Northumberland's great coastal castles, with English warships pursuing the Spanish Armada. The needle points to the wind direction in real time. It's been telling the wind since 1913 and has only stopped once (for restoration).

In farmland overlooked by the castle is a pretty little walled **garden** designed by Gertrude Jekyll in 1911. She had originally intended to create a kitchen garden but instead it became a summer flower garden with roses, sweet peas, fuchsias and delphiniums, which continue to bring colour and scent to the isolated enclosure.

SPECIAL STAYS

Hunting Hall Beal TD15 2TP ☏ 01289 388652 ⌂ huntinghall.co.uk. I was greeted by three geese upon arriving at this 18th-century farm a short drive inland from Lindisfarne. For families looking for a countryside base with lots of free space for children to run around in and farm animals to visit, Hunting Hall's three old farmworkers' cottages are ideal. There's also a ford where children can go 'fishing'. Historically, the collection of farm buildings is very interesting and includes an old smithy and unusual hen house with niches in the stone work. The stone cottages – and a modern shepherd's hut in an orchard – are homely with plenty of country touches (floral fabrics, wood furniture, exposed beams, real fires), the kitchens are very well-equipped and all cottages have direct access to flower-filled gardens and meadows beyond. The owners are genuinely committed environmentalists and strive to make the buildings eco-friendly with solar panels, green paints, organic bed linen and an array of other green devices and furnishings.

FOOD & DRINK

Barn at Beal Beal Farm (on the mainland opposite Lindisfarne), TD15 2PB ☏ 01289 540044 ☺ daily ♿ 🐾. On the approach to Lindisfarne Causeway, this large family-friendly bistro and campsite (which also has a small playground) caters well for families. The site is said to be where the monks at Lindisfarne Priory kept their beehives. The busy café/restaurant serves good cold and hot breakfasts and lunches (summer veg risotto, fish and chips, sandwiches and soups) to visitors (and especially to those waiting for the causeway to open which you can see from the sunny terrace). There's a roast on Sundays and evening meals in summer (Thursday–Saturday; book ahead). The **Bothy Bar** next door is a snug drinking hole (☺ w/ends).

LINDISFARNE GOSPELS

It is remarkable that this exquisite illuminated manuscript, 1,300 years old, survived 600 years of battles, invasions and unrest in this once lawless region. The Gospels are considered one of the most treasured religious and artistic works in the UK and for that reason are stored for safekeeping at the British Museum in London. Durham Cathedral, Chester-le-Street and Lindisfarne all have facsimiles of the book; the last is displayed in The Lindisfarne Centre on Marygate (page 134). The highly decorative pages were painted using animal and vegetable dyes in one unified style by Eadfrith, who was Bishop of Lindisfarne in the late 7th and early 8th centuries.

Crown & Anchor Market Pl, Lindisfarne ✆ 01289 389215 ☺ lunch & dinners daily but seasonal times so check ahead ♿ side entrance 🐾. Friendly 200-year-old pub with a sunny beer garden and restaurant serving a medley of pub favourites (fish and chips, roast meats) and some Lindisfarne specials including lobster and a fish platter. Good craic at the bar with rosy-cheeked locals catching up over a beer. Good range of regional drinks.

Pilgrims Coffee House Marygate ✆ 01289 389109 ☺ daily, subject to the tides so times are variable ♿ 🐾. You may have seen packets of Pilgrim's beans in shops and cafés elsewhere in Northumberland. Well, this is where they are roasted. It goes without saying that this is the best place for a coffee on the island and one of the best places in the whole of Northumberland. But that's just the coffee. The family-run business also tempts customers with their cakes, scones and slabs of flapjack. Their signature 'Cuthbert Cake' is a saintly offering: a kind of oat-based flapjack packed with nuts, fruit and spices and topped with a lemon icing, best enjoyed on a sunny day in the enclosed walled garden.

✳ ✳ ✳

🚶 A HOLY COASTAL WALK: LINDISFARNE ROUND-ISLAND

❄ OS Explorer map 340; start: first public car park you come to on reaching the island from the causeway, ♥ NU125424; 5 miles; fairly easy

It takes a couple of hours to complete this circular trail, which is a beautiful walk with constant views of the sea, and culminates in the priory and castle. I've walked this route many times and hardly ever met anyone. The white sands on the north side of the island are all yours. As for the route, you hardly need a map; just a sense of the shape of the island and the location of the village and castle in relation to the dunes and causeway.

1 From the first ticketed car park you come to on reaching the island, head back down the road towards the causeway for 150yds, then take the footpath on your right by a kissing gate that crosses into farmland. Orchids bring a burst of crimson to the grassland in localised damp patches. At a fork in the path, continue ahead, following the England Coast Path marker. Bear right at the second fork.

2 At the third marker, instead of continuing ahead following the fenceline, bear left, away from the national trail, crossing a partially collapsed dry-stone wall and picking up a clear grassy track through the dunescape, bearing right. There are numerous trails here; just keep on in the direction of the white triangle day marker on the headland. Traverse the **bays** fringing the north of the island.

3 At **Emmanuel Head**, well-placed benches around the white day marker allow you to sit out of the wind and watch white horses galloping over the stone-strewn shores and gannets flying low to the waves. Turn south, with the Farne Islands, Bamburgh Castle and the Cheviots all within view, to meet the corner of a dry-stone wall. Continue ahead with the wall on your right, then crossing it at a gap. The path continues between two fencelines. At a kissing gate, bear right on the grassy path towards the castle.

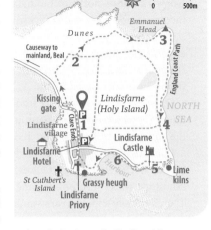

4 At a gap in the wall by a metal bird sculpture, walk on a raised embankment – an old **wagonway** used during the late 19th century for the transport of lime – which curves to the right for the castle. The **lime kilns** are said to be some of the best Victorian examples anywhere in England.

5 By the little footbridge, turn right down some stone steps and follow the gravel path under the **castle** walls. The three **upturned boat hulls** (now storage sheds) are much photographed. Once a common feature in many coastal communities, Lindisfarne is now one of the only places they remain in use.

6 With the castle behind you, continue to the harbour and the modern **Window on Wild Lindisfarne** building which serves as both a bird hide and information point detailing the island's special wildlife. Walk around the harbour and up and over the grassy heugh. Skirt the **priory** and turn right on to Church Lane, from where you'll find the entrance to the monastic complex. (The more direct return to the car park from the harbour is to continue through the village on Marygate then Chare Ends towards the causeway, passing The Lindisfarne Hotel on your right.)

* * *

30 GOSWICK SANDS, CHESWICK SANDS & COCKLAWBURN BEACH

A runway-straight stretch of desolate coastline shoots north for five miles from Lindisfarne to the distant outskirts of Berwick, and is blissfully free of people. It is one of the wildest and most pristine places for a long, meditative beach walk and is on the route of the Northumberland Coast Path. Apart from the golf club at Goswick and the view of Berwick, your contact with the built world is minimal. At low tide, the vast expanse of **Goswick Sands** north of Lindisfarne reveals itself. Take care here: the incoming tide progresses quickly across the beach.

The **coastal cycleway** (NCN Route 1), running along the inland edge of the dunes on a paved track, makes getting here by bicycle straightforward; drivers can park at several rough pull-in areas reached from Cheswick (signed off the A1).

One weekend in summer I stood at the top of one of **Cheswick's** high dunes (of which there are many, incidentally) and counted 12 people on the entire two-mile-long stretch of sand.

Cocklawburn Beach is a picturesque family-friendly cove reached at the northern end of Cheswick Sands, beyond some impressive limestone rocks (crumbling lime kilns are evidence of past industry). There's usually an ice-cream van here.

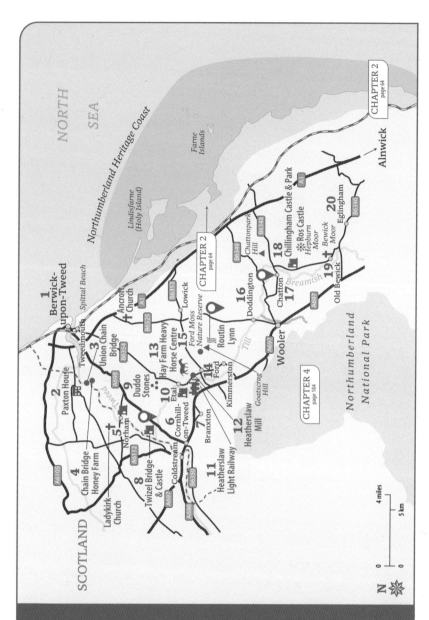

BERWICK & ALONG THE TWEED & TILL

3

BERWICK & ALONG THE TWEED & TILL

Scotland's second-longest river, the **Tweed**, forms the border with England from Coldstream to Berwick, where a colony of swans escorts the waterway for its final lazy run to the North Sea. One of the best salmon and trout rivers in Britain, it is wide and wooded for much of its length, making the Tweed popular with anglers, canoeists and walkers alike.

The most northerly town in England, **Berwick-upon-Tweed** (page 147) welcomes visitors from the south – by rail or road – across two memorable stone bridges. It's one of the most picturesque towns in the region, enclosed by Elizabethan walls and boasting some fine museums and independent shops.

Cutting a secretive course between the national park and the A1 is the **River Till** (page 164), which flows south north for over 30 convoluted miles through the plains lying between the Cheviot Hills and the arc of sandstone hills to the east before emptying into the River Tweed. Lush and sparsely populated, the valley of the Till is characterised by low-lying farmland overlooked here and there by craggy moors where Iron Age communities have left their mark. Highlights include the quaint estate villages of **Ford** (page 170) and **Etal** (page 165), **Chillingham Castle** (page 176) with its ancient parkland and wild cattle, **Heatherslaw Mill** (page 168) and **prehistoric rock art** in the hills around **Chatton** (page 174), as well as a couple of outstanding medieval river crossings and a secluded **waterfall** (page 173). For Wooler, the Cheviots and Northumberland National Park, see *Chapter 4*, page 185.

GETTING AROUND

Berwick is well connected by **road** and **train** as it lies close to the London–Edinburgh Great North Road (the A1) and the London–

Edinburgh East Coast Main Line (from Newcastle or Edinburgh by train takes around 40 minutes). **Public transport** along the Tweed and in the countryside between the national park and the coast, however, is limited to a few buses (see bus route map, page 18).

Cyclists (and motorists wishing to take in the views) should be wary of using the A-roads either side of the **Tweed**, which thunder with goods vehicles (as well as the busy north–south A697 connecting Cornhill-on-Tweed with Wooler). For a leisurely trip along the border, follow instead the **Tweed Cycle Way** (see below) via Paxton House, Horncliffe and Norham (this route works in the car too), although there is one short run on the A1.

South of the Tweed, you're best off taking the more scenic B-roads east of the River Till. What's more, many of the historic sites described in these pages are within ten miles of each other, making travel on two wheels both a practical and enjoyable way of exploring the area.

BUS

Berwick is easily reached from Alnwick and Newcastle via various coastal locations, by taking the X18 or the more frequent and direct X15.

For touring the **Tweed**, the **Scottish border** and parts of the **Till plains**, see the bus route map on page 18. One useful service is the 67, connecting Berwick with the likes of Norham Castle and Cornhill-on-Tweed every few hours. Between Berwick and **Wooler**, the 464 (via **Doddington**) and the 267 (via **Etal** and **Ford**) reach some of the attractions listed in these pages, but they are not particularly regular.

CYCLING

The **sandstone hills** east of the national park (roughly the area between the A697 and A1) have much to lure road cyclists with a fondness for steep climbs and descents. Between Doddington and Eglingham, for example, are some thrilling stretches of tarmac offering wide countryside views framed by the distant Cheviots. At some high points you can see both the hills and the coast with just a turn of the head. The 120-mile-long **Sandstone Way** from Berwick to Hexham encompasses many of the villages featured in these pages.

The 95-mile-long **Tweed Cycle Way** takes in some fine river and hill scenery as it passes through the Scottish Borders to Berwick, mainly on B-roads connecting places like Chain Bridge Honey Farm with Norham.

TOURIST INFORMATION

Berwick TIC & Library Walkergate ✐ 01670 622155 ☉ Mon–Sat ♿

WALKING

Along the Scottish border the landscape is agricultural in character, but what the area lacks in outstanding hill walks, it makes up for in **riverside trails**. For long yet gentle stretches, you can hike along the **Till** and **Tweed** rivers. The nine-mile walk along the south banks of the Tweed from **Berwick to Norham** passes several old fishing shiels and the suspension bridge at Horncliffe, for example, while the Till's wooded riverside path connects **Twizel Bridge and Etal** in five miles.

For more challenging routes, head for the **sandstone hills** between the national park and coastal plain. I've described a couple of short walks to see the **prehistoric stone sites** at **Chatton** (page 175), **Doddington** (page 174) and **Goatscrag Hill**, where a visit to the nearby **waterfall** is also recommended (page 173).

Also consider hiking a stretch of **St Cuthbert's Way** (page 187), perhaps from Wooler to Lowick (12 miles one way; return by bus 464), taking in the moorlands between Chatton and Doddington, and the **Kyloe Hills**. Other popular upland spots include **Bewick Moor**, **Hepburn Crags** and the **Bowden Doors** crags, which attract many climbers.

CYCLE HIRE & REPAIRS

Good Times Bike Hire Inland Pasture Farm, Scremerston, Berwick, TD15 2RJ ✐ 07774 398744 ⊘ goodtimesbikehire.co.uk ☉ Apr–Oct daily. Specialising in electric bikes. Order bikes online for delivery to your location or pick up.

TAXIS
A1 Cabs Berwick ✐ 01289 308524, 07760 774938 ♿
Woody's Taxis Berwick ✐ 01289 547009 ♿

1 BERWICK-UPON-TWEED

The salmon-fishers rowing in their boats from Spittal Snook, looked strange and spectral through the mist; and if Tweed had anything to say concerning his birthplace in the western hills, and his travel along the Border land, it was stifled by the gloom, and I heard it not.
Walter White, *Northumberland and the Border*, 1859

NORTHUMBRIAN FOLK MUSIC TRADITIONS

Geoff Heslop

The northeast of England is rich in music and we are fortunate that this music is very much still alive, with an increasing number of musicians performing and writing.

The history of music in the area probably begins for us in the Border Ballads, many of which were collected by Sir Walter Scott in the late 18th century. These songs tell of great events and foul deeds from the region's bloody past. Many reflect the activities of the infamous Border Reiver families during the hundreds of years of troubles until around the mid 17th century. These were collected together in the volumes of the *Child Ballads* (those collected by Francis James Child in the 19th century). Many of these ballads are still sung today, including *The Fair Flower of Northumberland* and *Johnnie Armstrong* – which tells the story of one of the most notorious Border Reivers.

We have our own instrument, the Northumbrian smallpipes, which is bellows-blown and has a distinctive sweet tone. There's been a revival in the instrument since the mid 20th century, largely due to the increase in the number of pipe-makers; there are now a large number of players of all ages, both in the North East and throughout the world, and many modern tunes are being written.

The two other contributors to the music of the area are the songs that came out of the industrial heritage of mining, shipbuilding and fishing and the music-hall songs of the 19th century.

Many fine songs were written reflecting the often-hard life of the workers and their families, but also the Geordie sense of humour in the face of it, such as *Keep Your Feet Still Geordie Hinnie* and *Cushie Butterfield*.

Geoff Heslop is a record producer who has recorded many of the most influential North East musicians over the last 40 years. He plays with his wife, Brenda, herself a songwriter, in their band, Ribbon Road (ribbonroadmusic.com).

Salmon are still caught on the Tweed in the time-honoured way using nets and traditional wooden boats, but on a sunny day, the river is nothing like as brooding as the description above. The same is true of the town itself, which is really a very cheerful place with its red-tiled Georgian houses gathered along the river's edge and colony of swans. The approach from the south is made all the more memorable by an old stone bridge that skims across the water in 15 low leaps leading you into the centre of Berwick in the most pleasing of ways. Here, you'll find a number of intriguing historic buildings, alleyways and museums, as well as a scattering of independent shops and places to eat.

Berwick has an uneasy identity because of its position on the wrong side of the river. Scottish or English? A lot of folk to the north and south are never quite sure because the northern banks of the Tweed are in Scotland, except at Berwick. At least that's the case today. But, this is a town that has yo-yoed from one side of the border to the other some 13 times. It doesn't help that Berwick's football team plays in the Scottish league and that the town has various other allegiances to north of the border. It's understandable, therefore, that many locals don't affiliate themselves to either country, preferring the description 'Berwicker'. Their accent is equally non-committal: neither Northumbrian nor Scottish Borders.

Border disputes in the Middle Ages eventually led to the complete fortification of the settlement under Elizabeth I. These distinctive 16th-century ramparts (see below) remain largely intact and are said to make Berwick an outstanding example of a fortified town.

A WANDER ON BERWICK'S ELIZABETHAN RAMPARTS

Berwick's 500-year-old ramparts encircling most of the town make for a great **walk**, offering views through Berwick's streets and out to sea. Without deviation, the circuit takes an hour or so, but most likely you'll want to hop off and on and see places of interest as you go. Information panels explain the form of the curtain wall, moat and impressive artillery bastions.

The **Berwick Barracks** (page 151) are a must-see on the easternmost side of the ramparts but do allow time for the **Holy Trinity Church** on Wallace Green (opposite the barracks). The mid 17th-century building is one of very few churches constructed in Cromwellian England and is strikingly different from any other church you will see in the region, particularly because it has no tower or spire. The interior is a mix of Gothic and Classical styles.

When you reach **Scot's Gate**, one of the main entrance archways into the town, you are pretty much in the centre of Berwick. If you continue

THE LOWRY TRAIL

Berwick's many cobbled lanes and irregular-shaped buildings caught the eye of L S Lowry who painted some of his most memorable street scenes here from the mid 1930s until his death in 1976. Download **The Lowry Trail** map at ⬨ berwickpreservationtrust.co.uk/lowry-trail.

south on the ramparts towards the river, you'll reach **Meg's Mount** (the westernmost bastion on the ramparts and one of Berwick's finest vantage points).

Berwick Barracks

Parade ✆ 01289 304493 ◷ end Mar–end Oct Wed–Sun; at the time of writing, the Barracks were closing for redevelopment. Check online for updates; English Heritage

The oldest post-Roman army barracks in Britain, dating to 1719, Berwick Barracks is now known for its museum spaces arranged around a quadrangle. This includes an exhibition space that traces the military history of the King's Own Scottish Borderers regiment, formed in 1689 to defend Edinburgh against the Jacobites. This isn't just a military heritage centre, however: in the clock building, you'll find the **Berwick Museum & Art Gallery** (✆ 01670 620277 ◷ Apr–end Oct Wed–Sun) ♿ ground floor only, request ramp) with its small, recreated garrison town and fine art gallery. **The Burrell Collection** (an offshoot of the magnificent Burrell Collection in Glasgow) includes paintings from the 16th century to the early 20th century from Britain, France and the Netherlands. Works include those by renowned French landscape painters, Degas and Boudin, alongside local artists such as James Wallace who painted scenes of everyday life in the 1900s, including salmon fishermen on the Tweed.

One of the most looked at pieces in the collection is Lindisfarne's old telephone exchange, which stands around 8ft high and is complete with all its many switches and plugs.

Annexed to the barracks and outside of the quadrangle by the ramparts' path is the **Gymnasium Gallery** (✆ 01289 330999 ⬦ maltingsberwick. co.uk ◷ Apr–end Oct Wed–Sun), a repurposed military gym dating to 1901 and now a small venue showcasing works by resident artists – largely sculpture, installations and conceptual art – as well as touring exhibitions by British and international artists. Only open for shows so do check online for upcoming events before visiting.

BERWICK'S CENTRE

If approaching Berwick's centre from the train station, you'll probably end up walking down **Marygate**, the town's high street. There's a **market**

◀ **1** Berwick's Old Bridge at dusk. **2** The altar in Holy Trinity Church, Berwick. **3** The 28 towering arches of Royal Border Bridge. **4** Spittal Beach.

FOOD & BEER FESTIVAL

Summer sees the return of the lively annual Berwick Food and Beer Festival (⌀ berwickfoodandbeerfestival.co.uk; day tickets cost a few pounds on the gate), organised by Berwick Slow Food. It's held in the grounds of the 18th-century Berwick Barracks (page 151) over a weekend in August (check website for future dates) and brings together the best regional food and drink producers and musicians for a weekend of tasting. There's even an animal farm to keep children happy.

held here on Wednesdays and Saturdays, mainly with clothes and fruit and veg stalls.

The **Town Hall** is easily the most prominent historic building on the street, and tours (⊙ Easter–Sep 10.30 & 14.00 Mon–Fri) include a visit to the jail on the top floor (note the 18th-century graffiti). Besides this, Marygate does not hold huge appeal for visitors, except perhaps for a couple of independent cafés, craft stores and **Grieve's bookshop** (entrance faces Church St ✆ 01289 306051), which stocks a large range of regional maps, as well as walking and travel guides.

Just off the high street, **The Maltings** (Eastern Ln ✆ 01289 330999) theatre and cinema on Eastern Lane puts on a varied programme of comedy, theatre, dance and family shows.

Sloping downhill from Marygate to the Tweed is **West Street** – a narrow, cobbled lane (worthy of a few photographs) with some lovely independent shops.

Set behind the river and Quay Walls at the bottom of West Street is wonderful **Bridge Street**, well-regarded for its run of great independent antiques emporiums, galleries, art shops and places to eat (many of which are closed on Sun and Mon). A few businesses really stand out, including **Tidekettle** where artist Lucy Baxandall handmakes paper and creates unique works inspired by geology and landscapes; **Marehalm**, a Scandinavian-inspired craft and interiors shop; and **Twenty Five**, a gallery run by artist Scot Robinson who paints local scenes.

Granary Gallery

Dewer's Ln (access from the Quay Walls above the riverside) ⌀ maltingsberwick.co.uk
⊙ Wed–Sun during exhibitions ♿

Restoration of Berwick's old 1769 granary (remarkably in use until 1985) began some time ago and the building eventually opened in 2010 to include a modern YHA, café and this art gallery on the second floor, which puts on a few well-regarded shows every year: Turner, the Fleming Collection and of course Lowry, with exhibitions coming round every so often in recognition of the Manchester artist's connection to Berwick.

ALONG THE RIVERSIDE: BERWICK'S BRIDGES & QUAY WALL

East Coast Main Line trains from Edinburgh to London creak across Robert Stephenson's 1850 **Royal Border Bridge**, offering a spectacular view of the Tweed. The clear problem here is that you only very briefly see its 28 towering arches, but the bridge's magnificence is sensed in the way it makes you feel at 126 dizzying feet above the river. It's such a Victorian pleasure.

The other way to get up close to those long, colourful stone legs is to stroll downhill on a leafy path that connects the station with the river. Cowering underneath the Border Bridge arches is the ruin of **Berwick Castle**, founded in the 12th century. Those ruthless Victorians bulldozed the fortress to make way for the bridge and station.

Continuing downriver on the promenade, you'll pass a boathouse and then **New Bridge** (opened 1928). Its sculptural undersides won't go unappreciated by photographers. Last in the trio of Berwick's bridges is the 17th-century **Old Bridge**, which leaps across the Tweed in 15 arches.

From the town end of the bridge, pedestrians can take a stroll along the river-facing **Quay Walls** to admire the handsome row of Georgian houses between Old Bridge and **The Main Guard** (Palace Green ☉ summer only; English Heritage), which stands by the southern ramparts. A small sandstone block with a portico supported by columns, the 18th-century building once operated as a guard house, a refuge station if you like, for soldiers manning the town's defences and enforcing the night curfew. There's even a lock-up, the 'black hole' as it was known, where the drunk and disorderly would spend the night. Now a small **museum** dedicated to narrating aspects of Berwick's history, it's open in the summer by the Berwick Civic Society.

TWEEDMOUTH & SPITTAL BEACH

Facing Berwick on the south side of the river is **Tweedmouth** – a largely residential area but with many 19th-century buildings near the river that serve as reminders of the area's once thriving grain, herring

CROWNING OF THE SALMON QUEEN

Paying homage to the historic salmon fishing industry on the Tweed, the annual Tweedmouth festival, **The Feast and Crowning of the Salmon Queen**, takes place to the sound of bagpipes with a street procession in mid-July starting at the Town Hall.

The schoolgirl queen is 'crowned' by the Mayor and paraded in a traditional coble fishing boat that is pulled through the streets to onlooking crowds. It's an enduring celebration (though previously she would have been rowed along the Tweed) dating to the 13th century and revived in the mid 20th century.

and salmon fishing industries. Here, where Brewery Lane meets Brewery Bank, is an intact run of 19th-century brewery buildings; it's rare to find all the elements of a **Victorian brewery** (drying sheds, malt kilns and the 'brewery tap' – the nearest pub to the brewery) as well preserved as this.

On Tower Hill, and with Tweed views, is **Tower House Pottery** (TD15 2BD ✆ 01289 307314 ◷ Mon–Fri; by appointment Sat & Sun). When I visited, the owners were immersed in their craft, painting vases, plates and cups with their trademark floral designs and local scenes.

Continue along Dock Road to reach Sandstell Road with its old **herring sheds** and **salmon fishermen's shiel**. **Spittal's beach** and its Victorian promenade (painted many times by L S Lowry) was once a popular seaside resort. It's still well visited by Berwickers who stroll along the paved promenade (&). The nearby sheltered cove of **Cocklawburn Beach** (page 142) holds more bucket-and-spade appeal, however.

❚❙ FOOD & DRINK

Fish and chip shops in Berwick are plentiful. I like the old-fashioned **A Corvi Fish Restaurant** (33–41 West St ✆ 01289 306149 ◷ Mon–Sat), which is very reasonably priced. **Coull's** (11 Castlegate ✆ 01289 331480 ◷ daily), and **Prior Chippy** (9A Grove Gardens, Tweedmouth ✆ 01289 308936 ◷ Sun–Fri) also have a good reputation.

Atelier 41–43 Bridge St ✆ 01289 298180 ◷ noon–22.00 daily; last food orders 20.15 🐾. Extremely popular café, bar and charcuterie with a lively ambiance and styling (vintage finds in every corner). This is a place for friends to feast over a sharing platter of meats and cheeses (Atelier are well known for them). Or choose from a long list of pâtés smothered over rustic bread. There's much more here, too: a hot smoked pig's cheek and pease pudding sandwich; a raclette and veggie toastie; cured Welsh lamb or venison; Scottish mussels.

Audela 64 Bridge St ✆ 01289 308827 ◷ evenings only Mon, Wed & Thu, lunch & dinner Fri–Sun ♿. A modern, upmarket restaurant with a small but tempting British/French menu infused with some ingredients sourced from the surrounding waters and hills: Berwick crab, Northumberland cheese, North Sea halibut, Borders wood pigeon and beef from near Lindisfarne. The three mains on offer when I visited were a fillet of beef with mash and shallots; halibut with a potato terrine, cauliflower and mushroom sauce; and a beetroot tarte tatin with goat's cheese.

Barrels Ale House 59 Bridge St ◷ from 17.00 Mon–Fri, from noon weekends. A characterful pub full of local chatter just off the Old Bridge. Inside, vintage skis and a big fish hang from the wall and ceiling along with a load of other curious objects. Punters sit on barrels and in an old barber's (dentist's?) chair enjoying a (cheap) pint of real ale.

The Corner House Café 31 Church St ✆ 01289 304748 ◷ Mon–Sat. On cold days, the flickering of flames from an open fire in front of Chesterfield sofas and the smell of home cooking lure pedestrians in off the street to this snug café. It's the sort of place you can hunker down in for a few hours reading the papers or one of the secondhand books pulled from a bookcase. Though not extensive, the menu includes soups, sandwiches and really, really good cakes – all made in-house.

Coxon & Coxon 22 Bridge St ✆ 07946 440537 ◷ Thu–Mon. A 'wine room' of old-world bottles for tasting, learning, buying and enjoying over a fabulous cheese and meat board.

The Green Shop 30 Bridge St ✆ 01289 305566 ◷ Mon–Sat. They pack a lot into this eco-store selling fruit and veg, local cheeses, ice creams and crafts, as well as an array of green and fair trade household goods and beauty products.

Mavi Turkish Restaurant 52 Bridge St ✆ 01289 309533 ◷ noon–22.00 daily ♿. A great little authentic restaurant always overflowing with diners. Booking recommended.

Mule on Rouge 17 Bridge St ◷ Tue–Sun (closes 14.00 Sun). Youthful coffee house with an artsy vibe, specialising in bagels, vegan and veggie food – and Bob Dylan tunes.

Northern Edge Coffee 7 Silver St ✆ 01289 306892 ◷ from 08.30 daily 🐾. With a coffee board that reads like a wine menu, you know you're in a very special coffee house; all arabica beans are roasted on site. This is simply one of the very best places in Northumberland to pick up your cup of ambition (and perhaps a bacon or sausage roll to go with it). Good flatbreads too: lemon and herb chicken or roast ham, Emmenthal and mustard for example. Sit inside – all vintage, off-beat vibes – or outside on a picnic table.

Northern Soul Kitchen 19 West St ✆ 07933 833165 ◷ Wed–Sat. 'Our menu is ever changing and depends on what food we have intercepted from landfill fate that day' reads the blackboard in this wee community 'pay as you feel' café. When I visited, there were some lovely looking plates of food coming out of the kitchen: halloumi and veg salad with flatbread; vegan chicken and chorizo toastie, and delicious cakes: chocolate brownie, orange sponge and strawberry loaf. Occasionally – just occasionally – you might see a closed sign and this message: 'sorry folks, no grub donated last night'. The only thing with a set price is the coffee – which is very good (from Pilgrim Coffee on Lindisfarne).

ALONG THE RIVER TWEED

Snaking along the border with Scotland, the banks of this fine fishing river are dotted here and there with stone huts called shiels that were once extensively used by salmon fishermen.

Places of note include the Palladian manor, **Paxton House** (where visitors can take part in traditional salmon fishing), the restored Victorian suspension crossing, **Union Chain Bridge**, the **Honey Farm** at Horncliffe, and **Norham** with its castle and Norman church.

2 PAXTON HOUSE
Near Berwick TD15 1SZ (bus 32 from Berwick stops at the reception) ✆ 01289 386291
⊙ house: mid-Mar–end Oct daily; café: until Dec ♿ café & partial access into house 🐾

On the Scottish side of the River Tweed – and reached quite marvellously by road from England by crossing the suspension bridge at Horncliffe – is this celebrated country house built in the Palladian style by James Adam in 1758. In 80 acres of landscaped parkland, it looks down through trees to the river below.

Much of the **interior** and its furnishings date to when the house was constructed, including the Chippendale furniture (Scotland's largest collection), French wallpapers and rococo plasterwork. Particularly memorable is the plasterwork in the dining room and the restored Georgian kitchen. Many of the paintings and antiques were amassed during the first owner's Grand Tour of Europe.

The impressive **picture gallery** holds some paintings on loan from the National Galleries of Scotland. One canvas of local interest in the house depicts the nearby Union Chain Bridge spanning the Tweed, with net fishermen in the foreground.

Seasonal highlights in the formal **gardens** include daffodil displays in spring, and flower borders in summer. Nearby, children can burn some energy in the **adventure playground** or get involved in den building. Garden games including croquet are also available. Incidentally, **campers** in the walled garden (how's that for a caravan site?) gain out-of-hours access to the grounds.

A pleasant downhill stroll through the wooded grounds leads you to the banks of the **Tweed** and a restored Victorian **boathouse**. Traditional fishing using large nets is still practised today, although only for research purposes. A few hundred years ago at the peak of salmon fishing on the Tweed, there were 84 netting stations; the **Paxton Netting Station** is the only one that remains today. On certain days in summer, visitors can help pull in the nets from the gravel shoreline in the time-honoured way, or take a **boat trip** to learn about the Tweed's wildlife.

3 UNION CHAIN BRIDGE

Vis Unita Fortior
Motto on the Union Chain Bridge connecting England and Scotland ('United Strength is Stronger')

The world's oldest vehicular suspension bridge at Horncliffe is a magnificent 449ft-long iron crossing above the Tweed, connecting England with Scotland. In 2021/2 the entire structure was dismantled and restored and it is now looking its very best with added infrastructure to enrich a visit, including walkways and new surfacing for vehicles to cross (one at a time). Two life-size bronze sculptures at either end depict the bridge's original designer on the English side and a modern-day engineer (Scottish side) to reflect the tremendous feat of dismantling the crossing and rebuilding it using aerial ropeways.

When first opened in 1820, hundreds descended above the banks of the Tweed to watch its designer, Captain Samuel Brown, cross the bridge with horses pulling carts laden with an estimated 20 tonnes – presumably as a show of its strength. Among those in the audience was the great Scottish engineer, Robert Stevenson (of lighthouses fame). A young Isambard Kingdom Brunel, accompanied by one of France's esteemed engineers, Charles Navier, visited a few years later. Clearly, this was a bridge causing quite a stir among the engineering giants of Europe – and rightly so: at the time it was the largest iron suspension bridge in the world.

Captain Brown knew a thing or two about structures made with decking that are designed to move, from his time in the Royal Navy. His flexible chain links are said to have been based on a ship's rigging blocks.

Find out more about the bridge at the honey farm (page 158) just up the road (where there is parking) and reached in a couple of minutes on foot.

4 CHAIN BRIDGE HONEY FARM

Horncliffe, nr Berwick TD15 2XT ℰ 01289 382362 ⊙ Apr–Oct daily; Nov–Mar Mon–Fri; free admission 🐾

No doubt you will have already come across Mr Robson's pots of liquid gold in farm shops, B&Bs and delis across the North East. You can buy (and try) all his varieties as well as some exceptional beauty products from the friendly **visitor centre** on the farm, some of which are made downstairs in the workshop. Bricks of beeswax stacked waiting to be turned into candles and balms tells you the stock upstairs is the real deal. As for the honeys, the Flower Comb Honey has a particularly sweet taste and scent (I've never found a flower honey as good as this anywhere in England). In the **shop** you'll see a working hive with an observation glass panel and, over a few rooms, an **exhibition** devoted to everything – really, everything – related to bee-keeping: history, practicalities, culture. Old skeps and honey pots from around the world are a wonderful addition to the displays. Bridge fans will also find one area devoted to the history and restoration of the Union Chain Bridge down the road.

"No doubt you will have already come across Mr Robson's pots of liquid gold in farm shops, B&Bs and delis."

Scattered across the farm's fields and inside a barn are a large number of **vintage vehicles** and agricultural machinery, including a wonderful coble boat from Seahouses, a number of tractors and trucks and an old double-decker bus – now a quirky **café** (⊙ Easter–Oct Tue–Sun & bank holidays) selling sandwiches, teas and locally made cakes and honey flapjack, with seating inside and out.

5 NORHAM

The attractive and ancient small border town of Norham is best known for its ragged **castle** (page 161) that rises above the River Tweed on a wooded eminence, keeping a watchful eye on Scotland.

The **town** grew around the castle from the 12th century but pretty much everything you see today, except for the medieval layout, lower stones of the market cross and parts of the church, dates from the 19th century. When Beatrix Potter visited Norham she was not impressed, writing that 'every tenth house is a Public'. Today only two pubs remain in business.

---

1 Union Chain Bridge over the Tweed. **2** Paxton House. **3** Norham Castle. ▶

Broad streets lead to a large green surrounded by a couple of food shops and stone houses, once the homes of farmers and fishermen and built of the same blushed local sandstone used in the construction of the castle. Round the corner on West Street, a gun maker's services the thriving country-sport industry in these parts.

But the story of Norham begins in a much earlier period with the founding of a monastic centre in the 7th century. A **church** has stood here since at least AD 830 though the present **St Cuthbert's** is of Norman origin and is one of a handful of exceptional churches in Northumberland that is really worth visiting. Even to the lay eye, St Cuthbert's has a strikingly long nave, chancel and churchyard (the largest in Northumberland, the church warden explained). Though restored over the centuries, a fair amount of stonework from the 12th century survives – notably the chancel arches (the alternate red and white stones match those at Lindisfarne) and south arcade, described by Pevsner as 'truly majestic'. Indeed, the mighty circular pillars and detail in the arches are impressive.

Before leaving the churchyard, allow time to marvel at the beautifully carved (and clearly Norman) window arches on the south side of the chancel. Note, too, the cluster of yew trees that likely mark the spot of the earlier Anglo-Saxon church, founded some 200 years after St Aidan crossed the Tweed here from Iona, on his way to establish a monastery at Lindisfarne.

A quiet lane round the side of the churchyard leads to the banks of the Tweed in little over 100yds, where a **riverside footpath** provides a scenic view of Norham Castle.

"Allow time to marvel at the beautifully carved (and clearly Norman) window arches on the south side of the chancel."

On the north side of the Tweed in Scotland, reached by crossing Norham's stone-arched bridge and turning right at the crossroads, is **Ladykirk church** (TD15 1XL), a very fine example of Scottish Gothic architecture (and completely different architecturally to St Cuthbert's). It was built on quite some scale in the late 15th century on the order of James IV of Scotland after he saw a vision of the Virgin Mary when falling from his horse in the nearby river, hence his crowned bust at the west end of the church. The lofty stone-vaulted nave and chancel roof are particularly striking, even to the lay visitor.

Norham Castle

Castle St ℘ 0370 333 1181 ⊙ Apr–Sep daily; Oct–Mar Sat & Sun 🐾 English Heritage

In medieval times, the bishops of Durham ruled Norham, and the castle, which started life in 1121 as a timber building, was their northern stronghold. It was rebuilt in stone towards the end of the same century with a keep and curtain wall and thereafter underwent many changes and additions.

Much of what remains dates from the 16th century, though fragments of the earlier stone walls and arches survive. Situated as it is on the border with Scotland, it was besieged many times (13 to be more precise) from its construction until it succumbed to James IV of Scotland in the days before the Battle of Flodden in 1513 (page 163). Since then it has been left to the elements and is now a ruin, albeit one still with a brute of a keep and a moat (now dry). Norham's crumbling walls first caught the eye of a 22-year-old **William Turner** in 1797 who went on to sketch and paint the castle many times throughout his career (always from the Scottish side of the Tweed). In one of his most famous works, *Norham Castle, Sunrise*, mist shrouds the fortress, which appears spectral above a luminous Tweed.

¶¶ FOOD & DRINK

Norham's 200-year-old butcher's shop, **Foreman & Son** (8 Castle St ℘ 01289 382260 ⊙ Tue–Sat) opposite the village green, sells rare-breed meats, wild boar sausages, pies packed with local venison, pigeon, pheasant or rabbit and filled sandwiches and bacon rolls to take-away. A few doors down, the **village store** (22 Castle St ℘ 01289 382205 ⊙ daily) is useful for basic pantry items, some fresh fruit and veg, ice creams, drinks and so on. A **bakery** on West Street (℘ 01289 382248 ⊙ mornings Tue, Wed & Sat) offers sweet treats and breads.

Masons Arms Free House 16 West St ℘ 01289 382326 ⊙ food served breakfast, lunch & dinner Mon–Sat, lunch & dinner Sun 🐾. A cracking, authentic country pub with a snug, wood-panelled interior and open coal fire; Allendale beers and much local cheer (though you'll have to cope with the Western saloon bar feeling of everyone turning when you walk in). Food is good: filled breakfast rolls; steak and chips, burgers, scampi and pizzas (also to take-away). No food on Thursdays but you are permitted to order fish and chips from the van outside and wash your meal down with a drink from the bar.

6 CORNHILL-ON-TWEED

Above the Tweed and moments from the Scottish border is this small stone village and useful stopping place. Indeed, the words 'post horses' above the porch of the 18th-century **Collingwood Arms** indicate how long the village has served as a rest point for cross-border coaches, traders and travellers.

Besides the inn, superb village shop (see below), café and Victorian church, there's not a huge amount to warrant a stay beyond lunch (unless you are exploring the surrounding countryside). That said, I would recommend a stroll to the banks of the Tweed, which is reached from either the English or Scottish side of the impressive **Coldstream Bridge**. Built in 1763, its five arches rise 60ft. There's a useful pull-in area on the north/Scottish side for motorists but do take care while crossing the road, which shudders with wagons. By a fingerpost signed for 'Lennel and Crow Green', steps lead to the shallow river's edge. On a hot day, a paddle and picnic are in order – so long as you aren't bothered by the road noise above; otherwise you may like to wander along the river trail to find a quieter spot.

¶¶ FOOD & DRINK

Collingwood Arms Main St ✆ 01890 882424 ☺ daily (lunch only on Sun) ♿ 🐾 bar only. This old coaching inn and upmarket hotel and restaurant nuzzles the Scottish border by the banks of the Tweed and is a good choice for passing visitors. Lunches are served in the bright, contemporary bar area (feels more like a café and serves light bites including sandwiches and burgers, as well as more substantial plates); evening diners sit in an altogether more plush room with parquet flooring and upholstered chairs. The menu, with some ingredients grown in the kitchen garden and from the local butcher in Norham, caters well for the hotel's 'sporting' guests so expect fish, venison and duck – but few vegetarian options.

Cornhill Village Shop Main St ✆ 01890 883313 ☺ from early morning daily (closes 13.00 on Sun) ♿. What an unexpected find! Superb take-away food (and bottled Cheviot beers) as good as this inside a village shop and post office was not what I was expecting when I pulled over by the A698. The smiley ladies behind the counter do wonderful things with pastry, eggs and meat infused with Borderland flavours to produce super pies, haggis, beans and tatties, sausage hot pot, chicken curry and macaroni cheese with crispy bacon. And look at those stonking wedges of homemade quiche, and wild boar sausage rolls stuffed with so much pig that one is good to share between two. And that's before you've glanced at the cakes.

7 BRANXTON

This unassuming hillside village three miles south of Cornhill and the Tweed, is mostly of interest for its proximity to the Flodden battlefield (see below), but it does have a wonderful little church. Sadly, the Cement Menagerie garden museum is no more but its life-sized animals created in the 1940s are now on display at Ayton Castle, north of Berwick.

A short walk or drive west out of Branxton on your way to the Flodden battle site, **St Paul's Church** stands on an isolated breezy hill with views of undulating grasslands all around (if travelling from the village, go left when you reach a fork in the road). The oldest part is the chancel arch that dates from the 12th century. Wounded soldiers are said to have been brought here following the 1513 battle fought on the nearby hillside, and it's said that the body of James IV of Scotland, wrapped in the Royal Standard, lay here before being taken to London.

BRANXTON & THE BATTLE OF FLODDEN

The last medieval battle in England – and the most significant in Northumberland – was fought on a hillside just outside Branxton village, four miles southeast of Coldstream on the Scottish border.

The 1513 clash between the Scots and the English was sparked by Henry VIII's attack on France, which put James IV of Scotland in the difficult position of renewing the 'auld alliance' between France and Scotland at the request of the Queen of France. And so a huge Scottish army left Edinburgh for northern England in mid-August, led by the king. They crossed the River Till over Twizel Bridge and took Norham after a siege lasting six days.

By the end of August, the Earl of Surrey, whom Henry VIII had left in charge of defending England, arrived in Newcastle and proceeded north with an army of 20,000 – to fight 30,000 Scots.

The two sides faced each other on 9 September 1513, at Branxton Hill: standards flying, knights in armour and men with arrows, swords and pikes at the ready. The Scots had the more advantageous position at the top of the hill, bearing down on the English along Pallin's Burn, but they missed a prime opportunity to advance. In the end, the English archers were devastating in their precision and the Scots with their cumbersome pikes were slaughtered in their many thousands – perhaps 9,000 men. The battle lasted just a couple of hours, resulting in victory for the English army. By dusk, the King of Scotland, many noblemen and thousands of men on both sides lay strewn across the hillside.

Every year a few hundred horseriders make the journey from Coldstream to Branxton Hill to pay homage to the fallen soldiers of 1513. Led by the 'Coldstreamer' carrying the town's standard, it's quite a spectacle to see them galloping over the fields. The Coldstream Riders' Association (⊘ scotlandstartshere. com/event/coldstream-civic-week) organise the annual event in early August, as well as a few other ride-outs in the same week, including to Norham.

If you continue away from the church for a third of a mile up the road, there's a parking area from where a footpath leads steeply up Branxton Hill to a memorial cross overlooking the village and famous **battlefield** site, which is dedicated 'to the brave of both nations'.

ALONG THE RIVER TILL

Tweed said to Till,
'What gars ye rin sae still?'
Till said to Tweed,
'Though ye rin wi' speed,
And I rin slaw,
Whar ye droon ae man,
I droon twa!'
17th-century verse

From the grassy plains east of the Cheviots, rising to the upland sandstone terrain bordering the A1, is this little-known corridor of Northumberland with much to offer walkers, cyclists and touring families. **Chillingham Castle**, prehistoric sites in the hills above **Chatton** and **Doddington**, and heritage attractions in and around **Ford** and **Etal** are among the area's highlights. From a number of beauty spots you gain an unrivalled profile of the Cheviot range.

Here we follow the deep, sinuous **River Till** from **Twizel** with its medieval bridge and castle, three miles east of Coldstream and Cornhill, where it joins company with the Tweed.

8 TWIZEL BRIDGE & CASTLE

Close to where the River Till flows into the Tweed (halfway between Cornhill-on-Tweed and Norham on the A698) is one of Northumberland's most striking medieval crossings. **Twizel Bridge** has five arched ribs on its underside supporting a single-span that curves over the lazy River Till. In the days leading up to the Battle of Flodden in 1513 (page 163), both the English and Scottish armies would have crossed this newly constructed bridge. Above the river and bridge, trees rise on a steep bank to meet **Twizel Castle** (once a medieval tower house and then an 18th-century folly), which peeps above the canopy. It's now a crumbling fortress draped in ivy but still commands attention. It's made of the pinky grey sandstone you find quite a lot round here.

9 DUDDO STONES

One mile northwest of Duddo village (between Norham & Etal). As you exit Duddo village on the B6354, the road bends sharply to the left. Turn off right here down a minor lane (after a red telephone box and Duddo Farm). Park in a lay-by on your right in 500yds ♀ NT931437

Five giant fists of stone thrust from the ground form this **Bronze Age circle** on a hilltop a few miles north of Etal. Dating from around 2000BC and standing between 5 and 10ft tall, they look most striking late in the afternoon when the sun picks out the grooves and ancient cup marks in the stones. Human remains were excavated from the central area in the late 19th century, suggesting the site had mythical or sacred value, as is common with stone circles elsewhere.

Duddo Farm permits access to the stone circle along a permissive path through a field of crops. The **walking route** is signed by a farm gate by the roadside (see directions above). It takes 30 minutes or so to reach the stone circle on foot, which you'll see on a hill three-quarters of a mile in the distance.

10 ETAL

Etal's single street, connecting a manor at one end with a ruined castle at the other, is strikingly unlike any other in the region with its two neat facing rows of whitewashed stone cottages and a thatched inn (the only

FORTIFIED CHURCHES

Many Northumberland churches of a certain age bare testimony to the cross-border clashes and clan conflicts that swept across the region from the 14th century and continued for the next few hundred years. Places of worship were not immune from assault – far from it – and so in the border parishes where the locals had had enough of the Scots, we find medieval and Norman churches reinforced with hefty walls and cheerless slit windows (**St John's, Edlingham** (page 209), **Old Bewick's Holy Trinity** (page 181) and **St Cuthbert's, Corsenside**, are good examples), stone roofs like **St Cuthbert's, Bellingham** (page 241,) and even protective towers known as **Vicar's peles**, which provided refuge to the clergy.

In a scattering of old churchyards, these defensive structures remain freestanding, notably at **St Andrew's, Corbridge** (page 348) and **St Michael and All Angels, Ford** (page 171); others lie further afield, as at **Ponteland** (page 281) and **St Cuthbert's, Elsdon** (page 244). But in the middle-of-nowhere hamlet of **Ancroft**, six miles south of Berwick on the B6525, the pele tower was actually raised out of the Norman nave. Its ground floor is tunnel vaulted.

thatched pub in Northumberland). More Suffolk than Northumberland you may think. The village was laid out in the mid 18th century (though the houses have since been rebuilt) and it draws a similar reaction as Ford because of its old-world character.

Opposite Etal's main street on the other side of the B6354, **St Mary's Chapel** stands in the grounds of Etal Manor. The gated driveway gives the appearance that the parkland is private, but you are permitted to walk to the chapel. The building dates to the mid 19th century and was constructed in memory of Lord Frederick Fitz-Clarence, the one-time lord of the manor (and illegitimate son of the Duke of Clarence, later William IV). He is interred below a prominent tomb carved with a sword and foliated cross, which is reached via a small door to the left of the organ.

Visible from the same road is a **cricket ground** where matches are held on weekends in summer. A women's team plays on Saturdays.

Raised on a bank above the River Till is **Etal Castle** (✆ 01890 820332 ☺ Apr–Jun Fri–Sun & bank holidays; Jun–end Oct daily; free admission 🐾 English Heritage), a 14th-century fortress boasting a substantial gatehouse and tower house, and a few lengths of curtain wall. You can wander across the grassy medieval courtyard within the castle grounds and peer into the exposed domestic rooms and floors of the **tower house** (the main living quarters of the castle). The **gatehouse** shows evidence of a portcullis (a replica now secures the castle entrance), and drawbar sockets reveal where heavy timber was used to strengthen the opening.

In the days leading up to one of the bloodiest conflicts in British history, the 1513 Battle of Flodden (page 163), Etal Castle fell to the Scots on their way to fight the English at Flodden – where they would be defeated.

A visit makes for a good day out when combined with a trip to Etal village and a ride on the Heatherslaw Light Railway (page 168), whose trains stop just below the castle car park before returning to Ford a few miles along the line.

¶ FOOD & DRINK

Black Bull Etal ✆ 01890 820200 ☺ lunch & dinner daily ♿ 🐾. Once a traditional boozer, the Black Bull was refurbished some years ago now and has a rather stark and modern

---

◀ **1** The Heatherslaw Railway tracing the River Till. **2** Twizel Bridge – one of the county's most striking medieval crossings. **3** The ruins of Etal Castle. **4** St Paul's Church, Branxton. **5** Milling demonstration at Heatherslaw Mill.

café-like interior, though there's lovely outdoor seating and it retains its character externally with its thatched roof, a feature shared with no other pub in Northumberland. On the food front, it's all pretty standard pub grub: scampi, lasagne, fish and chips, sausage and mash, as well as sandwiches and jacket potatoes etc.

The pub is run by Cheviot Brewery and their cask ales are of course on tap (Harbour Wall is their best-selling beer; it's a pale ale, quite zesty), but you can also drive a few miles up the road to the **Cheviot Tap Room & Microbrewery** (TD12 4TP ✆ 0191 389 7102 ☉ noon–22.00 Fri & Sat, noon–17.00 Sun 🐾) where there's a shack-like bar with outdoor seating and great pizza nights on Fri & Sat (make sure you book).

Lavender Tearooms Etal ✆ 01890 820761 ☉ May–Oct daily; Nov–Apr Sat–Thu ♿. Busy café, post office, pantry and gift shop, selling coffees and light lunches made with some local ingredients including Doddington's cheeses, and scones from Norham. Try their Northumbrian Singin' Hinny, a large, fluffy scone that's almost bread-like and is extremely filling. Or their signature lavender cake – a sponge infused with flowers. Outdoor seating with a view of the immaculate village is perfect on a summer's day.

11 HEATHERSLAW LIGHT RAILWAY

Stations at Heatherslaw (between Ford & Etal TD12 4TJ) & below the castle in Etal village ✆ 01890 820317/820244 ⌂ heatherslawlightrailway.co.uk ☉ Easter–end Oct & around Christmas, hourly service between 11.00 & 15.00 (until 16.00 in summer); trains depart Heatherslaw on the hour & Etal at half-past the hour ♿ 🐾

Small carriages packed with families trundle behind the 15-inch-gauge steam engine for the two-mile ride from Heatherslaw Mill to Etal village (you can also make the trip in reverse). A one-way trip takes about 20 minutes.

It's a pleasant journey through farmland with the River Till in view the whole way. Willows, alders and oaks crowd the riverbank, where herons take flight as the train approaches. You may like to time your journey to stop for lunch in Etal before returning to Heatherslaw, either by train or along a path running parallel to the B-road at the top of the village. Watching the engine on the turntable at Heatherslaw station has long been a highlight of family trips here with my kids.

12 HEATHERSLAW MILL

Between Ford & Etal, TD12 4TJ ✆ 01890 820488 ☉ Easter–end Oct daily

A visit to Heatherslaw, the only working water-powered cornmill in Northumberland (at one time there were 140 in the region), makes for a great family day out and can be combined with a trip on the narrow-gauge railway whose station is on the other side of the river from the mill (reached via a footbridge).

A mill has stood here since the 13th century, although the present three-storey building dates to the Victorian era. For a few pounds you can explore the inside and join a **guided tour** of every stage of the milling process, beginning with raising the sluice gate (children are invited to help). Moments later the 16ft water wheel (viewed through a glass floor panel) begins to turn, powering various cogs and grinding stones until milled flour exits a chute in great poofs.

"Here children can dress up, sweep the floor, lay food on the table and rock a baby to sleep."

Upstairs, an **exhibition room** chronicles the social history of agricultural labour in the area and includes displays of machinery and an engaging **children's corner** that features a recreated labourer's bedroom and kitchen furnished as it might have looked in the 19th century. Here children can dress up, sweep the floor, lay food on the table and rock a baby to sleep.

A ground-floor **shop** sells various crafts and gifts including bags of rye, wholemeal and spelt flour produced on site.

¶¶ FOOD & DRINK

Café at the Mill ✐ 01890 820488 ○ daily 🐾. Modern upstairs café (outside seating too) inside the historic Heatherslaw Mill whose head cook is committed to local farm produce, and so you'll find local beef and pork stuffed into the pies and hot baguettes (dripping in cider gravy, I might add). Pizzas, toasties, jackets and cheesy chips for fussy kids, and various homemade traybakes and cakes. Northumbrian teas and coffee.

13 HAY FARM HEAVY HORSE CENTRE

Hay Farm (between Ford & Etal), TD12 4TR ✐ 01890 820601 ○ Tue–Sun but phone before visiting ♿ 🐾

A short walk east from Heatherslaw Mill (under a mile) to see Hay Farm's Clydesdale horses is recommended for families and anyone who finds these friendly giants endearing (who doesn't?). On demonstration days, horses are ridden in their finery and you'll hear about their traditional duties when they worked the land. At other times, visitors are welcome to get up close to the animals in their stables, view the displays of horse-drawn machinery and take a ride on a carriage (no

HEAVY HORSES IN NORTHUMBERLAND

'It's a horse with a purpose,' says Vivienne Cockburn from the Milfield Heavy Horse Association at Hay Farm near Etal (page 169). 'Clydesdales worked the land all over Northumberland and moved agriculture forward. They were used for everything: in forestry, haulage, shipping, agriculture and even by milkmen, but now they're a rare breed.'

At Hay Farm, crops were threshed and then taken to nearby Heatherslaw Watermill – a job involving the use of some 17 Clydesdales that worked out of the farm. The introduction of the tractor changed all that and by the mid 1950s, these powerful work horses became redundant. Thousands of Clydesdales were destroyed all over Northumberland.

Clydesdale horses returned to the Grade II-listed 18th-century farm in 2011, predominantly for the enjoyment of local people and to preserve the connection of the breed with the area. 'It's very rewarding seeing children listening to grandparents talking of their memories of these gentle giants and passing on a bit of history,' says Viv.

booking required ⊙ Jul–Sep 13.00–15.00 Tue, Wed, Thu & Sun but check online ⬧ hayfarmheavies.co.uk).

Built in the 18th century (with 19th-century additions), the farm's historic barns, stables, granary and engine house are an added attraction. During special events you can watch the horses pulling vintage machinery, sample regional foods, and watch craftsmen and women demonstrating traditional skills.

14 FORD

A sweeter little village than Ford could hardly be imagined outside of Arcadia.
W W Tomlinson, *Comprehensive Guide to Northumberland*, 1888

Ford stays in the memory: its immaculate main street with an old fountain at one end (now a planter but wouldn't it be fabulous if it spouted water again?) is a picture of rural peace and has remained unchanged for well over 100 years. The Victorian-styled lanterns are not original, but let's not get too picky.

Few cars – and usually none at all – park on the street (apparently residents park at the back) so it really feels like you are stepping back in time. Ford could be the set of a BBC period drama; all it lacks is a carriage, and a bonnet for the lady behind the post office/tea room counter. Take in the scene from the **tea room** (⬧ 01890 820230 ⊙ daily) gardens over a scone or slice of cake. The estate office told me: 'some visitors arrive at the village and it looks so perfect that they think it is private and they can't go in.' You can enter and parking is permitted on the main street, but do you dare pollute the view with your modern machinery?

Lady Waterford Hall (✆ 07790 457580 ◷ end Mar–Oct daily, Nov–end Mar by appointment ♿) was a school until the 1950s. The building – and the rest of the village – was commissioned by Louisa Anne, Marchioness of Waterford, who became the sole owner of the Ford estate on her husband's death. She was an accomplished painter and spent 22 years creating the striking pre-Raphaelite-esque frescoes inside the hall which I thoroughly recommend viewing if you are in the area. The paintings depict biblical stories but the figures are all local people who sat for Lady Waterford. At the time of writing, the Hall was open for **afternoon teas** (scones, cakes, traybakes, tea and coffee) every Thursday during the summer.

"Ford could be the set of a BBC period drama; all it lacks is a carriage, and a bonnet for the lady behind the post office counter."

St Michael's and All Angels Church stands by the side of Ford Castle gazing at the distant Cheviot Hills. It dates to medieval times but was restored in the mid 19th century, and has some curious features including the two faces either end of the arcades. The little man with a beard near the porch is medieval; his facing friend is Victorian. At the back of the church (inside) are a few medieval memorial stones on the ground. One is said to show the Northumbrian bagpipes complete with a chanter and bellows.

In the churchyard are a number of very old gravestones from the early 18th century and a tiny memorial stone dated 1641. In the sloping field is the ruin of a **vicar's pele tower** (page 165).

Opposite the church is the **Old Dairy** (TD15 2PX ✆ 07393 212690 ◷ Wed–Sun & bank holidays), now a café (page 172) and sizeable, higgledy architectural antiques emporium selling an assortment of period furniture, fixtures, fireplaces, old garden tools, vintage jugs, maps and oddments.

Ford Castle is a staggering 13th-century fortified mansion with three surviving corner towers and an imposing gateway and curtain wall. Unfortunately, it's not only closed to the public but is also mostly hidden by trees; the best views are from St Michael's churchyard. In the weeks

FORD & ETAL ESTATES

Rivalry between the manors of Ford and Etal are legendary in these parts (during one bloody conflict in the early 1400s, the heir to the Lord of Ford was killed by the neighbouring family). A century of feuding between the two families, the Manners and Herons, came to an end around the time of the 1513 Anglo-Scottish battle at Flodden (page 163) and the two estates became united under the Joicey family in 1908. The same family continues to manage the two villages and associated attractions, including Heatherslaw Mill (page 168), Lady Waterford Hall (page 171) and the light railway (page 168).

before the Battle of Flodden in 1513 (page 163), James IV of Scotland is said to have spent a few nights with Lady Heron in the fortress (her husband having been previously captured by the Scots). As the king took his leave, he set the place alight.

¶ FOOD & DRINK

The Old Dairy Opposite Ford Castle, TD15 2PX 🕿 07393 212690 ⊙ Wed–Sun. Adjoining a great **antiques emporium** housed in a 1930s milking parlour, this little **café** with a couple of tables serves coffees, teas and a few cakes (homemade fruit cake and a blackberry sponge called 'Black Magic'). Don't overlook the outside tables and marble **champagne bar**, which invites visitors to enjoy a glass of fizz while taking in the fabulous view of the Cheviots. You weren't expecting that were you?

15 FORD MOSS NATURE RESERVE

A mile northeast of Ford village, a lane branches off the B6353; half a mile along this paved lane you'll see a track by a wicket gate – this is the entrance to the reserve. You can park on the roadside verge here ♀ NT970375; Northumberland Wildlife Trust

Enclosed by a thick band of pine trees a few minutes' drive from Ford village is this rich lowland peat bog. Don't let those last two words put you off – it's a tranquil reserve inhabited by many birds and plants, and is a very pleasant place for a **walk and picnic**, though it can be quite overgrown in parts.

The central area lies in a hollow (once a lake formed after the last ice age) and is covered by heather, thick sphagnum mosses, hare's-tail cottongrass and patches of cranberry and bog myrtle. The insectivorous round-leaved sundew grows here (see photo on page 199).

The most prominent feature is a tall brick chimney that marks where a coal mine once operated. A path (part bridleway, part permissive footpath) runs around the perimeter of this basin but you might have to machete your way through parts where it's overgrown. You can take a longer **walk** that encompasses Goatscrag Hill and Routin Lynn (see below). A spectacular view and prehistoric rock carvings await those who make the climb.

* * *

A SECRET WATERFALL & PREHISTORIC ROCK CARVINGS: ROUTIN LYNN & GOATSCRAG HILL

❋ OS Explorer map 339; start: between Doddington & Ford, 2 miles east of Kimmerston on an unclassified road to Lowick, ♀ NT983367; 1 mile; easy

Take the family on a fairy-tale adventure to this secluded waterfall hidden deep within an ancient woodland (not to be confused with Roughting Linn near Chatton). Combined with a visit to Goatscrag Hill to search for prehistoric animal carvings etched into the walls of a rock shelter, this makes for a rewarding afternoon. But it's only one for the sure-footed as the descent to the river is really steep and a bit of a scramble in places.

There are two ways to reach **Routin Lynn**: either walk from Ford village or Ford Moss Nature Reserve (page 172), picking up a bridleway via Broom Ridge and Goatscrag Hill; or drive along the aforementioned road from Kimmerston to Lowick. After two miles you'll come to a crossroads where there's a fingerpost on the left signed for 'Goats Crag'. Park opposite.

Though few visit this magical waterfall, it really deserves seeking out – and even the climb adds to the sense of discovery. In wet and wintery weather the path is pretty perilous, however.

Start from the pull-in area by the crossroads. A fingerpost points down a wide track. After a couple of hundred yards, a narrow trail snakes off to your left (if you reach the cattle grid, you've gone too far) into an enchanting **woodland** with oak and beech trees hiding a glorious display of bluebells in spring (NB: this path may be re-routed during forestry works). Descend sharply to reach a prominent old beech tree. Turn right here and follow the sound of water to **Routin Lynn**, the prettiest of falls, cascading down a cliff face into a wide pool just deep enough to take a plunge. In summer the waterfall may be more of a rain shower spraying into the basin where a paddle is all you'll manage but you can walk behind the waterfall (and only get a little bit wet).

Retrace your footsteps to the farm track, turn left and go over the cattle grid, heading north into open countryside. The trail soon swings to the west for the short uphill walk to **Goatscrag Hill**. Locate the more westerly of two main rock shelters at the foot of the hill and search for the **rock carvings** of four animals with horns and antlers on the rear wall. Some years ago a

Bronze Age cemetery was unearthed here that concealed the remains of ashes, including some stored in two pottery vessels.

Climb to the top of the craggy massif and search for **cup-and-ring decorated rocks** – and a spectacular view of the Cheviots on one side and the North Sea on the other – before retracing your path back to the woods.

More prehistoric rock carvings are found back near the crossroads (♀ NT983367). About 25yds north of the road, and reached by a path through woods, is a huge stone slab in a clearing which is covered in cup-and-ring motifs of differing shapes including one resembling a sun with radiating lines. It is said to be the most decorated stone in Northumberland and the largest panel of prehistoric rock art in England.

* * *

16 DODDINGTON

At some point on your travels around Northumberland, you've probably come across **Doddington Ice Cream**. It's produced in the village of the same name, five miles north of Chatton. Attractive as it is with its stone cottages and leafy surrounds, Doddington does not have a huge amount to merit a special visit, unless you really like **prehistoric rock art** – or ice cream (sold by the tub from outside the farm) and are prepared to scout around a bit for the **cup-and-ring marked stones** on nearby Dod Law.

If you're up for the hunt and **walk**, first take a lane off the main B6525 at the south end of the village. It's signed for the golf course and is on the other side of the road from the turning for the church. A hundred yards ahead past a driveway with a cattle grid, you'll see on your right a stile into a field. Head uphill on to Dod Law. After about 150yds, start looking for the decorated stones.

Doddington's parish **church** (originally 13th century but much altered since) is found in the far southwest corner of the village where it stands peering across farmland to the Cheviot Hills. Note the little watch house that was built in the early 19th century to protect the dead from body-snatchers.

17 CHATTON & AROUND

Pleasantly surrounded by verdant farmland, **Chatton** village is close enough to the Cheviots and Northumberland's sandstone hills to make this a good base for hikers. An arc of hills dotted with prehistoric sites rises to the east providing many opportunities for walks within a few miles of the village. Note, too, that some of the highest-quality accommodation in north Northumberland is found in and around the village and includes the Georgian mansion, **Chatton Park House** (⊘ chattonpark.com).

Chatton holds appeal to the passing traveller owing to its good pub, **The Percy Arms** (see below), village shop and proximity to Chillingham Castle.

⑪ FOOD & DRINK

The Percy Arms Chatton NE66 5PS ⌀ 01668 215244 🐾. A mixture of locals and visitors gather around the bar on weekend lunchtimes in this old pub restaurant and hotel for a drink (local cask beers on tap). After breakfasts (served to non-guests too), food is served from noon until 21.00 (lunches in the bar area and evening meals in a more refined dining room next door). Pub pleasers on the menu include cod and chips, steaks, pies and burgers, and a lighter lunch menu of sandwiches and jackets. Sunday roast dinners served from noon until late. Forgo breakfast is all I can say.

* * *

⚘ ROCK ART & WILDLIFE ON CHATTONPARK HILL

※ OS Explorer map 340; start: B6348, 1 mile east of Chatton ♀ NU074287; 1½ miles; moderate

The reward for a short climb to Chattonpark Hill is rich ground flora, birdlife and views that you can absorb while searching for prehistoric rock carvings, thought to be some of the best examples anywhere.

SCENIC ROUTE TO THE COAST

If you are heading to the sea, I recommend the scenic B6349 that takes you across a memorable bridge and over Belford Moor. **Weetwood Bridge** (a couple of miles east of Wooler on the B6348) spans the River Till and is one of the most elegant medieval bridges in Northumberland, with a wide arch made of blushed sandstone. Its height above the water, rose masonry, splayed parapets, conical finals to its piers and view of the Cheviots are not easily forgotten, particularly when viewed en route to Wooler. There are also a few old metal lattice and stone bridges around here, including the early 19th-century **Fowberry Bridge**, set in woodland by **Fowberry Tower** (once a 15th-century tower house but now chiefly a late 18th-century manor).

A useful pull-in area by the side of the B6348 marks the start of this walk. Set foot by the footpath sign on a heavily vegetated woodland path. Go through the farm gate ahead and turn right along a rough dirt track, enjoying the sound of birdsong in the old beech and sycamore trees. Continue uphill with conifer **woodland** to your left and under the boughs of a couple of old ash trees until you reach open land.

You'll come to two farm gates. Go through the left-hand one and head uphill, crossing rough **grassland** grazed by sheep (tuck your trousers into your socks as there are ticks about). Skylarks will accompany you the whole way to the top of the hill, and you may also see yellowhammers and buzzards.

You could spend a few hours searching the quartzy grey stones for motifs (this would take even longer in late summer when bracken covers everything), but here are a couple of grid references to make things easier: ♀ NU07572906 and ♀ NU07632926.

The other prominently decorated stone in the area is found within the remains of an earthen **hillfort**, located beyond the trig point to the north-northwest (which you will see once you've climbed over a fairly prominent stile). A deep **cup-and-ring** impression (and some fainter marks) decorates the lone panel at ♀ NU07222940.

Now, if that's not enough rock art for you, there are some staggering stones under the overhang of nearby **Kettley Crag**, north-northeast of Chattonpark Hill. The rock at ♀ NU07462981 is densely covered with many cups, rings and gutters.

* * *

18 CHILLINGHAM CASTLE & PARK

NE66 5NJ ✆ 01668 215359 ⊙ Apr–end Oct (last entry 16.00)

> **Forgive any disorder by thinking and knowing that I rescued a roofless, floorless wreck of a castle, with a jungle having taken over the garden and grounds.**
> Sir Humphry Wakefield Bt, 2002

Chillingham is one of the eeriest and most atmospheric castles in England. It was besieged on numerous occasions during medieval times and many a captured Scot and Border Reiver were executed here. A word of caution: this is not like the castles at Alnwick or Bamburgh and you won't find polished cabinets displaying rare porcelain, dining rooms dripping in crystal and gold and immaculately laid-out rooms. I find it enthralling because it is not any of those things. Certainly, one of Chillingham's greatest appeals is that you can touch a lot of what is on display and, in some rooms, even rummage through the owner's collections.

Many kings were entertained here, including Edward I who stopped off on his way north in 1298 to capture William Wallace (better known to Hollywood film enthusiasts as *Braveheart*). It wasn't until 1348 that Chillingham became fully fortified. It's formed of four square-angled towers enclosing a central courtyard. The walls are embattled and the whole edifice looks tremendously intimidating with its stern, grey walls, dark windows and ominous central staircase leading to the **Great Hall**. Now picture the above on a dark October evening as you enter Chillingham on a ghost tour and you can imagine the impression it makes.

Cruel things have happened to prisoners held in the **dungeons** at Chillingham. 'If you were a Scot back in the 14th century and you were caught and brought to Chillingham Castle, it was a death sentence,' a guide told me. Still visible in the dungeon are lines carved by prisoners on the walls representing the number of days they had been in captivity. The recreated **torture room** contains skeletons in cages and various authentic medieval torture devices including an iron maiden, scold's bridle (a metal mask usually forced over the head of a woman accused of gossiping or 'nagging') and executioner's block. It's chilling stuff, and children (and adults) might find it harrowing. On the family ghost tour I attended, I was grateful to the guide for pretending some of the torture devices were fake, but between you and me, they're mostly the real deal.

Chillingham Castle is much frequented by ghost hunters who claim it is one of the most haunted castles in Europe. Many apparitions and strange goings-on have been reported by visitors: objects being thrown around rooms, violently swinging lanterns and slamming doors. **Ghost tours** sell out far in advance and should be booked online (⊘ chillingham-castle.com/ghosts). Tickets include an atmospheric tour of the castle with guides detailing hair-raising stories in each room and culminating in a ghost 'hunt' with the use of a pendulum to communicate with one of the resident spirits. It is thrilling stuff and my children still talk about their chat with Lady Mary a year on.

"Chillingham Castle is much frequented by ghost hunters who claim it is one of the most haunted castles in Europe."

Stone, spiral staircases connect the various **rooms** – all of which hold an eclectic assortment of objects: a Stone Age burial cist, the skins of wild cats, a collection of rocking horses and so on. Furnishings are medieval or Tudor styled with wall tapestries, banners, armoury and the heads of various beasts hanging from the walls, including a colossal pair of antlers once belonging to an elk that lived half a million years ago. On one of my visits to the **King James I Drawing Room**, it was winter time when the property is usually closed to visitors; the guide pointed to the yellow drapes over the windows that I can only describe as looking full. 'If I drew those curtains, hundreds of bats would fall out,' he said. Time for a walk in the splendid **Italianate gardens** – the formality of the clipped topiary bushes and planting schemes a contrast to the rooms inside the castle.

Chillingham Park & cattle

NE66 5NP ✆ 01668 215250 ☉ Easter–end Oct; four tours daily.

> At the first appearance of any person, they set off in a full gallop; and, at the distance of two or three hundred yards, make a wheel round, and come boldly up again, tossing their heads in a menacing manner: On a sudden they make a full stop, at the distance of forty or fifty yards, looking wildly at the object of their surprise.
>
> Ralph Bailey describing a Chillingham bull in Thomas Bewick's *History of Quadrupeds*, 1792

The history of this ancient 365-acre **parkland** dates to the founding of the Chillingham estate in the 13th century. When the wooded parkland was enclosed, its population of wild white cattle also became cut off; they have remained isolated from the outside world ever since.

Chillingham **cattle** are thought to be the last surviving native wild herd in Britain and are descended from the wild ox that used to inhabit the forests covering much of the British Isles in prehistoric times. They certainly have a wild appearance with their unruly looking woolly coat and fierce horns.

The herd is currently just over 100 animals strong but the population fluctuates from year to year. Over the hard winter of 1946 numbers plummeted to just 13 individuals. To prevent their near-extinction again, hay is provided during the winter; otherwise they are completely

---

1 Lady Waterford Hall is decorated by beautiful frescoes painted by Louisa Anne, Marchioness of Waterford. **2** Look for yellowhammer on Chattonpark Hill. **3** The Great Hall in Chillingham Castle. **4 & 5** On our Goatscrag Hill walk, look for prehistoric cup-and-ring carvings and find the pretty waterfall of Routin Lynn. ▶

left to fend for themselves. 'They live and die by their own strengths as they have done for hundreds of years,' the park warden told me.

The best way of seeing the cattle is to join an hour-long **tour** through the parkland, which encloses many ancient trees. You may see a bull fight, which is quite a spectacle. Because the animals are potentially dangerous, you can't visit the park without a guide.

Chillingham church

St Peter's is really worth visiting before or after a tour of the parkland and is easily reached from the estate car park. Twelfth-century masonry survives in the nave but the most distinguished piece of stonework in the simple building is the mid 15th-century tomb of Sir Ralph Grey and his wife. Intricately carved saints and angels surround the tomb chest; on top lie the figures of the couple – still with some visible paintwork. During the Wars of the Roses, Grey had his son executed for supporting the wrong side though he escaped being hanged, drawn and quartered and instead suffered the somewhat better fate of being beheaded.

On leaving the church door, turn left and seek out the small 18th-century headstone commemorating an estate gardener, which stands by the south chapel wall. The relief of a rake and spade makes it fairly easy to spot.

SEVEN CASTLES

Chillingham Castle shelters below an impressive area of craggy moorland that rises above the Till plains, offering some of the most expansive views in the whole of Northumberland. **Hepburn Moor**, **Bewick Moor** and **Bewick Hill** are well known to rock climbers and bouldering enthusiasts but anyone can enjoy the rugged scenery by following the steeply ascending lane connecting Hepburn Farm (a mile or so south of Chillingham Castle) with North Charlton by the A1.

From the Forestry England car park at Hepburn (a quarter of a mile beyond Hepburn Farm), it's an uphill climb of half a mile along tarmac to where a footpath strikes off to your left through the heather to the prominent double-ramparted earthwork, **Ros Castle** (♀ NU080253). At 1,000ft above sea level, Ros provides an outstanding view of the county; on a clear day you can see seven of Northumberland's castles: **Warkworth**, **Alnwick**, **Dunstanburgh**, **Bamburgh**, **Lindisfarne**, **Ford** and **Chillingham** and an unparalleled panoramic vista of the Cheviots – catch them at first light for a truly memorable sight.

19 OLD BEWICK

Many whizz past Old Bewick on the A697 but those taking a meandering route through the countryside or the high road to the coast might want to stop here. The hamlet itself is quaint enough, with its old farm buildings and cottages, and there's a hillfort just behind the settlement, but it's the **Holy Trinity Church** tucked away up a lane half a mile north of Old Bewick (signed from the road) that you should really see. Its hugely thick walls, slit windows and Romanesque chancel arch are clear giveaways as to its status as one of the oldest churches in Northumberland; it is Saxon in origin with enough of its structure surviving from the 11th century to describe it as Norman. One of the most interesting features is the carvings on the capitals of the chancel arch: the two heads gnashing their teeth may be a representation of the pre-Christian green man.

The ancient **churchyard**, enclosed by a burn and many firs and old yews, makes a wonderful sanctuary for wildlife. Snowdrops put on a dazzling display in February.

20 EGLINGHAM

Eglingham's stone houses stand either side of a sloping through-road. There's not a huge amount to see from a visitor's perspective, but what it lacks in attractions it makes up for with its pub, which serves good food and ales (see below).

St Maurice Church has been much restored over the centuries, but it does have a Norman chancel arch. Its font dates to 1667 and bears the words 'wash and be clen'. One of the bells in the tower is called Anthony. It is apparently inscribed in German with the following words: 'Anthony is my name. I was made in the year 1489.'

¶¶ FOOD & DRINK

Tankerville Arms NE66 2TX ℰ 01665 578444 ☺ evening meals daily, plus lunches Fri–Sun ♿ 🐾 bar only. Just the kind of country inn visitors will want to fall into after a day hiking in the hills, with its 19th-century stone walls and low beamed interior. It's full of period quirks, complete with a fire lit many months of the year, antique prints on the walls and old-fashioned wooden furniture throughout. Good local ales served at the bar and excellent traditional pub fodder – mainly roasts, steaks and seafood dishes served with veg; local produce dotted about the menu too. Sunday lunches tend to get booked up a few days before.

The award-winning Slow Travel series from Bradt Guides

Over 20 regional guides across Britain.
See the full list at bradtguides.com/slowtravel.

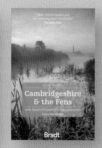

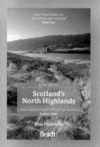

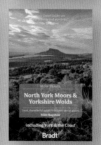

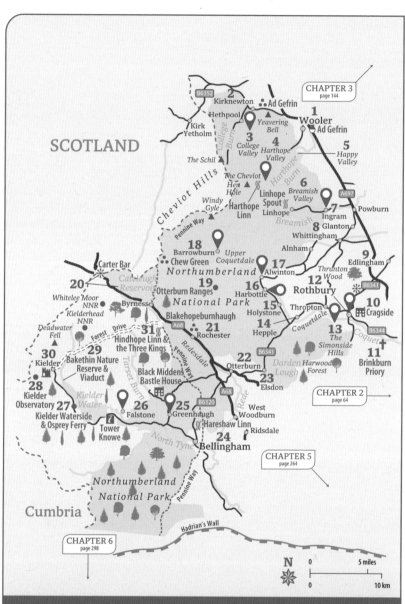

CHAPTER 3 page 144

1 Wooler
Ad Gefrin

2 Kirknewton
Ad Gefrin

Hethpool

Kirk Yetholm

SCOTLAND

3 College Valley

The Schil

Cheviot Hills

The Cheviot
Hen Hole

Windy Gyle

Harthope Linn

Yeavering Bell

Harthope Valley

Harthope Burn

5 Happy Valley

6 Breamish Valley

Linhope Spout
Linhope

Breamish

7 Ingram
Powburn

8 Glanton

Whittingham

Alnham

9 Edlingham

Pennine Way

18 Barrowburn
Chew Green

Upper Coquetdale

Northumberland

17 Alwinton

Thrunton Wood

12 Rothbury

Carter Bar

Catcleugh Reservoir

20 Whitelee Moor NNR

Kielderhead NNR

Byrness

19 Otterburn Ranges

National Park

16 Harbottle

15 Holystone

Thropton

Coquetdale

13 The Simonside Hills

10 Cragside

B6344

11 Brinkburn Priory

Deadwater Fell

Forest Drive

30 Kielder

29 Bakethin Nature Reserve & Viaduct

31 Hindhope Linn & the Three Kings

Blakehopeburnhaugh

21 Rochester

Redesdale

Pennine Way

Harwood Forest

14 Hepple

22 Otterburn

23 Elsdon

Darden Lough

CHAPTER 2 page 64

28 Kielder Observatory

27 Kielder Waterside & Osprey Ferry

Kielder Water

Tower Knowe

26 Falstone

25 Greenhaugh

Black Middens Bastle House

Tarset Burn

24 Bellingham

Hareshaw Linn

West Woodburn

Ridsdale

North Tyne

Pennine Way

Northumberland National Park

Cumbria

CHAPTER 5 page 264

CHAPTER 6 page 298

Hadrian's Wall

N

0   5 miles
0   10 km

NORTHUMBERLAND NATIONAL PARK & KIELDER FOREST

4
NORTHUMBERLAND NATIONAL PARK & KIELDER FOREST

Isolation, inky black skies, glacial valleys and buxom hills characterise much of Northumberland National Park – the most sparsely populated of all the national parks in the country; a place you can feel truly alone and experience the closest thing to wilderness found anywhere in England. The deeper you venture into the **Cheviot Hills** (page 189), your chances of walking all day alone, viewing the Milky Way with the naked eye or encountering rare upland wildlife notably increase.

Kielder (page 253), England's largest forest, is a vast uninhabited expanse of conifer trees and moorland that merges with the Cheviot Hills on the western edge of Northumberland. Its remote location, upland terrain and large reservoir make the area popular with mountain bikers, watersport enthusiasts, families and wildlife watchers.

Kielder's astonishingly black night skies make this a prime location for astronomers who are well catered for at the spectacular **Kielder Observatory** (page 257).

Heading eastwards, waterfalls, heather-covered hillsides, prehistoric rock art and defensive farmhouses and towers dating mainly from the 16th century feature more prominently in the **Redesdale** (page 234) and **Rothbury** (page 207) landscapes, particularly around the **Tarset Valley** (page 249), **Elsdon** (page 238) and the **Simonside Hills** (page 218), all of which are popular with cyclists and walkers.

The market town of **Rothbury** (page 213) is well located for visits to all these places and boasts high-profile historic attractions on its doorstep, including **Cragside** house (page 209) and **Brinkburn Priory** (page 211).

Five hundred years of cross-border warfare and clan fighting made this stretch of upland countryside a very dangerous place to live. Those

TOURIST INFORMATION

Tower Knowe Visitor Centre Kielder NE48 1BX ✐ 01434 240436 ☺ Easter–end Oct daily ♿

Wooler TIC The Cheviot Centre, 12 Padgepool Pl, Wooler ✐ 01668 282123 ☺ Mon–Fri, morning Sat ♿

lawless years ended after James I came to the English throne in 1603, but parts of Redesdale (from Otterburn to Carter Bar on the Scottish border) still have a wild edge. Dark forests, lonely fells, rough farmland and Cheviot moors dominate the landscape, enticing those who savour solitude.

And then there's **Hadrian's Wall**, the most important Roman monument in Britain, laced along the southern fringes of the National Park. I've devoted a whole chapter to the Roman sites in *Chapter 6*.

GETTING AROUND

A car or touring bicycle is essential for exploring the hills. Some towns and villages on the eastern edge of Northumberland National Park can be reached by **bus**, notably Rothbury (the X14 from Newcastle via Morpeth is particularly useful; see bus map on page 18 for other routes) and Wooler (464 from Berwick), but if you're heading deeper into the Cheviots without a car, you'll need to cycle or hitch a ride along one of the tracks that runs through the larger valleys. The only **train stations** of help are at Morpeth and Berwick-upon-Tweed.

CYCLING

The major **Cheviot valleys** (Upper Coquetdale, Breamish, Harthope and College) have paved tracks tracing their respective rivers through the hills. Also consider the old **drove roads** (page 220) crossing the Cheviots, especially Salter's Road from Alnham, which is paved.

Cycling in **Coquetdale** using Rothbury as your base is a good option with the choice of off-road forest tracks maintained by Forestry England at Harbottle, Harwood and Thrunton woods (collectively known as the Rothbury Forests), and some fabulous B-roads that will appeal to the freewheeling-cyclist. **Kielder Forest**, too, is well known to mountain bikers for its well-maintained forest trails, graded according to difficulty.

The Pennine Cycleway (355 miles from Berwick-upon-Tweed to the Peak District) follows the River Tweed before turning south along the eastern edge of the national park via the picturesque villages of Alwinton and Elsdon and onwards to Hadrian's Wall.

CYCLE HIRE & REPAIRS

At the time of writing, the bike hire centres at Kielder had closed down but plans are afoot to reopen a new hire station at Kielder Waterside.

Coquet Cycles (page 67). Alnwick-based mobile repair service.

WALKING

With remote scenery and the highest summits in Northumberland, the **Cheviot range** is an obvious destination for the hill walker. Four major valleys named after their respective rivers (the **Coquet**, **Breamish**, **Harthope** and **College**) all have similar appeal with smooth-sided slopes overlapping each other for as far as the eye can see, eager whisky-tinted burns, waterfalls here and there, and a tremendous sense of remoteness and space. I've detailed some popular routes in the hills of all the major valleys in the section on the Cheviot Hills (page 189). You'll need ❋ OL16 The Cheviot Hills and OL42 Kielder Water & Forest.

The rivers running through each Cheviot valley are a destination in themselves and many visitors come just to picnic by the water's edge or paddle among the rocks (particularly in Breamish and Harthope valleys). There are few villages and hardly anywhere to buy food or pick up supplies so you might want to make a stop in the likes of Wooler

LONG-DISTANCE PATHS

The **Pennine Way** crosses remote moorland on its course through the Cheviots, traversing a number of famous peaks including The Cheviot (page 200) and Windy Gyle (page 228) before reaching Redesdale, and skirting the eastern edge of Kielder.

St Cuthbert's Way (62½ miles from Melrose in Scotland to Lindisfarne) takes in outstanding hill and coastal scenery on its easterly course from the Cheviots to Lindisfarne. At one point (close to St Cuthbert's Cave) you can see both the hills and the sea.

The 97-mile **St Oswald's Way** (page 301) encompasses Hadrian's Wall countryside before picking up the **Northumberland Coast Path** (page 67), another well-worn trail to Lindisfarne.

and Rothbury beforehand. For that reason, both towns make popular bases for walkers. Rothbury is also well situated for the walker wishing to explore the rugged heather-clad **Simonside Hills** (page 218), pretty much on the doorstep of the town.

Walks in **Redesdale's hills** (page 234) are not as well known and can be challenging. Come prepared, as it is pretty wild, boggy and lonesome in a lot of places, particularly Kielderhead National Nature Reserve (page 254). If you don't want to hike out into the wilderness, there are a number of waymarked routes in and around **Kielder Water** (page 253) as well as a number of easy woodland and waterfall walks, including **Hindhope Linn** (page 260) and **Hareshaw Linn** (page 246). Also in the Redesdale area is the stunning **Tarset Valley** (page 249), offering some rewarding low-level river and meadowland trails.

Northumberland National Park's useful website (⊘ northumberland nationalpark.org.uk) has a comprehensive walking section that includes the excellent 'Rangers' Favourite Walks' leaflet, available to download and also at tourist information centres. Free **guided ranger walks** (summer only; no booking required) are also listed online and available in leaflet format.

For **walking holidays**, guided and self-guided walks, the long-established **Shepherds Walks** (page 303), based in Rothbury, is recommended. Also consider **Northern Adventures** ⊘ northernadventures.co.uk, a Northumbrian company employing local guides on some classic national park and coast routes.

HORSERIDING

Bridleways (some on ancient drove roads) cross the Cheviots, linking the valleys and making this a superb place to visit on horseback. Northumberland National Park has a few maps detailing circular routes by horse on their website (⊘ northumberlandnationalpark.org.uk).

For guided horseriding trips in the Cheviots, try **Kimmerston Riding Centre** at Wooler (☏ 01668 216283 ⊘ kimmerston.com).

TAXIS

Bellingham Taxi ☏ 01434 220570
Border Villager Taxi Wooler ☏ 01668 482888
Ricky's Taxis Coquetdale ☏ 07718 585508
Tarset Valley Taxis North Tyne & Redesdale ☏ 01434 240835, 07711 400152; Take bicycles.

THE CHEVIOT HILLS & WOOLER

Wherever you wander in north Northumberland, the Cheviots are almost always brooding in the distance, guarding the frontier with Scotland. There's no mistaking this stonking corridor of smooth humps down the western edge of the county, which are strikingly rounded and unlike all the other hill ranges in northern England.

The slopes of these long-extinct volcanoes are dominated by dwarf shrubs and grasses and, except for a few plantation woodlands, the Cheviots appear at first quite featureless. It's not until you set foot on them that the character of individual hills and valleys becomes apparent with their wooded ravines, ancient trackways, Iron Age hillforts and waterfalls. In terms of altitude, you'll find some of the highest hills in England here with six summits over 2,000ft.

Though seemingly desolate, the **vegetation** covering the Cheviot plateaux forms an internationally important blanket bog habitat characterised by sphagnum mosses, cotton grasses, sedges, cloudberry, bilberry and heather. In ravines, alpine flowering plants including rose root, dwarf cornel and alpine willow herb flourish. The insectivorous sundew grows where the ground is particularly damp.

Deep **valleys** radiate from the highest peak, **The Cheviot**, which marks roughly the centre of the range. **Breamish**, **Harthope** and

LOCAL WORDS

caad cold
burn stream
haar sea mist
haugh flat land by water (pronounced 'hoff')
heugh jagged hill
hope sheltered valley eg: Linhope, Harthope
kirk often seen in place names eg: Kirknewton, Kirk Yetholm (Old Norse origins, meaning 'church')
knowe small hill
law hill
linn waterfall
lonnen lane

lough mountain lake (Northumbrian equivalent of 'loch', pronounced 'loff')
muckle big
Northumbrian 'burr' used to describe the local pronunciation of 'r'
shiel shepherds' or fishermen's huts
stell sheepfold (round, stone enclosure)
tup ram
whaup curlew (somewhat onomatopoeic if you've ever heard curlews in the breeding season)
yon that
yow ewe

College valleys are named after their respective rivers that rush eagerly off the hillsides. For the most part, they are all rocky and fairly shallow with shingle banks and rapids and the odd pool suitable for bathing.

Horseriders, cyclists, walkers and back-country hikers will find miles of lonely footpaths and bridleways in the Cheviots and a handful of quiet paved tracks snaking deep into remote countryside, with no through roads. This is not the Cotswolds and you won't find quaint villages or many places to pick up supplies, so come prepared. Isolation and remoteness is what brings you here. Those day trippers who come looking for cream teas and gift shops quickly turn around and head back out.

1 WOOLER

Nestled below some impressive hills on the edge of Northumberland National Park is the old market town of Wooler, promoted as the '**Gateway to the Cheviots**'. Indeed, Wooler is blessed with some very fine upland and river scenery and walks within just a few miles of its centre. If you are heading into the Cheviot valleys or hiking the long-distance trail, St Cuthbert's Way (page 187), which passes through the town, this is your last opportunity to pick up supplies (note that the Co-. op is conveniently open until 23.00).

Wooler itself is a pleasant workaday town built of stone and sits surrounded by an area of green hills and fields known as **Glendale**. Incidentally, Wooler provided inspiration for the fictional town of Greendale in the *Postman Pat* stories, and visitors will find its **high street** just as agreeable: old-fashioned independent shops sit side by side including a step-back-in-time sweet shop, butcher, baker, pharmacy, at least three antiques emporiums, a post office (of course), an excellent deli (page 192) and two independent bookshops well-stocked with an array of local guides and maps.

For **tourist information**, head to the Cheviot Centre on Padgepool Place (page 186), at the far end of High Street.

Every August Bank Holiday Monday sees the **Glendale Show** (⬧ glendaleshow.com) in farmland south of Wooler. It's one of the largest country shows in Northumberland with sheep and cattle competitions, musicians, local food producers, vintage vehicle enthusiasts and plenty of entertainment to make for a good family day out.

To reach the start of some very fine **hill walks** (particularly Harthope and College valleys), you need to venture several miles out of Wooler, but do not overlook the countryside closer to the town. **Wooler Common** and **Humbleton Burn** are within a mile of the town centre (signposted from Ramsey's Lane) and are ideal places for a short family walk or picnic. A longer hike could encompass **Humbleton Hill** and its Iron Age hillfort (for tremendous views). **Happy Valley** (two miles from Wooler; page 202) is another delightful spot with a well-worn woodland trail by a merry little river. Waterfall lovers (and wild swimmers) should seek out **Carey Burn Linn** (♀ NT976250) not marked on OS maps, a mile from its namesake bridge, found on the road through Harthope Valley.

Ad Gefrin museum & whisky distillery

South Rd, Wooler, just off the main A697 ✆ 01668 281554 ☺ daily ♿

'Reawakening Northumbria's Golden Age' on the edge of Wooler is this important **museum** with a shop, restaurant and distillery. The eye-catching buildings are crafted to a design based on the timber royal court that once stood not far from here (page 192). Interactive and visual displays narrate the national significance of the Northumbrian Saxon court during a period of intense religious, artistic and cultural growth. Historical weaponry, jewellery, stonework and other artefacts help enrich this story. A highlight is the Castle Eden Claw Beaker – one of the best-preserved Anglo-Saxon glass artefacts in Britain.

An adjoining building houses a large **whisky distillery** open for (tasting) **tours**. Visitors learn all about the process involved in producing Northumberland's only single-malt whisky. Book tours online (⌂ adgefrin.co.uk/distillery) or by calling the number above.

For many, however, Ad Gefrin is simply a very enjoyable space to meet for coffee or lunch, with an outdoor seating area and seasonal Anglo-Saxon events with actors in costume and live music. The smart **restaurant** offers one of the best dining experiences in Wooler (see below).

¶¶ FOOD & DRINK

Local food shops are plentiful along Wooler's high street and include a butchery, bakery, Co-op store and a scattering of tea rooms selling sandwiches, scones and coffees.

Ad Gefrin South Rd, just off the main A697 ✆ 01668 281554 ☺ daily ♿. Background Northumbrian bagpipe music sets the tone for this smart bistro on the edge of Wooler, housed in a modern heritage centre with a whisky distillery (see above). The bright modern dining area with high ceilings, wooden slatted walls and outdoor seating is a highly appealing choice for lunch with table service or casual drinking at the bar. The day starts with a simple brunch menu (served 10.00–noon Thu–Sun) of filled breakfast rolls, scones and Pilgrim's coffees from Lindisfarne. For lunch, it's gourmet burgers, haddock and chips, risotto, hot sandwiches or light bites (soup, quiches, salads). Book Sunday roasts and afternoon teas in advance.

The Good Life Shop High St ✆ 01668 281700. Glass jars of herbs, seeds and nuts line the shelves of this health food deli and shop which also sells cheeses from local Doddington Farm, ham, olives, bread, biscuits etc. It smells of good things inside and the chatty Scottish owner will guide you through all the best Northumbrian produce on display.

Grinders Coffee Shop High St ✆ 01668 283762 ◷ closed Tue ♿. Grinders stands out for its cakes (freshly made; always something different) and substantial lunches: a beef brisket served with smoked cheese on sauerkraut and rocket; venison burger; haggis and melted cheese on chips; pan haggerty (a Northumbrian potato and onion-based pie). It's not cheap, I'll admit, but the portions and quality of the food are very good.

Milan Restaurant High St ✆ 01668 283692 ♿. Great modern Italian set back off the High Street (reached via the arch by the Black Bull) serving bowls of pasta, plus pizzas and a few seafood and meat dishes including Glendale chicken (stuffed with black pudding). Book at least a day or two in advance for tables on weekend evenings.

2 KIRKNEWTON

The hamlet of **Kirknewton** stands at the head of College Valley and is noted for its very interesting church, dating from the 13th century. Externally, **St Gregory's** looks Victorian and, indeed, it was mostly rebuilt in the latter half of the 19th century. However, its tunnel-vault chancel is very old (likely 13th century) and it houses a 900-year-old stone relief of the Adoration of the Magi mounted into the chancel arch.

Several paces west of the tower is the gravestone of Josephine Butler (1828–1906), a social reformer and feminist who devoted herself to many causes including the education of women and the rights of sex workers.

Yeavering Bell & Ad Gefrin archaeological site

Paulinus at a certain time coming with the king and queen [at] the royal country-seat, which is called Adgefrin, stayed there with them thirty-six days, fully occupied in catechising and baptising; during which days, from morning till night, he did nothing else but instruct the people resorting from all villages and places, in Christ's saving word; and when instructed, he washed them with the water of absolution in the river Glen, which is close by.

Ecclesiastical History of the English Nation, Bede AD731

Northumberland's largest **Iron Age hillfort, Yeavering Bell** (south side of the B6351 between Akeld & Kirknewton ♥ NT928293), pronounced 'Yevering', crowns a double-peaked conical hill over 1,000ft high, close to the hamlet of Kirknewton. Apart from a superb view across the Cheviot tops in one direction and to the North Sea in the other, a scattering of rocks indicates where over 100 roundhouses used to stand within the protective walls of the huge stone rampart. This flattened perimeter wall would have once stood up to 8ft tall.

A well-trodden **walk** to Yeavering Bell begins between Kirknewton and Ad Gefrin archaeological site (just off the B6351). Follow a paved track signed for 'Torleehouse' for a mile before picking up St Cuthbert's Way, climbing away from Kirknewton. After a quarter of a mile, a signpost points to the summit of Yeavering Bell. To vary the return, take the permissive path descending off the northern slope of the hill back to the road. Incidentally, the old name of Yeavering is derived from the Welsh for goat ('gafr'), which is nice because the primitive breed still roams Yeavering Bell to this day and you may well see **wild Cheviot goats** on this hike. I've seen them in the fields by the roadside not far from Ad Gefrin.

"A scattering of rocks indicates where over 100 roundhouses used to stand within the protective walls of the huge stone rampart."

In open grassland below Yeavering Bell, a mile east of Kirknewton on the B6351, a prominent stone monument by a lay-by will catch your eye. Remarkable historical events were staged hereabouts 1,300 years ago when great timber halls and buildings fit for the kings and queens of Northumbria formed the centrepiece of the Anglo-Saxon summer royal palace, **Ad Gefrin**. It was here that Bishop Paulinus performed some of the earliest conversions to Christianity in the Kingdom of Northumbria over a period of 36 days, an account of which was recorded by Bede (see quote opposite). The site was discovered in 1949 and excavated over the following few decades. Today, the area is turfed over and there's not a lot to see but the significance of the Saxon court is brought to life at the modern **Ad Gefrin museum** (page 191) in Wooler.

3 COLLEGE VALLEY

Reached from Westnewton (near Kirknewton on the B6351); vehicle access through the valley is limited to 12 permits a day, issued by College Valley Estates for £10 per car on a first-

WILD CHEVIOT GOATS

Scarce and feral, the shaggy, long-horned goats in the Cheviots are descendants of the earliest primitive goats that were domesticated over thousands of years successively from the time of Neolithic farmers onwards. Though not as timid as you might imagine, they still have a wariness that is to be expected of a breed that has roamed these hills for a very long time. There's no mistaking the animals with their multi-coloured fleeces and wild look. Male goats are particularly conspicuous with horns up to 3ft in length.

Four herds inhabit Northumberland National Park: at **Kielderhead NNR**, **Upper Coquetdale**, and **Yeavering Bell** and **Newton Tors** near College Valley. Each herd is directed to the best grazing grounds by an old nanny who knows the hills well.

come, first-served basis. Book online at college-valley.co.uk. Without a permit, you'll need to leave your car in the parking area at Hethpool.

This six-mile-long glacial valley is the most isolated of all the major valleys in the Cheviot range. Its seclusion is helped by the control of cars entering the valley. Sheep rule this road.

The paved track from the hamlet of Hethpool makes for a wonderfully scenic cycle ride or drive through the valley, which is blocked at the southern end by a wall of cloud-nudging summits protecting the frontier with Scotland. You'll pass the odd plantation woodland and thick patch of gorse, a few old shepherds' houses – now mostly converted into holiday cottages – a bunkhouse (see below), sheep everywhere, and an isolated village hall about halfway through the valley.

Cuddystone Hall is a plain 1960s building with a nice big bell. It's occasionally the scene of a night of dancing and celebration, this being the most remote place to legally tie the knot in Northumberland – if not England. Outside the hall is a **memorial** to the World War II airmen who died when their planes crashed into surrounding hills. If you hike to any of the crash sites indicated on the memorial, you'll find metal debris still lying in situ.

Mounthooly Bunkhouse (college-valley.co.uk/accommodation/bunk-house), at the southern end of the valley, occupies a prime spot for exploring some of the most impressive hills and crags in the Cheviot range, including the **Hen Hole** (page 196) with its trio of waterfalls

◄ **1** Looking down over Wooler. **2** Walking through College Valley. **3** A demonstration at Ad Gefrin museum. **4** Yeavering Bell is Northumberland's largest Iron Age hillfort.

known as the **Three Sisters** (page 197), **Bizzle Crags**, a magnet for serious climbers owing to its many rock buttresses, and the awesome whale-back **Schil**, which offers what Alfred Wainwright described as an 'exquisite view' of the valley. Another favourite aspect is from **Auchope Cairn**, looking across to Scotland in one direction and down through the Hen Hole and the head of the valley in the other.

Hen Hole

> Hen Hole is so deep and narrow that sunshine never enters it, and often at midsummer there is still a small patch of snow – called the Snow Egg... [T]here is a tradition of a party of huntsmen being led to their doom here by mysterious music.
>
> Arthur Mee, *The King's England: Northumberland*, 1952

This rocky, ice-sculpted chasm hides around the corner at the head of College Valley, luring walkers into its deep cleft. It's well known to ravens, peregrine falcons and, in years gone by, golden eagles.

The demanding 4½-mile **hike** to the top of The Cheviot via the Hen Hole (see Walk 2 mapped on page 201) from the head of the valley at Mounthooly criss-crosses College Burn the whole way to **Auchope Cairn** and requires hands and feet at times but is fairly easy to navigate. The burn splashes from ledge to ledge for 1,500ft until it reaches the valley floor, and at one point forms a trio of small waterfalls called

SHEILA & THE FLYING FORTRESS

A snowstorm was battering the Cheviots on 14 December 1944 when nine US airmen were flying back to their base following an aborted bombing raid. Flying low over the hills to avoid the plane icing up, they crashed into the north slope of the Cheviot (West Hill) near Braydon Crag. Two of the airmen were killed instantly but three managed to make their way to Mounthooly – now the bunkhouse at the head of College Valley.

Shepherds John Dagg and Frank Moscrop heard the plane come down and managed to locate the survivors huddled together in a peat gully with the assistance of John's Border Collie, Sheila.

The two shepherds each received a British Empire Medal while Sheila was awarded the animal equivalent of the Victoria Cross, the Dickin Medal, the first ever civilian dog to receive the award.

The dying wish of the pilot of the B-17, who passed away in 2005 at his home in Fort Lauderdale, was that his ashes be scattered at the site of the plane crash where fragments of the wreckage still lie. The request was fulfilled by relatives later that year.

the **Three Sisters** where hardy children (my kids at least) strip off and dabble in the icy water.

From the falls, take the less severe route round the side of Hen Hole to meet with the Pennine Way (and Scotland over the fence) on the ridge line. It's a straightforward hike to the summit of **The Cheviot** via **Auchope Cairn**, which offers a terrifying view down Hen Hole's funnel. When I last walked this route one hot June day, my children made a snowman at the top. It seems the 'Snow Egg' (see opposite) is not a myth (the phantom musical notes said to haunt the Hen Hole escaped us, however).

To vary the return to Mounthooly, retrace your path to the top of Hen Hole and continue on the Pennine Way via a mountain refuge and then across **The Schil** before descending to the valley floor via woodland. The round hike is 11 miles.

An even **longer walk** that makes for a strenuous and fulfilling hike follows an unclear path off the north side of The Cheviot, descending to the hamlet of **Goldscleugh** then by lane with the **Lambden Burn** for company to **Dunsdale cottage**. The final few miles to Mounthooly are via the side of a hill and through woodland.

Hethpool

Hethpool is an eye-catching hamlet at the entrance to College Valley with a country house and two pairs of Arts and Crafts cottages built in the early 20th century.

Behind Hethpool House is a stand of mature oaks (no public access) known as the **Collingwood Oaks**, which are named after Admiral Collingwood (of the Battle of Trafalgar fame) who is said to have pushed acorns into the ground believing the trees would supply timber for the battleships of the future. Little did he know that metal would replace wood by the time his oaks matured. To mark the bicentenary of his death in 1810, a new oak woodland was planted near the road on the approach into Hethpool.

On the first Sunday in August you may see a small crowd gathering hereabouts for the annual **College Valley Show**, which features terrier racing, sheepdog trials and folk music.

Wanderings from Hethpool

Stunning views of College Valley await the wanderer setting foot from Hethpool. Of particular interest are the hillfort trails, of which there are quite a few around the entrance to the valley, including to **Yeavering Bell** (page 192) and the equally strenuous climb to the top of **Great Hetha**, noted for its hillfort, as well as a stupendous view of the tops of many peaks. Also consider following **St Cuthbert's Way** along Elsdon Burn to **Ring Chesters** – another fort reached after a steep ascent. Less strenuous is the short circuit to **Hethpool Linn** (see below).

* * *

🚶 A FAMILY WALK TO HETHPOOL LINN

❄ OS Explorer map OL16; start: Hethpool ♥ NT895282; 1½ miles; easy; waterproof boots a must

Hethpool's waterfall is not a true cascade, but the rushing College Burn pounding through a rocky chasm in a wooded glen is camera-pleasing stuff nonetheless, and this walk makes a very pleasant hour-long diversion.

Opposite **Hethpool's cottages**, by a sharp bend in the road, follow a 'St Cuthbert's Way' (SCW) sign over a cattle grid and down the gravel track. Cross the river and turn immediately left, following the SCW sign through gorse. A stony track leads uphill and through a farm gate. Take in the view of White Hill behind Hethpool, the rippled turf revealing medieval agricultural terraces, and the facing Collingwood oak woodland (page 197) clothing a steep hillside.

Go through another farm gate and follow the marshy track through a young mixed **woodland**. In 500yds, bear left following the SCW marker then a few paces later go through a gate, again following the SCW sign. Ignore the next SCW sign and instead continue on a descending footpath to the river.

Glimpsed between the boughs of old oaks, the burn pools beneath the walls of the **gorge**, sprouting with ferns, mosses and gorse. Cross the stile. From the footbridge over the gorge, the river surges through the chasm, all white water and roar.

On crossing the bridge, follow the path uphill for about 30yds, ignoring the track on your right.

You'll come to a paddock; strike off left and cross a plank footbridge. Go through a gate a short way ahead and turn immediately right then left following the fenceline. A couple of hundred yards ahead, go over the stile and turn right for Hethpool's cottages.

* * *

1 The pretty hamlet of Hethpool at the entrance to College Valley. **2 & 5** Cotton grass and sundew are just some of the plants that thrive in this environment. **3** Harthorpe Valley and burn with gorse flowers in full bloom. **4** The walk to Hethpool Linn is family friendly. ▶

4 HARTHOPE VALLEY

Behold a letter from the mountains, for I am very snugly settled here, in a farmer's house, about six miles from Wooler, in the very centre of the Cheviot Hills, in one of the wildest and most romantic situations ... All the day we shoot, fish, walk, and ride; dine and sup upon fish struggling from the stream, and the most delicious heath-fed mutton, barn-door fowls, poys, milkcheese, etc.
Sir Walter Scott in a letter to his friend, 26 August 1791

Scott penned the above letter from the remote farmstead at **Langleeford** by Harthope Burn that is regularly passed today by walkers exploring this glacial valley. Three of the highest peaks in the Cheviot range are within reach of the day hiker from here: The Cheviot, Hedgehope Hill and Comb Fell. Even those cycling along the valley bottom or pottering under trees by the river will find Harthope Valley as enchanting as Scott did over 200 years ago, with river birds and trout in abundance, sheep and grouse on the slopes and small waterfalls here and there.

Harthope Burn is wooded for much of its course and plenty of grassy areas invite a picnic and paddle. Those who can tolerate the cold waters will find bathing holes every so often, including the magical **Harthope Linn** (♥ NT927203), a secluded plunge pool passed en route to The Cheviot, where the brave – having made it down the steep slopes to the water – shower under a small fall overhung with mountain shrubs, trees and ferns.

Walks in Harthope Valley are plentiful and include the hike from Langleeford to Harthope Linn described opposite. Continuing beyond the waterfall is the most direct hike to **The Cheviot** (outlined on page 202). Another popular route is to **Hedgehope Hill** (the perfectly rounded massif dominating all the other hills on the approach through the valley), passing the impressive **Housey Crags** (a destination in themselves) from where there are great views of all the major summits peering down through the valley.

The Cheviot

There is something quite captivating about The Cheviot, partly because of its height (at 2,674ft, it is the highest mountain in Northumberland) and partly because it is located right in the middle of the Cheviot range with beautiful valleys and many high summits nearby. And, I suppose, there is a certain draw about a brooding hill that holds on to its cap of snow into summer. When The Cheviot is not sulking under a swirling smoke-machine-like fog, you can see all the mountain ranges from the Lake District to the Lothians. But, the best views are from the approach and not the summit itself which is pretty underwhelming: a table-flat squelchy quagmire only passable because of the solid Pennine Way stone slabs.

Northeast of the highest point lie the fragmentary remains of a **B-17 bomber** that crashed into the mountain during World War II (page 196).

Some of the most popular **hiking routes** to the top are through College Valley and around the Hen Hole (page 196) or from Harthope Valley via Hedgehope Hill and Comb Fell, or by following Harthope Burn upriver from Langleeford, the route described below.

* * *

🚶 TOP OF THE CHEVIOT VIA HARTHOPE VALLEY

❄ OS Explorer map OL16; start: Langleeford, Harthope Valley 📍 NT949220; 8½ miles; moderate. Rough car park ½ mile downriver from Langleeford farm

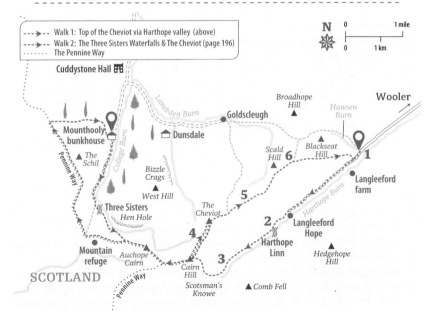

This is a stunning, classic Cheviot hike to the summit of the highest peak in Northumberland with tremendous hilltop and valley views the entire way (and a waterfall on the outward leg). Make sure you take a map, warm outdoor clothing (at any time of the year) and a compass in case a fog rolls in.

1 From the parking area in a grassy area by the river, walk half a mile upriver to **Langleeford farm**. Go through the gate (ignore the footbridge over the burn) and follow the stoney track uphill with the river on your left. After a mile, the trail swings round the isolated farmstead, **Langleeford Hope**, and through a damp copse on a raised boardwalk. With the farm behind you, ascend across open ground on a less distinct path for half a mile.

2 **Harthope Linn's spout** plunges into a dark pool not far from the path but it can be difficult to find in the summer when the vegetation is at full height. From the waterfall, continue uphill for a couple of miles (though it feels much further because of the gradient), picking your way along the winding path, which criss-crosses the burn. As you climb, the stream bubbles in peaty hollows as it becomes narrower and quieter, until Harthope Burn disappears altogether.

3 On meeting a fence line at **Scotsman's Knowe**, a fingerpost points to **Cairn Hill**, the top of which is reached after a killer 500yd climb. Enjoy a tremendous view looking back down the valley of rounded slopes merging into each other, the North Sea in the distance.

4 Cross the stile and turn right on the Pennine Way, following the famous stone slab path across the boggy massif of **The Cheviot** for three-quarters of a mile. Its summit is marked by a prominent trig point at 2,674ft.

5 Continue on the flagstone path, crossing a ladder stile and descending off The Cheviot along a well-trodden track following a fence line on your left for 1½ miles to the top of **Scald Hill**, The Cheviot's shoulder.

6 Walk downhill off the plateau of Scald Hill, keeping close to the fence line for another 500yds, then, just before the fence bends left, strike off right (♀ NT933221) following a line of grouse butts on a clear downhill track back to the valley basin. Turn left on the road for the 500yd walk back to the car park.

* * *

5 HAPPY VALLEY

Some two miles south of Wooler; there are two rough parking areas at either end of the valley: Carey Burn Bridge & Coldgate Mill (reached by following Cheviot St from Wooler town centre to a ford); Middleton Hall has an official parking area, but you'll need to make your way on foot to the river.

Is Happy Valley as idyllic as it sounds? In an area with so many wooded glens and jazzy burns, Happy Valley has a lot of competition, but it is a gem and easy to reach from Wooler. It's not on the scale of Harthope Valley (a continuation of Happy Valley) or Breamish Valley, but it has its own charms and can be walked in under an hour.

From Coldgate Mill, a **footpath** follows **Coldgate Water** upriver through woodland for a mile or so before the scenery opens into rough grazing pastures with gorse bushes and shrubs. Look out for hares. The final stretch to the junction with **Harthope Burn** is picturesque, with heavily wooded slopes rising from the valley bottom and glimpses of the river, which flows leisurely round shingle banks and boulders – and appears at its happiest.

6 BREAMISH VALLEY

One of the big three valleys in the English Cheviots, Breamish Valley (sometimes known as Ingram Valley) is quite different from the U-shaped Harthope and College valleys in that its shallow river takes a more meandering route through the hills on its way east. For that reason it doesn't have quite the same tunnel views, but visitors will instead feel embraced in an amphitheatre of hills.

A major draw are the hillforts and Linhope's **waterfall** (page 206), both of which are accessed from a single-track road running through the valley. You can drive as far as Hartside; thereafter the road to Linhope is just for residents. On the way there are plenty of places to pull over and place a picnic rug by the **River Breamish**. On warm days, families paddle in the shallow water, and children throw stones from shingly banks.

"It doesn't have quite the same tunnel views, but visitors will instead feel embraced in an amphitheatre of hills."

A favourite location is **Bulbys Wood car park** (a mile or so upriver from Ingram) where the river runs wide, offering hours of water play (and a rope swing on my last visit). There are toilets here, places to picnic and a little information hut.

As you hike or take the car for a walk through the valley, note the ancient and medieval cultivation terraces on many slopes. This whole area has been farmed for thousands of years; the evidence of which is all about you: **Bronze Age burial cairns**, abandoned medieval villages and an impressive concentration of **hillforts**, built some 2,300 years ago. The most prominent examples are at Wether Hill and Brough Law (page 204) near Ingram.

A network of Hillfort Trails developed by the national park authority direct you to many of these archaeological sites but if you can't walk, a local initiative, the **Ingram Valley Farm Safari** (✆ 07379 651819 🖱 ingramvalley.co.uk/ingram-valley-safari) will take you on a three-hour off-road adventure with a local guide to see the hillforts, wildlife and landscapes of the area.

An **archaeological display** (page 207) next door to the Ingram café provides a good overview of the human history of the valley and a map outlining the above-mentioned trails.

✳ ✳ ✳

🚶 INGRAM HILLFORTS TRAIL

✳ OS Explorer map OL16; start: Bulby's Wood car park ♥ NU007163; 2½ miles; easy

This short, family-friendly walk to one of the most impressive Iron Age hillforts in Northumberland offers fabulous views through Breamish Valley. The return passes ancient cultivation terraces and the farming landscape of today where you may see the local shepherd rounding up sheep.

For the most part, this route is clearly marked with 'Hillfort Trail' signs but a map is helpful as there are extensions of this walk and arrows pointing in multiple directions at times.

1 Opposite **Bulbys Wood car park** (half a mile west of Ingram) a fingerpost points up a steep permissive path to Brough Law and to the most impressive ancient settlement in the valley. **Brough Law hillfort** is a huge rampart of loose tumbledown rocks about 70yds in diameter that would have enclosed timber roundhouses 2,300 years ago. With skylarks overhead in spring and far-reaching views, this is a wonderfully peaceful spot – and a good place to catch your breath.

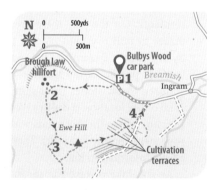

2 Retrace your footsteps to the path and turn right. A 'Hillforts Trail' marker post ahead guides you across the wide grassy path over the plateau of **Ewe Hill** for half a mile (ignore a fork in the path).

---

1 Aerial view of Brough Law hillfort in Breamish Valley. **2** Competitors in Powburn Country Show. **3** Linhope Spout, Breamish Valley. ▶

BLUE LEMON FILMS

Tel: 016 8 217
www.a cott.c

LEN SMITH

COXY58/S

3 At the next fork, turn left and climb over the brow of the hill in front. In 500yds or so, bear left, continuing your descent off the hillside on a grassy path. Clearly defined **cultivation terraces** line the hillsides hereabouts.

4 Join a wide stony vehicle track and continue downhill for a few hundred yards to meet with the main road. Turn left and continue for a quarter of a mile to return to the car park. Look back at the hillside to see the agricultural terraces.

✳ ✳ ✳

Linhope Spout waterfall

Tucked below conical Ritto Hill and surrounded by some hefty summits, the secluded hamlet of **Linhope** hides under trees by the confluence of the River Breamish and Linhope Burn. The **walk** to the waterfall, a mile or so from Linhope, is straightforward with a short ascent and descent at either end but note that there is no public parking at Linhope (Hartside, three-quarters of a mile away, is the last official place to park).

From **Linhope**, cross the burn and take the farm track uphill, tracing the side of a stand of conifers and passing through a gate. Keep the trees and fenceline on your right; fingerposts will steer you on the right track. Once in open grassland, bear right following a descending track into a wooded ravine. Simply follow the water upriver to **Linhope Spout**, which plunges 60ft through a secluded rock cleft into a dark pool. In freezing conditions, icicles the size of swords hang from the rocks. In summer, with midge repellent at the ready, strip off for an invigorating shower. Rocky steps by the side of the fall lead to the top for an alternative view. Tramp across the hillside and rejoin the farm track for the return to Linhope.

7 INGRAM

This peaceful hamlet at the foot of the valley is a useful starting point for exploring the surrounding hills. A **café** (see opposite) and an **archaeological exhibition** are housed in the old school, the latter featuring displays chronicling the history of farming and settlement in the valley over the last several thousand years, as well as earthenware discovered during digs at nearby Iron Age hillforts. Also note the Neolithic ring-marked stone at the entrance to the building. A **gift shop** annexed to the café showcases original artworks and local crafts, including blankets and handmade soaps and creams.

Ingram's **church** dates in part to the early Norman period. The tower and rounded tower arch hold some of its oldest masonry. To the left of the altar, a curious stone carving of some legs features the diminutive figures of monks. In the churchyard, look out for a very old headstone only a few feet high featuring a man and woman holding hands, and a couple of headstones with skulls and crossbones near the porch door.

Ingram and nearby Powburn each put on **country shows** in the summer. **Ingram's** (second Saturday in September) is more intimate with family-oriented events, as well as the usual sheepdog trials and horticultural displays. The **Powburn Show** (⊘ powburnshow.com; first Sat in Aug) features Cumberland and Westmorland wrestling, food and craft stalls, pony jumping, livestock displays and so on.

Not far from the entrance to the valley, by the side of the A697, is a wonderful affordable antiques emporium. There's quite a lot to rummage through at the **Hedgeley Antique Centre** (Hedgeley Service Station, A697, Powburn ⊘ 01665 578142 ⊙ daily ⅅ but tight spaces inside) and some corners are better than others, but you'll generally find rustic wooden furniture (church pews, trunks, chests of drawers – that kind of thing), as well as linen, antique prints, secondhand books, china and oddments.

FOOD & DRINK

The nearest place for a decent evening meal is Eglingham's **Tankerville Arms** (page 181).

Ingram Café Breamish Valley NE66 4LT ⊘ 01665 578100 ⊙ daily ⅅ 🐾. Serves coffees (using beans roasted locally) and a small selection of light lunches (soup and sourdough, sandwiches etc) in a modern café with garden tables to the rear. The owner bakes all her own cakes and scones.

ROTHBURY & THE SIMONSIDE HILLS

Descending into Rothbury from Northumberland's arc of sandstone hills (roughly the area between the A697 and A1), road users dip in and out of a string of villages, historic houses and archeological sites set in outstanding countryside.

To the south of **Rothbury** – a prosperous town on the eastern edge of the national park with an esteemed National Trust house –

grasslands lie sheet-flat to the **River Coquet**, which has carved a heavily ribboned course through the low-lying meadows under the gaze of the **Simonside Hills**. East of Rothbury the river curls around the 12th-century **Brinkburn Priory** before continuing on its journey to the sea at Warkworth. For the upper reaches of the Coquet ('Upper Coquetdale'), see page 219.

8 WHITTINGHAM

Are you going to Whittingham Fair?
Parsley, sage, rosemary and thyme.
Remember me to one who lives there,
For once she was a true love of mine.

Wandering north of Thropton (which is west of Rothbury) on quiet back lanes, you may chance upon this peaceful village on the edge of the national park. There's a traditional **country show** held on the third Saturday in August, which was immortalised in the above ballad – at least it was until Simon and Garfunkel sang the now more famous *Scarborough Fair* version.

Whittingham's well-kept stone houses line either side of a green bank studded with trees. At the southern end of the village is a fetching **memorial fountain** dedicated to a local earl who stands on a plinth looking rather downbeat with his faithful Border Collie.

Whittingham Tower, near the centre, is an impressive 14th-century fortified house constructed with huge sandstone blocks that was remodelled somewhat in the 19th century. Now a family home, it was once a refuge for villagers during the centuries of cross-border fighting before it became an almshouse ('for the use and benefit of the deserving poor,' notes the inscription above the doorway).

Following the River Aln westwards to Little Ryle, you'll come to **St Bartholomew's Church** by the side of the road. The interior is notable for its surviving Early English architecture, but the most remarkable feature of the building is its tower, the lower part of which is Saxon.

9 EDLINGHAM

'Eadwulfingham' to give the hamlet its Anglo-Saxon name, lies equidistant between Rothbury and Alnwick (not to be confused with Eglingham further north) in outstanding countryside. It's not so much the hilltop hamlet that is of interest; more its distinctive church and castle that are hidden somewhat from view at the end of a lane (reached from the B6341).

The stern-looking 14th-century tower of **St John the Baptist Church** provides a visual reminder of the lawlessness that pervaded the Northumberland countryside during medieval times. Invasions from the north were not uncommon and villagers and the priest may well have sheltered in the defensive-looking tower, which lacks a belfry (you might as well open the door to attackers) and has slits instead of windows. The earliest masonry visible is Norman, seen in the south porch doorway (and its barrel-vaulted ceiling), nave and chancel arch.

Edlingham Castle stands in a striking position on a hillside close to the church with ragged moors and the **viaduct** of the defunct Alnwick–Cornhill railway as its backdrop. All that remains of the mid 12th-century building, which once had a moat and barbican, are its foundations, a few walls and part of its defensive tower, built in 1340. A severe chasm has formed in one of the walls, giving the structure a dramatic profile.

10 CRAGSIDE

Rothbury NE65 7PX ✆ 01669 620333 ◷ house: end Feb–early Nov & Dec daily; gardens, woodland & tea room: year-round daily ♿ café but limited access to the house & paths 🐾 outdoors & café; National Trust

> The electric light has been introduced into the house by the distinguished owner, who has utilised the power of a neighbouring burn to work the generating machine ... Words are inadequate to describe the wonderful transformation which Lord Armstrong has made on the barren hillside as it existed prior to 1863. Every natural advantage has been utilised by the great magician.
> W W Tomlinson, *Comprehensive Guide to Northumberland*, 1888

Tyneside industrialist, innovator and 'great magician' William Armstrong was ahead of his time when he began devising ingenious electrical gadgets for his 19th-century country house on the outskirts of Rothbury. Cragside lays claim to being the first private house in the world to be lit by hydro-electricity. Water generated the electricity that lit Joseph Swan's novel filament lightbulbs; electrically powered gongs announcing dinner, buzzers to call servants, and a fire alarm system were to follow. There's even a passenger lift for workers to transport coal through the house and an automatic meat spit in the kitchen.

Externally, Cragside is part Gothic, part Tudor with many gables, tall chimney stacks, high-pitched roofs and timber additions. When viewed through a parting in the trees from the Debdon Burn, the house looks majestic crowded by so many lean conifers and reaches skywards like a Bavarian castle.

Armstrong (and his house) was famous in his lifetime and he hosted many dignitaries at Cragside, including the Prince of Wales and his family in August 1884 who came to inspect the intriguing new technologies. The **Drawing Room** was completed just in time for the royal visit. It's the grandest room in the house with a huge intricately carved marble fireplace, ornate plasterwork and a number of important paintings including a Turner watercolour. Reporting on the royal visit the *Newcastle Daily Journal* had this to say: 'The château itself was a blaze of light. From every window the bright rays of the electric lamps shone with the purest radiance.'

The rest of the house is rich in Arts and Crafts detailing, including William Morris stained glass and wallpapers, and extensive oak furnishings. Some highlights include the **kitchen** with its lift and huge range, the **Turkish baths** (especially the fine blue tile work in one plunge pool), and, of course, the **library** which was the first domestic room in the world to be lit with Swan's lightbulbs.

The grounds

Built into the hillside, Cragside makes use of the sandstone and varying heights to create romantic vistas. The wider landscape is very much part of its appeal and there are no walls shutting out the moors, burns and crags. The lakes are manmade, however, and all the Scots pines, firs, redwoods, azaleas and rhododendrons were planted by Armstrong – well, technically by some 150 gardeners. They are said to have dug in seven million trees and bushes.

Narrow paths below the house wind through heathers and alpine plants and past a couple of cascades in the largest sandstone **rock garden** in Europe. A slender 1870s **footbridge** with elegant ironwork reaches across the Debdon Burn at some height, offering a superb view of the mansion. A short walk leads to more **formal gardens** where hardy and tender plants from around the world bring an unexpected vibrant colour palate to the otherwise natural tones seen elsewhere. The beautiful **glasshouse** used for cultivating fruits must be seen. Note the turntables under each earthenware pot that enabled the fruits of fig, orange, grapefruit and apricot trees to evenly ripen (with the aid of an underground heating system).

Armstrong's Victorian enthusiasm for efficiency, order and punctuality is not just reflected inside the house. The Gothic **clock tower** near the formal gardens helped regulate the hours of estate workers – all 300 of them at one time. It has two mechanisms: one to operate the clock and the other to chime a bell that sounded at meal times and at the start and end of every working day.

Within the wider grounds with its 40 miles of garden and woodland footpaths, a scenic **carriage drive** circumnavigates the whole estate via a couple of lakes.

At **Tumbleton Lake** by the visitor centre, there's a good **tea room** in a courtyard with all the usual National Trust offerings: scones, sandwiches and a handful of hot dishes made with seasonal produce. Sought-after picnic tables overlook the peaceful lagoon.

11 BRINKBURN PRIORY

Near Longframlington (5 miles east of Rothbury) NE65 8AR 𝒟 01665 570628 ☉ Easter–early Nov Wed–Sun 🦽 🐾 English Heritage

Standing in a hollow at the bottom of a wooded track, the Norman doorway to the church appears through a parting in the trees offering an enchanting first glimpse of this wondrous **priory**. Built in the 12th century, and once inhabited by Augustinian monks, Brinkburn stands today as one of the most intact priories of its age in England since restoration in the 19th century. Its isolated location, completely hidden from view in a loop of the River Coquet, only adds to the sense of awe. This is particularly so late in the afternoon when sunlight pours through the stained-glass windows of the church – cathedral-like in its proportions – enhancing the colour and swirling patterns in the sandstone. You can hear the river (inhabited by otters) and thrushes singing outside, but every afternoon on the third Sunday of the month in summer, local choirs, string quartets, Northumbrian smallpipes players – and other groups – fill the priory with music. A **summer music concert** here is not to be missed (booking usually not required).

Architecturally, Brinkburn is celebrated for its Transitional style that blends Norman and Early English and dates from the end of the 12th century to the beginning of the 13th. A good example is the

aforementioned entrance seen on the approach, which shows chevron detailing typical of the Norman style, and above, an arcade of three Gothic arches of the Early English style.

Inside the **church** – the only intact building in the monastic complex and which continued in use as the parish church after the Dissolution of the Monasteries under King Henry VIII – there are no screens or obstructions to distract from the elegant tiers of lancet windows and lofty pointed arches. The 150-year-old **organ** was commissioned and donated by the Armstrongs of nearby Cragside (page 209).

Outside are a few remains of priory buildings, but mostly your attention will be drawn to the **manor house**, which was built out of the ruined monastic buildings and reconstructed in the 19th century. Its interior has been stripped out, but a number of features remain partially intact including some decorative plasterwork and the elegant floor-to-ceiling doors of the ballroom that open into the garden. Its very emptiness has a deeply evocative quality and English Heritage have put the spaces to good use in recent years to house art exhibitions.

¶¶ FOOD & DRINK

The Anglers Arms Weldon Bridge NE65 8AX ✆ 01665 570271 ♿ but narrow doorway 🐾. Nestled in a secluded spot by the River Coquet, this traditional 18th-century free house (with rooms upstairs) is a lovely choice for a weekend lunch on a warm day, with outdoor tables on a sunny terrace and in the beer garden (next to a large children's play area). Inside, the traditional interior is full of the quirks and trinkets of an old English country inn. Carnivores are well catered for and you'll find various cuts of meat on the menu, a fair few fish dishes and all the usual pub favourites. Sunday lunches come recommended. Take-away fish and chips for two is good value for £25.

St Oswald's Way passes the inn, leading even casual walkers to the wooded banks of the River Coquet. Early morning hikers, take note of the breakfast menu, which includes Craster Kippers.

12 ROTHBURY

Forested hills to the north and east shelter the capital of Coquetdale from the boisterous winds that punish the fell tops. To the south, beyond

◀ **1** Views of the Cheviot Hills from Lordenshaws hillfort. **2** Rothbury on the River Coquet. **3** Brinkburn Priory. **4** The stern-looking 14th-century tower of St John the Baptist Church in Edlingham. **5** Cragside – the first house in the world to be lit by hydro-electricity.

BRIDGES ACROSS THE RIVER COQUET

Three striking multi-arched bridges span the Coquet from Rothbury to just beyond Brinkburn Priory. The oldest is in **Rothbury** town centre, parts of which are thought to be 15th century. East of Brinkburn, the mid 19th-century **Pauperhaugh Bridge** crosses the Coquet in five graceful arches. This is a good bridge from which to watch trout and salmon leaping over the rapids below in the autumn. Look out for goosanders and dippers from here to **Weldon Bridge** – the last crossing in the trio – which is best viewed from the riverside path. It dates to 1760 and has the added attraction of an inn (the Anglers Arms, page 213). Follow St Oswald's Way along the south side of the river to gain the best views of Rothbury's bridges and riverside.

the River Coquet, green vales slope gently upwards until they come to an abrupt halt by the foot of the Simonside Hills. You can see why this market town makes an excellent base for walkers.

Rothbury itself is popular with visitors and has a couple of galleries and cafés and a celebrated National Trust house on its doorstep (Cragside, page 209) and its attractive **town centre** holds much visual appeal: two rows of stone townhouses and traditional shops arranged either side of a green bank. A number of businesses go back several generations including a hardware shop and ironmongery established in 1888, and a quaint toy shop that has been in the same family for 100 years. There's an excellent deli (page 217) selling local produce, a bakery, outdoor clothing shop, pharmacy, a scattering of pubs and cafés and a superb butcher. Many rural towns must have once been like this.

All Saints Church is a few paces from the market cross – dedicated to Lord Armstrong of nearby Cragside – on the triangular green, and it is worth visiting for its Anglo-Saxon font alone. The present-day church was largely rebuilt by the Victorians but the chancel contains 13th-century masonry and an astonishing 1,200-year-old rectangular **font pedestal** (the bowl is 17th century) carved with a tiger prowling through forest, and the haunting faces of the apostles looking up to Christ.

Heading west along the High Street is the **Coquetdale Art Gallery** (Front St ✆ 01669 621557 ☉ mid-Mar–mid-Dec Mon–Sat, afternoons Sun) occupying the old court building above the police station. Run by volunteers since the 1970s, the gallery showcases paintings (a few hundred at any one time), woodwork, basketware, jewellery and textiles produced by some 130 regional craft workers and artists. All the stock is highly affordable and there's a huge range of works.

Walks from Rothbury

There are good walks right from the town centre including the steep climb to the **Rothbury Terraces** – a rugged heather-clad hillside above the High Street which offers uninterrupted views of the facing Simonsides. The route starts from the tight alleyway between the Narrow Nick pub and the Co-op store (you'll see the public footpath on Ordnance Survey map 332 and the obvious circuit of the hillside that routes back into Rothbury at the western end of the town).

A gentle, multi-use **riverside path** (&) from one end of Rothbury to the other is accessed from below All Saints Church (in the town centre) or from the western/Thropton end of Rothbury, signed off the B6341 (where there's a car park). Look out for sand martins, herons and kingfishers. At Rothbury's multi-arched sandstone road bridge in the town centre, the riverside path continues downriver for another mile or so on rough ground through historic **Thrum Mill** (now a private dwelling) where the river rushes through a stunning carved gorge.

Two miles south of Rothbury, along **St Oswald's Way**, are the well-known prehistoric rock carvings at **Lordenshaws** (page 218). The views alone are worth the trek here. Keep on the same trail and you'll be into the **Simonside Hills** proper where miles of trails await (the hike to Simonside is a popular route; page 217). It's a bit of a slog to the Simonsides from Rothbury on foot so you might want to drive or get a taxi (page 188) as far as the Lordenshaws or Simonside car parks.

Closer to Rothbury is the National Trust's **Cragside estate** (page 209) with many miles of footpaths for walkers wishing to explore the craggy hillside and forests that form the backdrop to Lord Armstrong's historic house.

¶ FOOD & DRINK

You are never more than a minute's walk from a café, restaurant or pub in Rothbury. Picnickers will find a cluster of local food stores on the High Street, as well as the **Co-op** general store.

For evening meals, no restaurant particularly stands out, though you could try **The Turks Head** (High St ☎ 01669 620434 ☉ daily) for pub meals (a fairly average

TWO SCENIC ROADS

ROTHBURY TO ALNWICK

A high road over the hills to the coast connects two of the most popular market towns in Northumberland. From Rothbury, the B6341 climbs steeply past Cragside and through Debdon Woods before reaching open heather moors. There are several pull-in places along the road from where you can take in the view of the Cheviot Hills. Don't miss Edlingham's church and castle (page 209).

ROTHBURY TO BREAMISH VALLEY

From Rothbury, follow the B6341 for a couple of miles towards Thropton. Just before you enter the village, turn right at the Cross Keys Inn on an undulating road due north through the old-world villages of Whittingham and Glanton to Powburn. All routes climb quite high, offering a tremendous view of the Cheviots rising above a timeless pastoral landscape: field upon field divided by hedgerows, old stone farm buildings, horses in paddocks, hares sprinting across pastures, foraging partridges and so on. This is also a great bike ride. Early mornings are particularly memorable, especially in winter when the Cheviots are covered in snow and the lowlands look silvery green under a covering of frost.

restaurant with a sunny back garden and children's play area). Better still is to head out of town to the **Anglers Arms** (page 213), or the **Three Wheat Heads** at Thropton (see below). I had breakfast at the **Newcastle House Hotel** (Front St ✆ 01669 620334 🐾), with a view of all the comings and goings in the town centre from their sunny patio. The food (from eggs on toast to a full Northumbrian) was perfectly decent. **Bewicks** (✆ 01669 621717 ☉ daily ♿ 🐾) next door is another pleasant café (and evening bar) for coffee, breakfast and light bites.

The Narrow Nick High St (next to the Co-op) ✆ 07979 101332 ☉ from 16.00 Mon & Sun, from 14.00 Tue–Fri and from noon Sat 🐾. Named after the alleyway it rubs shoulders with, this fantastic micro-brewery is as quirky as the (tiny) pub itself. Take your pint to a salvaged bus seat and enjoy the cheerful local banter. Friendly staff and great range of beers, ciders and gins (try the local Hepple Gin).

Three Wheat Heads Thropton ✆ 01669 620262 ☉ from 11.30 daily ♿. Old, well-regarded country pub two miles west of Rothbury with a great Sunday carvery (book ahead). Traditional low-ceiling interior – nothing fancy – but take a look at that view of the Simonside hills! On warm days, you'll want a table in the pub garden to take in the panorama. Sunday roast portions are huge, and a choice of four meats with all the trimmings. At other times, there's a wide selection of meat, fish, pasta and vegetarian dishes and a good-value children's/small appetite menu.

Tully's Of Rothbury High St ☏ 01669 620574 ◷ Tue–Sun. Over a hundred years ago, Tully's used to make deliveries of groceries through the Coquet Valley by horse and cart; today the tradition continues (using modern transport) but most trade is across the counter in the original Rothbury store. The shelves in this fabulous pantry store and delicatessen are packed with sweet treats, dry goods, local beers and gin, and picnic food items. Fresh meats, Northumberland cheese and fresh sourdough made locally.

* * *

A BREATHTAKING CLIMB TO THE TOP OF SIMONSIDE

❋ OS Explorer map 332; start: Forestry England car park at Simonside, 4½ miles southwest of Rothbury by road ♀ NZ037997; 4¼ miles; moderate

A memorable hill walk south of Rothbury through Forestry England woodland and heathland followed by a stiff climb over sandstone outcrops to the top of one of the best-known summits and viewpoints in the national park. This route is generally well-marked with red arrows.

1 From the **Forestry England car park** at Simonside, locate a wooden barrier across the forest road; go round it and follow the ascending track. After half a mile, you'll reach a T-junction; turn right, passing a tall metal mast. Keep on the wide gravel track for another 550yds.

2 At a junction, bear left in the direction of the red arrow. Continue through forest and then into an open mosaic landscape of heath and young conifers.

3 At a fork by a marker post, bear left and continue up through the bracken. Catch your breath and take in the stunning views of Coquetdale behind you. Keep plodding

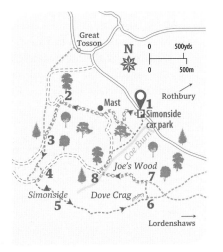

upwards through a rocky gully. There are a few paths hereabouts but they all open by the road.

4 Emerge from the heath by a red forest road. **Simonside** looms above. Turn right and continue for a few hundred yards to a national park information board. Strike uphill here and climb to the sandstone crags at the top. A magnificent view of Coquetdale awaits.

5 Stone flags cross the heather plateau connecting the summit of Simonside to **Dove Crag**, a mile east. Stay on this stone path the whole way.

6 Just past the summit of Dove Crag, the flagstone path bears right at a prominent fork in the direction of Lordenshaws. Do not continue on this stone path; instead descend off the hill along a sandy path for 300yds through heather and young trees, which opens by a junction with a wide stony track.

7 Turn left. There's no marker post at this junction but you'll pick up the red arrows further ahead. Continue for half a mile on a clear track.

8 At a junction with a red forest road, turn right by **Joe's Wood** and, 200yds later, turn right again and off the forest road by a marker post in the bracken. Enter woods, with the sound of a burn trickling through the understorey, and pick your way along the descending track through trees, following the red arrows all the way back to the car park.

* * *

13 THE SIMONSIDE HILLS

A ramble along this whale-backed sandstone massif south of the Coquet at Rothbury is a favourite with hill walkers. The views are magnificent: miles of grasslands and forests stretching all the way to the North Sea, and the blue humps of the Cheviots in the distance. To the south, if the light is favourable, you can see Tyneside.

What makes the Simonsides so distinctive, apart from the striking profile against the sky and famous prehistoric rock carvings at **Lordenshaws** (see below) are its rocky outcrops. For the most part,

PREHISTORIC ROCK ART

Northumberland is renowned for its numerous 5,000-year-old **cup-and-ring grooves and marks** carved into stone slabs. Fist-size with a series of concentric circles formed around a central depression, many are astonishingly well defined. Good examples are seen at **Weetwood Moor** (east of Wooler), **Chattonpark Hill** (page 175), **Routin Lynn** (page 173) and **Doddington Moor** (page 174). The most visited cup-and-ring marked stones in

Northumberland are scattered in grassland close to **Lordenshaws** car park near Rothbury. They look particularly impressive when the sun is low in the sky and the lines really stand out. The remains of a medieval deer-park wall, and ridge and furrow ripples in the fields indicate where medieval farmers ploughed the land.

Lordenshaws car park is four miles south of Rothbury and reached via an unclassified paved lane off the B6342.

however, the hills are covered in an expanse of heather with patches of bracken, cowberry and bilberry, and peaty bowls and gullies here and there. Red grouse are easily startled and will take off with their characteristic 'go back, go back' call. In August, the Simonsides turn fuchsia when the heather flowers.

UPPER COQUETDALE

Seasoned travellers to Northumberland National Park go dreamy-eyed when you mention Coquetdale. It's a much-sung dale with lush scenery and has parts that feel wonderfully remote. I'm really talking about **Upper Coquetdale** – roughly the extent of the River Coquet from its jingly beginnings in the southwestern corner of the Cheviots at Chew Green, past **Barrowburn**, **Alwinton**, **Harbottle**, **Holystone** and on to Rothbury, 30 miles from its source.

The higher reaches are classically Cheviot-like: heavy moors, sparkling burns, flower-filled hay meadows and the occasional stand of conifer trees; but further south around Holystone the landscape becomes wooded (now with ancient broad-leaved trees) before entering the open flood plains at **Hepple**.

WALKS IN UPPER COQUETDALE

A paved, potholed road extends for 12 lonely miles from Alwinton to the Roman camp, Chew Green, on the Scottish border, following the River Coquet much of the way and making for a memorable cycling or road trip (page 233) through the valley.

Many popular walks start and end from farmsteads and hamlets along the river and you don't have to wander far before you feel the swelling moors enclosing all around; every time you turn back, the hills seem to have shuffled in that bit closer.

I've described a couple of enjoyable short routes including at **Harbottle** (page 225), **Alwinton** (page 227) and **Barrowburn** (page 230) but there are many more paths direct from rough parking areas through the valley. The car park at Wedder Leap, Barrowburn, is a popular start point for hikes to **Windy Gyle** (page 228) for instance. For those who keep going through the valley, following the Coquet upriver, the likes of Buckham's Bridge offer more in the way of lonesome walks. You're unlikely to meet any other souls on a hike over **Deel's Hill** for

OLD DROVE ROADS

Footpaths, cart-tracks, packhorse routes and livestock trails have criss-crossed the Cheviots for as long as these moors and valleys have been farmed. Each tells a story of industry, society and conflict; they connected communities, provided access to the best pastures and markets for trading but also brought tribes into conflict.

Some have prehistoric origins; others, like **Dere Street**, were built by the Romans, and a good number are medieval or date to the time around the Union of the Crowns when relatively peaceful times promoted cross-border trade. During the 18th and early 19th centuries, tens of thousands of animals (mainly cattle) were seasonally driven across the border along the likes of **Clennell Street**, connecting Morpeth with Kelso, and **Salter's Road** from Alnham (which connects with Clennell Street on the Scottish border), once used by those in the salt trade.

Some drovers travelling from Scotland also traded in illicit goods, especially whisky (duties on the liquor were higher in England thus promoting an illicit trade), and **whisky stills** were hidden in rocky outcrops in a number of places. A mile or so west of Barrowburn, where Rowhope Burn meets the Coquet, there was once an 18th-century inn (evocatively named Slymefoot) that was notorious for receiving smuggled spirits.

Clennell Street, Salter's Road and **The Street** are some of the best-known routes that are still used by farmers and, nowadays, also by ramblers, mountain bikers and horseriders. They are largely wide tracks (grassy, dirt or paved) that tend to take a drier route over the hills, avoiding bogs.

Popular **walks** include the stretch of Clennell Street that runs north of Alwinton above the River Alwin, and The Street to Windy Gyle (page 228).

example. In reality, few visitors will venture beyond Alwinton (a popular base for walkers because of its pub and excellent hill walks direct from the hamlet).

Also consider walks away from the Coquet itself, such as to **Bleak Law** from the hamlet of **Biddlestone** (halfway between Alwinton and Alnham) via the remote **Biddlestone Chapel** and Loundon Hill.

The River Coquet forms the northern boundary of the **Otterburn military training area** (page 233), which covers the southern moors in the Cheviot range. Countryside and hills north of the river are yours to explore at any time; south of the river, there are restrictions. Red flags indicate the ranges are closed to the public. Most visitors explore the hills to the north anyway because the signed walking trails are on that side. If you want to experience the desolate moors to the south, check access restrictions first (page 234).

14 HEPPLE

Hepple is an unassuming old place six miles west of Rothbury with a post office, 14th-century **pele tower** and a beautiful **churchyard** offering an unparalleled view of the Simonsides. I am somewhat biased (my dear grandmother is buried here) but I can hardly think of a more peaceful spot or a more stunning valley view than from Hepple's churchyard. No one will mind you eating your sandwiches here. Note the names inscribed on the headstones: Scott, Laidler, Blythe, Milburn and Hall, of course – all strong border-country names with a heritage linking them to the Reiver clans of long ago.

Christ Church itself is a simple Victorian building with the odd medieval cross slab about and a 12th-century font bowl. However, it's that view of the shingle-banked **River Coquet** twinkling through the wide valley basin under the gaze of the heathery Simonsides that is really worth pulling over for.

Incidentally, **Hepple Gin**, which you may have spotted in pubs and shops across the region, is a local family-run business whose distillery is based in the village.

15 HOLYSTONE & LADY'S WELL

Plantation forest blankets the hilly ground between the small villages of Holystone and Harbottle, west of Rothbury, but amid the conifer trees is a remnant patch of ancient oak woodland (North Wood), which hosts a memorable chorus of birdsong on spring mornings.

Whiling away the years in a secluded spot below the woods is **Holystone**, a tranquil village consisting of a church, a scattering of pretty cottages and a famous Roman well where 3,000 Northumbrians are said to have been baptised during the Easter of AD627 by St Paulinus, Christianity having only just reached England (page 192). It's a pleasant, ten-minute walk along a signed farm track to **Lady's Well** – a rectangular stone basin with a Celtic cross at one end. A medieval statue of St Paulinus watches over the pool, which is fed by a spring. Sadly, there are no obvious remains of the Augustinian nunnery that once stood in Holystone prior to the Reformation.

A wander along the quiet lane heading south out of Holystone leads to **St Mungo's Well** – an early 19th-century stone pant. It's very peaceful here by the merry little burn and you may find the forests and swelling moors ahead draw you involuntarily further out of the village and into

ADDERS

Britain's only venomous snake loves a sunny clearing on a heather or bracken slope. An adder will quickly slip away into the vegetation if you get too close but sometimes they will coil and give you a hiss. It's their way of saying 'back off' – and you should do just that. Anyone who is bitten should seek urgent medical help. Bites can be fatal to pets.

Few people would be stupid enough to approach an adder, but I did hear a tale of a soldier on the Otterburn Ranges who thought it would be funny to pee on a basking adder. Well, you can guess what happened.

the **Otterburn military training area** (open to the public at certain times; page 234), a stunning and vast area of open moorland that must be seen (when red flags aren't flying).

To **walk** to **North Wood**, turn off the aforementioned lane at the Forestry England Holystone picnic site and follow an uphill trail through the trees. Return to Holystone by skirting the edge of broad-leaved North Wood in a southwesterly direction, enjoying the wide views of Coquetdale and the Simonside Hills. Descend through farmland to Campville where **Dovecrag Burn** is glimpsed below a steep ravine. Scottish outlaw Rob Roy is said to have sheltered here. Follow the paved lane back to Holystone.

Woodhouses Bastle

Reached by a grassy track off the Hepple to Holystone road is one of the best examples of a border fortified farmhouse. It keeps watch at the top of a grassy vale and probably dates from the 16th century. As is typical of bastle houses (page 235), the walls are hugely thick and the windows are small holes and slits. You can see into the ground floor, with its stone-vaulted ceiling.

16 HARBOTTLE

🏠 **Kidlandlee Holiday Cottages**

The 12th-century **Harbottle Castle** (originally a motte and bailey) teeters on the edge of a grassy summit above the village's main street.

◄ **1** The impressive Drake Stone near Harbottle. **2** Adders love to find sunny spots on the moors to warm up. **3** There are four herds of wild goat in Northumberland National Park, including one in Upper Coquetdale. **4** St Paulinus watches over Lady's Well in Holystone.

Built as a defence against the Scots, it now lies completely ruined, with crumbling walls and scattered stones.

Creating a striking silhouette on the facing hillside is the **Drake Stone** – a huge free-standing rock (said to have healing properties) near a glacial tarn. Drake Stone is even more impressive close up and I recommend the **hike** to the top (page 225). My Victorian guidebook describes how, until 'recent times', poorly children were cured of their illness by being passed over the Drake Stone – a custom linked to when this stone was sacred to Druids. The same book notes that infant mortality in Harbottle is 'almost unknown'.

> *"Creating a striking silhouette is the Drake Stone – a huge free-standing rock near a glacial tarn."*

A small **village show** on the first Saturday in September brings together the finest sheep, veg, cut flowers, jams and crafts produced in the local area. Rapper sword dancers and folk musicians entertain the crowds who also come to watch wrestling and children's events or pick through the car boot sale.

SPECIAL STAYS

Kidlandlee Holiday Cottages Harbottle NE65 7DA ✆ 01669 650472 ⌂ kidlandlee. co.uk. Upper Coquetdale is one of the most stunning valleys in Northumberland National Park and you can hardly find a more superb location for walkers or cyclists than this collection of stone cottages and converted barns (all modern and above average for the area in terms of comfort and price) set within open countryside. Off-grid and with their own filtered water supply from a bore hole and walks from the doorstep, this is a place to get away from it all.

FOOD & DRINK

The Star Inn ✆ 01669 650221 ◷ from noon daily ⚲ 🐾. Two hundred years ago, drovers stopped at this coaching inn on their way to and from Scotland. The Star now welcomes a different clientele with walkers and locals keeping the place busy with food orders throughout the week. A revamp in recent years has given the pub new life with B&B rooms upstairs, a modern interior and wood-fired kitchen housed in the old brewery producing great 'hand-stretched' pizzas, bowls of pasta and a few meat and fish dishes (steaks, fish and chips etc).

A small **shop** in the courtyard is stocked with cans of baked beans, cereal, bars of chocolate and fresh cake. There's a tourist information leaflet stand and the shop also sells Ordnance Survey maps and the day's papers.

* * *

⚑ A CLIMB & SWIM: DRAKE STONE & HARBOTTLE LAKE

❋ OS Explorer map OL16; start: Harbottle Forestry England car park, 400yds north of Harbottle castle car park, on the left ♥ NT921044; 2 miles; moderate

- -

This is a stunning, short hike (and a good family-friendly route) to a huge 30ft-high boulder resting on top of a heathery slope facing Harbottle village. A secluded tarn lies just beyond the Drake Stone, should you wish to cool off on reaching the top. Return through woods and then along lanes with an Alpine-like view of Alwinton in meadowlands.

1 From the **Forestry England car park**, take the footpath signed for the Drake Stone (a temporary sign may be in use), past the red Ministry of Defence sign and through a couple of gates. Climb for half a mile up the heather and bilberry-covered slope, keeping close to the dry-stone wall on your right the whole way and making for the monstrously large grey rock on the hilltop.

2 At the **Drake Stone**, take in the view of fields rising from the valley and the distant Simonside Hills, then, with your back to the giant rock, retrace your path several paces before crossing over a stile in the direction of the tarn and picking up the lakeside footpath. Walk the length of **Harbottle Lake**, where a dip is recommended (there are plenty of launching areas and there's rarely anyone about, but the water is very deep in places so take care).

3 At the end of the lake, turn uphill through heather, keeping close to the fenceline on your right. Enter West Wood and follow a line of concrete posts for half a mile.

4 Step out of the wood by a gate and cattle grid. Turn right down the track, savouring the view of Alwinton nestled below some bulky hills, and fields dotted with sheep and Belted Galloway cattle.

5 After half a mile, go through a gate and turn right on to the road for a third of a mile to reach the car park.

* * *

17 ALWINTON

Alwinton's lane of low-rise stone cottages, farm buildings and pub trail away from the meeting of two good trout rivers – the Coquet and Alwin – and the route of the ancient drove road, **Clennell Street**, which once extended from Morpeth to Kelso. The recently upgraded pub, the Rose & Thistle (see below), is a welcome sight for hikers striding off the surrounding hills. Indeed, several highly worthwhile **walks** start from Alwinton's car park (where there are public toilets), including two circuits snaking deep into the Cheviots along Clennell Street. One follows the Usway Burn on the return leg, and the other routes via Copper Snout. I've described a shorter river and hill route on the opposite page.

St Michael and All Angels Church stands half a mile south of the village offering wonderful views of the facing hillsides – and access along a footpath from the churchyard to some early 19th-century **lime kilns**. Reconfigured from a Norman chapel, the present church is curious for its highly unusual flight of steps from the nave to the chancel, which allowed for the creation of a crypt for the prominent local Clennell family. Not much masonry survives from the 11th and 12th centuries, but you will find some Early English features dating from the 13th century, including the north arcade and piscina in the chancel; the rest is Victorian.

The annual **Alwinton Border Shepherds' Show** in October is traditionally the last of the season in Northumberland. It's also one of the largest (and oldest) fairs in the county. Expect all the usual displays: sheepdog trials, craft tents, food stalls, Cumberland and Westmorland wrestling and bagpipe music.

¶| FOOD & DRINK

Rose and Thistle Alwinton ✐ 01669 650226 ☉ Wed–Sun and bank holidays ⅙ ❤.
Famous for hosting Sir Walter Scott when researching material for *Rob Roy*, this old stone pub is equally well-known for being a bloody nice place to fall into after a hike in the hills. It used to be a cosy place with agreeably outdated décor but a recent overhaul of the interior has created a brighter, more modern ambience and a fancier food menu (haggis bon bons anyone?). But the view of the Cheviots from the restaurant remains fabulously scenic and you can still play darts and billiards, or sit outside in the sun with a pint of local ale and moan about the price of beer and the words 'artisan sourdough bread'. Sunday roasts, fish and chips, divine puddings and Northumbrian cheeses.

* * *

🚶 ALWINTON AND THE RIVER ALWIN

❊ OS Explorer map OL16; start: Alwinton car park ♀ NT919063; 5 miles; moderate

Shepherds and traders of bygone centuries used the wide, time-worn drovers' track on the first leg of this walk to travel to and from Scotland. The return is along a gravel road that follows the lively River Alwin to Clennell Hall.

From Alwinton's car park, walk back through the village until you reach the green by the river. Cross **Hosedon Burn** by way of a footbridge and turn left. You'll see a fingerpost signed for **Clennell Street**. Once you've passed a farm on your left, the track continues steeply uphill by the side of buttercup meadows. Many low summits are now in sight. It's very peaceful up here with only the song of skylarks, bleating sheep and the occasional 'tuk, tuk' of a distant tractor carried in the wind.

Ignore the footpath to your right and continue upwards and over a stone wall by a farm gate using a ladder stile. Follow the path as it skirts **Castle Hills**, an Iron Age settlement.

Where the main track bears left, strike off right by a marker post and go through the gate ahead. Bear diagonally left to the bottom corner of the field by a young plantation. Go over the stile by a farm gate and follow the thin trail ahead along the side of the hill. Note the old sheepfold and the silvery River Alwin in the valley below.

At a marker post, bear right on a wider grassy track, descending to the valley bottom.

Begin the return leg by crossing a stile on to the forest road and turning right. Follow the River Alwin for 1½ miles towards Clennell Hall, crossing the river three times. Now a hotel with a bar serving food open to non-guests, **Clennell Hall** (✎ 01669 650377 ♿) goes back many centuries and features its old defensive tower.

The forest road skirts Clennell Hall. By some farm buildings and a cattle grid, cross the river via a footbridge (signed to Alwinton).

Turn left and head up the bank and then cross the field in front by way of stiles on both sides. Turn left on to Clennell Street and retrace your steps to Alwinton.

* * *

18 BARROWBURN

Barrowburn **farmstead** stands by the River Coquet, six miles upriver from Alwinton, and marks the start and end points of several popular Cheviot walks. Access is along a paved road with plenty of turns, potholes and free-range sheep about to ensure motorists maintain an average speed of 15 miles per hour. But who wants to zoom through this

HILL FARMING & COMMUNITY IN BARROWBURN

Until the current owners took over Barrowburn farmstead, the land was farmed by a fifth-generation hill farmer, Ian Tait, who had lived here since birth. There are not many buildings at Barrowburn except for the farm, old schoolhouse and community hall by the parking area.

Over a cup of tea and scone one winter's day some years ago, Ian told me about how the community once centred around these scattered buildings. 'The building downriver [by the car park] used to be a dance hall. It's used for storage now and is full of hay, but if you were to look under the hay, you'd see a beautiful sprung wooden floor.' It was here that the local farmers and their families used to dance to border folk songs, including the Barrowburn Reel.

'The school was the focus of the community,' explained Ian. It was opened by a gypsy in the late 19th century (page 229) and closed in the 1970s. Farmers' children (including himself) used to travel from all around to the simple stone building on the hillside. 'There was only one teacher and all ages were taught in the same room: big kids at the back and younger kids at the front. If the weather was bad in winter and most children couldn't get to school, we used to sit in front of the fire in the teacher's house next door, drinking hot Ribena and doing our maths.'

'School trips were not just for the children,' Ian recalls. 'The whole community would join us and we'd all go off to the beach at Tynemouth for the day.'

valley – with some of the most stunning grasslands and hill scenery in the whole of Northumberland in view – anyway?

The **meadows** behind the farm are particularly striking: a blaze of yellow, green and purple in June and July when yellow rattle, buttercups, eyebright, clovers, wood crane's-bill and knapweed come into flower. Mountain bumblebees like it here. Heading up the track, perhaps on a walk to Murder Cleugh (page 230), you'll pass the Deer Hut (no longer available to hire) and a stone camping barn next door (not generally open to the public except to those booked on a retreat; ⊘ nightfold.org). The latter is the **old school** that was opened by one of the famous Kirk Yetholm gypsies in the late 19th century (page 229).

Windy Gyle

Rising over 2,000ft, Windy Gyle straddles the Scottish border and is one of the highest hills in the Cheviot range and well known to hikers (and mountain bikers). For **Pennine Way** walkers, crossing the remote peak is one of the most memorable moments on the entire path. From the windswept summit at **Russell's Cairn**, all the major hills are in view: Shillhope Law, Hedgehope Hill, The Schil and The Cheviot.

In the 15th and 16th centuries, wardens appointed by the king to control the lawless border country used to meet in the Cocklawfoot/ Windy Gyle area to settle disputes. These rendezvous sometimes ended in bloodshed, including one meeting in 1585 during which Lord Francis Russell, son-in-law of the English warden, John Forster, was murdered.

TALL TALES, GYPSY KINGS & PRESIDENTS

Spend enough time in Northumberland's hills and walking its ancient tracks used by travellers, traders and soldiers of long ago and you'll hear accounts of clan skirmishes, murders, illicit goings on, malevolent dwarfs (the infamous 'Simonside Duergars') and plenty of apparitions of course. Some of these tales are immortalised in place names (Murder Cleugh, Russell Cairn and Winter's Gibbet to name a few). One of the most curious stories I heard in the Cheviots was told to me one winter's afternoon in Upper Coquetdale by the old farmer at Barrowburn, Ian Tait.

It concerns a poacher in the mid 19th century who was chased by a couple of gamekeepers to his home. The story goes that the poacher hid his shotgun in his son's crib but it accidentally went off, shooting the child through the arm. On hearing the story – and realising the child would never be able to work on the land – the landlord's wife paid for the child to receive an education. His name was Andrew Blythe (the Blythes were a famous gypsy family in Kirk Yetholm just over the Scottish border) and he eventually made a living travelling the Cheviot Hills teaching shepherds' children how to read and write. He opened the schoolhouse at Barrowburn (the stone building above the remote farmstead (page 227) and was the schoolmaster there for 50 years, as his gravestone in Kirk Yetholm describes.

There's another tale about the Blythes that sounds a bit too good to be true but is intriguing nonetheless. The Blythes were related to the gypsy royal family, whose kings and queens lived in the Gypsy Palace at Kirk Yetholm (a cottage, incidentally, with a fascinating history if you're ever in the area).

One hundred years earlier, in 1752, 18 gypsies from Northumberland (including members of the illustrious Blythe clan) were transported to South Carolina from Morpeth jail. Two centuries later, a man named William Blythe, who was said to be a relative of one of these Northumberland gypsies in South Carolina, was killed in a car crash in 1946, three months before the birth of his son, William Jefferson Blythe. The boy's mother remarried, and so the boy changed his name to William Jefferson Clinton, better known as Bill Clinton, the 42nd President of the United States.

Russell's Cairn, which marks a Bronze Age burial site 15yds in diameter, is named in his memory.

A strenuous, well-known **walking route** for experienced hikers is the eight-mile circuit of Windy Gyle that begins and ends a mile west of Barrowburn where Rowhope Burn feeds into the Coquet. This is a superb trail, offering some of the most outstanding views in the whole of the Cheviot range, but it's a tough old climb. It begins on the historic drove route, The Street, which meets the Pennine Way on the Scottish border for the eastward hike to the summit at Russell's Cairn. The return is made by following a track high above Trows Burn and then tracing Rowhope Burn back to the main road. There are other well-trodden routes to the summit of Windy Gyle, as a glance of an Ordnance Survey map reveals, including one that passes Murder Cleugh (see below) – another scene of brutality on these slopes.

* * *

⚲ UPPER COQUETDALE HILL WALK: BARROWBURN TO MURDER CLEUGH

❋ OS Explorer map OL16; start: Wedder Leap car park ♀ NT866103; 5 miles; moderate

This is a stunning river and hill walk with plenty of big landscape views, wildflowers and points of interest along the way.

1 From **Wedder Leap car park**, walk north up the road to the remote **Barrowburn farmstead**. By the farm buildings, cross the burn using the wooden footbridge and follow the farm track past wildflower meadows to a copse on the hill above the farm.

2 At the two buildings known as the **Deer Hut** and **Old Schoolhouse** (marked as a bunkhouse on Ordnance Survey maps), follow the stony track leaving Barrowburn behind you. Stay on the farm track as it dips downhill to trace the **Hepden Burn** upriver.

3 After 400yds, the track pulls away from the river and climbs to a plateau. Go over the ladder stile and press on to a stand of conifers, a quarter of a mile ahead.

4 The Usway Burn trickles through the valley below on the right. Keep to the right side of the trees through a recently felled forest (plenty of stumps here to sit with a flask of tea).

5 Grassland saddles the whaleback hill ahead but don't follow its spine; rather take the track to the right (signed with a blue bridleway marker) along its flank.

6 Cross a stile by a farm gate and pass a wooden hut a few paces ahead. An indistinct grassy track to your left descends to **Hepden Burn** and then climbs to meet with the forest road where you turn left, but you may find it easier to follow the gravel track by a fingerpost 100yds ahead of the hut, which crosses Hepden Burn in a hairpin loop. Whichever route you take, you are now on the Forest Road to Murder Cleugh.

7 Turn left off the **Forest Road** along a boggy path, keeping close to the forest fenceline. You'll meet once again with the Forest Road in a hundred yards or so. On your left, in a sunken corner, there is a farm gate in a muddy patch.

8 Cross the fenceline, using the stile a few strides uphill of the gate, and enter tussocky grassland. Ten yards beyond the gate on your left and by the trees and fenceline is a **memorial stone** that reads: 'Here in 1610 Robert Lumsden killed Isabella Sudden.' Which must have left countless walkers pondering 'why?'. If you really want to know, he reportedly killed her by hurling stones against her stomach. His punishment when the authorities finally caught up with him some 14 years later was a month in gaol and a fine. That's justice, 17th-century style, for you.

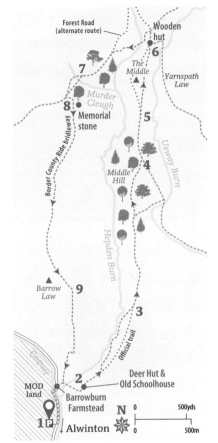

The return over **Barrow Law** is special, with the humps of several summits bouncing around and a far-reaching view of the River Coquet channelling a silvery course through the valley. But, you first need to locate the Border County Ride bridleway – a grassy track – across the hillside, which is not easy with so many sheep trails carved into the grassland. From the memorial stone, head up towards the brow of the hill and pick up the bridleway for 1½ miles, which trails below the summit of Barrow Law.

9 The Coquet comes into view as you begin your descent towards Barrowburn, which is entered by a metal gate across the farm track. Continue through the farm and retrace your steps to the car park.

* * *

19 OTTERBURN RANGES

It may be England's second-largest live firing range but this area of open moorland is also one of the most unspoiled stretches of countryside in Northumberland, covering 90 square miles and one-fifth of the national park. This vast area has not been improved or farmed since it came under the management of the Ministry of Defence in 1911, which explains why the waterways and grassland habitats are in such good condition and wildlife thrives. Otters, black grouse and merlin are some of the more unusual upland inhabitants; curlews, lapwings and skylarks accompany visitors in spring.

"This area of open moorland is also one of the most unspoiled stretches of countryside in Northumberland."

The ranges are often closed to the public (during training exercises), but the rest of the time (when red flags are not flying) you can enjoy some of the most spectacularly remote countryside and roads in England (access permitted for cars). This is great cycling country with uninterrupted moorland views framed by the humped Cheviot Hills, and dead-quiet roads. If travelling across country between Rothbury and Redesdale/Kielder and have the time, I can't recommend this route enough.

You can also make a highly memorable **loop of Upper Coquetdale** by following a quiet lane ('Burma Road') west out of Holystone and into the ranges. Continue across the moors to the Roman camp at Chew Green via Ridlees Cairn (stunning hill views from here) before picking up the riverside track that traces the Coquet downstream past Barrowburn and Harbottle. For both road trips, make sure you take OS maps OL42 and OL16 to ensure you take the correct turnings at junctions.

Archaeological relics on the ranges include prehistoric burial cairns, lost medieval villages, bastle houses, Roman camps and lime kilns. One of the most interesting of the 75 Scheduled Monuments is the **World War I practice trench** near Silloans, which brings to mind those at Ypres and the Somme (♀ NT836027; site not marked on OS Explorer maps). Access is from Bushman's Road but you must be escorted to the site (groups should call the number on page 234 to speak to the MoD and

---

◀ **1** An upland flower meadow. **2 & 3** Black grouse and merlin are just two of the many species you might be lucky to spot on the Otterburn Ranges. **4** The Otterburn Ranges are one of the most unspoiled stretches of countryside in Northumberland.

ACCESS TO THE OTTERBURN RANGES

The Controlled Access Area is roughly southwest of the River Coquet to the River Rede/A68 at Byrness and as far south as Otterburn; when red flags are flying, you must not enter the zone. Firing times are published on the Ministry of Defence's website (𝒟 01830 520569 𝒹 gov.uk/government/publications/otterburn-firing- times). When the ranges are open to the public and red flags are not flying (usually one weekend every six weeks & every day between mid-Apr and mid-May), during lambing season, visitors must still keep to the military roads and waymarked paths; there are no access restrictions on MoD land north of the River Coquet.

arrange a visit). Armchair travellers may like to take a trip on Google to see a bird's-eye view of the trenches, which appear as deep zig-zagging fissures in the ground.

REDESDALE & UPPER NORTH TYNEDALE

Rough are Redesdale's fells, rough are the grasslands and old fortified farmhouses, and rough is Redesdale's history. This is core Border Reiver country, once a lawless place in the late medieval period, which retains its wild look to this day. The moorland scenery either side of the River Rede between **Otterburn** and the Scottish border at **Carter Bar** is pretty desolate, with only the occasional farm surrounded by fells and tussocky grasslands, and a scattering of settlements guarding the Roman road into Scotland (Dere Street). As you near the Scottish border, the landscape becomes particularly moody and typically Cheviot-like with bulky hills muscling into one another and views for many miles around. Snow posts appear on roadside verges.

Further south around historic **Elsdon**, the **Woodburns**, **Ridsdale** and **Bellingham,** the sheep-grazed grasslands are interspersed with the odd heather slope, many fields of buttercups and Forestry England woodland. Lapwings tumble above damp meadows and the pitiful cry of the curlew is always in earshot in spring. My car once broke down on the road between Bellingham and West Woodburn and I spent a very enjoyable hour watching a meadow filled with courting curlews. Other good places to break down on a sunny day in spring would be the lanes winding through the likes of **Thorneyburn** and **Greenhaugh** in the beautiful **Tarset Valley** countryside, or above the **River North Tyne** between Bellingham and Kielder Reservoir. Cyclists and walkers will enjoy many a bird-filled sky hereabouts.

20 CARTER BAR & CATCLEUGH RESERVOIR

Scotland bursts upon the traveller coming over the brow of the hill at **Carter Bar**. From the lofty vantage point at 1,400ft above sea level you can see the Lammermuir Hills to the north. There's a large parking area where many people stop to take in the view and stretch their legs. A path to the west winds up boggy Carter Fell and into **Whitelee Moor National Nature Reserve**. From here, Catcleugh Reservoir comes into sight.

Heather slopes, wooded cleughs, peat bogs and tussocky pastures characterise the hilly ground all the way to the Scottish border. Burns run off the fells feeding **Catcleugh Reservoir** and the River Rede, which winds its way through the grasslands.

Catcleugh's sheet of water enclosed by trees provides an eye-catching vista (and hunting ground for ospreys). When the reservoir was being created in the late 19th century to supply water to Tyneside, a small community grew around Catcleugh to house construction workers, but was dismantled on completion of the reservoir. Only one timber hut, **Black House** (♀ NT74960317), remains and is now a small museum.

BASTLE HOUSES & PELE TOWERS

Murder, theft and arson were enough of a persistent threat in the borderlands during the 16th and 17th centuries to necessitate the construction of defensive farmhouses. These 'bastle houses' are dotted all over the border region, providing a visual reminder of the centuries of raids by clans known as the **Border Reivers** (page 240).

Bastles (from the French 'bastille' meaning 'fortress') are essentially two-storey dwellings with hugely thick walls, stone roofs and tiny upstairs windows. If an attack was feared, livestock was rounded up and locked in the ground floor before families climbed on to the second storey, sometimes by ladder or rope that was then pulled inside. See page 245 for details of some prominent bastle houses.

Pele towers (sometimes they are referred to as 'tower houses') are generally tall, fortified structures of several storeys associated with the estates of prominent landowners (and vicars). As well as protecting inhabitants, they served as lookout points and warning stations where beacons would be lit to alert locals of approaching invaders.

National park rangers open the site a few times a year – book tours online at ⊘ northumberlandnationalpark.org.uk.

The south window in nearby **St Francis of Assisi church** (NE19 1TR, half a mile south of Byrness village by the A68 ♥ NT771023) – a tiny place of worship on the Pennine Way dating in part to the 18th century – vividly commemorates workers who died during the building of the reservoir.

21 ROCHESTER'S ROMAN RUINS

It's fitting that the Otterburn military training camp should be sited in an area once well known to Roman soldiers. On the western edge of the Otterburn Ranges, the Roman road, **Dere Street**, shoots an arrow-

THE BATTLE OF OTTERBURN

Cowards had no place there, but heroism reigned with goodly feats of arms; for knights and squires were so joined together at hand strokes, that archers had no place on either party.

J Froissart *The Ancient Chronicles*, 1388

One of the most well recorded of all the Anglo–Scottish clashes in Northumberland is the Battle of Otterburn, famously fought by moonlight on 19 August 1388. It ended with a victory for the Scottish army, despite the death of their leader, the Earl of Douglas, and the capture of the legendary Henry Percy of Alnwick Castle (Shakespeare's 'Hotspur') and his sibling. The battle is immortalised in a couple of ballads: one English, *The Ballad of Chevy Chase*, the other Scottish. *The Battle of Otterbourne* contains the following verses:

It fell about the Lammas tide,
When the muir-men win their hay,
The doughty Douglas bound him to ride
Into England, to drive a prey ...
When Percy wi' the Douglas met,
I wat he was fu' fain;
They swakked their swords till sair they swat,
And the blood ran down like rain.

The location of the battlefield is not precisely known but the best consensus is that it took place just west of Otterburn, an area that still retains its open character. **Percy's Cross** stands in a small plantation by the side of the A696 and is thought to mark the spot where the Earl of Douglas was killed. It was already of some age when it was moved a couple of hundred yards in 1777. A worn trail leads visitors to the site.

straight course through the hills to the Scottish border. During the construction of this important supply road, Roman squads were housed in camps, some of which are visible to this day by the side of the route as earthen ramparts. The most easily accessible is **Brigantium** at Rochester, by the A68. A permissive footpath connects the camp with High Rochester and **Bremenium Roman Fort**, once an important garrison station on Dere Street. Houses now stand within the fort itself but its grassed-over perimeter wall is clear in places, with Roman masonry exposed here and there. Deeper into the Cheviot hills, where Dere Street crosses the Scottish border, lies **Chew Green camp** (♀ NT787084), its outline visible by the side of the road.

22 OTTERBURN

Otterburn's medieval castle manor, coaching inns, historic mill, pictorial countryside and convenient location near the junction of two major roads should make it an obvious stopping place for travellers, but if I'm honest, it's one of those places that sounds a bit better than it actually is.

The most prominent historic attraction is **Otterburn Tower**, a hugely impressive castellated manor house (now a wedding hotel) in landscaped grounds founded in the years after the Norman Conquest. The oldest part is the 14th-century tower, which is incorporated into the 19th-century manor.

Otterburn Mill

NE19 1JT ✆ 01830 521002 ⏶ otterburnmill.co.uk ⏲ daily ♿ 🐾

'The Queen has now made a selection from the patterns of Otterburn Tweed, which you kindly sent …' So began a letter from Buckingham Palace penned to the Otterburn Mill in 1939 pertaining to blankets for the young princesses, Margaret and Elizabeth. Since then orders for Otterburn Pram Rugs from the 18th-century mill have not stopped. The main difference now is that the chequered fabric (pastel pink, yellow and blue) is no longer woven at Otterburn, production having ceased in 1976. Blankets are for sale, however, in the on-site outdoor and country clothing **shop**.

Next to the shop is a **café** and **displays** of **old mill machinery**. Information panels describe the process of producing cloth from raw wool. To the rear of the mill by the car park is one of the most interesting mill relics. Timber and metal **tenter frames** dating to the early 1700s were used to stretch and dry washed cloth that was hung from tenter hooks (from where the expression 'to be on tenter hooks' originates). This is thought to be the only surviving example in the world.

¶ FOOD & DRINK

For a jacket potato or sandwich, try the café at **Otterburn Mill** (⌀ 01830 520225 ⊙ daily ♿ 🐾). Picnickers note the benches in surrounding fields. The friendly **Border Reiver newsagents** (⌀ 01830 520682 ⊙ until 15.00 daily 🐾) is well-stocked with provisions and doubles as a café selling all-day breakfasts, soups, quiches, scones and traybakes (great for passing cyclists, but the dining room itself is rather uninspiring).

For a more substantial meal, you really only have one choice in the village – the William de Percy Inn (see below).

William de Percy Inn Jedburgh Rd, Otterburn ⌀ 01830 576040 ⊙ daily ♿ 🐾. This luxury boutique hotel (also known as Le Petit Chateau) buzzes with wedding guests, especially at weekends, but the pub (also popular with locals and serving some regional ales) and restaurant are open to non-guests. Inside it's all rather faux swish with exposed brick walls, a lot of wood, dark paintwork and chandeliers. On the menu: pricey steaks, pies, burgers, fish and chips, and Sunday roasts, alongside a surprising choice of sweet and savoury crêpes.

23 ELSDON

> Hae ye ivver been at Elsdon?
> The world's unfinish'd neuk;
> It stands amang the hungry hills,
> An' wears a frozen leuk.
> The Elsdon folks like diein' stegs
> At ivvery stranger stare;
> An' hather broth an' curlew eggs
> Ye'll get for supper there.
> Opening to an old Northumbrian ballad by George Chatt

It's hard to find in Redesdale, or anywhere in Northumberland National Park, a more appealing village with such an intriguing past. Elsdon,

---

1 The remains of defensive bastle towers dot this region, a reminder of its turbulent past; pictured here Black Middens bastle house located between Elsdon and Kielder.
2 The earthen ramparts of Elsdon's motte and bailey castle. **3** Look out for the rare hen harrier over heather moorland. **4** Look for hunting ospreys on Catcleugh Reservoir. ▶

BORDER REIVERS

They were cruel, coarse savages, slaying each other as the beasts of the forest; and yet they were also poets who could express in the grand style the inexorable fate of the individual man and woman, and infinite pity for all the cruel things which they none the less perpetually inflicted upon one another. It was not one ballad-maker alone, but the whole cut-throat population who felt this magnanimous sorrow, and the consoling charm of the highest poetry.

G M Trevelyan, *The Middle Marches*, 1914

The border country from the late medieval period until the mid 17th century was the Wild West of Britain: a violent place marked by clashes between rival kinship groups in Scotland, Northumbria and parts of the North West, who had greater ties to family groups than to country. These allegiances provided a level of security to the border people who had suffered centuries of Anglo-Scottish warfare.

Some notorious families were the Armstrongs, Charltons, Elliots, Forsters, Dodds, Milburns and Robsons – surnames that remain common in the North East today. Reivers rode on horseback wearing steel bonnets and armed with swords, and travelled across the Cheviot Hills raiding farmsteads, stealing livestock and seeking retribution. Incidentally, it is because of the Border Reivers that we have the words 'bereaved' and 'blackmail'. The former speaks for itself, but the etymology of 'blackmail' is not as clear. The word is thought to originate in the border region (also used further north) where payments and goods were offered in return for immunity from raids.

A culture of **storytelling** developed in the hills, in which tragic love stories, raids and clashes were recalled in song. Recital of the melancholic border ballads died out during more peaceful times in the latter half of the 17th century, but some were recorded before they were lost completely; most famously by Sir Walter Scott in his *The Minstrelsy of the Scottish Border*. There's an extract of *The Battle of Otterbourne* in the box on page 236.

known as the capital of Redesdale, hides below hills rippled with the tell-tale signs of medieval farming, which form an amphitheatre around the village centre with its 14th-century church, green, and stone cottages. And 'hide' the village did for hundreds of years when inhabitants feared invasions from Scotland and attacks by Border Reivers.

Guarding the village in the northeast corner is an impressive Norman **motte and bailey castle** consisting of two large earthen ramparts. Architectural writer Pevsner describes it as the best example of its type in Northumberland. Access is up a lane, just past the metal road bridge as you're leaving Elsdon on the Rothbury road.

The other notable defensive structure is a medieval **pele tower**, once the residence of successive church vicars until the 1960s including Charles Dodgeson, great grandfather of Lewis Carroll. The fortified building – one of the most intact in Northumberland – dates from the 14th century. There's no public access, but visitors are permitted to walk some way up the drive to inspect its immense walls.

Until a few hundred years ago, Elsdon was an important staging post between Newcastle and Edinburgh, a place for travellers and drovers to rest in one of several inns facing the village green while their livestock grazed outside. Of the three public houses still standing, two have changed use but retain interesting features like the rustic sculpture of Bacchus sitting on a barrel above the doorway of the old **Bacchus Inn** (east side of the green). The **Bird in Bush** (page 243) is the only one still in business; its interior may have changed considerably over the centuries but it remains a convivial hub for villagers and visitors alike.

St Cuthbert's Church

There are two churches really worth visiting in Redesdale: one at Bellingham (page 244), the other at Elsdon. Both reflect in their walls those unstable times of cross-border fighting. On entering Elsdon's 14th-century church, notice the slash marks in the pillar on the left; they are said by 19th-century guidebook writer Tomlinson to have been made 'by the fierce bowmen of Redesdale in sharpening their arrows before leaving church.' It's an evocative image and an intriguing tale that seems to have endured. At least, the church-going locals I spoke to had heard the story.

There's so much more to uncover here: Roman and Saxon stones, medieval sarcophagi, some stunning examples of Northumbrian clear glass leaded windows and medieval sedilia (clergy seats). A shocking discovery was made in the 19th century by the north wall of the nave: a **mass grave** containing hundreds of human skeletons – all of them young men and boys. Could they be Englishmen who fell during the notorious Battle of Otterburn in 1388 (page 236)? And what about the **three horse skulls** discovered in the bellcote during restoration work in the late 19th century? Some say the animals may have been sacrificed as part of a Pagan ceremony during the construction of an earlier sacred building. More is known about a 650-year-old **sword** discovered on nearby Ministry of Defence land not far from the old Roman road, Dere

COCK-FIGHTING, BULL-BAITING & PAGAN TRADITIONS

'In consequence of the long isolation of the village amid moors and morasses, remote from the enlightening influences of civilisation,' wrote Tomlinson in his 1888 *Comprehensive Guide to Northumberland*, 'many pagan customs and superstitions were observed till within a very short time ago.' He continues, 'The Midsummer bonfires, through which cattle were driven to protect them from disease, were burning only a few years ago on Elsdon green – their origin, in the worship of Baal, being forgotten.'

Other bygone traditions include cock-fighting and **bull-baiting** (a ring would have once been fixed to the bull-baiting stone that remains in the green not far from the western end of Elsdon's church wall). At the southern end of the green is a **pinfold** that looks similar to a sheepfold, but was used to house stray livestock until their owners paid a fee for their release.

My Victorian guidebook notes that Elsdon's **village fête** at the end of August has 'long been obsolete'. Well, the tradition has since been revived and it's once again a popular family event with dog trials, folk music, clog dancing and more held on the village green during the August bank holiday.

Street, connecting Scotland and England. A replica stands in the church for visitors to attempt to lift. Made between 1200 and 1350, the 3ft-long weapon was designed for battle and may be the only surviving artefact from the Battle of Otterburn.

Winter's Gibbet

Besides horses' heads, bull-baiting, cock-fighting and a mass grave of fallen warriors, Elsdon's darker past is further revealed on a lonely hillside southeast of the village by an unclassified road to Morpeth.

"The superstitious folk of Elsdon are said to have rubbed wood chips from the gibbet on their teeth as a cure for toothache."

Winter's Gibbet (or 'Winter's Stob' as Northumbrians used to call it) is a wooden hanging post viewed eerily in silhouette by the side of the road at Steng Cross (on leaving Elsdon as if heading south to the A696, turn left at a prominent fork in the road which is signed for Winter's Gibbet).

Last time I passed, a torn flag was flapping madly in the wind from a chain attached to the post but there's sometimes a wooden head for added drama. My aunt, who lives nearby, tells me that the head periodically goes missing. It marks the spot (the gibbet is not original) where the body of William Winter was hanged in chains following his execution in Newcastle in 1791 for the murder of a local woman. Incidentally, she was killed at The Raw, an unmistakable bastle house on a farm three miles north of Elsdon (visible from the farm track).

The superstitious folk of Elsdon are said to have rubbed wood chips from the gibbet on their teeth as a cure for toothache in the 19th century.

Walks from Elsdon: The Todholes & Darden Lough

A number of enjoyable routes start in and around Elsdon, including a jaunt into the enclosing hills via two old farmsteads, **East** and **West Todholes** ('Toddles' not 'Tod-holes'), suitable for all walkers. Farm tracks and paths through fields connect both farms on a very pleasant 2½-mile circular ramble, best walked in early summer when the wildflower meadows are at their best. The start point is the rough car park as you leave Elsdon (in the direction of Rothbury), by the side of the B6341 (just past the metal road bridge). It's signed for 'East Nook/Hudspeth/Landshot/Whiskershiel'. If you look at Ordnance Survey map OL42, you'll see the obvious route, with the farm at Landshot your first port of call. Don't go as far as Whiskershiel Farm but turn off the paved track by a plank footbridge signed for 'East Todholes'. Soon after West Todholes, turn right, signed for 'Elsdon', which cowers in a hollow at the bottom of the vale.

If you continue on the Rothbury road (the B6341) for three or four miles, you'll come to a layby at **Grasslees Burn Nature Reserve** (♀ NY958981), the start point for a stiff four-miler to **Darden Lough**. Choose a hot day in August and enjoy the heather slopes in flower and a plunge in the mountain tarn at the top.

The ascent is sweaty stuff, but the route is fairly easy to navigate by following wooden marker posts. Allow around 2½ hours. The terrain is very uneven and boggy in parts. Again, the Ordnance Survey map of the area shows an obvious loop via **Darden Pike** – a craggy lookout with superb views for many miles around.

¶¶ FOOD & DRINK

Bird in Bush Elsdon ✐ 0191 816 1045 ◯ daily ♿ ❤️. Stone 18th-century inn opposite the village green. Inside, it's modern and not like the traditional pub you may have been expecting but the convivial atmosphere is just as you hoped: full of local banter, cyclists pulling up and walkers glugging pints of real ale on the green outside; and the food is decent too, with all the pub favourites plus Sunday roasts. Even if you only drop in for a coffee or cold drink, don't leave without a tub of homemade ice cream (their tea-tree honey and elderflower is outstanding).

24 BELLINGHAM

🏠 Hesleyside Huts

Land Rovers parked outside Bellingham's ('Belling-jum', by the way) Country Store and wagons passing with livestock should tell you that this town cradled by hills caters for the farming community. With the Pennine Way running right through the town, it also receives a fair number of hikers and cyclists, some of whom camp at the farm a few minutes' walk from the town centre, and stock up on supplies in the scattering of food shops and cafés hereabouts. There's also a good local hardware store stocked with camping and outdoor equipment, and a post office with maps and guides.

If you have time to potter about, there's a small **heritage museum** (page 246) and enchanting **waterfall** (page 246), both reached on foot from the centre of Bellingham.

At the western end of the High Street, **St Cuthbert's Church** is somewhat hidden behind the Black Bull Hotel and just beyond the **town hall** (the building with a distinctive green clock tower; a morning food and craft **market** is held here on the 3rd Saturday of the month). The church dates in part from the 13th century and has a colossal and highly unusual stone roof. It survived the lawless centuries that followed its construction, unlike many other medieval buildings that burned down when reivers were in town. Inside, you'll see the impressive barrel-vaulted roof spanning the nave in 15 stone ribs.

"With the Pennine Way running right through the town, it also receives a fair number of hikers and cyclists."

On exiting the church, a few steps to your right is a curious curved tomb called **The Lang Pack**, which is associated with a legend set in nearby Lee Hall. One night in 1723, the manor was left in the charge of servants who were visited by a pedlar looking for overnight accommodation. Permission was refused, but the servants agreed that he could store his large, heavy pack inside. After the pedlar left, they were alarmed to see the bag moving so they shot at it with a pistol. On opening the bag they found the body of a man wearing a whistle. Suspecting a raid, the servants armed

REDESDALE'S BASTLES

Some of Northumberland's historic fortified farmhouses – or 'bastles' (page 235) – have been converted into barns or more cheerful-looking cottages; a few stand on the loneliest of fells, all ragged and ruinous and instilling a tremendous sense of the region's lawless past. Many of the best examples are found in Redesdale, an area made even more atmospheric by the occasional sound of artillery fire from Otterburn's army training camp.

If you are prepared to hunt around a bit with a map, there are several clusters of bastles in the countryside between Kielder and Elsdon. Two of the best preserved are **Woodhouses** (page 223) and **Black Middens** (♀ NY772900). The latter stands near Kielder's Tarset Burn (signposted off the quiet lane from Greenhaugh to Comb). Black Middens is striking for its external stone steps leading to the first-floor entrance, hugely thick walls and holes in the doorway where a drawbar used to secure the opening. Incidentally, swifts nest in cavities between the stones between May and July. You'll find a good few bastles around here (an English Heritage board by the roadside shows you their locations). Continuing north up the Tarset Burn, you come to **Boghead Bastle** (♀ NY761910) at the bottom of a slope by Highfield Burn, which has a duct above the doorway that enabled those sheltering on the first floor to douse the entrance in water if it was set alight by raiders.

On the road between Bellingham and West Woodburn stand a couple of restored bastles among farm buildings at **Hole** and **Low Leam**. A pull-in area just east of Low Leam farm promotes access to the isolated bastle of the same name.

The striking ruin of **Shittleheugh Bastle** (♀ NY869950) keeps watch over open countryside marked by medieval ridge and furrow fields, a couple of miles northwest of Otterburn (reached by public right of way 400yds south of Elishaw on the A696). Only the original ground-floor doorway and striking gable ends remain intact. The walls stand to full height and look sculptural against the sky.

themselves before blowing the whistle to lure the dead man's accomplices. Sure enough, the gang appeared and were swiftly shot dead. Come morning their bodies had disappeared. The body in the pack is buried in the churchyard.

Outside the churchyard and reached via a stepped path (the Pennine Way) to the side of the Black Bull, is **St Cuthbert's Well** – or 'Cuddy's Well' as it usually goes by. It's a stout pant and not as old as it looks (probably 18th century) though the cover may be medieval. Spring water gushes from its spout into… a dog bowl, and it is also used in church baptisms according to the heritage sign.

One of the oldest and largest **agricultural shows** (⊘ bellinghamshow. co.uk) in Northumberland is staged just outside Bellingham on the bank holiday at the end of August. Expect all the usual traditional sheep and dog shows, folk music, food tents and plenty of activities for children including pony rides, face-painting and so on.

Bellingham Heritage Centre

Woodburn Rd ✆ 01434 220050 ◷ end Mar–end Oct Tue–Sun ♿ 🐾

Housed in Bellingham's old train station yard, this unexpected **museum**, which also serves as an informal tourist information centre, chronicles the upland industries and communities of bygone years. Displays on the Border Reivers and relics from the days of coal mining and traditional upland farming do a good job of narrating the dominant social and industrial traditions of Redesdale. There's also an old photography studio and large display of vintage cameras (quite random but intriguing nonetheless). The old **smithy** dates to 1834 and comes from nearby Stannersburn. It was formerly the workshop of an elderly man who had worked as a blacksmith for many decades. One afternoon in the 1970s, he locked up and decided not to return. Those who run the museum did a commendable job of rebuilding it exactly how he left it, still with a couple of unopened bottles of beer among his tools, of which there are around 500.

A fetching Intercity train carriage by the old station platform provides a fun venue for the **tea room** (page 248). There are outside tables too in a secluded spot.

Hareshaw Linn

Bellingham town centre, reached by following the riverside path/road opposite the police station; car park at the trail entrance

A highly picturesque stroll through trees leads to this 30ft-high waterfall close to Bellingham town centre. After an unremarkable first half mile to a picnic spot by the river (passing an old ironworks dam), the trail delves deeper into woodland, criss-crossing Hareshaw Burn many times. Continuing upriver, the trees become older and more heavily clothed in luxuriant mosses; jingling streams fall off the steep-sided

---

1 The Bellwether Gallery sells local craft and gift items. **2** A golden plover among the cotton grasses near Greenhaugh. **3** Harshaw Linn, Bellingham. ▶

gorge and huge boulders pile in the river. When I walked this trail in spring, all the usual woodland plants, including primroses, wood sorrel and dense patches of wild garlic, were in flower. Nuthatches, wrens and tree-creepers hid behind the trunks of oaks as I passed.

The waterfall is one of the most pleasing kind, not a tunnel of water but a cascade spraying in every direction on hitting rocks before entering a dark plunge pool.

It takes a couple of hours to walk there and back (three miles), but it's easy to navigate (no map needed).

SPECIAL STAYS

Hesleyside Huts Hesleyside Hall, Bellingham NE48 2LA ⌀ 01434 220068 ◈ hesleysidehuts. co.uk 🐾. Enchanting and luxurious, the seven luxury huts in the grounds of Hesleyside Hall are exquisitely designed with escapism and indulgence in mind (some with hot tubs, log burners and copper freestanding bath tubs). I love the diminutive chapel hut, the treehouse, and the watchtower – a modern interpretation of a Northumbrian pele tower (a nod to the Border Reiver heritage of the Charlton family who have lived at Hesleyside since 1343). For visitors looking for a truly decadent getaway, the Charltons also have three opulent bed and breakfast rooms available in the 18th-century family home. Surrounding the magnificent hall is Capability Brown parkland, which rolls towards the banks of the River North Tyne.

FOOD & DRINK

A couple of tea rooms and pubs serving food dot Bellingham's centre, including the **Cheviot Hotel** (Front St ⌀ 01434 211130 ⌖ ask for ramp 🐾), a popular inn with a town-facing beer garden offering pub food and real ales.

Tea on the Train The Heritage Centre Bellingham, Woodburn Rd (next to the TIC) ⌀ 01434 221151 ☺ daily ⌖ and also outdoor seating on the old platform. Take a seat in the vintage Intercity carriage and enjoy an inexpensive sandwich, scone and a cup of tea. Also serves afternoon teas.

First & Last Brewery Foundry Yard ⌀ 01434 239500 ☺ 16.00–21.00 Thu & Fri, from 14.00 on Sat, noon–18.00 Sun 🐾. Conversations merge across tables in this great little tap room on the edge of Bellingham, conveniently located for walkers visiting Hareshaw Linn. Serving inexpensive beers brewed on site, sit inside the snug little drinking room to partake in the local chit chat or outside on repurposed beer keg seats under a gazebo (midge repellent at the ready). Live music most Sunday afternoons.

Fountain Cottage Café & B&B Front St ⌀ 01434 239224 ☺ daily from 08.00 ⌖ 🐾. At the far north end of Bellingham's main street (B6320) is an old workhouse converted into a cheerful café (popular with cyclists) with outside tables, serving all-day breakfasts and a good selection of cakes, hot and cold lunches (sandwiches to burgers; jacket potatoes to fish goujons) and ice creams. The small building next door, incidentally, was once a mortuary. Lastly, if you're using the loo, check out the charming black-and-white photograph on the corridor wall titled 'Christmas Morning 1919', picturing locals outside the then post office opposite the café holding a great volume of parcels.

25 GREENHAUGH & THE TARSET VALLEY

Greenhaugh ('Green-hoff'), five miles west of Bellingham, stands in a remote spot en route to nowhere. As a result, this lovely little hillside village above the Tarset Burn, consisting of a stone street, friendly pub and farm selling fresh eggs by the roadside, generally goes unappreciated by visitors.

For those in the know, this is a wonderful destination for Sunday lunch when combined with a meadow and river **walk** in the exquisite **Tarset Valley** – a secluded wooded dale enclosed by sheep-grazed hills.

"For those in the know, this is a wonderful destination for Sunday lunch when combined with a meadow and river walk."

A three-mile-long circular trail to Thorneyburn via the Tarset Burn (page 250), for example, passes an upland hay meadow or three brimming with wildflowers from May. Even if you don't complete the full circuit, a wander down the lane from Greenhaugh to grasslands known locally as **The Bog** is worth it just to take in the colourful sight.

Thorneyburn's church on the west side of the valley, a mile by road from Greenhaugh, hides away in woodland above the Tarset Burn and is the only churchyard I know of in Northumberland inhabited by **red**

SCENIC ROAD: GREENHAUGH TO OTTERBURN

Heading east out of Kielder to the A68 and Otterburn, take the road signed for 'High Green' on approaching the junction at Gatehouse Farm (1½ miles north of Greenhaugh). Sheep stray into the quiet single-track road that ascends quickly into remote countryside, making for a spectacular journey across moorland. It's perfect for cycling, but you'll need good leg and lung muscles for the climb to 1,000ft. Once you're at the highest point, roughly where the Pennine Way crosses the road, the terrain flattens out with cotton grasses and heather and a tremendous view of the Cheviot hills before free-wheeling into the lowland farmland around Otterburn.

squirrels. Visitors are welcome inside the simple, aisleless nave to find out a little about the community and church built in 1818.

Three miles north of Greenhaugh, on a lonesome lane to Comb, stand a number of ruined **bastle houses** (page 245) close to the roadside. There's a pull-in area and trail map detailing their locations but Ordnance Survey map OL42 will come in useful.

On the other side of this road is **Sidwood**, a mixed Forestry England woodland populated by red squirrels and where there is a picnic area.

* * *

⚜ TARSET VALLEY WILDFLOWER WALK
❋ OS Explorer map OL42; start: Greenhaugh ♥ NY796871; 3 miles; fairly easy

This is an easy circuit in the valley of the Tarset Burn, which routes through glorious upland meadows stuffed with wildflowers in late spring and summer.

1 Just before entering Greenhaugh village from the south, take a farm track off to your left (signed for High Boughthill) through trees. The track opens in a few hundred yards with a splendid view of flower meadows by the riverside. Known locally as **The Bog**, these grasslands are designated a SSSI for their upland flora. Swathes of buttercups interspersed with cuckoo flower, ragged robin, yellow rattle, speedwell, pignut and many marsh orchids are a sight to behold from late May until early summer.

2 At a **ford**, cross the **Tarset Burn**. Either take off your shoes and socks and wade across for fun (careful, it's slippery) or go through the gate on your left and over the footbridge. If

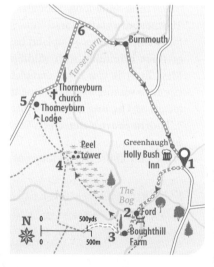

taking this dry route, follow a short length of boardwalk with the waterway on your right then cross the river by another bridge. On the other side of the ford, follow the farm track to **Boughthill Farm**, 150yds ahead beyond another wonderful flower meadow. Cross the farm courtyard, picking up the farm track on the other side, which you climb for 100yds to meet with a wooded area.

3 Where the track curves left, strike off right by a footpath marker post. Cross the stream in the hollow below and climb up the side of a hill (waymarked). Go through an opening in the dry-stone wall and bear immediately right through the gate in the adjacent damp field. Climb the tussocky hillside, which has nesting skylarks in spring, towards the spire of Thorneyburn church, which peeps above the treetops.

4 By a stile, bear right and head for a **ruined pele tower**, now barely more than a heap of stones, then bear left towards a house (Thorneyburn Lodge) in view ahead.

5 Turn right at **Thorneyburn Lodge**, on to a paved lane and through the farm gate. **Thorneyburn church** is a couple of hundred yards ahead. Red squirrels inhabit the churchyard, which is a wonderfully peaceful spot. After visiting the church, return to the lane and turn right along tarmac for 500yds.

6 At a T-junction, turn right and cross the Tarset on the road bridge ahead. Keep on the lane, heading uphill to a stone house on the corner (you can turn into the field here and rest above the river on some well-placed stones). The road bears right and continues through Greenhaugh, passing the welcoming Holly Bush Inn in half a mile.

* * *

¶¶ FOOD & DRINK

Holly Bush Inn Greenhaugh ✆ 01434 240391 ◷ from 16.00 Mon–Fri & from noon Sat, Sun & bank holidays. A small country pub full of friendly locals having a chinwag is always a good sign. It's been like this at the Holly Bush Inn (a former drovers' inn) for over 300 years. You can stay in one of the B&B rooms upstairs or just come for a drink of local ale or to dine in the good restaurant (fish and chips, scampi, curry, roast meats, a couple of veggie options and Sunday lunches – make sure you book). Even in summer, the wonderful range fire burns strong, and folk musicians sometimes pack into the small front room – a scene that will take you back a few centuries.

26 THE UPPER REACHES OF THE NORTH TYNE & FALSTONE

This is a beautiful corner of Northumberland that few visitors take the time to explore, so intent are most on reaching Kielder's forests and lakeland scenery at the head of the valley. Cyclists following the **Reivers Route** (NCN Route 10) between Lanehead and Falstone (or walkers on the **River Tyne Trail**) will, however, absorb every stone hamlet, moorland view and meadow from the quiet lanes and footpaths trailing above the banks of the River North Tyne. Motorists can follow this route too; just drop down a few gears and take it all in.

The old **Border Counties Railway** once ran a similar course through North Tynedale, connecting Hexham with almost every hillside village, and the sharp-eyed visitor may notice the disused line in a few places or recognise some of the Victorian cottages as station buildings.

Charlton was the first station stop upriver of Bellingham. The hamlet's name keeps alive the centuries-old connection of this whole area to the illustrious Border Reiver family of the same name whose ancestral seat (since 1343) is the impressive stone manor, **Hesleyside Hall**. Set in Capability Brown-designed parkland on the south side of the river, Hesleyside remains the home of the Charlton family to this day. While the house is not open to day visitors, the Charltons do offer luxury overnight stays (page 248). As for Charlton hamlet, it makes a useful stopping point on your travels, with the **Boe Rigg** restaurant (see opposite) and campsite offering food and beers to anyone passing through. Tucked away round the back of the restaurant in a converted hay barn is **The Bellwether Gallery** (⊙ Jan & Feb Sat & Sun; Apr–Dec noon–16.00 Wed–Sun & 🐾), a modern local craft and art gallery with plenty of inexpensive gifts for sale among higher-priced original works.

Continuing up the valley, travellers pass the hillside hamlet of **Lanehead** high above the confluence of the Tarset and North Tyne. The most scenic route for Kielder is to turn right then sharp left following NCN10 on a quiet lane through picturesque Tarset countryside via the old station house at **Thorneyburn** (note the level-crossing gates) and tootling through the stone hamlet of **Donkleywood**.

Falstone is a pretty village a mile or two ahead and stands at the gateway to Kielder. It's noted for its tea room, lively pub with a sunny beer garden, children's playground and peaceful setting by the North Tyne. The enclosed green by the river is a tranquil spot with picnic benches.

If you **walk** along the riverbanks (from the tea room, go to the end of the residential street and turn left on meeting the North Tyne), you'll come to a contemporary sculpture called **Stell** (a local word for sheepfold) that invites walkers to take a seat on one of two stone 'sofas'. The shallow waters hereabouts offer a few places for throwing stones and paddling. To return to Falstone, continue on the riverside path until you reach the stone bridge, where you should turn left along a meadow path back to the village. The whole route is just three quarters of a mile.

For the lower reaches of the North Tyne Valley, between Bellingham and Hexham, see page 267.

⅋⅋ FOOD & DRINK

The Blackcock Inn Falstone ✆ 01434 240200. Always full of jovial locals and a perfectly fine choice for a pub meal (usual pub grub, pizzas and inexpensive Sunday lunches). Catch the last of the day's sun in the beer garden or huddle round the coal fire in winter.

The Bellweather Gallery Charlton, nr Bellingham NE48 1PE ⊙ Wed–Sun ♿ 🐾. Tea room serving hot drinks and cakes within the gallery.

The Boe Rigg campsite Charlton, nr Bellingham NE48 1PE ✆ 01434 240663 ♿ 🐾 bar only but you can also eat here. Yes, it's primarily a campsite but the Boe Rigg, just off the main road between Kielder and Bellingham, has become as well known as a good drinking hole (local beers and a huge selection of whiskys) and restaurant that serves some great plates of food including breakfasts (full English, omelettes; book the night before) and mean burgers, chicken dishes, curries, fish and chips and so on for lunch and evening meals or to take-away. Nice views of the facing hillsides, kids playing badminton and free-range hens wandering about.

Old School Tearoom Falstone ✆ 01434 240459 ⊙ Thu–Tue ♿ outside toilet & a low step into café 🐾. Former Victorian school selling inexpensive breakfasts and cold and hot lunches. The tea room has free Wi-Fi and doubles as a small shop selling crafts and homemade jams, etc.

KIELDER WATER & FOREST PARK

A wide, black upland region, which looks wintry even in the sunshine... The song of the lark would be out of place here; the curlew's cry harmonises with the scene.
Walter White, *Northumberland and the Border*, 1859

England's largest forest, covering 230 square miles of remote, upland terrain, is one of the most isolated corners of England with the clearest night skies; yet it doesn't feel like England at all. As you motor into Kielder along the lakeside road, the tall Sitka spruce trees close in on you, and for a while the landscape takes on the appearance of the great Highland forests. The scenery is made all the more Scottish in character by vast areas of open moorland, ospreys and red squirrels.

Kielder is no untouched wilderness, however, this being a plantation forest surrounding the largest reservoir in northern Europe and supplying 25% of England's domestic lumber. It may be a relatively young landscape, created in the aftermath of World War I to replenish timber supplies, but it is still astonishingly scenic. The Campaign to Protect Rural England described Kielder as the most tranquil place in the country with the darkest night skies, and the whole of Kielder is now recognised as a **Dark**

Sky Park. On clear nights, I recommend a dusk walk to the **Observatory**. Halfway up is a large boulder by a modern sculpture called *Skyspace* where you can sit looking out over the trees and reservoir. As the light fades and only the silhouette of the hills and tree tops can be seen, the first planets appear. Stay here long enough and you will see more stars than you have seen anywhere else in England.

"Thigh-high heather, bracken and bilberry cover the peaty slopes, which are stunning in a wild, desolate way."

Architecture as art is a reoccurring theme at Kielder, with over 20 unique buildings and **sculptures** inspired by Kielder's landscapes dotted around the reservoir and forest. They include the aforementioned Observatory and Skypace enclosure as well as a giant timber head, stone maze, and a camera obscura within a stone hut. Pick up a printed guide at information points or see ⊘ visitkielder.com for locations.

North of Kielder Reservoir, an extensive area of moorland, part of the **Kielderhead National Nature Reserve**, stretches to the Scottish border. Thigh-high heather, bracken and bilberry cover the peaty slopes, which are stunning in a wild, desolate way: all those swelling hills creating

SUPPLIES & INFORMATION

Kielder is far from its nearest town (Bellingham) and has limited mobile phone signal and only a few places to eat. The only **petrol station** is a self-service machine (⊙ 24hr) in Kielder village (there's also a small **general store** and off licence here ✆ 01450 219018 ⊙ Apr–end Oct Tue–Sun). For food supplies, suncream and so on, your best option is the small shop at **Kielder Waterside** (page 256). There's a **post office** in Kielder village (✆ 01434 250245 ⊙ 09.30–16.00 Mon & Wed–Fri, 09.30–12.30 Tue & Sat).

All three of Kielder's **tourist information sites** are on the south side of Kielder Water. For full details, see ⊘ visitkielder.com.

Tower Knowe Visitor Centre (✆ 01434 240436 ⊙ Easter–end Oct daily ♿) stands by the main access road to the forest next door to a café overlooking the reservoir (page 261) and a wildlife-viewing station where you might spot ospreys. The large shop sells guides, gifts, maps and clothing.

Kielder Waterside (page 256) is a busy hub for visitors in the area with a restaurant, pub, small swimming pool and shop selling gifts, guides, basic provisions, kids clothing and free paper maps of Kielder.

Kielder Castle (page 259) is at the furthermost corner of the reservoir where there's an information point, café and children's play areas.

endless coloured folds, clouds rolling fast across big skies and the sun picking out individual moors to bathe in light.

This landscape is full of **wildlife** surprises: the sudden appearance of a merlin pursuing a meadow pipit, a wild Cheviot goat (page 195), exquisite day-flying emperor moths skimming the heather, and an expanse of cloudberries, their orange fruits ripe to eat. Breeding birds include golden plover, dunlin, red grouse, curlew and even ring ouzel.

OUTDOOR ACTIVITIES AT KIELDER

A superb network of trails for cyclists, walkers, horseriders and wheelchair users is maintained by Forestry England.

Circumnavigating the shoreline in 27 flat-ish miles on a paved surface, the **Lakeside Way** is the most accessible. It lends itself well to marathons (⊘ kieldermarathon.com) for obvious reasons. It takes around three to four hours to cycle the whole route.

Walks are plentiful around the reservoir and many routes encompass Kielder's **public art works** and wildlife hotspots. Pick up free *Wild Walks* **trail guides** in one of the visitor centres or download them from ⊘ visitkielder.com. Also consider countryside walks a short drive from Kielder at Greenhaugh for the scenic Tarset Valley (page 250), and Bellingham (page 246), and don't overlook the lovely Blakehopeburnhaugh waterfall walk (page 260), 12 miles northeast of Kielder Castle along the Forest Road.

Off-road **mountain bike trails** range from family-friendly green routes such as the Borderline Trail from Kielder village along an old railway line, to red routes like the Deadwater Trail (and its black route extension) that climbs to the summit of Deadwater at 1,900ft – the highest mountain-biking route in England. At the top you can see the Pentland Hills, south of Edinburgh, and the Lake District. Another exhilarating circular ride that actually takes you into Scotland starts out from Matthew's Linn and follows the Bloody Bush Trail to Newcastleton; the return is via the Cross Border Trail.

At the time of writing, you could no longer hire bikes at Kielder but a new hire station at Kielder Waterside will hopefully be open by the time you are reading this. Call ⊘ 01434 251000 for an update. Download routes from ⊘ visitkielder.com. Owing to storm damage and Forestry works, some routes may be closed. Check ⊘ forestryengland.uk/kielder-castle/cycling-and-mountain-biking-trails-kielder.

REWILDING KIELDER

Kielder has spearheaded a number of wildlife-breeding programmes in recent decades including for ospreys and water voles, while supporting the resident red squirrels, otters and important populations of birds of prey. Momentum is gathering for the reintroduction of lynx to their native habitat as part of a wider rewilding scheme (see ⊘ missinglynxproject.org.uk).

Thirty thousand trees (mainly broad-leaved) were planted along the Scaup Burn, around four miles east of Kielder Castle (following the Forest Drive), as part of the **Kielderhead Wildwood Project** launched in 2018. The task included propagating 500 native pine saplings from six very precious trees thought to be the only truly native Scots pines in England.

For **watersports**, contact the Calvert Trust (⊘ 01434 250232 ⊘ calvertkielder.org.uk ⊘ early Feb–Nov) for canoeing and sailing. The **Merlin Brae Water Ski Club** near Tower Knowe (⊘ 01434 250037 ⊘ merlinbraewaterski.chessck.co.uk ⊘ May–Sep Sat & Sun) offers waterskiing and wakeboarding lessons. Best to call at the weekend or email ✉ merlinbrae@gmail.com to make bookings as the club is operated by volunteers and is not always open.

Fishing permits and basic equipment for novices are available to hire or buy at Tower Knowe and Kielder Waterside.

Hidden in a handful of secluded locations are **wild camping** sites operated by Forestry England. There are no facilities; just a rough patch of grass to pitch up for a night. Campers must dig latrines. There are also eight **bothies**. For locations (a guarded secret) and to book, call Forestry England (⊘ 01434 221012).

27 KIELDER WATERSIDE & OSPREY FERRY

NE48 1BT ⊘ 01434 251000 ⊘ Feb–Dec; activities should be booked at the Kielder Waterside shop or online at ⊘ kielderwaterside.com

Kielder Waterside is a family-oriented hub halfway along the south shore of Kielder Water with forest lodges for hire. There's a pub and restaurant (page 261) here, reasonably well-stocked shop selling food, clothing, gifts, maps etc, and plenty to occupy children: a bird of prey centre (see opposite), playground, crazy golf, giant 'pillow' trampoline, bike hire, archery and a small swimming pool.

The **Osprey Ferry** (⊘ 01434 251000 ⊘ end Mar–end Oct Wed, Sat & Sun ⌂ 🐾) operates a 'hop on, hop off' service three times a day (check times and book at ✆ bookwhen.com/kielderwatersideferry or go to one of the visitor centres) and takes wheelchairs and a limited number of pushchairs. It stops at the Belvedere art installation on the north shore and Tower Knowe. Ospreys are frequently spotted flying and fishing over the water, particularly on early evening cruises. I enjoyed multiple sightings the last time I made the trip.

A short stroll from the waterfront is the **Kielder Bird of Prey Centre** (✆ 01434 250400 ✆ kielderbopc.com ⊙ 10.30–16.30 daily, until 15.30 in winter ♿). Outside flying demonstrations operate daily in the summer (⊙ 13.30 & 15.00), during which visitors can slip on a falconry glove and experience the thrill of a bird of prey swooping in to land on your hand. Private individual and family Hawk Walks last an hour.

28 KIELDER OBSERVATORY

Signposted off the main road, a third of a mile south of Kielder Castle; from the turn-off it's 2 miles uphill to the observatory ✆ 0191 265 5510 ✆ kielderobservatory.org ⊙ only for events (call to book or visit the website); parking (access track opened half an hour before events commence) ♿ partial access 🐾

No need to be an astronomy buff to come here: the enthusiasm of the staff and volunteers at the observatory will soon have you hooked. Even just the experience of travelling to this remote outpost, the hilltop views at dusk and the striking building are worthy of the drive alone.

DARK SKY PARK

Come nightfall, much of Northumberland is bathed in pitch-black skies due to the remoteness of the region and large expanses of uninhabited forests, hills and moorland – something that was recognised by the International Dark Skies Association who awarded Northumberland National Park and Kielder Water Forest Park the first **Dark Sky Park** status in England. It's an accolade the county shares with the likes of Death Valley in North America and is just one of three Dark Sky Parks in England. Within the zone, which covers 572 square miles of Northumberland, the Cheviot valleys and hills and the whole of Kielder offer some of the best spots for stargazing. See the 'Discover our Dark Skies' pages at ✆ northumberlandnationalpark.org. uk (under 'Things to Do') or visit the Kielder Observatory (see above).

Unsurprisingly, Kielder is considered the best place in England to see the **Northern Lights** because of its exceptionally dark skies and relative closeness to the North Pole. If the conditions are right (clear skies and a strong solar storm), you may see curtains of flickering green and pink light.

RICKFORDUK/S

DAN MONK/KIELDER OBSERVATORY

PHIL MADDOCKS/S

JOHN SPARKS/A

SS

The timber structure juts out of the hillside on stilts; inside, two roof shutters become 'your eye into the universe' when opened to reveal a dark sky dusted with millions of stars. Two huge telescopes crank into gear, turning on a huge circular track.

Even on cloudy evenings, the experienced team of astronomers do a superb job of engaging with visitors (huddled into a room by a log burner and sipping hot chocolates), using interactive technology to make sense of the scale and wonders of the universe. **Events** get booked up many weeks in advance, especially for family events like Space Kids and Aurora Nights.

29 BAKETHIN NATURE RESERVE & VIADUCT

Spanning the North Tyne near Bakethin Reservoir is a castellated **viaduct** dating to 1862 that is well used by cyclists and walkers following the Lakeside Trail, but was originally built to carry the now defunct Border Counties Railway on its journey from the Tyne Valley to Scotland. It was engineered with seven 'skew arches' shaped so the viaduct aligned with the river, which it crosses at an angle.

The viaduct is also one of the best places in Kielder from which to view ospreys, wildfowl and otters. In fact, this whole area is great for **wildlife watching**. Created during the construction of Kielder dam in 1979, the reserve wraps around the northern reaches of Kielder Water where a variety of amphibians, birds and mammals inhabit the wetland, woodland and grassland habitats.

30 KIELDER CASTLE, VILLAGE & FOREST DRIVE

The Duke of Northumberland's former hunting lodge, **Kielder Castle**, dominates the western end of the reservoir and marks the start points for a number of biking adventures into the forest including the awesome route to the summit of **Deadwater Fell**, standing at 1,900ft on the Scottish border, and which can also be hiked. There's an **information point** inside the castle (sometimes staffed with helpful Forestry England workers) and a café (page 261). A campsite, pub,

---

◀ **1** Kielder Water and Forest Park – some 230 square miles of remote, upland terrain. **2** The Kielder Observatory offers superlative opportunities for stargazing in this Dark Sky reserve. **3** Forty-seven sculptures dot the forests and shores of Kielder **4** There are mountain bike trails for all skill levels. **5** Red squirrels are prevalent in the forest.

FISH EAGLES

Ospreys returned to Kielder in 2009 after a 200-year absence and are now frequently sighted over Kielder reservoir between late March and early September, where they pull fish from the reservoir's depths. Early evening is the best time to see them, either from the Osprey Ferry or the Lakeside Way path, Kielder dam or the Bull Crag Peninsula.

To learn more about the birdlife and view nesting ospreys through powerful telescopes, a visit to the informative volunteer-run **osprey viewing station** at Tower Knowe (page 254) is a must.

lodge accommodation and **Kielder village** (post office with a cash machine, a B&B and a self-service petrol station) are all nearby.

The **Kielder Salmon Centre** (NE48 1HX ℘ 01434 250269 ☉ Apr–Sep daily ♿) at Kielder, run by the Environment Agency, is the largest salmon hatchery in England where close to a million fish annually are reared to restock waterways in the north of England including the Tyne – the top salmon river in England. Engaging displays explain the lifecycle of the fish and conservation of the rare freshwater pearl mussel, also grown at the centre. In autumn you may be able to see the salmon being 'stripped' of their eggs if you phone in advance.

From Kielder Castle to Blakehopeburnhaugh, the potholed **Forest Drive** traverses the upland landscape north of Kielder Water in 12 slow-going miles. If you're in a hurry to reach the A68, this is a terrible route; if you're happy to trundle along enjoying the outstanding moorland and forest scenery and perhaps stopping for lunch or a walk, Forest Drive is for you. At the halfway point, the Sitka spruce trees open up, permitting a long view into the hills with Kielderhead to the north and Emblehope Moor to the south. A couple of great short **walks** begin at the eastern end of Forest Drive, not far from the A68, where there is parking (see below).

31 HINDHOPE LINN & THE THREE KINGS

At the eastern end of the Forest Drive at **Blakehopeburnhaugh** (not the longest place name in England in case you are wondering; that is Cottonshopeburnfoot a mile north), a parking area marks the starting points to a couple of **walks**, including access to the Pennine Way.

Hindhope Linn is a magical waterfall in secluded woodland and is easily reached in just over a mile from the Blakehopeburnhaugh car park by following Blakehope Burn for 15 minutes or so along a well-trodden woodland path above a gorge and through trees, bilberry and bracken. Hindhope Linn's long spout plummets into a pool (at times deep enough for a dip) enclosed by trees, mosses and luxuriant ferns. It's a most enchanting setting.

Walking north from the car park is another well-marked trail of just over a mile to **The Three Kings (of Denmark)**, a circle of three upright and one fallen stones covered in lichens and thought to be between 3,000 and 4,000 years old.

¶¶ FOOD & DRINK

The best restaurant for a hot lunch or dinner in the Kielder area is **The Pheasant Inn** (page 262) at Stannersburn. There's a small **food shop** at Kielder Waterside (✆ 01434 251000 ⊙ 24hr ♿), but for a bigger shop, you'll need to make the trek to Bellingham or arrange for supermarket delivery to your accommodation (major supermarket chains deliver to Kielder lodges). The **post office** in Kielder village sells drinks and snacks and there's a good **mobile take-away café** at Kielder Castle (⊙ Tue, Wed & Fri–Sun plus additional days during some school holidays) with a range of burgers, pulled-pork sandwiches, hot dogs and chips to enjoy on one of the park benches around the castle. **The Kielder Tavern** in Kielder village (NE48 1ER ✆ 01434 250072 ⊙ daily ♿ 🐾) is a locals' pub serving burgers, Sunday roasts and standard pub fare.

The Café Tower Knowe Visitor Centre, near Falstone NE48 1BX ✆ 01434 240436 ⊙ Easter– end Oct 11.00–17.00 Thu–Sun ♿ 🐾. Imaginatively named bistro at the gateway to Kielder and on the Lakeside trail selling mainly pastries, coffee and good ice creams; a sheltered terrace overlooking the reservoir catches the afternoon sun. A gift shop and the **Osprey viewing hut** operate next door.

Forest Bar & Kitchen Kielder Waterside NE48 1BT ✆ 01434 251000 ⊙ Feb–Dec all day ♿. A decent pub and restaurant on the lakeside, popular with visitors, some who come for just a coffee with a view. Pizzas, burgers, fish and chips, all-day breakfasts, Sunday roasts, ice creams. It can get pretty crowded and noisy inside with hyper kids tumbling out of the little soft play

RED SQUIRRELS

At Kielder, our native squirrel has the upper hand over greys, making this their last stronghold (50% of the red squirrel population in England). A reliable place to see them is around the Kielder Castle entrance to Forest Drive. Chewed pine cones on footpaths are a sign that squirrels are about, but listening for them in the trees is the best way to spot them. Also try Kielder Waterside where there are feeders.

area, and you may have to wait for your food. Weather permitting, an outside table overlooking the reservoir may be more relaxing, or grab a take-away pizza.

The Pheasant Inn Stannersburn NE48 1DD ✆ 01434 240382 ⊙ Apr–Oct lunch & evening meals daily, Nov–Mar Wed–Sun. A good choice for Sunday lunch or dinner. Hearty traditional British mains and puddings, made with plenty of regional ingredients (fish from North Shields, Northumbrian meats, cheeses from Ponteland). The roast lamb is superb. And a great selection of local ales. All served in a 400-year-old unpretentious farmhouse with much rustic appeal (low beams, wooden furniture and old photographs of Redesdale life hanging on the walls) and not a bit of gastro pub décor. Book in advance. B&B rooms available.

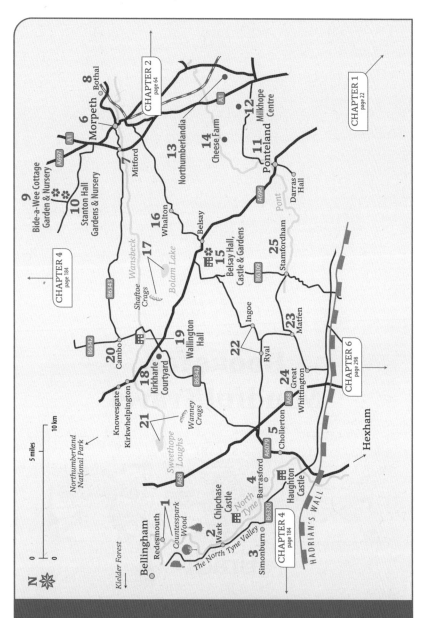

MORPETH & CAPABILITY BROWN COUNTRY

5

MORPETH & CAPABILITY BROWN COUNTRY

Lowland farmland surrounds settlements north of the River Tyne, including **Ponteland** (page 281) and **Morpeth** (page 272) – the most prominent towns in this tranquil corner of Northumberland – where a potter around a stately home followed by a cream tea or pub lunch are the order of the day. If you take the car for a wander, you'll find yourself dipping in and out of well-to-do villages, tootling along green lanes and glimpsing country houses between the trees and hedgerows. Here you'll find two of the region's finest manors (**Wallington Hall** (page 290) and **Belsay Hall** (page 283) and several intriguing gardens open to the public. Cyclists will enjoy the country lanes connecting all these places.

Those with an interest in historic gardens will know the celebrated 18th-century landscape designer, **Capability Brown**, was born at **Kirkharle** (page 289) – a rural farmstead west of Morpeth. The landscape for miles around is at times like a vignette of an 18th-century country estate where undulating meadows, waterways, ponds and ancient broad-leaved trees come together to picturesque effect as if planned by Brown himself.

GETTING AROUND

Unless you're on two wheels or don't mind tightly planning your holiday around the infrequent buses, you're going to need a **car** to access much of the countryside covered in this chapter. The only **train** station of help is at Morpeth (with fairly frequent services from Newcastle in under 15 minutes).

BUS

Reaching Morpeth is straightforward as there are regular services from Newcastle (X14) every day; accessing the wider countryside is more

> ### TOURIST INFORMATION
>
> **Morpeth Chantry** Bridge St ✆ 01670 623455 ☺ Mon–Sat ♿. Large, helpful TIC; also houses a shop selling local guides, crafts and artworks and Bagpipe Museum (page 273).

difficult and most of the places in this chapter are not on a bus route. See the bus map on page 18 for reaching Ponteland, Stamfordham and Matfen (page 294).

CYCLING

Cycling in the countryside covered by this chapter is a joy: there are plenty of quiet back roads around the likes of Ponteland, Matfen and Belsay, and high passes with far-reaching views of moors and forests as you travel west towards Kielder and Redesdale in North Tynedale. The enticing **Rievers Route** (NCN Route 10) takes in the best of both landscapes on its 172-mile coast-to-coast journey from Tynemouth to Cumbria's Whitehaven, connecting Ponteland on the outskirts of Newcastle with Stamfordham, Matfen and Kielder Water.

An exhilarating stretch of the 355-mile **Pennine Cycleway** (NCN Route 68) skirts the eastern edge of the Cheviots, entering some remote tracts of Redesdale around Elsdon and Bellingham before continuing south to Hadrian's Wall. Dense forests, upland farmland and river scenery await. It's also a popular route with weekend cyclists whose bikes you'll see stacked outside watering holes and cafés in many a country village and especially in the likes of Elsdon, Bellingham and Once Brewed.

CYCLE HIRE & REPAIRS

WATBike Thorneyford Farm, Kirkley, Ponteland NE20 0AJ ✆ 01661 825599 ☺ Mon–Sat. Repairs, bicycle equipment & cycle transport. Café (✆ 01661 871094 ☺ Wed–Sun).
Pedal Power (page 301)
Sims Cycle Workshop 7B Old Queens Head Yard, Morpeth NE61 1PY ✆ 01670 207459 ☺ Tue–Sat. Repairs and equipment.

WALKING

Travelling west through the central belt of Northumberland, the landscape increases in tempo from gentle farmland cosying up to stone villages in the lowlands to the remote moors, upland meadows and forests encountered as you near the national park.

Walks around Morpeth are not particularly demanding, but there are some pleasant strolls to be had along the River Wansbeck and around Bolam Lake, for example. **St Oswald's Way** long-distance path (page 301) enters fine farming countryside between Kirkwhelpington and Hadrian's Wall, taking in the pastoral scenery once so familiar to Capability Brown.

While there are some pleasant walks making use of footpaths crossing fields, bridleways and quiet lanes in and around Ponteland, the only really special route is to the top of **Shaftoe Crags** (page 288) where a spectacular panoramic view of central Northumberland awaits.

For a river walk, I can hardly think of a more scenic and peaceful place for a stroll than the upper reaches of the River North Tyne following the **River Tyne Trail** out of Kielder and through Redesdale, particularly between Redesmouth and Wark (page 268).

TAXIS

Broadway Cabs Ponteland ✆ 01661 822200
Just Taxis Morpeth ✆ 07957 495503
Phoenix Taxis ✆ 01670 540 222 ♿
SA Taxis Morpeth ✆ 01670 513513

THE NORTH TYNE VALLEY

From Kielder, the wild River North Tyne flows out of Northumberland National Park, across reiver country and through some enchanting old woods before merging with the Tyne north of Hexham. Here, we follow its course from the old railway village of **Redesmouth**, through **Countesspark Wood** and **Wark**, past a castle or two, and into the territory of the Romans just north of Chollerford. For the market town of Bellingham and the upper reaches of the valley in the Kielder Forest area, see *Chapter 4*.

1 REDESMOUTH & COUNTESSPARK WOOD

Once a station on the old Border Counties Railway line, a length of which is now submerged under Kielder Water, the hamlet of **Redesmouth** occupies a wooded bank above the confluence of the rivers Rede and North Tyne. Little known to visitors to the area (or indeed to anyone outside of Redesdale), this is a stunning beauty spot with wonderful woodland and river scenery.

An old English bluebell wood, **Countesspark** does not disappoint in spring. Broad-leaved trees crowd the banks above a secluded stretch of the River North Tyne, which is reached on foot from Redesmouth in 15 minutes or so. To **walk** there from the old railway cottages (if travelling west from the A68, look out for the hamlet on your left after the road sign for Redesmouth and just before the sharp descent to the river), follow the lane downhill to some derelict engine sheds (now used for hay storage). Turn left on to the dismantled line, with the old station house, platform and signal box (now converted into accommodation) ahead. Wildflowers flourish on the damp trackbed, which you follow for a few hundred yards to a ladder stile on your right that leads into the woods and to the **riverbank**.

"Wildflowers flourish on the damp trackbed, which you follow for a few hundred yards to a ladder stile."

This is a beautiful spot with some bathing options; note that the current is very strong in places so take care. Follow the North Tyne downriver, passing a quaint log fishing hut owned by the Duke of Northumberland. Salmon and sea trout are pulled from the water hereabouts. At a hairpin bend in the track, turn uphill to meet the railway line, where you turn left and follow the trackbed back to Redesmouth. This circular route is 1½ mile long.

2 WARK

Facing the verdant banks of the North Tyne, Wark is most memorably approached from the east across a slim metal bridge. It's pleasant here with a green bound by well-kept stone cottages and an award-winning pub. Note the mature chestnut tree; it was planted in 1887 to celebrate Queen Victoria's Jubilee.

¶¶ FOOD & DRINK

Battlesteads Hotel & Restaurant Wark ✆ 01434 230209 ⊘ breakfasts and evening meals daily & lunch Sun ♿ 🐾 garden only. So much more than a multi award-winning restaurant and hotel, Battlesteads plays an important role in the life of the village, putting on community events like a four-day summer **beer festival** and stargazing talks and events held at their **observatory**.

The restaurant (smart but informal dining) uses plenty of ingredients from the hotel garden, as well as salmon smoked on site; you could choose pan-fried rabbit with black pudding, followed by game meatballs with tagliatelle; or simply fish and chips. For afters, again it's all traditional bowls of deliciousness (with a twist): lemon posset with Earl Grey-soaked prunes for example. A Northumbrian cheeseboard always features. The **Sunday carvery** is very popular so book ahead. In summary, the food is so good and so reasonably priced that you'll want to stay here and spend your evening with a drink in the sun-filled conservatory or back garden.

3 SIMONBURN

I'll admit there's not a lot to *see* here; just some rustic terraced cottages facing a large green, a tea room and 19th-century St Mungo's Church, but if your idea of a pleasant Sunday out is moseying through tranquil countryside on quiet lanes to an old-world village with the promise of a cream tea, Simonburn is for you.

Simonburn Castle sits on a wooded mound half a mile northwest of the hamlet. Only fragments of masonry remain from the fortress, which was built in 1766 as an eye-catcher from Nunwick Hall to replace an earlier medieval tower.

The same distance in the other direction (northeast), you'll reach **Nunwick** – a flower-filled hamlet with a hall dating from 1760.

FOOD & DRINK

Simonburn Tea Rooms The Mains ☏ 01434 681321 ☺ Wed–Sun. On a summer's afternoon, a cup of tea, slice of cake or a scone while the children muck about in the garden is just the thing. Light lunches include soup, quiche and sandwiches (breakfast and evening meals available for non-guests of the B&B if booked in advance).

4 BARRASFORD & NEARBY CASTLES

Haughton Castle hides behind a bank of mature trees, only revealing itself for the briefest of moments as you pass through the quiet settlement of **Barrasford**, a couple of miles north of Chesters Roman Fort. The village has a pleasant riverside walk offering a rare glimpse of Haughton Castle's exposed turrets.

To reach the **river** and see the medieval manor house, cross the stile by the bridge at the eastern end of the village and follow the merry burn to the River North Tyne. It's a bit brambly and the long dew-laden grasses tend to be trouser dampening, but it's worth the tramp along the footpath for the views when you reach the wide, rapid-surfing North Tyne. At the riverbank, turn right by an old oak and follow the trail until you reach a cottage. The best view of the turreted castle is from this point.

Haughton Castle (a right of way goes through the grounds) stands on the west side of the River North Tyne, not far from Humshaugh, looking rather stern with its formidable embattlements and small cheerless windows. It was fortified in the 14th century and survived the next few hundred years of cross-border conflict before its transformation into a 19th-century country house.

Northwest of Barrasford, on the road to Wark, is **Chipchase Castle** (NE48 3NT 🖉 01434 230203 ⊙ call or check online ⊘ chipchasecastle. com for public opening times), next in the line of great Northumbrian country houses in the North Tyne Valley. Chipchase is a hugely impressive part-Jacobean, part-Georgian manor house with a medieval tower set within landscaped parkland. It forms the centrepiece of an estate that encompasses a stretch of the best salmon river in England (fly-fishing arranged through the castle). A small chapel stands alone in the grounds, and on the other side of the manor is a walled garden and nursery.

5 CHOLLERTON

Many visitors on their way to Hexham must have put on their brakes at Chollerton on seeing its old church and scenic position above a lush vale.

Inside **St Giles's**, the most intriguing stones are the pillars: round on one side of the nave; octagonal on the other. The former are Roman and no doubt came from one of the nearby forts. Also dating to this period is the old font on the right as you enter the church, which began life as a Roman altar. Note too the 19th-century old stable and **hearse house** by the road, its former function indicated by the stone horse mount. It's one of only a few remaining in the country. Inside is a little **museum** with information boards about the building (it once served as a post office) and local community.

Uphill from Chollerton is a wonderfully complete and unchanged **Victorian farm**. It retains its old windmill, blacksmith's forge, carriage house, farmhouse and a row of cottages (described by English Heritage

---

1 View along the river in Morpeth. **2** The Morpeth Cheese Shop is a local institution. **3** The pretty village of Simonburn. **4** Chipchase Castle is one of several impressive manors in the North Tyne valley. ▶

DAVE HEAD/S

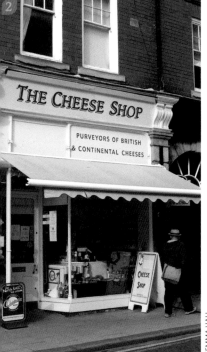

GEMMA HALL

DAVE HEAD/S

CHIVES/DT

as an important example of industrial farm housing). There's no public access but you can take in the assemblage of buildings by pulling over at the side of the A6079.

CAPABILITY BROWN COUNTRY: MORPETH & SURROUNDS

One of the busiest towns in Northumberland, **Morpeth** is a useful stopping off point for Great North Road (A1) visitors travelling to the coast or hills, with plenty of tempting independent shops and a pleasant river and parkland for walks. Venturing outside the town, green farmland encloses a scattering of places worth noting: a couple of small **animal parks** and **gardens** open to the public, and the odd village stranded in an earlier century.

6 MORPETH

This well-connected working town off the A1 rivals the likes of Hexham and Corbridge in size and energy, with a thriving local food and shopping scene, and plenty of historic streets, alleyways (page 274) and buildings to admire. Cocooned in a loop of the River Wansbeck, Morpeth's centre feels crowded – and sometimes jammed with cars – but step away from the high street and you'll find a quieter part of town. A wander down to the river, with its pleasant waterside and access to Carlisle Park provides a welcome breathing space (page 274).

THE GATHERING

Celebrating the region's heritage, traditions, food and arts, the Morpeth **Northumbrian Gathering** (northumbriana.org.uk) is a three-day festival staged in Morpeth's public squares and buildings over the weekend that follows Easter. The much-anticipated tradition has been bringing together folk ensembles, writers, food producers, dancers and craftsmen and women from Northumberland annually since the first Gathering in 1968.

Rapper sword dancers, entertainers and musicians occupy the streets, with plenty of local delicacies on offer from the farmers' market opposite the town hall and various competitions staged around town, including a bagpipe event in the Chantry. A Punch and Judy show, storytelling and a child-friendly ceilidh cater well for families. You can even try your hand at bell ringing in the historic clock tower, which opens to the public for tours.

A good spread of independent boutiques and cafés are dotted throughout the town – some tucked away down Morpeth's many alleyways. I'm particularly fond of the **Cheese Shop** (page 275) by the clock tower and **Rutherford's** independent department store on Bridge Street. Incidentally, the town's old newspaper office, the Morpeth Herald, faces Rutherford's on the other side of Bridge Street. The signage (**J. & J.S. Mackay**) and frontage have changed little since the first hand-printed paper entered circulation in the mid 1800s. A display in the window showcases antique printing tools and has a paper from the archives opened for passers-by to enjoy.

Market Place

Morpeth's landmark **clock tower** provides an eye-catching focal point in the centre of town. Its irregular-shaped stones (recycled from a medieval building) give the appearance of a building much older than its early 17th-century construction. Note the two figures at the top: they are known as Clarence and Cuddy and are said to do a commendable job of keeping an eye on the town.

A curfew bell is tolled every day at 20.00 (except on Wednesdays) – a tradition that's endured for over 300 years. Local bell ringers perform at civic events and during the Morpeth Northumbrian Gathering (see opposite), when the tower is open to the public (one of only three such tower open days a year). It's a tight squeeze up some ladders and through a trap door where the bellringing ropes hang loose, tempting visitors eagerly packed into the confined space.

A few paces away is the **Town Hall**, originally the work of Vanbrugh and built in 1714 but reconstructed in the late 1800s following a fire. The reception is in the old butter market. If you're passing, have a peek inside, especially to see the rather grand staircase.

Bridges & bagpipes

At the bottom of Bridge Street, by the river, the Grade I listed 13th-century **Morpeth Chantry** – the town's oldest building and one of only a small number of bridge chantries left in the country – crouches between the footbridge and the road bridge. It once operated as a toll house for the crossing, as well as a chapel dedicated to All Saints and a grammar school (the priest of the day had his work cut out). It's now the **tourist information centre** (page 266) and houses a large gift

ALLEYWAYS & YARDS

As you wander around Morpeth's streets, note the narrow passageways between buildings, many of which have intriguing names: Old Nag's Head Yard, Old Gaol Yard, Corporation Yard, Whalebone Yard and George and Dragon Yard. One alley is simply named Horse Entry. They take us back to the days when the town was a stopping point for horse-drawn coaches travelling from Edinburgh to London on the Great North Road. Inns provided shelter to travellers, and adjoining blacksmiths and stables (reached via alleys) took care of the coach horses.

shop showcasing local artworks, crafts, Northumbrian tartan, guides, maps and sweet treats.

The standout feature of Morpeth Chantry is the wonderful upstairs **Bagpipe Museum** (♿ via a lift), where visitors can enjoy the distinctive soft notes of the Northumbrian smallpipes, often performed live by musicians (third Saturday of the month), as they wander around the displays of historic instruments. Unlike Scottish bagpipes, the Northumbrian variety are bellows blown, a skill requiring much concentration; hence the far-away look on the faces of pipers as they perform. A smallpipes competition is held in the museum at the annual Morpeth Northumbrian Gathering festival (page 272).

Outside, the dainty **Chantry Footbridge** over the Wansbeck dates from 1869 and rests on the hefty piers of a 13th-century crossing. The three-arched road bridge opposite was designed by Thomas Telford and built in 1831. Pedestrians can use the footbridge for access to Carlisle Park and Morpeth Castle.

Carlisle Park, Morpeth Castle & the riverside

Rowing boats and swans glide along the wide River Wansbeck, enhancing the setting of **Carlisle Park** (⊙ until dusk) on the southern edge of Morpeth with its play areas, **paddling pool** (⊙ May–Sep) and gardens. There's a paved riverside towpath here (♿), plus a boat-hire operator close to Elliott footbridge (at the bottom end of Newmarket East Car Park), which is also a key access route from the town centre into the park for pedestrians.

The **William Turner Garden**, opposite the old Court House, celebrates the eponymous local Morpethian and 'father of English botany' in a series of raised beds containing medicinal herbs, each with a description of their health properties lifted from Turner's 16th century *A New Herball*. They include fennel used to treat dog and snake bites ('It is good drunken in wine for the biting of serpents') and Madonna Lily ('It scoureth the face and taketh away the wrinkles').

Close by is a small **aviary** with rescued tropical birds and a statue of suffragette **Emily Davison**, who is depicted tipping her food bowl – a reference to her hunger strikes in prison. She famously stepped out in front of George V's racehorse during the Epsom Derby in 1913 and later died of her injuries. Her gravestone in Morpeth's St Mary's Church bears the epitaph of the Women's Social and Political Union slogan: 'deeds not words'.

"It's a stiff climb to the top but the reward is a view over Morpeth's red-tiled rooftops."

Looming over the Turner garden is **Ha' Hill**, where an 11th-century motte and bailey castle stood until it was destroyed by King John in 1216. It's a stiff climb to the top but the reward is a view over Morpeth's red-tiled rooftops and the surrounding countryside. When the Ha' Hill castle was razed, it was replaced by **Morpeth Castle**, whose surviving 14th-century gatehouse is now a Landmark Trust holiday property.

Morpeth's imposing early 19th-century **Court House** (once the old gaol and sometimes mistaken for the castle) stands opposite the entrance to Carlisle Park on Castle Bank. It's held various functions over the years but it currently houses an **antiques emporium** (☉ daily) stuffed with curiosities.

¶ FOOD & DRINK

Picnickers will find plenty of places in **Carlisle Park** or by the riverside. Pick up almost everything you need for an al fresco lunch at the **farmers' market** (☉ first Saturday of the month) in the market place and from the well-stocked **Morpeth Larder** (✆ 01670 503302 ☉ daily) in Sanderson Arcade (reached via Bridge Street and opposite Rutherford's department store).

The Chantry Tea Rooms 9A Chantry Pl ✆ 01670 514414 ☉ Mon–Sat. A quaint lavender-painted tea room, opposite the TIC, popular with a largely older clientele. Best visited in the afternoon for tea, served in a proper china teacup, but also for breakfasts and light lunches.
The Cheese Shop 6 Oldgate ✆ 01670 459579 ☉ Tue–Sat ♿. I can't leave Morpeth without picking up my favourite regional cheeses at this specialist shop facing the clock tower. In addition to the Northumberland Cheese Company's bestselling Nettle, and

Doddington's Darling Blue, the counter features popular cheeses from elsewhere in the UK and across the Channel. Shelves of fine jams (the gooseberry is really good) and chutneys, biscuits and gorgeous homemade cheese scones ('made at dawn this morning') will fill your basket.

Lollo Rosso 40 Bridge St ✆ 01670 514111 ○ closed Sun ♿. Large, modern Italian always busy with locals because the food is consistently very good. Book ahead.

Market Place Café Market Pl ○ daily. It turns out there is so much more you can pile onto a slice of sourdough for breakfast besides avocado and bacon. Perhaps you'd like mushrooms with marmite butter and a fried egg? Or smoked mackerel with cream cheese, beetroot, horseradish and watercress? Specialising in breakfasts and brunch, this large modern café facing the clock tower is obviously doing many things right, judging by all the occupied tables. Needless to say: start your day here.

The Office Chantry Pl ✆ 07957 721066 ○ from 17.00 Mon–Sat, from 15.00 Sun 🐾. CAMRA award-winning snug watering hole by Morpeth Chantry TIC, with a fine selection of beers from local breweries. Bring your dog, drink Northumbrian ale, chat with locals and set the world to rights.

St Mary's Inn St Mary's Ln ✆ 01670 641111 ○ from 08.00 until late Mon–Sat, afternoon Sun ♿ 🐾. With a red-brick frontage reminiscent of an Edwardian hospital, this chic pub,

ZOOS & FARMS

Surrounded by farmland in the lowlands around Morpeth and Ponteland are a couple of small zoos and an animal farm that will keep children occupied for half a day or so (or provide a welcome stop off for families on the A1).

Housing farm and exotic animals, the **Northumberland Zoo** (5 miles north of Morpeth, NE65 9QH ✆ 01670 787778 ○ daily ♿ partial access) is a hit with families with Arctic foxes, snowy owls, lynx and snow leopards and a lemur woodland that you can walk through for close-up encounters. Admission tickets are pricey in comparison to the **Northumberland College Zoo** (NE20 0AQ; access off the North Rd if coming from Ponteland ✆ 0300 770 6000 ○ local school holidays daily, year-round weekends ♿) at Kirkley Hall, an agricultural college a couple of miles north of Ponteland with 150 species, including meerkats, wallabies, monkeys, various reptiles and farm animals. Peacocks and children wander freely. It's delightfully low key (and inexpensive).

Also with plenty of opportunities for contact with exotic creatures and all the familiar farm animals (bottle-feeding lambs and small animal petting area) is the **Whitehouse Farm Centre** (NE61 6AW ✆ 01670 789998 ○ school holidays daily; winter months varibale ♿), four miles south of Morpeth. Various rides and a couple of excellent adventure playgrounds will keep younger children occupied most of the day.

B&B and restaurant (wooden floors, real fires and smart décor with some vintage touches), south of Morpeth, serves good lunches, evening meals and Sunday roasts. Haddock and chips, homemade pies, sourdough pizzas, burgers or something from the grill. An extensive bar snacks and light lunch menu is served in the bar area, including hot sandwiches and a reasonably priced children's menu.

No 59 The Townhouse 59 Bridge St ✆ 01670 336833 ⊙ noon–late Thu–Sun. You know you're in for a treat at this upmarket restaurant (one of very few in and around Morpeth) when you glance at the starters: lobster, ox cheek, local gin cured salmon and Northumbrian game. Facing the Morpeth Chantry at the bottom end of the high street, The Townhouse operates a bar on the ground floor and upstairs restaurant with views of the Wansbeck. Dishes are carefully prepared with some local ingredients. Come here for a hunk of meat or Sunday roast and make sure you leave room for one of the chef's sophisticated puddings.

7 MITFORD

From Morpeth, road and river intertwine through woodland making for a pleasant journey with the Wansbeck dancing through the trees. A mile or so from Morpeth you'll come to a sharp bend in the road where **Lowford Bridge** carries the B6343 over the Wansbeck into Mitford. There's not much to distract besides its pub, old mill and a lone thatched cottage by the riverside (one of only a handful of thatched buildings remaining in Northumberland); the village's greatest appeal is the farmland setting, church and ruined castle.

St Mary Magdalene Church (⊙ Jun–Aug 14.00–16.00 Tue & Thu) faces the ruin of Mitford Castle about half a mile west of Mitford's Plough Inn. Both are reached by way of a lane off the main Mitford to Morpeth road (signed for Mitford church). You can also walk here from Morpeth (just a few miles) across meadows and along the wooded riverside. The church's oldest stonework dates from the 12th century and includes the priest's door and south arcade, but for the most part it appears solidly Victorian with a steeple and tall spire. Like the castle opposite, the church was destroyed by fire several times, notably in 1216 during King John's northern rampage.

Mitford Castle rises from a field guarded by crows and jackdaws and looks arresting on its green knoll, even in its crumbling state. As you can believe, it has been ransacked many times since its construction in the mid 12th century. For a closer peek, look out for a footpath post by a lay-by a couple of hundred yards west of the church, pointing into a field.

1

2

3

4

8 BOTHAL

Just over three miles east of Morpeth, the River Wansbeck meanders past Bothal Castle and its neat 19th-century estate village that ranks as one of the most pristine in Northumberland. You can make this journey on foot by following the riverbank trail the whole way.

Bothal's medieval church and uniform honey-coloured houses with their distinctive metal-patterned windows and maroon paintwork are hidden in a hollow, and the village as a whole feels cut off, certainly geographically, but in other ways too – seemingly frozen in a bygone century when landed estates exerted tremendous influence over local communities. They still do to an extent, but it's nonetheless a surprise to see a fresh coat of feudal paintwork here in the 21st century.

"The village as a whole feels cut off, certainly geographically, but in other ways too – seemingly frozen in a bygone century."

Mature broad-leaved trees (stunning in autumn) rise on a steep bank above Bothal, increasing this sense of seclusion. There's no visual link from the village to the **river**, but it is easily accessed by following a grassy lane from the memorial cross and **St Andrew's Church** (note the distinctive bell-cote). Those wishing to cross the **Wansbeck** have the choice of stepping stones or a wire bridge. It's beautiful down here and a nice spot for a swim.

Bothal Castle, which dates from 1343, is a beast with huge curtain walls, a tower and gateway, but because of its isolation few people seek it out – or even know of its existence. Unfortunately, it's not open to the public, but striking views are had when approached from the west by road (also from the riverside and the aforementioned track).

9 BIDE-A-WEE COTTAGE GARDEN & NURSERY

Stanton, near Netherwitton NE65 8PR ℘ 01670 772238 ☉ mid-Apr–Sep noon–16.30 Thu–Sat ♿ partial access

Bide-a-Wee is hidden away off a road to nowhere, roughly between Morpeth and Longhorsley. Undulating meadows grazed by sheep surround the gardens, which were formed out of an old sandstone quarry over two decades ago. Paths snake up and down and through the quarry where ferns drape from rock walls and over ponds crowded with

---

◄ **1** Bothal Castle dates from 1343. **2** The gardens at Stanton Hall. **3 & 4** Pretty Mitford and its 12th-century castle.

more shade-loving, moisture-licking plants. Elsewhere, herbaceous borders, swathes of cornflowers (this being the home of the national collection of *Centaurea*), and a wildflower meadow delight visitors.

Many varieties of perennials, grasses, ferns and shrubs are for sale at the on-site nursery. A small tea room offers a good local Ringtons brew and cakes.

10 STANTON HALL GARDENS & NURSERY

Stanton, near Netherwitton NE65 8PR ✐ 01670 772641 ☉ mid-Apr–Sep Tue–Sun

Quite wonderfully situated in the grounds of a 14th-century manor (a private home and not open to the public), the gardens at Stanton Hall are glorious in summer and many visitors come here as much to admire the terraces and planting schemes as to buy plants. Feeling inspired, you will no doubt want to make your purchases from the wide selection of plants and shrubs grown on site, with knowledgeable gardeners on hand to advise.

While the gardens lack the infrastructure of a ticketed attraction (though there is a lovely honesty café), this being an independent, family-run business, you'll find the nursery is a world away from a commercial garden centre. When combined with a visit to nearby Bide-a-Wee Cottage Garden (see opposite), a mosey through the gardens at Stanton Hall makes for a very worthwhile afternoon jaunt into the Morpeth countryside.

CAPABILITY BROWN COUNTRY: IN & AROUND PONTELAND

Country lanes in the vicinity of **Ponteland** dip in and out of well-to-do villages, including **Matfen**, **Great Whittington** and **Whalton**, and are popular with cyclists and those enjoying a motor in the countryside. I spent many memorable afternoons in years gone by with my grandmother around here, dawdling along byways, getting in the way of tractors, stopping to chat to cyclists, drinking tea in the Milkhope Centre, going to fêtes and so on.

Travelling north out of Ponteland on the A696 towards the birthplace of Capability Brown at **Kirkharle**, the landscape becomes increasingly rural and Brown-esque with miles of rolling farmland fringed here and there with a bank of mature broad-leaved trees and rivers coming in and out of view. Nowhere is this more true than at **Belsay Hall**, one of the finest country mansions in the North East.

11 PONTELAND

Ponteland ('Pon-tee-land') was once an antiquated village and it still holds on to some of its old roots by the ornamental bridge over the River Pont. Here stands **St Mary's Church** with its Norman tower, and **The Blackbird**, a mansion house that started life as a fortified tower in the 14th century before it became incorporated into the 17th-century manor. It's now a good restaurant (page 282) and pub. In addition to a scattering of decent places to eat and some boutique shops, there are some pleasant corners to stretch your legs by the river, and a **vicar's pele tower** on Main Street (opposite Waitrose).

A **disused railway line** runs for a mile or so through the Darras Hall estate into open farmland where you'll eventually come to a nice spot by the River Pont to picnic and for children to throw stones. The line is largely concealed by trees and housing but you can pick up the path from behind the Darras Hall shops (find the garage and the signage for the Reivers cycleway, NCN Route 10). The woods are full of birds, including bullfinches on my last walk.

"Ponteland was once an antiquated village and it still holds on to some of its old roots by the ornamental bridge."

While we're in **Darras Hall**, mention must be made of the estate itself. Today there are plenty of mansions to gawp at, this being a wealthy suburb of Newcastle and a popular residential area for Newcastle United footballers, but the original dwellings dating from the 1930s to 1960s formed part of this early 20th-century utopian suburb that was dubbed the 'Garden City of the North'. Cherry trees, ornamental conifers and rose bushes edge the manicured lawns and driveways. Think *Stepford Wives*... in rural Northumberland.

¶¶ FOOD & DRINK

A few cafés, pubs and restaurants dot the main road (A696) through Ponteland. In Darras Hall, there's Michelin dining at the Indian restaurant, **Haveli** (3-5 Broadway ✆ 01661 872727 ◷ Wed–Sun). The two restaurants reviewed below are best for an intimate family meal or for couples. For something more casual, try the sourdough pizzas at **Bawn** (11 Main St ✆ 01661 598054 ◷ 17.30–21.00 Wed–Sat, plus lunch Sat), a chic little place with a great menu (and good value kids' pizzas).

The Blackbird North Rd ✆ 01661 822684 ⊙ noon–21.00 Mon–Sat, noon–17.00 Sun (bar open until late) ♿ side entrance & downstairs only 🐾 bar only. The ground floor of this upmarket pub and restaurant dates to the 14th century when this was a fortified house; the rest is mainly 17th century. Expect all the usual gastro pub offerings and a pricey bill for posh burgers, haddock and chips, roast lamb, fishcakes and steaks, served in the bar, the more refined Tunnel Room or the smart dining room upstairs. Sunday lunches are popular so you'll need to book. There are a couple of hand pumps serving local beers and a good selection of gins.

New Rendezvous 3–5 Bell Villas ✆ 01661 821775 ⊙ evenings only. Really good Chinese cuisine and attentive service in the old blacksmiths; popular with locals including Newcastle United footballers and former striker Alan Shearer (staff will tell you of after-hours games of poker with players).

12 MILKHOPE CENTRE

Blagdon NE13 6DA (just off the A1, 9 miles north of Newcastle) ⊙ daily ♿

This rural 'retail park' shares similarities with Kirkharle further north (page 289). The concept is similar: small local businesses brought together in converted 19th-century farm buildings in a country setting. You'll find a few furniture shops and an art gallery but mainly you'll want to visit for the superb farm shop (see below) and busy coffee shop, the **Blacksmiths** (✆ 01670 789878 ⊙ daily ♿).

The **Blagdon Farm Shop** (✆ 01670 789924 ⊙ Tue–Sun ♿) is a veritable feast of local produce. The meat and cheese counters are particularly generous and they only stock meat from the estate or local farms. 'I can tell you which farm every piece of meat you see came from,' the lady behind the counter told me. All the big-name regional producers are represented; vegetables come direct from the estate's walled garden.

13 NORTHUMBERLANDIA

Fisher Ln, Cramlington NE23 8AU (just off the A1) ⊙ dawn to dusk daily ♿ 🐾

An outdoor parkland created from a former industrial site (or 'slag heap') is not novel in the North East, but this large complex of paths and hillocks is also an impressive landscape sculpture. On the ground it's hard to make out that all the undulating grassy slopes form an image of a woman, a quarter of a mile in length, lying face up. 'The Lady of the North', or, as locals prefer to call her, 'Slag Alice' (the name is a word play on 'Slack Alice', a local expression meaning a slovenly woman) makes a worthwhile stopping point if travelling along the A1, especially if the kids need a run around. From Alice's head and breasts you get a better sense of her form and can see Northumberland's hills and the North Sea.

14 CHEESE FARM

Green Ln, Blagdon (nr Horton Grange) NE13 6BZ 🖉 01670 789798 ⊙ 10.00–16.00 Tue– Sun (last food orders 15.00)

Foodies will have spotted Northumberland Cheese Company Nettle and Cheviot cheeses in pretty much every good deli in the North East; well, this is where they are produced, with Jersey cow milk. The stone barns include a viewing window where you can see the cheese-making machinery at work.

Upstairs in the old granary, a **café** offers light lunches, including cheese soup, ploughman's, toasted sandwiches and something called a Northumberland Stack (sausage and bacon topped with melted cheese), plus cakes and scones. You can purchase their full range of cheeses – all 16 of them – from the cheese counter as well as jars of chutney, honey, crackers and local bottled beers. The nettle (very creamy) and Cheviot (mouth-tinglingly sharp) varieties are very popular. Redesdale – a creamy sheep's cheese – is my personal favourite but it's not as easy to source away from the farm as the others. Outdoor courtyard tables (👩‍🦽 🐾) in summer make this café a popular spot with cyclists.

15 BELSAY HALL, CASTLE & GARDENS

Belsay NE20 0DX 🖉 01661 881636 ⊙ Apr–Oct daily; Nov–Mar Wed–Sun 👩‍🦽 gardens & ground floor of hall & castle 🐾 grounds only; English Heritage

A trip to Belsay offers something quite different to other stately homes in Northumberland: a Greek Revival mansion, luxuriant Picturesque-style gardens and a medieval castle tower – all set within many acres of undulating farmland. For a few decades now, English Heritage has staged some superb contemporary art exhibitions here and it's worth checking online for upcoming events.

Work began on the stone **Hall** – which is precisely 100-square-foot – in 1807 when the owners returned from a year-and-a-half-long honeymoon in Europe. Sir Charles Monck was passionate about Greek architecture and had exacting standards – both of which are clear as you tour the estate.

Raised like a Grecian temple on a platform above three steps, the **house** is distinguished by the plain grandeur of its façade, with almost no decorative masonry except for two huge Doric columns either side of the doorway. Some would say it's austere; others see beauty in those clean lines and smooth, honey-coloured sandstone blocks that are finely cut and set without mortar. The ancient Greek theme continues in the **Pillar Hall** – a square reception room surrounded by colonnades on two storeys (note the Doric columns on the first floor and Ionic columns downstairs). Guests were entertained at dances held in the elegant space – a spectacle not difficult to envisage.

Peeling (original Morris) wallpaper in the empty upstairs bedrooms gives the impression that the last occupants of the Hall have only recently left. In fact Belsay has been like this since the 1960s. Floor to ceiling sash windows frame the exquisite grounds outside, where ornamental trees poke through a dense bank of rhododendron, and sheep graze parkland beyond.

It takes about 20 minutes or so to walk to Belsay Castle, which is reached via a series of contrasting **gardens**. Formal terraces planted with shrubs and perennials fall away from the south side of the hall connecting to the **Magnolia Terrace** that must be appreciated in early spring for obvious reasons. Beyond the croquet lawn (you can watch matches here in summer), you leave behind the formal planting schemes around the house and enter the **Quarry Garden** – clearly Picturesque in style, as was the fashion of the time – an utterly enchanting place for a longer stroll (&). Created out of the hollows left behind when stone was excavated to build the hall, the quarry garden is deliberately wild in appearance with plenty of intentionally rustic features: stone archways, a grotto and exotic shrubs, ferns, palms and creepers sprouting and climbing over the roughly cut rock faces. Yews and Scots pines tower above the cliff faces, increasing the sense of height and seclusion.

Beyond the quarry, the path opens into the sun-filled parkland around a ruinous 14th-century **castle tower** – one of the finest pele towers in Northumberland, built as a retreat for the wealthy occupants

---

1 Northumberlandia – an outdoor parkland created from a former industrial site.
2 Pillar Hall at the stunning Greek Revival-style Belsay Hall. **3** Dancers at Whalton's Ba'al Fire celebrated on old Midsummer's evening . **4** Blagdon Farm Shop at the Milkhope Centre is a veritable feast of local produce. ▶

TOURING THE COUNTRY LANES AROUND BELSAY & PONTELAND

The unclassified roads north of Ponteland winding through Whalton, Ogle, Berwick Hill and Bolam Lake are a cyclist's delight. The odd car and tractor pass by, but mostly it's quiet enough to dawdle along, do a spot of birdwatching, stop for sandwiches and so on. There are no dramatic vistas – just fields bound by hedgerows, a farm or three and a couple of old hogback bridges.

West of Ponteland, the landscape becomes increasingly rural and undulating, with more old villages and tranquil lanes suitable for touring by **bicycle**. And many visitors do just that, following the coast-to-coast Reivers Cycle Route (NCN 10) linking Ponteland, Stamfordham, Matfen and Bellingham on its course to Kielder and the west coast beyond, hence all the bikes stacked outside country pubs in these parts. Unless climbing northwards to Ryal, the countryside is tame and the main cycle routes are fairly flat along leafy lanes.

of the manor during invasions from Scotland. Climb to the top floor for a great view. As with many of Northumberland's embattled manors, Belsay Castle is formed of a mansion house (built in 1614 and now largely in ruins) with the aforementioned tower at one corner.

ᵢ⁁ FOOD & DRINK

You have two choices for lunch at Belsay: the **English Heritage café** inside the grounds of the Hall (plain tea room selling light lunches), or the **Blacksmiths Coffee Shop** (NE20 0DU ✆ 01661 881024 ☉ daily ♿ 🐾 outside only) at the estate entrance. An outdoor table in a sheltered corner of grass at the Blacksmiths is just the ticket on a sunny day. Watch swallows skimming the surrounding fields over a bowl of soup, a scone or baked potato. When ordering, check out the huge bellows above the old range.

16 WHALTON

[O]ld men and women, young men and maidens, and the children, begin to gather in groups and watch the proceedings impatient till, as the Twilight deepens and the pile of [sticks] has been carefully prepared and examined, the word is given to 'light her.' Then the children joining hands will form a moving circle round the burning pile... [A]s the fire begins to burn and the flame mounts higher till it illuminates the whole village, a fiddle or some other instrument is heard and the young people begin to dance in the near neighbourhood of the fire.'

'The Midsummer Bonfire at Whalton' by Reverend J Walker, Rector of Whalton, 1903, printed in *Archaeologia Aeliana*

Well-to-do Whalton is considered a very desirable village: a broad sweep of neat stone cottages with a manor house, pub, ancient church and community spirit in bucket loads.

Expect all the usual gala attractions at the annual **Whalton Village Show** in September (birds of prey demonstrations, Morris dancing, local craft stalls, vintage cars, traditional Northumbrian music and so on), as well as extremely entertaining sheep races, in which the animals compete with a doll made out of a pair of stuffed tights strapped to their backs.

Traditional festivals also include the **Ba'al Fire** on old Midsummer's evening, 4 July, during which school children dance around a bonfire lit next to the Beresford Arms – the very same spot that the tradition has been observed for eons. The event has Pagan origins and is historically a sun-worshipping festival linked to the corn harvest. A fascinating record of the annual event was recorded by the rector of Whalton in 1903 (see opposite), who describes the event in detail, starting with the making of the bonfire – a community event in itself. In years gone by, corn was used to create a human figure known as the **Kern Baby** – or 'babby' – which was then thrown into the fire. The tradition was revived some years ago with the creation of a huge, clothed sculpture.

"A broad sweep of neat stone cottages with a manor house, pub, ancient church and community spirit in bucket loads."

With many churches, it's not until you step inside that they reveal their antiquity. This is true of **St Mary Magdalene** which externally has the appearance of a 19th-century church, but is almost solidly 13th century inside.

At the eastern end of the village is **Whalton Manor** (℘ 07881 938080 ⌂ whaltonmanor.co.uk ☉ gardens: mid-Apr–Sep 14.00 Wed; Oct–mid-Apr pre-booked visits; cash only; ♿ with assistance), which looks like a continuation of the fine stone houses it follows. It is claimed that the mansion is the longest manor house in England, but it is really four dwellings merged into one. Parts date from the 17th century, but mostly it was altered by Sir Edwin Lutyens in the early 20th century. The archway seen from the road is his doing. The old stable (still in use) about a cobbled courtyard is wonderfully unchanged. Most people who book a tour come to see the famous **gardens**, which were laid out by Gertrude Jekyll in 1908 and contain beautiful herbaceous borders.

🍴 FOOD & DRINK

Beresford Arms Whalton ✆ 01670 775273 ◷ daily for breakfast, lunch & dinner ♿
🐾 bar only. Modernised old coaching inn (offering B&B rooms) dating to the 1800s with a pleasant restaurant, though it feels more like a café than a traditional pub. Outdoor seating on a summer's day is the ticket. The food is very good and inexpensive and there's always several Northumbrian and Tyneside beers on hand pumps. Expect all the usual pub favourites, plus dishes like sausages with haggis mash, chalk stream trout with a seafood chowder and samphire. Sunday lunches are good value.

17 BOLAM LAKE & SHAFTOE CRAGS

Near Belsay NE20 0EU ✆ 01661 881234 ◷ year-round; café & visitor centre Sat & Sun, bank holidays & during school holidays ♿ paths can be muddy 🐾

Bolam Lake and woods is popular with picnickers, dog walkers and those in need of a soft drink and a slice of cake (there's a friendly café at the north end of the lake serving snacks, drinks and simple lunches as well as local guides and crafts).

The lakeside path (three-quarters of a mile; partly on a boardwalk) is very pleasant with views of swans and ducks in the large manmade lagoon crowded by mature trees. Red squirrels are occasionally seen in the woods around the café and visitor centre.

"With few areas of high ground, the mile-long circuit of Shaftoe Crags is well-known for its views."

A very different **walk** to **Shaftoe Crags** begins from the crossroads at Bolam West Houses (📍 NZ070823); reached by taking the road signed for Rothbury on the west side of Bolam Lake for about a mile north. Look out for a red post box by the crossroads; ignore Google maps as it may take you along the A696 Belsay road, which you should avoid.

With few areas of high ground for miles around, the mile-long circuit of Shaftoe Crags is well-known to locals for its views. From the pillar box at Bolam West Houses, take the rough, pot-holed track for about half a mile to a pull-in parking area (by a cattle grid), which is the start point for this circuit. A clear paved track leads to a small lake. From here, you head uphill to a trig point on a sandstone outcrop offering superb views over miles of Northumbrian countryside (a walker told me you can see Blencathra in the Lake District on a clear day). Cross to the other side of the crags in a kind of quarry-like bowl and trace the side of a dry-stone wall before descending across marshy farmland back to the parking area, finding the driest route you can.

18 KIRKHARLE COURTYARD

NE19 2PE, midway between Ponteland & Otterburn, just off the A696 🖉 01830 540362
🕙 from 10.00 daily ♿ partial access 🐾

Set in open farmland in the birthplace of Capability Brown is this tempting clutch of converted stone barns housing **shops** selling regional paintings, stained-glass art, homeware, jewellery and various hand-crafted items. There's also a larder shop stocked with a small selection of local produce (jars of honey, jams, sauces), and the wonderful **Running Fox café** next door. Fantastic breakfasts; soup, scones and chunky sandwiches, pies and quiches are brought to tables in a peaceful sparrow-filled courtyard. Inside it's warm and the smell of homemade food wafts from the kitchen.

"Inside it's warm and the smell of homemade food wafts from the kitchen."

Those interested in **Capability Brown** will delight in seeing one of his very early garden designs, finally realised here almost three centuries after he made his sketch for Kirkharle (see below). You can **walk** off lunch along a pleasant accessible gravel path (just over half a mile) through his parkland with its serpentine lake and grasslands.

In the other direction, it's a few minutes' stroll along the lane from Kirkharle's main car park to the **church** with a bell-cote where Brown was baptised. St Wilfrid's was one of three churches run by the Premonstratensian monks of Blanchland Abbey, the earliest parts of which date to the 14th century, including the piscina, sedilia and the aumbreys. Kirkharle was the ancestral home of the Loraine family for 400 years, hence all the stones inside recording the deaths of various family members, including Richard Loraine who died in 1738 at the age

LANCELOT 'CAPABILITY' BROWN (1716–83)

The great 18th-century landscape gardener lived at Kirkharle until he was in his 20s, and went to school in nearby Cambo. A plan for the landscaping of Kirkharle was found in the 1980s and is almost certainly Brown's work. The design was never realised – until 2010. It will be some years before the chestnut trees around the pond mature, but already the lakeside trail is a pleasant place for a wander, with views of sheep grazing in nearby pastures and house martins catching airborne insects over grasslands left uncultivated for wildflowers and invertebrates.

Brown went on to create many of the great country estates in England, including Hulne Park at Alnwick Castle (page 84).

of 38. According to his tombstone, he was 'a proper handsome man of good sense and behaviour' before he died of an apoplexy while 'walking in a green field near London'. Note too the horse steps by the churchyard gate. Romantics may like to imagine the local congregation crossing open grasslands for Sunday worship. Certainly, the surrounding countryside feels timeless – in a Brownesque way.

For a **longer walk**, take the cross-country route (signed 'St Oswald's Way') to **Kirkwhelpington**, a pretty village two miles north. The walk starts from the **Loraine Monument** next to Kirkharle Courtyard and is described on a nearby board. The memorial stone and information panel will tell you everything you might (not) want to know about how Robert Loraine met his death in this field in 1483.

19 WALLINGTON HALL

Cambo NE61 4AR 🖉 01670 773600 ☉ grounds & café: daily year round; house: variable in winter 🦽 🐾 outdoor areas; National Trust

Four grinning dragon heads greet you on the approach to Wallington – one of the great country houses of Northumberland. You could easily spend most of a day exploring the rooms, gardens and woodlands, and playing games in the grassy courtyard. Next to the Palladian clock tower is a café with lovely outside tables, a shop selling plants and herbs and a large enclosed green where children can freely run around.

The late 17th-century **manor** has many memorable rooms and features: the Italianate plasterwork of the drawing and dining rooms, a fine collection of Victorian dolls' houses, a

"A thin stream trickles through the green oasis landscaped with terraces of plants and shrubs."

cabinet containing 3,000 toy soldiers, wall tapestries and a complete **kitchen** dating to the early 1900s with a huge dresser and shelves of cookware, vintage cast-iron pans and jelly moulds. One room has been converted into a **reading room** for visitors to enjoy. It's particularly child friendly, with comfy sofas and a little den to hide away in with a book from one of the shelves.

The **central hall** was styled on an Italian Renaissance *palazzo* and is arranged over two levels with arcades painted with ferns and flowers. Guests once enjoyed high tea here surrounded by eight large pre-Raphaelite paintings still hanging today that were all created by William Bell Scott in the mid 1800s. His brief was to 'illuminate the history and worthies of Northumbria,' and so we see depictions of the Industrial Revolution on Tyneside ('In the nineteenth century, the Northumbrians show the World what can be done with Iron and Coal'), the construction of Hadrian's Wall, and Danes invading from the sea. In some, the action in the background tells the story, as in the *Grace Darling* painting.

Wallington's **walled garden** is reached at the end of a short walk through woodland and past an ornamental pond. A thin stream trickles through the green oasis landscaped with terraces of plants and shrubs. A kiosk serves ice cream, cakes and drinks at the far end of the enclosure.

On the wider estate, there are a number of **walks** and **cycle rides** (see ⌖ nationaltrust.org.uk/wallington for details) but the most popular route is reached from the Hall on a descending trail through woodland to the **River Wansbeck** (native white-clawed crayfish live in the water, red squirrels in the trees and beavers have recently been reintroduced to the estate). You'll pass a great children's **play area** before descending to the **Boathouse Lake**, where family members in times gone by would skate on the frozen ice during winter. Historical records recall one 'late-night Christmas skating party' with Chinese paper lanterns hung on the trees for illumination. '[It was] a magical atmosphere created by the globes of light around the pond with the dark sky filled with stars overhead,' recalled one family member.

The river eventually flows under Northumberland's most elegant **bridge** – a Palladian crossing on the southern edge of the estate. Wait until you see it bathed in evening light.

20 CAMBO

Cambo, the old estate village of Wallington, lies a short distance north of Wallington Hall, whiling away the years at the top of a hill. It boasts nothing more than a couple of rows of stone houses, a 16th-century pele tower, a church and a hilltop view of tumbling farmland, but a hamlet quainter than this is hard to find. Roses, daisies and sweet peas fill the cottage gardens and herbs drape over stone walls, adding to Cambo's English country charms.

The 19th-century parish **church** overlooks open countryside once so familiar to a young Lancelot 'Capability' Brown, who used to walk across these fields on his three-mile journey from Kirkharle to school. Apparently, one schoolmaster (after Brown's time) kept an annotated record of former alumni, which is decoded by the following rhyme:

The names distinguish'd by a star
Were the most docile by far;
And those with equi-distant strokes
Were secondhanded sort of folks;
But where you find the letter B
A humdrum booby you will see;
And where an exclamation's set,
The rascals went away in debt.

21 SWEETHOPE LOUGHS & THE WANNEY CRAGS

Sweethope Loughs (west of Knowesgate, signed off the A68 ⌁ 01434 618579), essentially one large trout-filled **lake**, is mostly hidden from sight by a ring of conifer trees, but a public right of way around the lake's southern edge affords views of the blue expanse. Ospreys occasionally help themselves to fish, but humans must obtain a fishing permit to take advantage of one of the best trout lakes in Northumberland. **Wild swimmers** can also enjoy the lake and its scenery by booking through the local wild swimming company, H2O (⌁ 07737 300470 ⌁ h2otrails.co.uk).

Of interest to walkers, climbers and birdwatchers will be the nearby **Wanney Crags** rising above Sweethope Loughs to the north (reached by a footpath from the single-track road along the northern edge of Sweethope Loughs (♥ NY944829), or by a rough track connecting to the A68, a half-mile south of Ridsdale (♥ NY907836); look out for the Forestry England sign 'Fourlaws' at both entrances). At the top of **Great Wanney**, find yourself a rock to sit on and enjoy Redesdale's countryside unfolded before you with the Simonsides and Cheviots both in sight.

'High o'er wild Wanny's lofty crest, where the raven cleaves the cloud,' begins an old local ballad. Ravens inhabit the crags here to this day. They try and nest every year, but often give up when rock climbers take advantage of the first fine days of the year in early spring. For this reason, choose where you sit carefully so as not to disturb the birds. Peregrines sometimes swoop by, and goshawks and other birds of prey are not uncommon.

---

1 The lakeside path at Bolam Lake offers very pleasant views. **2** Wanney Crags is of most interest to walkers, climbers and birdwatchers. **3** The 7ft-high prehistoric Stob Stone at Matfen. **4** Cambo is the old estate village of Wallington. ▶

North of Great Wanney, a wide track winds through heather and woodlands towards the A68. Keep to the track between Aid Moss and Aid Crag and avoid the rough public footpaths from March to August so as not to disturb rare nesting birds. On summer evenings you might be fortunate enough to hear nightjars hereabouts.

22 RYAL & INGOE

Generous views of the Northumbrian countryside reward cyclists puffing into **Ryal** from the south. The lovely hilltop **church** was originally built in the 12th century but has been much altered since. Inside, its porch is full of medieval grave covers set into its walls. As is commonplace, they are carved with shears representing a woman and a sword for a man. Beyond the churchyard walls, yellow and green fields bound by hedgerows and blocks of forests stretch far into the distance.

Cyclists heading west on the Reiver's route, NCN 10, can expect a few thrilling rollercoaster miles ahead through a beautiful pastoral landscape. A mile east in the other direction, **Ingoe** sits amid prehistoric monuments including a burial mound and the **Warrior Stone**, a similar standing stone to the one at Matfen (see opposite).

23 MATFEN

Matfen was developed as the estate village for Matfen Hall and is what many people would call a perfect 19th-century English village: unaltered stone terraces set around a broad green where a burn trickles merrily under a couple of sweet bridges in its own time. A small playground, simple café, pub, red telephone box (now a book exchange) and church complete the model village scene.

"Unaltered stone terraces set around a broad green where a burn trickles merrily under a couple of sweet bridges in its own time."

Rising above Matfen's rooftops is the 117ft-tall spire of **Holy Trinity Church**, which largely dates from the mid 1800s. Though rather plain internally, four intricately carved alabaster reliefs depicting shepherds and other figures crowding around a baby Jesus are worth a close look.

Matfen Hall is hard to see from the village itself unless you traipse around the churchyard, which I suppose was the intention of the architects of the day who would have intended to keep the estate village quite separate from the Hall. The early 19th-century country mansion, now a spa hotel and golf course, was recently refurbished, with no expense spared. Non-guests can book lunch and evening tables, indulge in cream teas with a view of the 300-acre landscaped parkland or simply stop by for a coffee or glass of wine. There really is no finer place for many miles around (see below).

Under a mile south of Matfen, by a prominent castellated house on Hope Lane, is a prehistoric standing stone, known as the **Stob Stone**. At 7ft high it's hard to miss on the road verge. Its numerous depressions or 'cup marks' are a Northumbrian speciality (page 218).

¶¶ FOOD & DRINK

The **Matfen village store** (✆ 01661 886202; daily ♿) serves breakfasts, coffees and light lunches and stocks pantry provisions and quiches, pies, scones and the like for picnickers.

Matfen Hall Matfen NE20 0RH ✆ 01661 886500 ⏱ daily ♿. From the galleried entrance hall, which oozes period sophistication with wall tapestries, a grandfather clock and Chesterfield sofas by an open fire, the elegant interior continues in the dining areas of this luxury 19th-century five-star spa and golf hotel. Despite the fine furnishings and attentive service, it all feels pleasantly unstuffy and relaxed.

I lunched in the glazed **Cloisters** (very well heated in case you wondered), an informal space but still with pristine white table linen and background piano music. The small menu (pork and veg, a burger, cod and chips and a few other plates, plus a sharing board of meats and cheeses) also includes lighter options, soup and sandwiches. For a special evening meal, book the **Emerald Restaurant** (⏱ evenings Mon–Sat, afternoon Sun), which takes the fine dining at Matfen up a notch with a five- and eight-course tasting menu. And make sure you allow time for the **1832 bar** – a stunning oak room with huge windows offering a wide aperture of the parkland. One final mention: the decadent Georgian blue **Drawing Room**: there is no finer place in Northumberland to take afternoon tea.

Set in 120 hectares of parkland (with its own golf course), Matfen Hall also offers one of the best independent hotel experiences in the North East, with opulent but very comfortable rooms.

24 GREAT WHITTINGTON

West of Matfen, across fields dotted with hay bales and tractors, Great Whittington is soon upon you. A plaque reads: 'Best kept village 1977'. Not that it has gone downhill since then: the gardens of Great Whittington's stone cottages are quite a sight in summer. Farmsteads, an old schoolhouse, coaching inn, blacksmith's and Methodist chapel combine with sandstone housing fronting a long green to form one of the most quaint rural villages in Northumberland – one delightfully free of visitors except the odd cycling and Sunday lunch party stopping at the Queen's Head (see below).

To **walk** off lunch, you could follow St Oswald's Way for under a mile in a southeasterly direction to Toft Hill, taking in an 18th-century **windmill** en route. Whittington Mill's sails have long gone but its stout, four-storey tower is a pleasing landmark amid flat fields.

¶¶ FOOD & DRINK

The Queens Head NE19 2HP ✐ 0191 691 0838 ☉ evening meals Thu–Sat, lunches Sat & Sun 🐾. An all-round great country pub with a satisfying menu to delight carnivores (grilled beef served Brazilian style on a wooden board, for example), but always something for vegetarians too. And the setting: a sunny beer garden and wonderful countryside views surrounding a pretty Northumbrian village. In winter, you'll want to tuck into your Sunday roast by the fire in this old coaching inn with exposed stone walls.

25 STAMFORDHAM

Two neat terraces, mostly of old stone, front Stamfordham's wide, long green, marked at its western end by the village's 1735 market cross (the covered building with four open arches). Unless pausing on your travels for a pint at the Swinburne Arms (mainly a sports boozer but with south-facing outdoor benches overlooking the green where cyclists gather on Sunday afternoons), there's not much to keep you for long in the village but you may enjoy taking a stroll to **St Mary's Church** which dates from the 13th century and, though it was largely rebuilt in the mid 1800s, a number of old features survive, including the chancel arch.

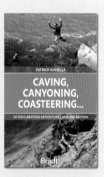

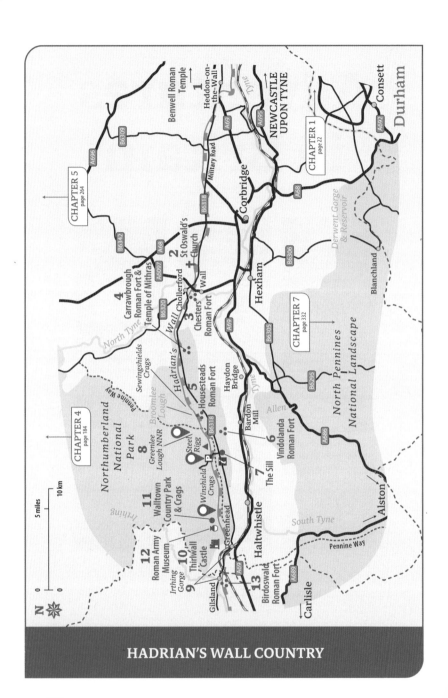

HADRIAN'S WALL COUNTRY

6

HADRIAN'S WALL COUNTRY

Climbing north out of the Tyne Valley, the hills begin their gallop towards Scotland but are momentarily stopped dead in their tracks by a frozen wave of igneous rock. This dramatic precipice is made even more impassable by a stone barricade ribboned along its uppermost lip. When built 2,000 years ago **Hadrian's Wall** stood 10ft high; today half its height remains in places. Spanning 73 miles from coast to coast across the neck of England, it is the region's most celebrated attraction – and an awe-inspiring feature of the rugged Northumberland landscape. According to English Heritage it is 'the most important monument built by the Romans in Britain'.

The best-preserved stretch, between Chesters and Brampton, rides the tops of the highest hills and rocky ridges where undulating grasslands roll into Cumbria and down through the Tyne Valley. This is superb walking country indeed.

GETTING AROUND

You can pretty much reach every town and visitor attraction along Hadrian's Wall by train from Newcastle then bus, though you'll have to plan your day carefully around the **Hadrian's Wall bus** service (page 300). Most likely you'll need to take a taxi (page 303) at some point. That said, it's possible to walk to Vindolanda from **Bardon Mill station** (two miles) along Chainley Burn, and you can also access the Wall in three miles from **Haltwhistle station** by following Haltwhistle Burn. You'll need ❀ OS Explorer map OL43.

The dead-straight **Military Road** (B6318) is the usual access point for the major Roman forts if driving. It runs parallel to Hadrian's Wall and offers views of the Wall and surrounding landscape, but cars fly along and cyclists should be very cautious. The old Roman road, the

> ### *i* TOURIST INFORMATION
>
> **The Sill: National Landscape Discovery Centre** (page 318). Tourist information centres also in Corbridge (page 348) and Hexham (page 354).

Stanegate (page 309), is a mile or so south of the Military Road and is a recommended alternative for **cyclists**.

BUS

The **AD122 Hadrian's Wall Country Bus** (⊘ gonortheast.co.uk/ ad122 for timetables) runs every two hours daily throughout the year and stops at the popular jumping-off points for the Roman ruins, including Chesters, Housesteads, Once Brewed, Vindolanda and Greenhead, and connects with Haltwhistle and Hexham railway stations for trains and buses to Carlisle and Newcastle (see the public transport map, page 18). One and three-day Discovery Tickets allow unlimited travel and can be bought from the driver. Disabled badge holders and the elderly with a bus pass can travel for free (buses have low-floor easy access).

In addition, the **Tynedale Links 681 bus** (⊘ gonortheast.co.uk) shuttles between Alston and Birdoswald Roman Fort via Haltwhistle, Greenhead and Gilsland a few times a day year round.

TRAIN

Northern Rail (⊘ northernrailway.co.uk) operates a regular daily service between Newcastle and Carlisle stopping at a few stations of some use for Hadrian's Wall visitors, including **Hexham, Bardon Mill, Haltwhistle** and **Brampton**. Hadrian's Wall Country Bus (see above) connects with Hexham and Haltwhistle stations.

CYCLING

Hadrian's Cycleway is well signposted (National Cycle Network route 72) on its 174-mile course from Cumbria's Ravenglass to South Shields on the River Tyne. In Northumberland, it mostly runs south of Hadrian's Wall; the off-road stretch along the Tyne through Newcastle to the North Sea is shared with the Hadrian's Wall Path for walkers.

Cyclists can make good use of the Newcastle–Carlisle railway to access Hadrian's Wall (see above), which is never more than a few miles north of stations on the line. Bikes travel free; two per service on a first come, first served system.

BICYCLE HIRE, REPAIRS, TRANSFERS & HOLIDAYS

Hexham-based **Ecocabs** (✆ 01434 600600 &) and **Advanced Taxis** (✆ 01434 606565) provide transfers for you and your bike.

The Cycle Hub Hadrian's Cycleway, Newcastle (page 25)
Eco Cycle Adventures Hexham (page 335)
Pedal Power ✆ 01665 713448 ⌂ pedal-power.co.uk. Hire bikes and book cycling holidays and transfers.
Trailbrakes ⌂ trailbrakes.co.uk. Also operates holidays.

WALKING

Ramblers will find no shortage of excellent hikes in and around Hadrian's Wall. The scenery doesn't really get going until your back is to Heddon-on-the-Wall, but from there on the landscape becomes increasingly remote, rough, ascending and unbound. By the time you clear Chollerford and Chesters Roman Fort on heading west, you enter the most memorable countryside on the whole of the Wall: undulating farmland, large glacial lakes, soaring craggy walls of dolerite and far-reaching views north across Redesdale's forests.

I've outlined a few short circular walks in these pages that take in some of the most popular stretches of Hadrian's Wall, but also consider making use of the Hadrian's Wall Bus AD122 for linear routes.

A stunning eight-mile walk along the Wall, taking in some of the finest vantage points on the national trail, runs from **Walltown Crags Country Park** to **The Sill** via Whinshield Crags and Steel Rigg. I

ST OSWALD'S WAY TRAIL

This stunning and varied 97-mile hike from the Roman wall at Heavenfield, near Chollerford, to the coastal isle of Lindisfarne embraces some fine upland scenery north of Hadrian's Wall to Otterburn before tracing the River Coquet on its journey to the sea at Warkworth. From here, the trail swings north, taking in the most unspoilt stretch of the Northumberland Heritage Coast and providing plenty of chances for a dip in the sea from one of the many sandy bays en route. Add four stonking medieval castles to the list of sights and you have the ingredients for a highly memorable week-long trip.

recommend walking eastwards so you can use the facilities and shelter at The Sill if you're early for the return bus.

Also see my summary of walking the full length of the **Hadrian's Wall Path** on page 304.

WALKING HOLIDAYS, BAGGAGE TRANSFERS & TAXIS

Shepherds Walks (✆ 01669 621044 ⌂ shepherdswalks.co.uk) is a reputable local company based in Rothbury offering self-guided trips along Hadrian's Wall. In addition to holidays, **Brigantes** (✆ 01756 770402 ⌂ brigantesenglishwalks.com) will also take your bags if you're walking independently.

Other baggage transfer companies include **Hadrian's Haul** (✆ 07967 564823 ⌂ hadriansbags.co.uk) and **Sherpa Van** (✆ 01748 826917 ⌂ sherpavan.com) but note that for many companies the service is confined to the spring and summer months.

Taxis in the area include **Advanced Taxis** (aka Hadrian's Wall Taxis ✆01434 606565), and **Ecocabs** (✆ 01434 600600 ♿).

HADRIAN'S WALL & ROMAN FORTS

When built on the orders of Emperor Hadrian in AD122, the **Wall** extended for 73 miles from coast to coast with a 25-mile extension south through Cumbria. It took three legions consisting of 5,000 men as little as, perhaps, a decade to build. But, they didn't just build a mighty wall with a deep channel on its north side: 16 **forts** were raised, as well as the **vallum** – a 20ft ditch with a mound either side running the length of the south side of the Wall. According to English Heritage, this immense earthwork likely functioned as 'the Roman equivalent of barbed wire'. Now, if it weren't for the colossal and visually more striking Wall, perhaps more would be made of the vallum in history books. It really is a remarkable feat in its own right.

Although the Wall had a defensive role, it mainly functioned as a barrier marking the northwest edge of the Roman Empire (Hadrian being more concerned with containing his kingdom than expanding it). It was, say English Heritage, a kind of Berlin Wall, and controlled the north–south flow of human traffic for some 250 years until the collapse of the Roman Empire in the 5th century.

◄ **1** Hadrian's Wall is 73 miles long, reaching from coast to coast.
2 Walkers at Milecastle 39.

WALKING THE HADRIAN'S WALL PATH

Perhaps I am the first man that ever travelled the whole length of this Wall, and probably the last that ever will attempt it.
William Hutton, 1801

The 19th-century poet and historian, William Hutton, is considered the first person in modern times to have walked the Wall from Bowness-on-Solway to Wallsend, Newcastle, and though his journey (at the age of 78) was so arduous that he suspected no one would follow in his footsteps, today the route is clear and well-marked, attracting thousands of hikers annually. And it's not a difficult path – 84 miles easily walked in a week. Facilities have proliferated since the opening of the well-signed **Hadrian's Wall Path** (HWP) in 2003, and hikers will find a number of options for a bed and places to eat, plus companies offering bag transport (page 303).

What many visitors would call 'the best bit' is the well-preserved central section of Wall within Northumberland National Park. That said, just because the Wall breaks up and often vanishes altogether either side of the central section, that isn't to say the walking isn't scenic. The Solway Estuary is birdwatching heaven, and the tumbling farmland through the Tyne Valley is quite dreamy in parts. Even Wallsend has a certain appeal: it is as manmade as Sewingshields Crags is wild, but there is something very raw about the industrial scenery with its cranes and old shipbuilding yards at Swan Hunters.

But, back to 'the best bit'. Between **Sewingshields Crags** and **Greenhead** the landscape is all Wall, basalt and grassland with plunging views of inky lakes and distant forests. Through this landscape, the Wall rollercoasters for 12 spectacular, thigh-busting miles, holding the Roman masonry to the sky and out of the reach of builders of past centuries.

To this end, a number of guarded posts were built along its length, one every Roman mile (1,620yds). Between these **milecastles** were two observation towers – or **turrets**. Some, like Milecastle 37 west of Housesteads with its broken arched gate, are impressive to this day. Little kindles the imagination more than on a wet, misty morning when the Wall rises and falls through the fog and the walker is forced to seek shelter on the inside wall of a milecastle. One can only imagine what the Roman soldiers thought about being stationed on this remote ridge.

"One can only imagine what the Roman soldiers thought about being stationed on this remote ridge."

Despite the 'recycling' of Wall stones following the retreat of the Romans, the central section, between Chesters and Brampton, is well

At any time of year the **weather** can be foul in the uplands of Northumberland and, just like soldiers 2,000 years ago, you may find yourself huddled under the Wall sheltering from the wind. Chill-proof clothing is recommended throughout the year.

A word on **mud**: at bottlenecks on the central section of the HWP, the ground oozes with squelchy mud so you'll be grateful for your boots (and gaiters), even though there are long stretches on relatively dry grassland and paved surfaces (through Newcastle for example) where walking shoes will suffice.

Most people walk east to west (Heddon-on-the-Wall is a popular **starting point**), usually because Newcastle is better connected than the west coast, but purists won't like starting a walk at a place called Wall*end*!

Villages to refuel at include tea rooms at all the major forts, the odd café, pub and mobile coffee van, but you may have to walk a couple of miles off the Wall in remote parts for refreshments. **The Sill** (page 318) is an important resource for Wall walkers at the mid-way point, for food, a bed, supplies and information.

A scattering of very good **B&Bs** welcome hikers within walking distance of the Wall but they get booked up many months in advance. **Campers** are reasonably well catered for but most sites are a few miles from the path. Wild camping really isn't an option as the HWP is busy with walkers and the surrounding farmland well controlled. Various **tour operators** (page 303) offer packages for walkers and cyclists.

Even though the route is well signposted, you should take ❋ OS Explorer **maps** 314, 315, OL43 and 316. You'll be grateful when a weather front rolls in. Many **guides** to the HWP include route notes alongside maps, including the excellent *Trailblazer* guide.

preserved, owing in part to its isolation and the private acquisition of a long length by landowner John Clayton (page 307) from the 1830s.

Chesters, **Vindolanda**, **Housesteads** and **Birdoswald** all have their highlights and some superb on-site museums housing Roman treasures. Also worth visiting are the ruins in **Corbridge** and **Segedunum** in Wallsend, Newcastle. Archaeologists and volunteers at Vindolanda continually find new items during their annual summer digs.

The preservation of the forts and Wall in this central section has been greatly assisted by the rough, inaccessible countryside. Of course, this is also what makes Hadrian's Wall exceptionally good walking and cycling country, and an increasing number of visitors come here to take on the 84-mile **Hadrian's Wall Path** or 160-mile **Hadrian's Cycleway**.

BENWELL ROMAN TEMPLE

Broomridge Av, Benwell, Newcastle NE15 6QP; free admission; English Heritage

Only the committed will seek out the ruins of a small Roman temple built around AD180 on a residential street between the west end of Newcastle and Heddon-on-the-Wall, but it's a visit worth making. Sure, there are more impressive Roman structures in the region, but the setting in the middle of an ordinary modern estate couldn't be more unexpected or intriguing.

The first thing to note is the location: you're standing on a hill with a view across the Tyne valley which was seized upon by the Romans as a prime spot for a fort, known as **Condercum**, the fragmented outline of which appears on the north side of the West Road, a short walk from the temple.

As with other forts along Hadrian's Wall, a civilian settlement developed outside the garrison. Within it were places of worship, including this simple, rectangular **temple** dedicated to a Celtic deity, Antenociticus (the adoption of a local god by Roman settlers was not unusual). When the site was excavated in 1862, Antenociticus' head, still with his thick mop of hair, was uncovered along with the temple's altar stones. The original stones are displayed in Newcastle's Great North Museum: Hancock; the two altar stones on site are concrete casts.

It is surprising that this temple has survived at all in such a heavily urbanised environment (even the Mithras Temple, in remote countryside, is only somewhat better preserved; page 310) but remarkably there are more Roman finds a couple of streets west on Denhill Park, notably a short section of the **vallum** – a defensive ditch running parallel to the length of Hadrian's Wall – still with its stone crossing. This **Vallum Causeway** once provided access over the earthwork and is the only one visible along the Wall and therefore of quite some archaeological significance.

1 HEDDON-ON-THE-WALL

As you approach Heddon from the east, look out for the long stretch of Hadrian's Wall crossing a field on the left of the Hexham Road. Note too that on entering this pleasant village high above the Tyne Valley, locals greet you in the street. Welcome to Northumberland.

The friendly village centre is reached by turning left where the Wall ends. Make sure you visit **St Andrew's Church**, parts of which date to the Saxon period. A wide Norman arch spans the sanctuary and a large fragment of a Celtic cross rests to the left of the altar.

⑪ FOOD & DRINK

The Swan The Towne Gate ✆ 01661 853161 ♿ ramp at side entrance 🐾 some areas. Popular, family-friendly gastro pub in the centre of Heddon serving traditional pub food all day (from scampi to sausage and mash) and Sunday lunches. When the sun's out, sit in the beer garden and take in the Tyne Valley views.

2 ST OSWALD'S CHURCH & THE BATTLE OF HEAVENFIELD

Heavenfield NE46 4HB ♥ NY937696; 1½ miles east of Chollerford; access from a lay-by on the B6318 Military Rd & then by walking 200yds across a field

> **Oswald set up the sign of the holy cross and, kneeling down, prayed God to send his heavenly aid to those who trusted in him in their dire need. This place is pointed out to this day and held in great veneration.**
> Venerable Bede's account of the Battle of Heavenfield in his 8th-century *Ecclesiastical History of the English People*

It was on this site in AD635 that Oswald, the future King of Northumbria, raised a cross ahead of the **Battle of Heavenfield**, during which his small army defeated the Welsh king, Cadwallon. His victory led to the development of Christianity in Northumbria, first with the establishment of a monastic community at Lindisfarne under St Aidan (page 138), and then throughout the region from the Forth to the Humber. The church commemorates this important moment.

St Oswald's was likely rebuilt three times, the last in the late 19th century to become the small, modest building you see today, commanding a splendid spot that is best appreciated from the north side of the churchyard. From this vantage point, farmland sweeps northwards, drawing the eye to the Cheviots and beyond.

Inside, observant visitors will notice the old gas lights (the church is cut off from the grid) and that there is no separation between the nave and chancel. Close to the font is a Roman altar stone, which was fashioned into a socket for a cross many years ago.

St Oswald's Day on 5 August is celebrated with an annual pilgrimage from Hexham Abbey to Heavenfield.

3 CHESTERS ROMAN FORT
 Carraw

Chollerford NE46 4EU ✐ 01434 681379 ☉ Apr– end Oct, as well as school holidays, daily; w/ends only at some other times ♿ most of the site including the museum
🐾 English Heritage

Mondays were dig days in the diary of John Clayton, a wealthy Northumbrian landowner who amassed thousands of Roman artefacts between 1840 and 1890 from ruins unearthed on his estate at Chesters, including this cavalry station. When he died, aged 98, he owned the central section of Hadrian's Wall, five forts, almost 12,000 coins, 5,000 items of pottery, 97 altar stones and 39 statues, among many other finds. It is thanks to him that so much of the Wall's length remains continuously intact and that many Roman artefacts survive at all. Prior to Clayton's land purchases, Wall stones were widely plundered (almost every field boundary, farmhouse, church and B&B in the area contains Roman masonry). Clayton put a stop to that and placed the most precious discoveries in his garden 'Antiquity House' – later rebuilt and opened to the public posthumously in 1896 within the grounds of Chesters fort.

"The fort itself stands on a hugely picturesque vale sloping away from the museum to the River North Tyne."

The **museum** is reached first on entering the English Heritage-run site. And what an astonishing collection it is: rows of statues, altars and stone reliefs side by side on shelves along with wooden cabinets containing tools, jewellery, trinkets, bottles, pottery and fragments of painted glass. Particularly important pieces in the collection include a full-height statue of Juno, the swirl patterns and folds in her tunic still remarkably clear.

The fort itself stands on a hugely picturesque vale sloping away from the museum to the River North Tyne. At its centre is the colonnaded courtyard of the **headquarters** building, still with its paved flooring and well (notice the phallic good luck carving). Next door is the **commanding officer's house**, complete with its private bathhouse. To the left are the remains of three **barrack blocks**. This being a cavalry station, the barracks housed both Asturian horsemen from northern Spain and their animals (in an adjoining stable).

A large **bathhouse** lies outside of the fort wall by the wooded riverside and represents the best example of its type in Britain, as well as being one of the most intact Roman structures on the whole of Hadrian's Wall. You gain an idea of how soldiers would have moved from the changing room (the large room with a row of arched niches that may have been used for hanging clothes or could even, an expert at English Heritage told me, have held statues of the seven days of the week) into progressively warmer chambers. Treatment rooms include a sauna, a steam room and hot and cold pools. Like all Roman bathhouses, it was a place to wash (using oil, not soap) and socialise. At Segedunum Roman

THE STANEGATE

In the years before the construction of Hadrian's Wall, the Romans built a military road between Corbridge and Carlisle. The line of the Stanegate (a medieval name meaning 'Stone Road') runs 1½ miles south of Hadrian's Wall but is not to be confused with the much busier B6318 Military Road running fairly tight to the Wall.

The eight-mile stretch of the Stanegate from **Fourstones** (page 362) to Vindolanda via **Newbrough** (page 363) makes a very pleasant route to Hadrian's Wall from the Hexham area and offers views of upland meadows and pastures the whole way. It's also on the Hadrian's Cycleway (NCN Route 72).

Fort (page 45) in Wallsend, a replica bathhouse has been created based on the ruins at Chesters.

By now you will have appreciated the view of the wide River North Tyne, which forms rapids as it rushes on its way to join the South Tyne at Hexham. From the viewing platform below the bathhouse, you can see the abutments of two **Roman bridges** on the south bank. For a closer look, cross the multi-arched 18th-century road bridge at Chollerford (wonderful river views here) and take the path immediately off to the right through a gate. Note another good luck phallus carved onto the eastern bridge abutment.

SPECIAL STAYS

Carraw Military Rd, Humshaugh NE46 4DB ℰ 01434 689857 ◌ carraw.co.uk ♿. Very close to the Hadrian's Wall Path and within a few miles of Chesters Roman Fort are two exceptionally comfortable cottages (one sleeps ten; the other four) facing open countryside. Both cottages are modern and unfussy inside with lovely views of the Tyne Valley and distant Pennine moors.

¶¶ FOOD & DRINK

There's not a huge choice of places to eat directly in the vicinity of Chesters Roman Fort and the Wall. I'm rather fond of **The George Hotel** (Chollerford NE46 4EW ℰ 01434 681611 ♿), which reminds me of outings with my grandparents as a child. Back then it was considered a posh hotel; today, it's a little less refined, but it's an okay place for lunch or an evening meal: cod and chips, burgers and a few meat and veg dishes, and there's a stunning view of the River North Tyne and its old bridge from the garden. Alternatively, the **Red Lion** at Newbrough (page 364) is a lovely pub.

Within the grounds of Chesters Roman Fort is a small **tea room** (Easter– end Oct ♿) serving cakes and hot and cold drinks.

4 CARRAWBROUGH ROMAN FORT & THE TEMPLE OF MITHRAS

Humshaugh NE46 4DB; 5 miles east of Housesteads

In a landscape dominated by extensively excavated buildings, it may be surprising to know that many Roman structures remain buried under turf. In recent years, the land on which this **fort**, known to the Romans as **Brocolitia** and constructed around AD200, has come under the guardianship of English Heritage which many Roman enthusiasts hope will pave the way for closer examinations of the site in years to come.

For the time being, visitors must be content with the earthen outline of the garrison station, which once housed around 500 soldiers and is typical in its playing-card shape. It sits tight to the Military Road (in fact the northern wall would have once stood where you now see tarmac) and is signed off the B6318.

You're unlikely to pull over for the fort alone, but this site is special for what has been exposed outside of the fort walls in the civilian settlement or 'vicus', notably a temple dedicated to the god Mithras and a nearby Roman well dedicated to Coventina.

When discovered in a corner of a field west of the fort in 1876, the **Coventina Well** – a rectangular basin constructed around a spring – contained some 16,000 Roman coins, 22 altars and clay incense burners and many other artefacts, some of which are housed in the museum at Chesters Roman Fort (page 307). They include a wonderful stone relief of the goddess reclined holding a water lily. There's nothing to see in situ today but the field remains decidedly marshy underfoot – a nice reminder of the spring waters still flowing underground.

The **Temple of Mithras**, on the other hand, is well preserved and open to visitors. My advice is to wear wellies as the short two-minute walk from the car park, across the fort ramparts to the ruins, is damp and muddy in parts.

Mithraic temples were intentionally dark and windowless in order to conjure the cave in which the god Mithras killed a sacred bull and banqueted with Sol. Now roofless and with its walls much reduced in height, you have to use your imagination a bit. I once visited in the half

---

1 St Oswald's Church, Heavenfield. **2** Vindolanda was built several decades before Hadrian's Wall. **3** The bathhouse at Chesters Roman fort. **4** An aerial view over Housesteads reveals the extent of the site – it is the most complete Roman site in Britain. ▶

SS

JAIME PHARR/S

CDK PHOTOS/S

WIRESTOCK CREATORS/S

light of an early spring evening when no one else was around and found the site really quite atmospheric. Above the tussocky grassland, snipe were 'drumming' – an eerie sound if you've ever heard it – and perfectly suited to the location and the secretive cult of Mithraism with its dark initiation ceremonies. Inside the temple, the three altar stones (the originals are held in Newcastle's Great North Museum: Hancock) would have formed the focal point for meetings and Mithraic feasts.

5 HOUSESTEADS ROMAN FORT

Off the Military Rd (B6318), near Haydon Bridge NE47 6NN ✆ 01434 344363 ⊙ daily
♿ only museum 😺 English Heritage

Housesteads is the most complete Roman fort in Britain and the most visited of the four main garrison stations in Northumberland, owing in part to its dramatic position commanding the lip of an igneous cliff. Built in the years following the construction of Hadrian's Wall, the fort sits snug to the stone barricade, teetering on the edge of the Roman Empire.

After a stiff hike up to the fort, your first calling point is the **museum** with its small collection of Roman altars, stone reliefs of gods, pottery, jewellery, leather shoes and medical tools recovered from the fort's hospital. One of the highlights is a 4ft sculpture of Victory (one of four discovered at Housesteads) – her wings half opened, tunic fluttering in the wind. A video shows how the fort was constructed.

CHARIOTS TO TRAINS

Take a close look at the stone floor in the east gate entranceway at Housesteads Roman Fort, which reveals two heavily worn grooves created by Roman carts over the years, coming in and out of the fort

The distance between the channels shows that the Roman cart wheels were just shy of 5ft apart – the same axle dimension adopted in the centuries after Roman rule. It is also, not coincidentally, the same width as standard railway gauges in Britain today (4ft 8½ inches).

Before the invention of steam engines, horses pulled carts on wooden tracks, like the recently discovered Willington Waggonway unearthed on Tyneside (page 46), so it is thought the same standardised axle length was applied when these wooden rails were replaced by metal ones and 'iron horses'.

It's funny to think that the great Victorian railway engineers based at Wylam, some 20 miles away from Housesteads, developed the railway line based, by default, on the measurements of Roman carts.

As with other garrison stations along Hadrian's Wall, Housesteads is typical in its arrangement of buildings with its centrally located **headquarters**, **granaries** (still with their sturdy buttressed walls), **hospital** and **commanding officer's residence**. The last consists of rooms arranged around a courtyard and has an excellent example of Roman under-floor heating technology. The surface, now mostly removed, was raised on rows of pillars under which hot air circulated.

The well-preserved **latrine** in the southeast corner of the site often fascinates visitors most. The room is oblong with a raised central area and a gutter running around its perimeter which was flushed by water piped into the building. Two wooden benches with holes for around 30 bums once bridged the gap between the central stone plinth you see today and the outer walls. It is thought soldiers cleaned themselves using a kind of natural sponge made of moss attached to the end of a stick. The functions of the trough and bowl are not known for certain though plenty of people have made guesses.

The four **gates** around the curtain wall are of interest, particularly the west gate, still with its door pivot holes, and the east gate with its stone flooring deeply worn by the wheels of carts (page 312).

* * *

STEEL RIGG & SYCAMORE GAP CIRCUIT: A CLASSIC HADRIAN'S WALL WALK

❀ OS Explorer map OL43; start: Steel Rigg car park; ♀ NY750676; 4 miles, or 5 miles to include Winshield Crags; moderate

This well-trodden circular walk takes in some of the most photographed scenery in Hadrian's Wall country and gives you two perspectives of the Wall: from the Whin Sill looking north into 'barbarian' country, and from the farmland below the crags gazing up at the Wall ribboned along the edge of the spectacular escarpment. If you extend the route to Winshield Crags on your return, you'll also experience one of the most breathtaking views in the whole of the region, from the Cumbrian Mountains to the east coast. But, gone, sadly is the arresting sight of the famous Sycamore Gap tree, felled under the cover of darkness in 2023 by some local rogue.

1 From **Steel Rigg car park**, turn left on to the road and walk 100yds downhill to a gate by a fingerpost on your left where you pick up the national trail. Follow the footpath through grassland towards **Peel Crags**. Your first challenge is the climb to the top – one of the most

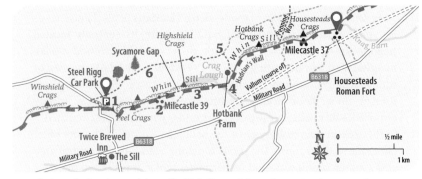

photographed vantage points on the Wall. The next few miles are tough as you criss-cross the Wall and make a series of steep ascents and drops, but the views from the dramatic whin escarpment of glinting Crag Lough below are tremendous.

2 Just beyond Milecastle 39, descend steeply to the **Sycamore Gap** tree stump in a natural hollow where visitors have left tributes to one of the most famous trees in Britain. Cross the Wall and continue on your way, now with Hadrian's barricade on your right.

3 The Whin Sill cliffs of **Highshield Crags** fall away to your left – a mere trip and stumble from the path so put your kids on a short leash for this bit. Walk through the woodland ahead and descend to the damp grasslands lying flat to the banks of **Crag Lough**.

4 Pass through a gate and cross the lane, picking up the Wall path on the other side, which is signposted for Housesteads. A wide grassy track guides you to **Hotbank Farm** where the return leg of this walk begins. Enter Hotbank Farm by way of stone steps over a dry-stone wall by a gate and cross the farm courtyard to a gate on the other side. You are now in barbarian land: a damp, open expanse of grassland with superb views of the Whin Sill.

5 Go straight on where the path forks, tramping to the ladder stile you can see in the distance. Cross the stile, turn left and continue for a few miles across farmland, jumping across a couple of streams and a few field boundaries on your way. Ahead, keep tight to the dry-stone wall on your right for three-quarters of a mile to a prominent copse where you pick up a farm track which winds its way to a road in another three-quarters of a mile.

6 Exit the farmland over a ladder stile and turn left onto tarmac. It's a bit of an uphill slog back to the Steel Rigg car park. Now, see that building at the bottom of the lane on the Military Road? That's the Twice Brewed Inn where a very good beer and plate of food awaits.

If you still have vigour in your legs and are thirsty for more wild Wall scenery, you can continue past the car park and turn right by a gate (signed) to make the stiff climb to **Winshield Crags** – one of the finest vantage points on the whole of Hadrian's Wall and, at 1,132ft, the highest point on the Wall trail.

* * *

6 VINDOLANDA ROMAN FORT

Near Bardon Mill NE47 7JN ✆ 01434 344277 ⊙ daily; check times online ♿ entrances at the top of the hill for the fort, and the bottom for the museum and café 🐾. The museum and fort are connected by a wide, gravel slope but the incline to the museum is too steep for most wheelchairs so you'll need to drive round

> We found posts sticking up in the ground then some funny little oily fragments of wood. There were two of these stuck together which I peeled apart with my hands; there were all these weird ink hieroglyphics on it. I just couldn't believe it... We didn't realise it at the time, but we had hit anaerobic deposits – in other words no oxygen down there, no bacteria, therefore everything was preserved exactly as the Romans had left it.
> The late Dr Robin Birley, Archaeologist and Director of Excavations at Vindolanda, on discovering the famous Roman writing tablets in 1973

Set on a natural table above a wooded ravine and surrounded by gently curving hills a mile south of Hadrian's Wall is this fort and fascinating archaeological museum housing some of the most important Roman finds ever recovered.

The Roman military station and village are reached first on entering Vindolanda from the north and were built in AD85, several decades before the construction of Hadrian's Wall. Over the following centuries the site was rebuilt several times and continued as a settlement, with shops and domestic dwellings, after the retreat of the Roman Empire.

Discoveries are still being made by experts and volunteers involved in Vindolanda's active **archaeological research programme** that began in the 1970s, and you may well see the team at work during the spring and summer, unearthing stones and buried artefacts, as you walk around the outdoor site.

Archaeological finds in recent years include two leather boxing gloves, a new hoard of writing tablets, and a gold coin dating to AD64–65 that bears the image of the Emperor Nero (its value to a Roman soldier was over half a year's salary; pity the soldier who dropped the coin in the ground).

When I last visited, one of the lead archaeologists on a dig enthusiastically exclaimed: 'we found yet another phallic image – the second phallus carved on to this road!' **Phallic symbols** were etched into paving stones or on boxes for good luck and a number of such images have been found over the years, including on the bridge abutment opposite Chesters Roman Fort (page 307). Vindolanda also holds a very rare carved wooden penis, thought to be the only one uncovered in the Roman world – the function of which can only be guessed. It's now on display in the museum.

Inside the **fort** walls, which would have once been at least 16ft high, are the remains of the commanding officer's quarters, a granary, barracks and the headquarters building. Equally as absorbing is the 'vicus' or **civilian settlement** outside the western fort gate with its food and textile shops, domestic dwellings, tavern and workshops facing each other along a main street. Drains (still channelling water today) line either side of the road and are covered with stone slabs at intervals marking the entrances to individual buildings. Taking a moment's pause, you can imagine the smells, bustle and noise along what was essentially a high street.

After exploring the ruins and the convincing replica stone **tower**, a path downhill leads to a wooded ravine and Vindolanda's outstanding **museum**. A delightful stream – the Chainley Burn – runs through the gardens, where there is outdoor seating for the **café**.

The first exhibit on entering the **museum** is a wall of Roman leather shoes that will stop you dead in your tracks. There's something intensely moving about the display, which brings to life the soldiers, their families and everyday preoccupations that we can relate to today, not least keeping your feet dry on boggy ground.

But the most treasured artefacts here are the **Roman writing tablets** (page 317) discovered on site beneath a protective layer of clay in 1973. They are the earliest collection of written material in Britain and provide a glimpse of life in Roman Britain. Most of the 1,400 tablets recovered thus far are stored in the British Museum in London but a number are displayed in a darkened room here. A short film tells the fascinating story of their discovery, with archaeologist, the late Robin Birley, excitedly describing the moment he realised their significance.

The rest of the museum is devoted to a remarkable array of other **artefacts** excavated at Vindolanda, including many ceramic vessels, tools, animal bones and weapons, as well as intriguing domestic items such as a brush made from pig hair, basketware, a lady's wig and jewellery. A particularly compelling display of terracotta bathhouse tiles contain depressions – paw prints, hoof marks and a human footprint – inadvertently stamped on the wet clay while the tiles were drying. Another standout find is a fragment of a bronze blade-like instrument (a 'calendrical clepsydra') with holes punched along its length and the

THE ROMAN WRITING TABLETS

I want you to know that I am in very good health, as I hope you are in turn, you neglectful man, who have sent me not even one letter ...

Are we to return with the standard ... to the crossroads all together or just half of us ...

My fellow-soldiers have no beer. Please order some to be sent ...

Letters written by Roman soldiers recovered from Vindolanda

Thanks to the damp, anaerobic soil at Vindolanda, a large number of leather, textile and wooden items that would otherwise have quickly rotted away survived here for almost 2,000 years until their discovery by archaeologists in 1973. What excited the team most were the hundreds of small writing tablets, about the size of postcards. At first, archaeologists thought they were wood shavings, until they noticed a script scrawled across the fragments of birch, alder and oak. The eminent archaeologist at Vindolanda, the late Dr Robin Birley, said at the time of the discovery, 'If I have to spend the rest of my life working in dirty, wet trenches, I doubt whether I shall ever again experience the shock and excitement I felt at my first glimpse of ink hieroglyphics on thin scraps of wood'.

Among the tablets are the quartermasters' book-keeping records listing supplies for the garrison, the correspondence of commanding officers, and messages of a more personal nature: letters to family members and notes accompanying parcels. Perhaps the most treasured card is the famous **birthday party invitation** from Claudia Severa to Sulpicia Lepidina; it is the earliest record of female correspondence and Latin handwriting in Western Europe and is held in the British Museum for safekeeping.

It was probably only a matter of time before archaeologists at Vindolanda came across a message that would disclose a derogatory term Romans used to refer to native people. Tablet number 164 revealed the slang word *Brittunculi*, meaning 'wretched Britons'.

word 'SEPTEMBER'. It is thought to be a Roman water clock and is the only example ever found in Britain.

Unlocking Vindolanda's Wooden Underworld is a stand-alone exhibition space devoted to the 1,500 wooden objects discovered here, from kitchen utensils to a toy sword and toilet seat.

Excavations are ongoing and adults over the age of 16 can join the team on an **archaeological dig** for one week or longer. Applications open in early November each year for the following season.

Taking the footpath from the back entrance of the museum, you can **walk** to the stables at Low Fogrigg and back in under an hour by following the bubbling Chainley Burn through woodland and across grassland. You can extend this route to the lovely village of Bardon Mill (a mile south of Vindolanda), with its historic pottery and Victorian train station, by continuing along the river (this is also a good way of reaching Vindolanda if you've come by train from Newcastle).

Outside the museum café on the Roman road (the Stanegate) stands a hefty cylindrical stone pillar – the **Chesterholm Roman Milestone** – just inside a farm gate. It is thought to be the only one of its kind in Britain still in its original location.

7 THE SILL: NATIONAL LANDSCAPE DISCOVERY CENTRE

🏠 **YHA The Sill**

Once Brewed NE47 7AN; the Hadrian's Wall Country Bus (AD122) stops right outside (page 300) ✆ 01434 341200 ⊘ thesill.org.uk ☉ Easter–Oct daily ♿

Seemingly built into the land is this modern stone- and glass-walled Northumberland National Park visitor centre on the Military Road, half a mile south of Hadrian's Wall. The roof is imaginatively planted with Whin Sill plants to reflect the special local flora. Inside, it's spacious and bright and offers visitors a great starting point for a visit to Hadrian's Wall – and a useful stopping place for long-distance hikers, this also being a YHA and on the Hadrian's Wall bus route. A shop on the ground floor is stocked with local guides, maps, artwork, gifts, and deluxe walking socks made in Northumberland. Also here is a free exhibition space devoted to 'landscape' with some interesting short videos relating to different aspects of the Northumberland countryside: music heritage to dry-stone walling.

"The light-filled café upstairs is a fabulous place to enjoy the scenery and watch the changing weather."

The light-filled **café** upstairs is a fabulous place to enjoy the scenery and watch the changing weather over a coffee or light lunch.

🧳 SPECIAL STAYS

YHA The Sill Military Rd, near Bardon Mill NE47 7AN ✆ 01434 341200 ⊘ yha.org.uk ♿. You can hardly find a more convenient, budget option for visiting Hadrian's Wall, which snakes across the Whin Sill escarpment half a mile away. Also close by are Vindolanda and Housesteads Roman forts. Housed in a modern building – which chiefly operates as a tourist information centre and café – YHA The Sill sensitively blends into the landscape. It's a great choice for solo hikers or families (there are 16 four-bed rooms and a number of two and three-bed suites). The Hadrian's Wall bus, AD122, stops right outside, shuttling visitors to all the major Roman attractions in the area.

¶ FOOD & DRINK

The Sill (page 318)
Twice Brewed Inn & Brewhouse on the Military Way road, nr Bardon Mill NE47 7AN ✆ 01434 344534 ⊙ breakfast, lunch & evening meals daily ♿ 🐾. Stumble into this popular family pub half a mile off the Wall and glug a pint of Sycamore Gap, congratulating yourself on navigating a four-mile Wall walk in fog and waning light with three young children. Well, that's how I last experienced the Twice Brewed. Fog or no fog, children or no children, Sycamore Gap is a beautiful beer brewed on site – a tradition dating to 1464. But there's more to enjoy at this friendly brewhouse, mid-range restaurant and B&B with all the usual pub favourites on the menu: homemade sausages, great pizzas, fish dishes, steak, scampi and burgers. I had venison ('shot close by' the waiter mentioned) with goats' cheese and a red onion marmalade. For a lighter lunch, choose from a selection of hot and cold sandwiches. Do book ahead, especially for Sunday lunches (served unusually late from noon until 21.00) and evening meals.

8 GREENLEE LOUGH NATIONAL NATURE RESERVE

📍 NY747690; access from Gibbs Hill farm parking area, 2 miles north of The Sill

Migrant wildfowl in autumn and winter lure birdwatchers to Northumberland's largest freshwater lake, which pools below Hadrian's Wall and the towering Whin Sill escarpment on which it rides. But, this wetland landscape is probably most biologically interesting in late spring and early summer when the reedbeds host nesting sedge warblers and reed buntings, and the fen and wild flower habitats fringing the lough are at their most verdant, attracting many butterflies, bees, moths, dragonflies and damselflies.

A boardwalk curves around the wettest parts of the **lake** to a bird hide, but to reach the walkway you must first walk a mile across uneven, damp fell ground that becomes increasingly squelchy underfoot as you approach the lough (see walk, page 321). Skylark song will accompany you the whole way in spring. Cotton grass, sneezewort, bog asphodel, marsh cinquefoil and swathes of honey-scented meadowsweet in July crowd the first stretch of the walkway before giving way to head-height reeds thereafter.

Flower meadows stuffed with yellow rattle, buttercups, clovers and vetches slope to meet the northern edge of the water. Look out for ringlet butterflies here. From the **bird hide**, you may see otters feeding on native white-clawed crayfish, particularly if visiting on a summer's evening. Ospreys are also not infrequently spotted taking fish from the inky depths.

You may only catch sight of a few flying species of course, but as you move through the swaying reeds that hum, hiss and chirp with insects, amphibians and birds you cannot locate, you will at least think you've found the most tranquil place in all of Northumberland.

* * *

🚶 GREENLEE LOUGH WILDLIFE WALK

❊ OS Explorer map OL43; start: Gibbs Hill car park; 📍 NY748691; 4 miles; easy

An exciting variety of birds and insects inhabit the fen, reedbed, lake and hay meadow habitats on this rewarding walk under the gaze of Hadrian's Wall.

1 Turn right out of **Gibbs Hill car park** and cross over a quaint humpback bridge before entering grassland by a fingerpost signed 'Greenlee Nature Reserve'. Cross the rough grassland ahead (and pass through three wicket gates) using the line of electricity poles to guide you. On reaching a wood, keep close to its boundary line.

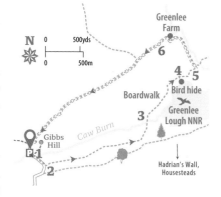

2 The last electricity post marks the rough location of the **boardwalk**. The plant life becomes more interesting from here on, with cotton grass, marsh cinquefoil and meadowsweet dominating in summer. Look out too for common blue damselflies and common darter dragonflies. At a junction in the walkway, turn right, skirting around the **lough**. The stems of reeds are head height in places and it's here that you may see a sedge or

---

◀ **1** Greenlee Lough NNR is Northumberland's largest freshwater lake inhabited by **3** sedge warblers and **4** otters. **2** The Sill National Landscape Discovery Centre is a great starting point for information about Hadrian's Wall.

grasshopper warbler or reed bunting. A waymarker at the end of the boardwalk points to the right. Keep to the fenceline and go through a wicket gate by the corner of a mixed woodland, entering a **hay meadow** swaying with yellow rattle and buttercups in summer. A **bird hide** overlooking the lough is reached via a stile at the end of the woods.

3 Climb away from the lake, keeping the dry-stone wall on your right. At a fingerpost, turn left and make for **Greenlee Farm**, which is reached along a track and over a ladder stile. Catch your breath and take in the view of the lough, Whin Sill crags and distant Pennine moors.

4 Skirt the farm, following a track round to the left. Pass through a farm gate and turn left at the top on to a stony farm track that will lead you in two straightforward miles back to the car park via a number of stiles. Depending on the time of year, your journey will be accompanied by the calls of curlews. At a junction in the track by the farm, turn right and you'll soon see the car park as you round the corner.

✳ ✳ ✳

9 GREENHEAD & GILSLAND

On your way out of Northumberland and into Cumbria, two pleasant villages are reached in quick succession. **Greenhead's** riverside setting, stone terraces, church and village hall make it a welcome stop for ramblers, cyclists and motorists but there's very little to warrant a stop beyond pausing for refreshments in the road-side café or Greenhead Hotel (page 323) opposite.

Gilsland is a quiet Cumbrian stone village, which sits in a dip in the hills and is reached from Greenhead by following a road high up over hilly farmland, or on foot along the Hadrian's Wall Path. The village was popular in Victorian times with visitors who came by train to enjoy the sulphur-rich waters just north of the settlement at Gilsland Spa (page 323).

Opposite Gilsland Green, on Hall Terrace, is a 17th-century cottage – and former hostelry – known as **Mumps Hall** that is now the **House of Meg Tea Rooms**, a popular spot with Wall walkers. It is famed for the legend of a notorious landlady nicknamed Meg of Mumps Hall who murdered and robbed many passing travellers in the 18th century.

South of the railway line, Milecastle 48 (also known as the **Poltress Burn Milecastle** after the river it watches over) is said to be one of the most intact of all on the Wall. Though its walls are not particularly high, you can see the foundations of rooms. A signpost on the railway bridge by the B6318 points you in the right direction. The up and down route takes about 15 minutes to walk and is reached via a playground and under a viaduct where the Poltress Burn makes its merry way.

FOOD & DRINK

The Greenhead Hotel Main Rd, Greenhead ✆ 016977 47411 ⊘ May–Oct 07.00-22.00 daily, Nov–Apr Wed–Sun. 🐾. Recently refurbished hotel (with revamped hostel in the converted church opposite) catering well for Wall walkers and visitors to the nearby Roman ruins. Food available all day but you'll have to be content with bar snacks or a bowl of chips between the main mealtimes. Dishes include various cuts of meat served with veg, risotto and a fish dish or two, and vegan and kids' menus too. Local ales in the bar.

Greenhead Tea Room Greenhead ✆ 016977 47400 ⊘ Mon–Sat. Serving food all day (filled baps, burgers, soups, toasties and cakes) and all the usual coffees, plus milkshakes.

Gilsland Spa & Irthing Gorge

Gilsland Spa Gilsland, CA8 7AR

High above the wooded gorge of the River Irthing, Gilsland Spa mansion (now closed but plans are afoot to revamp the hotel) occupies a secluded spot popularised in the 19th century for its sulphurous spring and romantic woodland setting laced with footpaths. It is said that Sir Walter Scott met his future bride here, a tale that fuelled a surge in Victorian tourists, aided by the opening of a railway station a mile away in the village of Gilsland. My 1859 travel guide notes stalls selling 'knickknacks [sic] and curiosities' but there's none of that

"Gilsland Spa mansion occupies a secluded spot popularised for its sulphurous spring."

infrastructure or footfall today and the train station has long since closed so most likely you will be able to enjoy the scenic gorge largely undisturbed, with its old trees wrapped in thick moss, towering walls sprouting with foliage and splashed by little waterfalls here and there.

To **walk** to the spa, take the path from the hotel car park (signed), descending through trees to the River Irthing which glints between the boughs of broad-leaved trees in the ravine below. It's a wide, muddy walkway and not really suitable for wheelchairs owing to the gradient. At a prominent bend take either track, but turning left on the main trail is the most direct route for the **spa** waters, which dribble from a tap into a stone basin by the side of a footbridge. Sulphurous fumes lead the way.

To vary the return, take the riverside path downstream and then the ascending trail on your right, just past a stone ruin. Incidentally, if you were to continue a short way ahead you would soon reach a derelict bathing pool, still with its stone steps and handrail.

For a **longer walk**, cross the footbridge by the spa spout and enter Woodland Trust land (on your left after crossing the bridge). In a few hundred yards, cross another footbridge and continue upstream to a large boulder and two small rounded ones by the river: the **Popping Stone** (presumably the large one) is said to be where Scott 'popped' the question to his lover. The tale is without evidence but that didn't dissuade 19th-century visitors (or indeed, modern-day walkers) from making the journey to pose for photographs. A couple of miles further upriver via Collering Wood and across open countryside is **Crammel Linn waterfall**, which sprays 25ft over a craggy sandstone outcrop in the Irthing into a broad pool.

10 THIRLWALL CASTLE
Half a mile north of Greenhead, off the road to Gilsland and on the Hadrian's Wall Path

All crumbling now, Thirlwall Castle still commands attention at the top of a hilly mound a mile or so north of Greenhead village and a short diversion off the Pennine Way and Hadrian's Wall Path. Stern and imposing with small windows and 9ft-thick walls, the robust block born out of a 12th-century building was clearly reconstructed with defence in mind when nobleman John Thirlwall strengthened his family home using recycled Roman stones in the 1330s. These were violent times and inhabitants with any wealth were reinforcing their piles to protect against attacks from the Scots and hostile Reiver clans notorious in these parts until the Union of the Scottish and English crowns in 1603.

The ruins are easily reached by a 15-minutes' walk from Thirlwall View car park (on the B6318) by following a footpath into a meadow, over the Newcastle to Carlisle railway line, and along Tipalt Burn (a nice spot for throwing stones) or from the national trails connecting Walltown Country Park with Thirlwall Castle via grasslands in half a mile. This is a lovely **walk**, incidentally, which can be made into a varied two-mile circuit: Walltown Country Park to Thirlwall Castle (Hadrian's Wall Path & Pennine Way) then a wander along Tipalt Burn (taking the Pennine Way) to Greenhead followed by a visit to the Roman Army Museum before returning to the country park. A map of this route is displayed in the country park car park.

11 WALLTOWN COUNTRY PARK & WALLTOWN CRAGS

The hard dolerite cliffs Emperor Hadrian seized as an ideal boundary for his empire is formed of Whin Sill stone, which did not go unnoticed by the Victorians for its durability, and it was extensively quarried at Walltown from 1876. Today the disused quarry forms a scenic park around a lake with picnic benches and a visitor centre. **Walltown Country Park** is popular with families, many of whom will be content to stroll through the trees and grasslands and around a couple of ponds buzzing with dragonflies to a sculpture known as the Peace Labyrinth. To give your legs a longer stretch and take in one of the finest lengths of Hadrian's Wall, follow the circuit described below round the quarry lake and up on to the Walltown Crags.

Laced along the top of the Whin Sill cliffs, a short climb from Walltown Country Park near Greenhead, is one of the most impressive lengths of Hadrian's Wall, standing over 7ft tall in places – or, as I counted, 12 rows high. From the rocky escarpment of **Walltown Crags**, Northumberland National Park is laid before you with the Cheviot Hills framing the panorama to the north.

* * *

🏃 WALLTOWN CRAGS CIRCUIT

✻ OS Explorer map OL43; start: Walltown Country Park car park; ♀ NY668659; 2½ miles; moderate

Arguably one of the most scenic stretches of Wall landscape along the whole of the Roman frontier (and far less crowded than other famous vantage points on the national trail), Hadrian's Wall rollercoasters over the high Whin Sill cliffs of Walltown Crags, offering far-reaching views of Northumberland. The return is across farmland below the Wall.

From the **visitor centre** in the Walltown Country Park car park, pick up the wide gravel trail that curls under a Whin Sill outcrop and around the quarry lake, climbing uphill through birch woodland to meet Hadrian's Wall at the top of the cliffs.

Catch your breath once you reach the Whin ridge and take in the expansive view and Roman masonry. Trace the Wall eastwards, noting how in places, natural rocks in the landscape have been incorporated into the Wall, and passing **Turret 45a**.

Turrets usually appeared two to every Roman mile (0.9 English miles) providing shelter for Wall soldiers, but it is thought this well-preserved tower, which appears to have been built as a freestanding structure before construction of the Wall, may have functioned as a signalling station.

Half a mile ahead, the national trail dips into a hollow and continues eastbound over a ladder stile towards Turret 44b where more fabulous Wall scenery comes into view. To return to the visitor centre, however, turn right in the hollow and before the stile and make your way along the quiet, paved track passing **Walltown Farm** on your right. Continue across sheep-grazed land and skirt the woodland in the distance.

Once over a cattle grid, a muddy footpath runs parallel to the road. A short distance ahead, steps in the path climb upwards before descending to the visitor centre through woodland. Continuing on the lane, however, would take you back to the Country Park via the Roman Army Museum – a slightly longer route.

* * *

12 ROMAN ARMY MUSEUM

Carvoran, Greenhead CA8 7JB ✐ 016977 47485 ⊙ Feb–Oct daily, Nov–Jan w/ends only ♿

Vindolanda's sister **museum** delves into the world of the fierce and unstoppable Roman army in all its spear-thrusting, shield-bearing magnificence. Different aspects of the Roman military are highlighted in this engaging space that details the life of Hadrian and the wider context of the Roman Empire. Life-size models of soldiers, including one in combat on horseback, will impress even the most casual of visitors.

One of the most remarkable exhibits is a black hair-moss helmet crest, the only one ever found. Elsewhere you'll see Roman shoes, cloak brooches, spear tips, and coins depicting the heads of the many Roman emperors.

The *Edge of Empire* is a compelling 20-minute film depicting the brutal training and routines of Wall soldiers and includes the re-enactment of an ambush by native Britons and special effects to recreate the Wall and forts.

Under grassland to the west of the museum, lies **Magna Roman Fort**. The garrison station and surrounding landscape, including the vallum and Milecastle 46, are the subject of a five-year archaeological investigation that began in 2023. An online blog at

---

1 Walltown Crags and Country Park. **2** The remnants of Thirlwall Castle are located close to the village of Greenhead. **3** Exhibits in the Roman Army Museum. **4** Crammel Linn waterfall, near Gilsland Spa. ▶

(⌖ romanarmymuseum.com/magnafort) details the programme of excavations and provides a fascinating insight into modern-day archaeology: the tools, methods and conservation processes. It's something of a race against time to understand the site and retrieve Roman artefacts before they become exposed to oxygen and begin to degrade – a process accelerated by our warming climate. Visitors can view the dig site on tours (call the museum ahead of your trip for dates and times).

⑪ FOOD & DRINK

The Milecastle Inn Military Rd, near Haltwhistle NE49 9NN ✆ 01434 341248 ☺ daily. This is just the kind of pub you want to stumble into after a long day, with its cosy, low-beamed interior, open fires, local beers on tap and unassuming interior where even the most dishevelled Wall walker will feel welcome. Meals are a little pricey, nudging £10 for lunchtime sandwiches and jackets, and £20 for evening mains: cod and chips, meat and veg dishes, burgers (also a vegan option) and macaroni cheese though the children's meals are more reasonably priced.

13 BIRDOSWALD ROMAN FORT

Gilsland, Cumbria CA8 7DD ✆ 016977 47602 ☺ daily ♿ 🐾 English Heritage

> One of our student archaeologists excavated a metal ring. I told her to keep digging along the trench and she found another ring, and another. She was shaking. We knew the rings must have been supporting wooden piping and that this was probably the Roman bathhouse [for the fort].
>
> Tony Wilmott, senior archaeologist for Historic England recalling a recent dig at Birdoswald Roman Fort

What is particularly intriguing about this remote Roman fort on the line of Hadrian's Wall are the layers of history visible above ground spanning 1,900 years of occupation from the second century AD, with Roman and medieval structures overlooked by an 18th-century farmhouse.

"The military station and farmhouse stand amid several miles of undulating grassland and Roman Wall scenery."

At the top of a wooded escarpment above the scenic River Irthing, the military station and farmhouse stand amid several miles of undulating grassland and Roman Wall scenery. Ripples in the ground reveal medieval plough marks, and a particularly well-preserved stretch of the great Roman earthen structure, the **vallum** (page 303), lies to the

WALL WITH A VIEW

Between Housesteads and Birdoswald Roman Fort, the upland terrain offers tremendous views of the Whin Sill backbone, Wall and distant hills. From all the prominent 'crags' (Sewingshields, Housesteads, Hotbank, Highshield, Peel, Winshield, Cawfield and Walltown), many miles of open countryside span the panorama: the swelling Pennine moors to the south; the bottle-green forests of Wark and Kielder to the north, and the Cheviot Hills beyond. And then there's the immediate scenery: the Wall trailing along the uppermost edge of 100ft-high curtains of volcanic rock; below, flower meadows and farmland grazed by sheep enclose steely lagoons.

Winshield and **Peel crags** are easily reached from the Steel Rigg car park, a mile or so north of The Sill. It's a stiff 15-minute hike to the top of Winshield Crags at 1,132ft (the highest point of Hadrian's Wall), but the sight of the Wall snaking for many miles with all the loughs and crags in view will stay in the memory. Also with parking nearby is **Walltown Crags** (page 325) near Greenhead – a quieter stretch of the Roman frontier but with spectacular views. For easy access to a long length of Roman wall, I recommend a visit to **Birdoswald Roman Fort** (page 328).

west of the fort. In the other direction, the longest continuous stretch of **Hadrian's Wall** trails across grassland towards a wooded ravine (and is immediately accessible from the road and by following the Hadrian's Wall Path).

Birdoswald (or 'Banna' to the Romans) is typical of a Roman **fort**. Rectangular in form with a curtain wall enclosing military buildings: a central headquarters with a Mediterranean-style inner courtyard, a commanding officer's house, granaries, barracks and a roofed drill hall where soldiers would practise combat skills. With the exception of the two 3rd-century granaries and part of the drill hall's long outer walls (which would have once measured some 47yds in length), the footings of most of these buildings remain under turf.

The **farmhouse** (largely mid 18th-century with a Victorian tower but the oldest parts date to the mid 17th century) occupies the northwest corner of the fort overlooking the outlines of a Roman workshop, a 16th-century defensive **bastle farmhouse** (page 235), and timber posts marking where a later **Dark Age timber hall** once stood.

Compared with Chesters, Housesteads and Vindolanda, the fort at Birdoswald has fewer buildings visible above ground, but its curtain wall and double **gateways** are remarkably well preserved, particularly the east portal flanked by two (now ruined) towers and a pier supporting a single arch stone (a 'voussoir' if you want the proper word). Look at the ground and you'll see fist-sized depressions for the gate pivots on which the doors were hung. Their considerable diameter gives an indication of the weight and height of the wooden portals.

Beyond the fort, the 30 miles of Hadrian's Wall to the west was originally an earthen construction but was later replaced with stone. You can see this older **Turf Wall** by exiting the fort through the south gate and following the **footpath** west where you will also enjoy plunging views of the wooded River Irthing.

"Remarkably, it was just in the last few years that archaeologists discovered what they think is the bathhouse for the fort."

When reading this account of the Birdoswald ruins, keep in mind that only around a quarter of the Roman site has been excavated, with many buildings in the civilian areas outside of the garrison yet to be uncovered. Remarkably, it was just in the last few years that archaeologists discovered what they think is the bathhouse for the fort but there's so much more under your feet. Put it this way, as the senior archaeologist at Birdoswald explained: if a Roman soldier were to visit today, he'd comment: 'I remember when all this land was houses and shops and buildings'.

Behind the farmhouse, a pleasant courtyard with old farm buildings (constructed with Roman stones of course) has been repurposed into a tea room, shop and **exhibition**, the last of which caters well for families and includes a short film highlighting how Hadrian's Wall would have once looked. Also in the small museum space are displays of items uncovered during digs. Note the urns discovered in a Roman cemetery at Birdoswald in recent times.

¶¶ FOOD & DRINK

The courtyard café at **Birdoswald Roman Fort** is a lovely spot for a slice of cake and hot drink or light lunch (sausage baps, soups, salad).

Slack House Farm Gilsland CA8 7DB (½ mile north of Birdoswald Roman Fort & 1½ miles west of Gilsland on the B6318) ✆ 016977 47351 ♿. I've travelled miles out of my way to pick up a tub of Dianne's rich, nourishing live natural yoghurt made with unpasteurised, unhomogenised milk, and her raw milk cheese. These are premium products made with a lot of love, care and respect for animal welfare and the environment. Made on site to a 1688 recipe, the milk is taken straight from the herd of brown and white Ayrshire cows in the nearby fields and immediately worked for up to five hours. The cheese is then left to mature for up to six months.

Phone ahead to check the farm shop (which also sells raw milk in bags and free-range eggs) is open. Otherwise you can pick up produce at local farmers' markets and shops (the butcher in Haltwhistle for example).

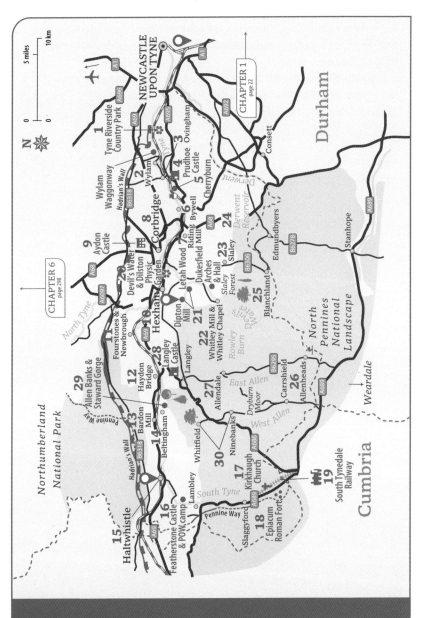

THE TYNE VALLEY & INTO THE NORTH PENNINES

7
THE TYNE VALLEY & INTO THE NORTH PENNINES

From Carlisle to Newcastle, road, river and railway ribbon across the neck of England through a wide, fertile valley with pockets of woodland and a scattering of farms and settlements hunkered by the water's edge. The countryside is not remote and neither is it dramatic, but there is much beauty in this broad-sided valley that is filled with light, owing to the relative flatness of the land. **Hexham** (page 354) and **Corbridge** (page 348) are the most prominent and historically interesting market towns on the Tyne.

A few miles south, the **Hexhamshire** (page 375) countryside offers many fine river walks and glimpses of a rural landscape (and economy) of yesteryear: old stone farms, secluded hamlets, water mills, wooded lanes and relics from the 18th- and 19th-century lead-mining industry.

The astonishingly beautiful **North Pennine hills** (page 382) roll across the Northumberland–Durham border with heather becoming increasingly dominant the further south you venture. From some moors, you can see Scotland. For the most part, however, Northumberland's Pennine dales are characterised by wooded gorges, flower-filled hay meadows and a pastoral landscape reminiscent of parts of Yorkshire with dry-stone walls criss-crossing farmland.

GETTING AROUND

Undoubtedly, the most reliable and frequent public transport option in the Tyne Valley is the **train**, though Hexham, Corbridge and Haltwhistle are also well serviced by **bus** from Newcastle (685). Roman Wall visitors make good use of the **Hadrian's Wall Country Bus AD122** (page 300), which connects with services in Haltwhistle and Hexham. As for travel in the North Pennines, you can get around by bus (page 18), but you're best off with your own vehicle – or a bicycle.

TRAIN

The Newcastle–Carlisle train (⊘ northernrailway.co.uk), also known as the (slightly misleading) Hadrian's Wall Country Line, runs a couple of times an hour daily between Newcastle and Carlisle. Railway and river intertwine the whole way and the train stops at most riverside towns and villages in the Tyne Valley: Newcastle, Wylam, Prudhoe, Stocksfield, Riding Mill, Corbridge, Hexham, Haydon Bridge, Bardon Mill and Haltwhistle, before shuttling on to Carlisle via Brampton and Wetheral. A Day Ranger ticket allows unlimited travel. The surrounding green and yellow fields dotted with sheep, cows, woods and farmsteads are just lovely. On the downside, it's no Bullet Train and it rattles along like a tin can.

CYCLING

The River Tyne corridor offers the day cyclist some pleasant, straightforward routes along the river. I've described the popular **Newcastle to Wylam** cycle ride on page 345. I recommend stopping at The Boathouse pub (page 340) which is conveniently located right next to Wylam station and makes for a rewarding end to a half-day excursion. If you can't manage the return ride, take your bike on the train. Services run hourly back to Newcastle from various stations in the Tyne Valley, including Wylam and Prudhoe.

Thigh-busting moors and long exhilarating downhill stretches abound in the North Pennines. Hundreds of cyclists take on the

THE HEAD OF STEAM

The **Newcastle–Carlisle railway**, dating from the 1830s, was one of the earliest railways ever built. The stations have retained much of their original Victorian character and North Eastern Railway Company architecture, particularly at Wylam, Prudhoe, Hexham and Haltwhistle. Waiting rooms with tall chimneys, big station clocks, signal towers, water tanks and decorative iron footbridges painted cream and red add to the historic appeal of the villages and towns the stations serve.

At **Haltwhistle station** – such an evocative name but nothing to do with the railways – all the above come together, making it one of the most interesting on the line.

TOURIST INFORMATION

Online, the **North Pennines National Landscape** website (⊘ northpennines.org.uk) contains helpful information about the countryside, geology and wildlife of the region. The National Landscape office also produces many high-quality walking, cycling and information guides, available to download or buy (⊘ 01388 528801).

Alston Town Hall, bottom of Front St ⊘ 01434 382244 ⊙ Easter–Sep Mon–Sat; Oct–Easter Mon–Fri ⅁
Corbridge Hill St ⊘ 01434 632815 ⊙ 10.00–15.00 Wed, Fri & Sat ⅁
Hexham Hexham Library, Queens Hall, Beaumont St ⊘ 01670 620450 ⊙ daily ⅁

140-mile **Coast to Coast** (Whitehaven to Tynemouth via Alston and Allenheads) and the 150-mile **Pennine Cycleway** (NCN Route 68; Appleby or Penrith to Berwick-upon-Tweed via the North Pennine moors, Redesdale and Wooler) every summer and you'll find good facilities along the way. There are many day rides of course: around the reservoirs, along disused railway lines (see a description of the **South Tyne Trail** on page 369, which follows the Pennine Cycleway), and country lanes above wooded gorges. See ⊘ ecocycleadventures.co.uk for suggested routes across the region. Five guides produced by the North Pennines National Landscape office can be downloaded from the cycling pages at ⊘ northpennines.org.uk.

 CYCLE HIRE & REPAIRS

In addition to the places listed below, there are a couple of options in Newcastle (page 25).

Eco Cycle Adventures Unit 7A, Haugh Ln Industrial Estate, Hexham ⊘ 01434 600600 ⊘ ecocycleadventures.co.uk. Transport for bikes and luggage; bike hire; online route descriptions.
North Pennine Cycles Nenthead ⊘ 01434 341004. Repairs, bike hire and shop.

WALKING

There are plenty of options for **river walks** around the towns and villages in the **Tyne Valley**. Beautiful mixed woodlands crowd smaller waterways like the West Dipton Burn and Devil's Water just south of Hexham – both of which offer walkers several miles of riverside rambles. Further west is Allen Banks (page 395), one of the most stunning wooded valleys in Northumberland.

The **North Pennines** presents some of the best opportunities for moorland and valley walks in England. From the River Tyne, the **Pennine Way** shoots due south roughly following the course of the River South Tyne from Lambley to Alston before climbing across some of the country's highest and most desolate fells; **Isaac's Tea Trail** makes a circuit of the beautiful Allen valleys (page 397).

Taxis

Advanced Taxis Hexham ✆ 01434 606565. Offer bike transfer.

Alston Taxis Alston ✆ 07990 593855

Diamond Private Hire Haltwhistle ✆ 07597 641222

Ecocabs Hexham ✆ 01434 600600 ♿. The fleet includes a large number of vehicles run on biodiesel. Ecocabs service the whole of Northumberland and offer bike transfer, luggage transport and tours.

THE TYNE VALLEY

The further west you venture through this wide, low-sided valley upriver from Newcastle, the views of farmland and glimpses of church towers and manor houses peeping through the trees become increasingly prevalent. Certainly from Newburn onwards, the scenery is are predominantly rural and verdant. Some of the greenest and most tranquil stretches of the River Tyne are found here and are easily reached by following the riverside path out of Newcastle city centre (page 345), or by taking the train to Wylam or Prudhoe.

"Road and railway lace in and out of a string of historic towns and hamlets, drawing visitors to their medieval centres and celebrated buildings."

Little effort is needed to lure passing travellers to **Wylam** and **Ovingham** with their affluent old railway terraces, riverside settings and free-house pubs. **Prudhoe** holds less immediate visual charm but does boast a ruined **castle** and wonderful National Trust farm, **Cherryburn**, the former home of nature engraver Thomas Bewick.

From Ovingham to the western edge of Northumberland, road and railway lace in and out of a string of historic towns and hamlets with the likes of **Hexham** and **Corbridge** drawing visitors to their medieval centres and celebrated buildings, notably **Hexham Abbey**, parts of which were built using stone from the ruins of **Corbridge Roman Town**.

1 TYNE RIVERSIDE COUNTRY PARK

From Newcastle the Country Park is signed from the A6085; car park off Grange Rd, NE15 8ND (close to the Big Lamp Brewery & Keelman pub)

You'd never guess a coal mine once stood on this 200-acre meadow and wetland parkland near Newburn, unless, that is, you notice clues in the landscape (the remains of four beehive coke ovens at Blayney Row, for example). Today, the site, which extends to the south side of the Tyne at Prudhoe, is popular with dog walkers, families and those cycling and walking Hadrian's Wall.

From Newburn, two trails keep tight to the riverbank (one exclusively for walkers). The Tyne flows lazily here, tugging the branches of overhanging shrubs and trees. If visiting at dusk, you'll walk under the noisy flight path of hundreds of jackdaws and rooks roosting in nearby trees.

¶¶ FOOD & DRINK

The Keelman's Lodge Grange Rd, Newburn ✆ 0191 267 1689 ◷ breakfast until 10.00 & noon–21.00 daily ♿. The large playground next to an outdoor seating area shouts 'family-friendly pub'. The Keelman is not really in the countryside as such, but the leafy riverbank setting is somewhat rural. The building dates to the mid 19th century and was formerly a water pumping station. Fairly inexpensive pub dinners: scampi, fish and chips, steaks, pies, burgers and so on; the **Big Lamp Brewery** serves a decent pint.

2 WYLAM

Wylam produced a number of the great railway pioneers of the 18th and 19th centuries. George Stephenson and Timothy Hackworth were both born here and William Hedley, who was raised in nearby Newburn, worked at the Wylam Colliery and tested his famous steam engine prototypes on the Wylam Waggonway (page 338). After visiting the wagonway and historic railway station at Wylam (page 338), anyone with an interest in railway history should visit the **Wylam Railway Museum** in the library (Falcon Terrace ✆ 01661 852174 ◷ Tue & Thu, 10.00–noon Sat ♿ to the rear, accessed from Dene Rd), which houses one-twelfth scale working models of early locomotives, the *Puffing Billy* and *Wylam Dilly* and other interesting artefacts in the small museum.

19TH-CENTURY RAILWAY TOWNS

Mining and industrial production over the last few hundred years greatly changed the character and fortunes of settlements in the Tyne Valley and North Pennines. These industries expanded with the aid of the railways in the 19th century and towns and villages grew as a result. Many places, particularly along the Tyne corridor, have retained their characterful uniform terraces of sandstone and brick, village greens and stone bridges. The largely unchanged 1835 railway station buildings at **Wylam** are wonderfully nostalgic and anyone with even a fleeting interest in railway architecture may delight in knowing this is one of the oldest railway stations in the world still in use.

The village itself makes for a pleasant stopping point on your travels along the Tyne. Grand stone houses and brick terraces either side of the river reflect the affluence that came with being a railway town in the 19th century.

Wylam's **town centre** is on the north side of the Tyne and accessed by following Main Road north from the river and memorial green. It's attractive enough with a few restaurants, shops, a post office and a couple of pubs.

Two **bridges** span the Tyne here. The more striking is the 1876 railway bridge (now only open to cyclists and pedestrians) at Hagg Bank (west of Wylam Station, reached from the riverside path). The single-span structure is reminiscent of Newcastle's Tyne Bridge, which was built half a century later. The crossing further east by the train station directly links the two sides of Wylam town and retains its 1899 toll house.

Wylam Waggonway

Today it is a wooded recreational path a few miles long between Wylam and Blayney Row but at the turn of the 19th century this wagonway (that then extended to Lemington) played an important role in the development of modern railway travel.

Wagons were used to transport coal from Wylam Colliery to ships docked at Lemington staiths on the River Tyne, some five miles away. Originally, they were pulled on wooden rails by horses, until the owner of the colliery, Christopher Blackett, set his mind to making the transfer of coal more efficient. In 1808, he replaced the wooden rails with cast-iron ones and enlisted the engineering skills of his colliery manager, William Hedley, to develop an engine to replace his horses. Hedley experimented with different designs until the ***Puffing Billy*** was unveiled in 1814. The stout locomotive (now housed in the Science Museum in London) was created with the assistance of two local engineers, Timothy Hackworth and Jonathan Forster, and is the oldest surviving steam locomotive in the world. The train carried coal along the Wylam Waggonway for 50 years, but its greatest contribution to the Industrial Revolution was in demonstrating that smooth iron wheels could run on flat iron tracks without derailing. This was an important step in the evolution of the modern train, enabling the locomotives of the future to travel at high speeds. A small replica engine is housed in the nearby railway museum (page 337), located at the Wylam end of the wagonway.

Halfway along the wagonway is **George Stephenson's Birthplace**, a small limewashed stone cottage built for mining families around 1760 (owned by the National Trust and open for special events only, including for organised walking tours along the wagonway. Book online at ⊘ nationaltrust.org.uk). The great railway engineer was born here in 1781 and in his early days he would have watched horses outside pulling wagons laden with coal from Wylam Colliery. Stephenson lived with six other family members in one room of the four-bedroom building.

Bradley Gardens

Sled Ln, Wylam ✆ 01661 852176 ⊙ Tue–Sun & bank holidays (closed Tue after a bank holiday) ♿ 🐾 outside only

Tucked away down a quiet lane south of Wylam train station, this enchanting 18th-century walled garden houses a tea room, nursery and a couple of upmarket gift and home interiors stores. A wonderful

THE SALMON RUN

For a month from mid-October, salmon turn upriver and embark on an arduous journey to their breeding grounds. The Tyne, being the number-one salmon river in England and Wales, is a good place to witness the spectacle (try Hexham weir or Wylam Bridge).

In the early 1800s, the Tyne was, as it is today, very good for salmon. On one day in June 1833, between 400 and 500 salmon were fished from the river and taken to market in Newcastle. However, by the 1950s there were virtually no salmon, owing to pollution. Cleaner water and the hatchery in Kielder (page 260) have reversed the salmon's fortunes dramatically and record numbers have been recorded in the Tyne in recent years.

Victorian **glasshouse** houses the tea room where middle-aged ladies take lunch and admire the flowerbeds, walkways draped in climbers and the view of the green hills rising beyond the garden walls.

¶¶ FOOD & DRINK

In Wylam you have the choice of a couple of pubs, cafés and restaurants including **Bistro en Glaze** (Main Rd ☎ 01661 852185 ☉ variable but usually Thu–Mon 🐾), a snug bistro serving breakfasts, Sunday lunches and evening meals, mainly Italian and British family favourites. Traditionally made sourdough pizzas are served at **The Wood Oven** (Main Rd ☎ 01661 852552 ☉ evenings Wed–Sun, plus brunch Sat & Sun &); known as 'Monty's' to locals, this really good pizzeria now also serves a British brunch menu.

For an outstanding pub lunch, consider making the journey to locally renowned **The Feathers Inn** (page 344).

Bradley Gardens (page 339) ☉ Tue–Sun & 🐾 outside only. Well-healed residents of the Tyne Valley book tables in advance at this secluded glasshouse café in a restored walled garden a short drive from Wylam. Besides the peaceful location and attentive service, the food – all cooked on site – is really very good, whether you've come for breakfast (eggs six ways, full English, granola, filled rolls), a hot lunch (chicken pie, fishcakes, quiche, haddock risotto, soup) or simply a coffee with a wonderful fruit scone. Their blackberry jam, incidentally, is homemade and absolutely delicious. It's available to buy in jars but they sell out quickly. Afternoon teas must be booked at least 24 hours in advance. Divine cakes and, yes, all freshly made too.

The Boathouse Station Rd ☎ 01661 853431 🐾. A cracking, much-loved traditional pub next to Wylam's historic railway station, and a CAMRA shining star in the Tyne Valley with 11 local cask beers and plenty of local chitter chatter on tap. Laid-back atmosphere, open fire – there's just so much to like about this well-known, somewhat dog-eared boozer.

3 OVINGHAM

Mature trees and bushes crowd the banks of the Tyne at Ovingham ('Oving-jum') where fly-fishermen whip the water with their lines and kayaks take it in turn to whoosh down the rapids. By any Northumbrian standard, this lively sizeable village holds much old-world appeal, particularly around the church with its red phone box, cottage gardens and old (now sadly closed) streamside pub, the Bridge End Inn.

St Mary's Church is built on the site of an early Saxon building of which the tower is the only relic. It is thought that part of the west side of the tower was built using Roman stones and the structure may

OVINGHAM GOOSE FAIR

The tradition of selling birds and other livestock at the village's annual Goose Fair dates to the 13th century, but seems to have died out some time in the early 20th century only to be revived in the late 1960s. The fair is now held on the third Saturday in June. Visitors are entertained with Morris and Rapper dancers and traditional Northumbrian folk music, with a procession beginning from the old Goose Fair Cross. Cakes, plants, ice creams and crafts can be purchased from stallholders, while children can have their faces painted and participate in the fancy dress competition and maypole dancing. It's all good, traditional country fun.

have been designed with habitation in mind during the post-Roman centuries when invasions were feared. As you walk to the main doorway, you'll see the grave of the celebrated 18th-century nature artist, **Thomas Bewick**, who lived at Cherryburn (page 343) over the river and went to school in Ovingham.

When I visited, I was drawn from the busy streets into the churchyard by the sound of children singing along to a piano. Despite the commuter traffic outside and the mini scooters stacked in the church porch (the same entranceway that Thomas Bewick used as a canvas for his chalk drawings when he had run out of notebook pages), there was something quite old-fashioned about the scene.

Whittle Burn is crossed by way of a fetching old packhorse bridge formed of two narrow stone arches. From here you can trace the waterway upriver along a quiet footpath. Nineteenth-century records of Whittle Burn note the occurrence of fairies. If a quiet woodland with a shallow, stony stream and overhanging trees is the kind of place that attracts fairies, then this should indeed be a favourite haunt.

4 PRUDHOE CASTLE

Prudhoe NE42 6NA ✎ 01661 833459 ◷ Apr–end Oct Wed–Sun & bank holidays ♿ access to ground floor of the house; some outside areas difficult 🐾 English Heritage

Prudhoe's ruinous 12th-century stronghold pokes through trees at the top of a steep bank and is easily the most striking historic attraction in the town (pronounced by locals as 'prudha'), which is largely a modern place above the south side of the River Tyne.

Built as a military fortress to defend the Tyne more than 900 years ago, Prudhoe is said to be the only castle in the north never to be taken

by the Scots. Its 12th-century **gatehouse**, 10ft-thick **curtain wall**, elevated position and moat no doubt provided good protection, and the ruins remain impressive to this day, even more so close up than from a distance.

Originally the stronghold of the Umfravilles – an important landowning family in Northumberland – it was later inherited by the powerful Percy family of Alnwick Castle and left to decay in the mid 17th century after the Union of the Crowns brought relative peace to the border region.

The **manor** house was originally built as a gentleman's residence in 1810 by the 2nd Duke of Northumberland and is now used as an exhibition space. Artefacts include arrowheads, cannonballs, fragments of medieval chainmail and horse bits which all help narrate the history of Prudhoe: its sieges and significance in controlling the north on behalf of the Norman kings of England.

On exiting the castle, take in the superb Norman stone archway and crumbling ruins of an 18th-century **mill** by the riverside.

5 CHERRYBURN

Station Bank, Mickley, Stocksfield ✆ 01661 843276 ⊙ mid-Mar—end Oct Thu & Fri ♿
🐾 National Trust

> The eventful day arrived at last ... I can only say my heart was like to break; and, as we passed away, I inwardly bade farewell to the whinny wilds, to Mickley bank, to the Stob-cross hill, to the water banks, the woods, and to particular trees, and even to the large hollow old elm, which had lain perhaps for centuries past, on the haugh near the ford we were about to pass, and which had sheltered the salmon fishers, while at work there, from many a bitter blast.
>
> *A Memoir of Thomas Bewick Written By Himself*, 1862

The year was 1767 and 14-year-old Thomas Bewick was leaving his birthplace on the banks of the River Tyne to begin an apprenticeship at an engraving workshop in Newcastle. His fondness for the family home at Cherryburn and the woods and rivers surrounding the farmhouse

◄ **1** Cyclists on the Wylam Waggonway outside George Stephenson's birthplace. **2** St Andrew's Church in Bywell has an extensive collection of medieval grave slabs. **3** The remains of 12th-century Prudhoe Castle. **4** Pages from Thomas Bewick's *A History of British Birds* at Cherryburn.

stayed with Bewick his whole life. Though he is most famed for his woodcut blocks of birds and his celebrated 1797 book, *A History of British Birds*, on every other page of the book there is a vignette depicting rural scenes typical of the Tyne landscape in the 18th century: boys sail toy boats on the river in one picture while in another a farmer cuts his meadow with a scythe. There is humour too, like the man holding on to a cow's tail while crossing a river with a drunkard on his back.

Bewick's engravings evoke nostalgia for the rural way of life and draw us seamlessly into his childhood in the Tyne Valley where fishermen stand knee-high in water, men play the fiddle and it is almost always summertime.

The National Trust looks after Bewick's much-loved **Cherryburn** and makes much of the stone cottage, cobbled courtyard, cottage garden, wildflower meadow and farm outbuildings huddled near the Tyne. It's a very appealing museum with displays of Bewick's works and a fascinating print room with demonstrations. Children will enjoy the natural play areas outside and the cherry orchard (with active beehives in summer).

From Cherryburn, you can **walk** through countryside and along the river to Ovingham and Wylam on the north side of the Tyne where Bewick went to school.

¶¶ FOOD & DRINK

The Feathers Inn Hedley-on-the-Hill, Stocksfield ✆ 01661 843607 ◷ **restaurant**: lunchtime & eve Thu–Sat, lunch Sun; **pizzeria**: Mar–Sep eve Fri & Sat; **bakery**: 10.00–noon Sat 😾 bar only except Fri eve. Go out of your way to locate multi-award-winning and Michelin-rated The Feathers. Almost everything on your plate is sourced in the North East from 60 local suppliers: Haydon Bridge beef, local roe deer, wild North Sea salmon, Slaley Wood mushrooms and Lindisfarne oysters. Lunch and evening meals are a cut above most other decent Northumbrian country pub restaurants. You could start with a pear, chicory, walnut and Darling Blue (Northumbrian blue cheese) salad and follow with roast pheasant. For afters, a classic British bowl: bread and butter pudding perhaps. And the bill? Around £20–£25 for evening mains is excellent value for food of this quality. Also come here for Sunday lunches. Outside seating can't be booked but you'll need to get in touch a week or two in advance for an indoor table on a Sunday. No gastro pub décor here – just traditional wooden pub furniture, exposed stone walls and a log burner.

Wor Local Micropub 10 Front St ✆ 01661 598150 ◷ from 16.00 daily 😾. Should you find yourself at a loose end in Prudhoe – an unlikely scenario but you never know – do seek out this lively little community pub with a large range of gins and cheap pints of local ale and cider. The beers are as authentic as the locals who pile into this compact boozer housed in an old computer shop, filling it with daft banter.

* * *

⅄ NEWCASTLE TO WYLAM BY BICYCLE OR ON FOOT

❇ OS Explorer map 316; start: Newcastle quayside; 10 miles; easy/moderate

This easy, off-road cycle path takes you west along the Tyne Valley under Newcastle's famous bridges and into tranquil countryside. It follows the well-signed **Hadrian's Cycleway** (NCN Route 72). The footpath for walkers (**Hadrian's Wall Path**) follows the same route, except between Scotswood and Newburn Bridge (the section you may wish to cover by bus 22 from Newcastle Central Station because it follows a busy road).

From Newcastle's quayside, follow the promenade upriver from the **Tyne Bridge,** noting the historic **Dunston Coal Staiths** (page 48) on the Gateshead side of the river. In winter, shelduck, teal, lapwing and the odd curlew dabble under the wooden structure at low tide.

The mile-long stretch to the ancient woodland of **Denton Dene** is a big, busy concrete affair (albeit one on a foot- and cycle path), but once you enter the Dene's woody confines, the Scotswood Road and its juggernauts seem far away. If you've heard the famous North East song *The Blaydon Races*, you'll recall the often recited line: 'There were lots of lads and lasses there, all with smiling faces, ganning along the Scotswood Road, to see the Blaydon Races.'

Just after Blaydon Bridge, the cycle path turns to the river and follows it closely to Newburn and, not far away, the 120ft-high **Lemington Glass Works cone** – the only one of four late 18th-century brick cones still standing here and one of the last remaining in England.

The **Tyne Rowing Club**, founded in 1852, is just beyond the Newburn Bridge. After a very pleasant half mile through the **Tyne Riverside Country Park** (page 337), the path swings north where you will meet with the old **Wylam Waggonway** (page 338) for the final leg to Wylam via George Stephenson's birthplace cottage (page 339).

Return the same way or by train (bikes permitted) from Wylam. If you continue west for another couple of miles to lovely **Ovingham**, you'll cross Wylam's eye-catching old railway bridge at Hagg Bank and a manmade limestone grassland inhabited by chalk-loving butterflies. NCN Route 72 passes Prudhoe train station on the south bank of the Tyne, from where you can return to Newcastle.

* * *

6 BYWELL

Technically Bywell is a village but all visitors see today are a few houses, the castle and hall (both glimpsed through private gates), and two churches separated at a junction by an old market cross; nonetheless Bywell makes for a pleasant diversion while motoring through the Tyne Valley. This is especially so if you're travelling on two wheels as the lanes hereabouts are wonderfully peaceful. But why two churches within such close proximity? Experts say they may have existed in two separate villages many years ago.

St Andrew's (usually open) is fascinating on account of its extensive Saxon stonework. According to Pevsner it has a 'first-rate Saxon tower, the best in the county' constructed in places with recycled Roman stones. Let's overlook nearby competitors, even if we're flexible with the county borders (St Andrew's at Corbridge, Ovingham's church and St Paul's of Bede fame at Jarrow come to mind), and instead admire the 9th-century tall tower with its irregularly shaped stones and rounded windows that give it a characteristic Saxon appearance. The base of the cross in the chancel is also Saxon and retains some fine stone detailing but the rest of St Andrew's mostly dates to the 13th and 19th centuries. Note the extensive collection of medieval grave slabs set into the exterior walls and displayed inside.

"Bywell makes for a pleasant diversion while motoring through the Tyne Valley."

As for **St Peter's** (open on the third Sunday of every month for morning service) – identified by its comparatively squat, wide tower – well, it's largely 13th century (with some Norman masonry) and was built on the site of a Saxon church. Its wonderful churchyard, with a profusion of snowdrops in February, slopes to the banks of the Tyne.

The other prominent building in Bywell is the **castle**. I say 'castle' but it's really just the gatehouse to a castle that was never built. Still, its castellated turrets are pretty impressive and the roofless building is of considerable age (early 15th century). It's said that Henry VI took shelter here on fleeing the 1464 Battle of Hexham and left behind his sword, helmet and crown.

7 RIDING MILL

When you arrive by train from Newcastle, Riding Mill feels like the first stop in the Northumberland countryside. There are no attractions to speak of in the village except for a couple of defensive bastle houses in Broomhaugh, a Methodist chapel, the 17th-century Wellington Inn (see below) and the old mill-house opposite, but the leafy setting, stone cottages and closeness to the River Tyne make this a pleasant stopping point. The last time I visited, some neighbours were trying to catch some escaped hens. It's that kind of a place.

The construction of the Newcastle–Carlisle line made it possible for Tyneside businessmen and their families to live in the countryside, hence the tall townhouses you see today that were built with Victorian commuters in mind.

If you have half an hour to spare, there's a lovely circular **walk** from the station to the river and back through woodland filled

"The last time I visited, some neighbours were trying to catch some escaped hens."

with spring flowers and the notes of tits and thrushes. From platform one on the north side of the line, take the paved footpath for a few hundred yards to **Broomhaugh**. Turn left at the Methodist chapel and continue to the end of the street where a dirt path near an old bastle house leads to the banks of the Tyne. Turn upriver and follow a well-trodden muddy path, turning left into woodland just before a tributary. Ahead, cross the stream at some stepping stones and then pick your way uphill through the trees and back to the station platform (aim for the houses peeping through the canopy).

¶¶ FOOD & DRINK

Wellington Inn Main Rd ✐ 01434 682531 ☉ lunch & dinner daily, plus breakfast Fri–Sun ♿. Printed wallpaper depicting fox-hunting and rural scenes, old black-and-white photos and the smell of a wood fire places this large pub with seating inside and out in the category: 'reasonably upmarket country pub restaurant', known for its family Sunday roasts. At other times, the menu is a medley of classic pub dinners.

Wheelbirks Ice Cream Parlour Stocksfield NE43 7HY ✐ 07717 282014 ☉ Tue–Sun ♿ 🐾 outside only. In the summer you'll want to eat in the orchard where the kids can run free. Ice cream may be on your mind, but don't overlook the lunch menu, which is really quite good and includes a range of hot and cold sandwiches, soup, burgers and jackets. As for the ice cream (made with rich Jersey milk produced by the doe-eyed cows you can see grazing outside), expect all the usual favourites and a few unusual tastes, alongside milkshakes made with raw farm milk. You can also pick up bottles of unpasteurised milk to take-away. Exceptionally family-friendly with plenty of play areas (inside and out).

8 CORBRIDGE

The broad main street is lined with houses and gardens instead of shops, and it is not difficult to imagine that at any moment a mail coach might come rattling through on its way from Newcastle to Carlisle and draw up at the friendly-looking Angel Inn.

The King's England: Northumberland, 1952

On entering this handsome market town along its principal thoroughfare, the large double-fronted houses of butter-coloured sandstone make quite a first impression, and it is clear why Corbridge is a popular visitor destination. In the **town centre**, art galleries sit next to an upmarket delicatessen on Hill Street, where you'll also find the **tourist information centre** (page 335); ladies chat outside jewellery shops on Middle Street; and several cafés, a florist and bookshop circle the busy Market Cross. A number of shop fronts have original 18th- and 19th-century wood detailing and a few are among more than 60 listed buildings in Corbridge.

Corbridge has not always been so prosperous, however. In the 14th century, the town was attacked and ransacked by the Scots on several occasions, and the Black Death later wiped out much of the remaining population. For several hundred years, Corbridge remained a small, insignificant settlement, until 1835 when the Newcastle–Carlisle railway opened and wealthy Tyneside businessmen gentrified Corbridge into the smart town it is today. Most of the streets date to this period though the layout is medieval.

There were several earlier booms in the town's history that ought to be mentioned, notably under Roman rule and again in the 13th century, when Corbridge was said to be (regionally) second only to Newcastle in wealth.

The Tyne flows fast over rapids as it passes Corbridge under the town's 1674 **bridge** – the only one still standing after floods in 1771 washed away every crossing along the Tyne, except for this magnificent seven-arched structure. Access the tranquil riverbanks by walking down the path at the side of the bridge.

St Andrew's Church

Before you enter St Andrew's, note the **vicar's pele tower** in the churchyard, which dates to around 1400. It now houses a rather special micro-brewery (page 353) but in the centuries of long ago, clergymen would have taken refuge inside the defensive tower during attacks

CORBRIDGE'S ANTIQUE SHOPS

Tucked away to the side of Corbridge's filling station on Main Street is a run of three tempting antiques shops. **RE** (✆ 01434 634567 ⊙ daily (afternoons only on Sun) ♿) is a huge emporium of vintage, recycled, repro and new household and garden finds housed in an old workshop. The open-plan space is divided into kitchen, bathroom, textiles, haberdashery, china and garden areas with new and old often sharing the same display cabinets. To give you an idea of what to expect, I last left here with several Edwardian terracotta pots rescued from a walled garden, some coloured twine, a jelly mould, four handmade wooden spoons and an enamel bucket.

Next door is the **Corbridge Antiques Centre** (✆ 01434 634936 ⊙ variable but usually from 11.00 or noon–16.00 Tue–Sun ♿), home to more than 30 dealers selling reasonably priced furniture, china, ornaments, garden pottery, jewellery, vintage toys and so on, over two floors. You'll want to spend a bit of time rummaging through the stock: a mixture of the 'just old' to the truly antique.

Lawrence Stephenson (✆ 01434 633663 ⊙ Tue & Thu–Sat) is an altogether more refined space with selected pieces of furniture (mainly mahogany tables, cabinets and drawers) from the Regency to Victorian eras with some lower-priced items.

on the town. English Heritage ranks it as the best example of its kind in Northumberland.

The walls of St Andrew's date mainly to the 13th century, though there is evidence of Norman construction as you enter the south porch, and the **tower** is Saxon ('the most important Saxon monument in Northumberland except for the Hexham crypt,' says Pevsner). Perhaps most striking is the 16ft-high **Roman arch** that forms the entrance to the baptistry. Like many buildings in Corbridge, we can hazard a good guess as to where this stone treasure was sourced. Also impressive and standing over double the height is an Early English archway dating to the 13th century.

As you depart the church grounds, turn right to see the exterior of the Saxon tower and the intriguing 700-year-old **King's Oven** built into the church wall. A plaque explains that it was 'the communal oven for the baking of the village's bread and meat.'

Corbridge Roman Town

Corchester Ln ✆ 01434 632349 ⊙ Apr–Oct & school holidays daily; Nov–Mar Sat & Sun ♿ museum & the Stanegate (though it's very uneven) 🐾 English Heritage

Before Hadrian's Wall, the Roman garrison town of Coria at the western edge of Corbridge, built circa AD85, was an important settlement at the junction of two major Roman roads: Dere Street and the Stanegate. It also held a strategic position at a crossing of the River Tyne and later acted as a supply town for Hadrian's Wall.

Over 350 years the site developed into a civilian settlement with workshops, granaries, meeting halls, a temple and public amenities. Here, traders, civilians, officers and soldiers jostled along what we would recognise today as a high street but the town was abandoned by the early 5th century, with the retreat of the Romans.

Looking down one of the principal throughfares, the **Stanegate** (page 309), which runs an east to west course through the town, stone guttering and the foundations of market buildings remain visible either side of the wide street, along with the huge floor of a **granary** to your left, still with its raised floors to allow ventilation. It's considered the best preserved in Britain. It is not difficult to imagine the noise and hubbub of soldiers and their families picking up supplies and the sound of water trickling from what was once an elegant **fountain** fed by an aqueduct.

"It is not difficult to imagine the noise and hubbub of soldiers and their families picking up supplies."

Facing the Roman town is a modern on-site **museum** charting the Roman occupation in AD43 to the collapse of the empire some 400 years later. It houses some wonderfully preserved domestic and military objects and a fine collection of stone monuments, including a relief of the sun god and another (rather amusing) depiction of Hercules brandishing a club. A clear highlight is the freestanding **Corbridge Lion**, a bushy-maned beast poised on top of a captured goat – or is it a cow? Experts believe it was originally a mausoleum statue, later repurposed into a water fountain with a spout routed through the animal's jaw.

Domestic items are always fascinating and include a game board with stone counters, complete with a shaker made from bone and a dice (interestingly with a duplicate number and no number six), children's feeding bottles and a doll's leg carved from bone. In the

1 Pretty Haydon Bridge on the South Tyne. **2** A postcard perfect cottage in Beltingham. **3** A stone terrace in the historic town of Corbridge. **4** Corbridge Roman Town. ▶

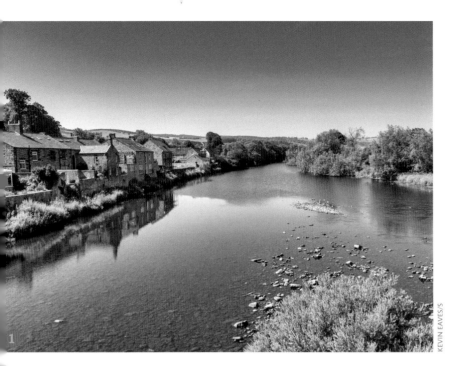

KEVIN EAVES/S

NORMAN PRICE/A

GEMMA HALL

SS

same cabinet is a glass flagon with fluted opening and still, amazingly, with its curved handle intact.

Many are drawn to Corbridge's **Lorica Segmentata** body armour, said to be the most complete of any Roman find. You can see how the individual plates were designed to flex allowing a soldier's arms and torso to move.

FOOD & DRINK

A scattering of cafés, pubs and restaurants dot the streets around St Andrew's Church. The queues snaking round the corner from **Grants** (1 Market Pl ☏ 01434 633044 ☉ daily) opposite the market cross indicate the popularity of this award-winning bakery and patisserie. Outdoor seating facing the marketplace takes in all the town's goings on. Also with outside chairs and serving coffees but in a quiet corner of the marketplace is **The Pele** (see opposite).

Upmarket restaurant, **Sycamore**, in the old Town Hall (2–3 Princes St ☏ 01434 239454) was due to reopen at the time of writing and is worth checking out (informal dining, high-end British cuisine). And for a really special pub lunch, consider **The Rat Inn** at Anick (page 362), a couple of miles west.

Angel Inn Main St ☏ 01434 632119 ☉ daily ♿ but disabled toilet a pig to reach 🐾. Claiming the (unverified) title of 'the oldest inn in Northumberland', the Angel's doors have been welcoming drinkers on Corbridge's principal street for hundreds of years – since 1569 to be precise, though the current building dates to 1726. The plush furnishings, open fires and gastro-pub menu draw in a loyal local crowd. Northumberland beef, North Sea fish, local game and posh burgers are always on the menu, alongside a few specials. Sunday lunches are popular so do book ahead. Also note the good-value light lunches: fish finger or hot beef sandwiches, lamb skewers and fishcakes for example. Also, take-away fish and chips (order from the bar). To drink, there's always a couple of local cask beers from the likes of Allendale and Anarchy breweries.

The Black Bull Middle St ☏ 01434 632261 ☉ daily ♿ 🐾 bar only. Popular 18th-century pub in the centre of Corbridge with plenty of character: low beamed ceilings, stone walls, a coal fire, old black-and-white photos of the village and real ales from the likes of Allendale and Hadrian Border Brewery. Traditional comfort food: pies (venison, steak, mushroom), fish and chips, a seafood grill, lasagne, burgers, steaks and some specials. A safe bet, always very good.

Brockbushes A69 roundabout east of Corbridge NE43 7UB ☏ 01434 633100 ☉ daily ♿. A pick-your-own strawberry and raspberry farm (online booking essential ⌂ brocksbushes. co.uk) with an on-site butchery, shop, tea room and play barn (new buildings under construction at the time of writing).

The Corbridge Larder & Café 18 Hill St ☎ 01434 632948 ⏲ daily. Simply one of the best delicatessen and pantry stores in Northumberland, and super little café whipping up all-day breakfasts, hot lunches and original sandwiches stuffed with local produce to sit in or take-away. Cheese fans are in for a treat at the deli counter, which boasts a comprehensive regional selection. Elsewhere, shelves are stocked with chocolates, biscuits, honeys, local beer, Corbridge gin and much more – all produced in the North East. Follow the smell of hearty food upstairs to the **Heron Café** (always busy). A noticeboard lists the provenance of local produce. Loosen your belt for the Larder full-English breakfast; for lunch, keep it simple with soup and a stottie sandwich or scone (made at dawn) or go for something a bit special: pear, Northumberland blue stilton and crème fraiche sandwich or smoked mackerel with homemade horseradish mayo.

The Pele St Andrew's Church, Market Pl ☎ 01434 632905 ⏲ 10.00–23.00 Thu–Sun 🐾. An eccentric pub in a 700-year-old fortified tower and one-time refuge for the clergy of St Andrew's during the centuries of ransacking and violence. Enjoy local ales, gins and coffees in this very special microbar – cleverly laid out over three floors with a central light well.

Pine Vallum Farm, East Wallhouses NE18 0LL (5 miles northeast of Corbridge) ☎ 01434 671202 ⏲ eve Wed–Sat, lunch Sun. A converted cow barn in farmland by Hadrian's Wall vallum earthwork is the setting for a rare food experience in Northumberland: a 20-course tasting menu by Michelin-rated chefs who craft foraged (knotweed, woodruff, meadowsweet, hand-dived scallops) and homegrown produce and rare-breed meats in an open kitchen into works of gastronomic art. With wine, expect to pay in the region of £200 per person.

9 AYDON CASTLE

Aydon, a few miles north of Corbridge NE45 5PJ ☎ 01434 632450 ⏲ Apr–end Oct Wed–Sun ♿ ground floor only 🐾 English Heritage

> **Aydon has no keep, and that gives it its outstanding architectural importance. Here is a very early case of a fortified house, rather than a castle.**
> Nikolaus Pevsner, *The Buildings of England: Northumberland*

Elevated on a fist of farmland overlooking a wooded ravine is this impressive 13th-century fortified manor house considered one of the most intact and formidable of its period.

When built in the 1290s by wealthy Suffolk merchant Robert de Raymes, Aydon Castle was originally unfortified, Northumberland at that time being a peaceful corner of the country. Little did he know that within a few decades, the Scots would come charging down the hills ransacking villages and towns in the Tyne Valley, igniting centuries of intermittent conflict on the Borders.

Robert was forced to house a garrison and strengthen his gentleman's residence with a battlemented courtyard and high **curtain wall** enclosing three sides of the manor (the south was already protected by the steep bank of a ravine). He must have regretted ever making the move north. English Heritage describe Aydon Castle as 'a memorial to one of the most disastrous miscalculations in the history of English real estate.'

Despite the added protection, Robert the Bruce's army was still successful in pillaging and burning Aydon Castle during their attacks on Corbridge in the early 1300s. As for Robert de Raymes, he died of the Black Death in 1349.

Continual occupation for the best part of 700 years until the late 1960s helped preserve the original 13th- and 14th-century hall, kitchens, courtyards, garderobes and bedrooms. Though unfurnished, you get a good sense of how the house evolved and the functions of individual rooms, such as the **kitchens** still with their huge medieval fireplaces, and a blocked-up window and doorway to protect the manor from invaders during turbulent years. Note, too, details including the (19th-century) pigeon holes cut into the second kitchen walls allowing birds to nest (and later be eaten), bread ovens, and chutes from the latrines that disposed of waste into the ravine below.

As you wander around the rear of the castle where it teeters on the edge of the steep wooded bank, you'll see the aforementioned chutes, as well as an eye-catching **chimney** with a circular shaft and little windows for the smoke to escape – a good example of the high standard of fittings in the original manor. Close by is an enclosed **orchard** (once a kitchen garden) with picnic tables.

10 HEXHAM

The Tyne Valley's principal town rears above the river on a wooded plateau like an Italianate village. Only Hexham's 13th-century abbey tower and tallest stone buildings break the canopy, leaving most of the old stone streets hidden from view. Reaching the historic centre from the Tyne obviously involves a climb, the most pleasant route being a pedestrian walkway opposite the railway station.

On entering the **marketplace** – a busy square with a higgledy mix of Victorian, Georgian and medieval buildings – it is clear why Hexham was once voted England's favourite market town by *Country Life* magazine. The criteria were charm, accessibility and sense of community, all of which are apparent to the visitor.

Hexham was burned and pillaged many times over the 1,300 years since it began life as a monastery on a terrace above the Tyne. In the Middle Ages, farming and lead mining were the major industries, but Hexham later became a centre of leather production and was famed for its gloves known as Hexham Tans. According to A B Wright in his 1823 *History of Hexham*, some 280,000 pairs were produced annually in the town (one of which visitors to the abbey museum can inspect in a display case). Wright also notes the presence of two woollen manufacturers, two rope makers (one survives on Argyle Street), 16 master hatters and a 'very considerable brewery'. I suppose it would have had to be of some size in order to supply some of the 32 inns and pubs in the town. A number of those historic taverns are still extant and serving ale today.

A tour of Hexham's old town

A wander through the streets radiating from the marketplace reveals the shops and industries of bygone times. The prominent stone-pillared shelter in the square is known as the **Shambles** – a medieval meat market. Goods are still sold here but you are more likely to find potted plants and clothes. A **farmers' market** runs on the second and fourth Saturday of the month.

"The Tyne Valley's principal town rears above the river on a wooded plateau like an Italianate village."

The stonking walls of the **Moot Hall** – a tower house dating to at least the early 15th century – demand attention. Once a courthouse, it now has many functions, including hosting weddings and an art gallery. A vaulted passageway leads to Hallgate and **Hexham Old Gaol** (page 359). Where the road winds round the side of the gaol, you'll find a couple of fine art galleries and a coffee house butting up against the prison walls.

One of the most fascinating streets in Hexham, **St Mary's Chare**, is tucked away down a passageway opposite the Shambles. It stands on the site of an old chapel from which the street gets its name. Go through the alley and then turn around at the old-fashioned sweet shop to see the outline of one of the chapel's windows. The cobbled lane ahead has many Victorian shopfronts housing **independent cafés and shops** including **Cogito Books** ($\mathscr{D}$ 01434 602555 $\odot$ Tue–Sat), recommended for local guides, OS maps and its children's area. Hidden somewhat to the side of a narrow alley is an enchanting clock repair shop where grandfather clocks stand in the passageway ticking away the days.

Running parallel to St Mary's Chare is **Fore Street**, a busier pedestrian street with an equal number of old shopfronts, but fewer independent businesses. **The Old Pharmacy** is a curious building: its black and red frontage with decorative grapevines was designed by a Belgian refugee in 1916 and looks incongruous – and far too special to be a high street clothing store (White Stuff at the time of writing).

Snaking downhill from the marketplace is **Market Street** – a road with many jewellers and hairdressers and the huge antiques emporium, **Ashbourne House Antiques** ($\mathscr{D}$ 01434 607294 $\odot$ Tue, Wed, Fri & Sat noon–16.00), which is stuffed with china, bric-a-brac, copper pots, furniture and architectural salvage. You can find anything here, from a cast-iron Victorian radiator to a hookah pipe.

Continuing downhill, Market Street soon becomes **Gilesgate**. Look out for a narrow alley on your left just past Bouchon Bistrot restaurant. Where now you see a large courtyard, car park and a shallow stream, until the 1920s animal skins were soaked in large **tanning pits** here to produce leather gloves. An information panel does a good job of making sense of what you can still see today. To return to the marketplace, retrace your steps up Gilesgate until you reach the impressive 12th-century arches of the **Priory Gatehouse**. A walkway snakes round the side of the abbey from where you gain good views.

Filmgoers should head to the independent picture house, **The Forum Cinema** on Market Place, not least to admire the Art Deco café interior: high ceilings with geometric features, and gold and mint paintwork. At the other end of Hexham's market square is the **Queen's Hall Arts Centre** (Beaumont St $\mathscr{D}$ 01434 652477 $\odot$ Mon–Sat $\mathring{\&}$), which puts on regular dance, music and theatre performances.

Hexham Abbey

Market Pl $\mathscr{D}$ 01434 602031 $\odot$ 11.00–17.00 daily $\mathring{\&}$

You may find the view of the abbey from the street a little underwhelming, but wait until you step through the door. What appears from the outside to be a rather stout, manly building with a squat tower, is elegant and lofty inside.

Founded in AD674 by Wilfrid, Bishop of York, the abbey was originally built as a monastery, but quickly became a church. It was said to be of greater beauty than anything 'this side of the Alps'. Today, the only surviving part of Wilfrid's wondrous building is the **crypt**, reached by descending a stone staircase in the nave. The warren of tight passages and chambers was constructed using Roman masonry from nearby Corbridge, in which you can see carvings and lettering.

Danish raids in the 9th century damaged the original Saxon building, which was restored as a priory some 200 years later (the remains of the priory **cloisters** lie in the abbey's southwest grounds). Most of what you see today dates to the 12th and 13th centuries.

The best vantage point inside is from the broad stone staircase in the south transept. The **Night Stair** used to lead to the canons' dormitory and today provides visitors with a superlative view of the crossing and choir. Lancet windows in the north transept and the three tiers of arched windows opposite drive the walls skywards, creating a sense of space and height. At the bottom of the Night Stair is a **Roman tombstone** with a startling engraving of a standard-bearer on horseback trampling over a cowering Briton. A few steps up – number six to be exact – is supposedly spotted with molten lead which had dripped from the abbey roof when the building caught fire during a famous 13th-century attack by the Scots.

Many more treasures are found in the aisles and around the altar, including an Anglo-Saxon chalice and a **frith stool** (a bishop's throne) that may have been built for Wilfrid in the 7th century. A number of Saxon grave covers and rare medieval wood-panel paintings are nearby.

In the chancel, you'll find the **Dance of Death** painted across four panels; Death is depicted in each hovering next to a cardinal, king, emperor and pope. Above the altar in the **Leschman Chantry Chapel** is an unusual wood painting of Christ emerging from a coffin. Kneeling at the head of the coffin is **Prior Leschman** whose stone effigy (carved with a hooded robe pulled over his eyes) is also in the chapel. Lastly, note the curious stone-carved figures on the side of the chapel, depicting a jester, harpist and bagpipe player.

Housed in a former monks' workshop near the Refectory Café is an engaging **museum** (☉ daily; free entry ♿) plotting the history of the abbey and town from Roman times to the present day. Highlights include nine 16th-century wood panels depicting the Passion of

CHEMIVAL/S

SS

Christ, the story of the discovery of the lost crypt in 1725, and an 8th-century carved stone pillar showing one of the earliest depictions of Christ's crucifixion.

Also intriguing are a number of artefacts discovered during the restoration of the floor of the choir stalls in 2013: sweet wrappers and drawings of Spitfires belonging to choir boys around the time of World War II that must have fallen through the floorboards.

Abbey Grounds, Hexham House & the Sele

Every corner of this pleasure ground commands a good view of the abbey and the church. It is now the mall of the fashionables, the privileged playground of the lower classes, and the place of exercise and amusement for all.

This 1823 observation of Hexham's historic parkland largely rings true today. Twenty acres of green space surround the abbey on all but one of its sides, divided into three distinct areas: the **Abbey Grounds** with its 20th-century bandstand; a large open area of grassland called the **Sele**; and the gardens and bowling green in front of the Georgian mansion, **Hexham House**. To the side of the bowling green is a wooded area with a lively burn that trickles through a 13th-century archway and under the boughs of oak and fir trees.

Hexham Old Gaol

Hallgate ✎ 01670 624523 ☉ Apr–end Oct daily during school holidays & Wed–Sun at other times &

'No, people weren't sent here to be punished,' the steward at the oldest purpose-built prison in England (completed 1333) said, correcting my false assumption. 'This was a holding cell until suspected criminals were tried. If found guilty, *then* they were punished.'

It's hard to see how being kept in a windowless stone cellar living on scraps of charity food for sometimes over a year (trials of prisoners were only held every quarter so you can imagine the backlog of cases) cannot be seen as a punishment. Perhaps that is why records show that 75% of prisoners in the Middle Ages were found not guilty when they were shackled and walked the few hundred yards to the Moot Hall where they were brought before a judge. For the remaining 25%, stocks, the ducking

---

◄ HEXHAM: **1** Colourful Market Street. **2** Hexham Old Gaol. **3** The abbey interior.

stool, branding and the whipping post were some of the punishments they could expect – if they weren't hanged. Executions were performed behind the Moot Hall in the marketplace but were rare because the Archbishop of York ruled Hexhamshire, and the Church was not in favour of the death penalty. The Archbishop was, however, in favour of collecting fines and 'board and lodging' from inmates who also had to pay for extra luxuries like bedding and fuel for fires. The gaol was in use until the 1820s.

The stone tower, made with hugely thick walls of recycled Roman stones, has four levels open to visitors. Each floor has an **exhibition room** dedicated to a different aspect of local history: the Border Reivers, rural life and the history of the gaol itself. The **dungeon** is reached by way of a glass lift that doesn't open but pauses long enough for visitors to gawp at the impenetrable walls and imagine being imprisoned in the cold, dark surroundings.

¶¶ FOOD & DRINK

Hexham's medieval streets are overflowing with bistros, restaurants, food shops and pubs. I've listed some favourites here and offered suggestions of places to eat outside the town centre, including some very good country inns nearby.

A few cafés to consider in addition to those listed here: **Hextol Tans** (11 St Mary's Chare ✆ 01434 605253 ⊙ Mon–Sat ♿ 🐾) for low-cost vegan and vegetarian breakfasts and lunches and **Muro Lounge** (Fore St ✆ 01434 620195 ⊙ daily ♿ 🐾) with its quirky interior, extended opening hours (long after most other places have closed) and extensive 'something for everyone' menu.

Bouchon Bistrot 4–6 Gilesgate ✆ 01434 609943 ⊙ lunch & dinner Tue–Sat ♿. Upmarket traditional French restaurant with starched white tablecloths and a menu requiring some studying unless 'baked fish quenelles "Lyon Style"' means something to you. Starters include scallops, a plate of fine French cured meats and monkfish cheeks; and for the main event: sea trout, duck, steak or mussels with potatoes cooked various ways and vegetables. For food this good, the prices are very reasonable (around £20 for mains). A two- and three-course fixed menu is even better value at just a few pounds more.

Danielle's Bistrot 12 Eastgate (off Battle Hill) ✆ 01434 601122 ⊙ lunch & dinner Tue– Fri, dinner Sat. No-fuss restaurant serving good Mediterranean and British dishes on bare candlelit tables; popular with locals. Come here for seafood and meat dishes.

Dipton Mill Inn Dipton Mill Rd (a couple of miles south of Hexham), NE46 1YA ✆ 01434 606577 ⊙ lunch & dinner Mon–Sat, lunch Sun 🐾. Small old drovers' pub and 17th-century former mill set by a secluded wooded river on the outskirts of Hexham. It's a traditional country inn in every way: low ceilings, a couple of real fires lit for most of the year and brassware scattered about. Beers come from the landlord's Hexhamshire Brewery. The food is okay: mince and dumplings, steak pie, chicken and veg as well as sandwiches, and old-fashioned British puddings. On a summer's day you'll probably want to sit outside in the beer garden by the burn.

The Garden 20 Hallgate ⊙ daily 🐾. Butting up against the Old Gaol in a quiet corner of Hexham, with a sunny courtyard and relaxed interior – all mismatched 70s furniture, house plants and botanical prints. Friendly, youthful team serving good coffees, bagels and traybakes.

The Grateful Bread Bakery 10 Market St ✆ 07719 922408 ⊙ from 08.00 Tue–Fri & from 09.00 Sat, closes 'when the bread runs out'. I find myself buying a loaf here even when I don't need any. All those shapely loaves of sourdough piled in the window – they look too good to pass by. Hexham sourdough is their signature white loaf but there's an exceedingly good malted brown sourdough, rolls and a few other artisan breads. Pick up some local jam or honey to go with your bread or a freshly made sandwich (ham and pease pudding, goats cheese and red onion relish, coronation chickpea and mango chutney).

Heart of Northumberland 5 Market St ✆ 01434 608013 ⊙ 16.00–late Tue, noon–late Wed–Mon 🐾. A good choice for a country pub lunch or dinner in the heart of Hexham. Late 17th/early 18th-century house refurbished with a sophisticated wood-panelled interior, leather-upholstered benches, and wooden chairs and tables. British pub classics with local produce dotted about the menu: fancy burgers served with Hexham-baked buns, Northumberland sausages and mash, steaks from Hadrian's Wall countryside and a few veggie options: soup with stottie bread, or a veg, lentil and nut Wellington. Great Sunday roasts too. Regional ales on tap.

Little Mexico 4 Market St ✆ 01434 622329 ⊙ Tue–Sat 11.00–19.00 (until 21.30 Fri & Sat). A shot of tequila sunshine in the centre of Hexham. Order a bottle of Sol and a wonderfully authentic street-food lunch (burritos, nachos, quesadillas, ceviche), sit back and soak in the youthful, Mexicano vibes. The juice bar is tempting: exotic blended cold-pressed fruit juices and smoothies. Also evening cocktails – the usual Mexican suspects plus Pisco Sour. I never, ever see this egg-based cocktail in the UK. Olé for Little Mexico (even if it is Peruvian).

Marketspace Coffee 14 Market Pl ✆ 07946 379887 ⊙ 08.00–16.00 Tue–Sat. Bags of Pilgrim's Coffee roasted on Lindisfarne pack the shelves of this small coffeeshop in the centre of Hexham. Coffee connoisseurs take note. I love the simple wooden stools and haberdashery-style counter with trays of knobbly homemade sweet and savoury bites: flapjack, brownies and cookies, filled croissants, and toasties made with sourdough from the bakery a stone's throw away.

The Natural Grocer 13 Cattle Market ☏ 07833 609530 ⊙ 10.00–21.30 Thu–Sat (closes 20.00 on Thu), 11.00–15.00 Sun. Pantry, off-license, tapas restaurant – the Natural Grocer promises much and delivers in all three areas with its ground-floor pantry stocked with jars and packets of North East produce, a Northumbrian cheese counter, and fab wine and bottled beer shop.

Upstairs is the main **restaurant** (Fri & Sat evening meals) – all stripped wood, upholstered chairs, mustard, teal and chandeliers – with exceptionally good bowls of food coming out of the kitchen: Andalusian lamb, seafood crowd pleasers (sardines on toast, garlic prawns), Asturian bean stew, and a sharing charcuterie and cheese board loaded with quality cuts of meat and Spanish queso. Breakfast, brunch and lunch menus are more of a mix of Spanish tapas and British regulars: sandwiches, mushrooms on toast, cured meat, pancakes and omelettes.

The Rat Inn Anick NE46 4LN ☏ 01434 602814 ⊙ food served noon–20.00 Wed–Sat & noon–15.00 Sun 🐾 but check by phone. Many locals rave about this award-winning, Michelin-rated old drovers' inn (low beamed ceiling, flagstone floors) occupying a tranquil spot high above the Tyne. Enjoy exceptional, good-value British/French food made with the very best regional produce. Listed on a blackboard is the provenance of cuts of meats (all of them local and sold by the ounce; once purchased they are struck off the board). The interior is not at all fancy – in fact it is all a bit of a mishmash of styles and furnishings – but this is a laid-back pub with no pretensions, despite the impressive menu. Sit in the sunny garden or inside next to the blazing cast-iron range. Ales are from local micro-breweries. Book ahead to secure a table.

Refectory Café Hexham Abbey ☏ 01434 602031 ⊙ daily ♿. A pleasant spot inside the abbey for an inexpensive sandwich, cake or scone; best of all are the tables in the sheltered courtyard, which catches plenty of rays and backs onto Hexham's park. Afternoon teas should be booked in advance.

Salute St Mary's Chare ☏ 01434 604607 ⊙ Mon & Wed–Sun. Casual, authentic Italian restaurant serving homemade ravioli, gnocchi and fish dishes. Secluded courtyard seating.

11 FOURSTONES & NEWBROUGH

Lying on the north side of the A69 and high above the River South Tyne means these two villages are somewhat cut off from visitor traffic pootling through Hexham or Corbridge – so they must be sought out. Unless, that is, you are cycling the Hadrian's Cycleway (NCN Route 72), in which case you will pass straight through the centre of both on the old Roman road, the **Stanegate** (page 309).

Fourstones trails along the side of a vale rising out of the Tyne Valley, gazing south across to the distant Hexhamshire countryside. A scattering of stone and brick cottages and a curious turquoise clapboard chapel dating to the late 19th century catch the eye. **St Aidan's** (☉ 14.00–16.00 Tue & Thu, 10.00–16.00 Sun) is thought to be one of only two wooden 'flat-pack' Victorian mission churches in the UK, ordered by the local vicar from a catalogue in 1875 to provide a place of worship for the hundreds of workers employed in the local coal mine, quarry, paper mill and lime kiln.

Continuing west on the Stanegate, **Newbrough** is reached in quick succession after one mile and holds plenty of rural charm with its flower-filled stone terraces and old pub (page 364), connected to its lovely outlying church by a footpath across meadows.

The lane to the side of the pub climbs north to Carr Edge woodland – the site of the Lookwide Campsite, the first official **Scout camp** led by Lord Baden-Powell in 1908 (a year after the famous Brownsea Island experimental camp). To locate it, follow the road for 1½ miles, then turn off right along a track on a prominent left bend in the road (signed for Carr Edge farm & B&B); a memorial cairn in the woods beyond the farmhouse marks the spot but the walk (half a mile from the turn-off) is a bit of slog, albeit with a lovely view of spring lambs bouncing around in fields.

"Sweeping grasslands to the north rise into a tsunamic wave along the crest of the Whin Sill escarpment."

A more varied and pretty countryside **walk** of half a mile connects the lane running round the side of the Red Lion with **St Peter's Church** on the Stanegate. From the Red Lion, take the lane heading north uphill. A footpath on the left after 300yds (signed for St Peter's Church) leads along a narrow, wooded path to a rushing stream (Meggie's Dene Burn). Cross over the stone footbridge and turn immediately left, through a gate following the stream downriver for 50yds before striking off across a meadow then over a lane. Pass through a couple more gates and down steps to a wooden bridge over a burn, then through another metal gate and across a grassy field before entering the pretty churchyard from the rear. On leaving St Peter's through the quaint lych gate, turn left on to the Stanegate for the short amble back to the Red Lion.

Continuing west on the Stanegate, the Roman road climbs into exposed countryside with **Grindon Lough** soon coming into view. Sweeping grasslands to the north rise into a tsunamic wave along the crest of the Whin Sill escarpment and Roman frontier.

¶¶ FOOD & DRINK

The Red Lion Newbrough ✆ 01434 674226 ♿. Old pub on the main road through the village and a good choice for an evening meal, Sunday roast or drink on your travels in Northumberland. Welcoming staff and great food (the vegetable and bean hotpot comes highly recommended, as do the roasts with perfectly cooked veg) in a small, simply furnished restaurant room annexed to the main bar. Also offers modern B&B rooms upstairs.

12 HAYDON BRIDGE

Two bridges connect this quiet town, which straddles the River South Tyne, including the graceful, six-arched pedestrian crossing built in 1776. From here you gain a good view of Haydon Bridge's old stone houses rising directly from the river, and the hills beyond.

'Haydon', as it's known to locals, is certainly attractive and a good choice for a pub lunch, but there's not a huge amount going on here to linger beyond lunch. If you do go for a wander on the north side of the river, perhaps along Ratcliffe Road to the General Havelock Inn (see below), look out for number 1A, which was bought in 1962 by Monica Jones, the long-term girlfriend of Philip Larkin. According to the poet's biographer, Andrew Motion, some of the couple's happiest times were spent in Haydon and the surrounding countryside: 'They lazed, drank, read, pottered around the village and amused themselves with private games. The place always cheered them both up.'

A sulphurous **spa** popular in Victorian times is reached on a short walk east from the Anchor pub (south side of the bridge) via a tranquil riverside path.

¶¶ FOOD & DRINK

General Havelock 9 Ratcliffe Rd ✆ 01434 684376 ⊙ daily but no food on Mon or Sun evenings ♿ 🐾. A favourite drinking hole of the poet Philip Larkin when visiting his girlfriend, Monica Jones, who lived a few doors down the terrace (a black-and-white photo inside records one such occasion). The pub's painted black so you won't miss it – and every local knows this is one of the best places to eat in the Tyne Valley. With that in mind, make sure you book. The pub and restaurant are, in all honesty, rather dated, but like many who come here, I like the lack of pretension and, certainly, the interior styling does not reflect the quality of the food, which is very good indeed. Everything is made on site, even the breads, pastries and ice cream, but the menu is tiny with a handful of mains: steak, fresh fish landed at North Shields the same day, pies, sausage and mash and one veggie dish. A sunny beer garden overlooks the South Tyne, but in winter, you'll want to sip your pint by the fire.

13 BARDON MILL

By road or railway between Haydon Bridge and Haltwhistle, you will pass Bardon Mill, a sweet sparrow-filled village with a useful store (there's a little café here too), train station, post office, inn and green set either side of a burn.

Errington Reay & Co pottery (✆ 01434 344245 ⊙ daily but closed Sun during winter ♿ 🐾) stands on the site of a 17th-century woollen mill and has been firing clay since 1878, first producing ceramic chimneypots and piping before branching out into plant pots. Look at the roofs of houses in the village and you will see that some are an unusual design, looking a little bit like an upside-down plant pot. Known locally as the 'Marriage Save Pot', it was developed at the pottery and remained in production until quite recently. It was a successful solution to the problem of smoke billowing back down chimneys into homes, which was a frequent nuisance in this exposed village.

Once there were a number of potteries in the Tyne Valley but they closed when the manufacture of cheap, plastic water pipes took off. Errington Reay survived by clever adaptation of their machinery to make garden pots. Five hundred are produced here every week, all hand-finished by a couple of men sitting at potter's wheels, and traditionally made using a salt-glaze (one of very few potteries in Britain still producing pots in this way). You can look inside the huge kiln at pots on shelves waiting to be fired. In the large outdoor yard,

ROMAN RINGERS

The clanking of metal on metal accompanied by good-hearted cheers was once a familiar sound in pub yards in many corners of Northumberland among farmers and miners gathered for a game of quoits.

Traditionally played after work, the game is simple enough, though proceedings can become pretty animated: competitors throw a steel ring (weighing over 4lbs) aiming for a metal spike in the centre of a clay pit 33ft away. Two points are scored for circling the post (a 'ringer') or being the closest to it.

Some say quoits was introduced to Britain by the Romans.

In recent decades, the game has had a bit of a resurgence and there are now 27 teams playing across three divisions in the North East.

A few pubs to see the action (usually May–Sep) include: **The Blue Bell**, Corbridge, the **Wallace Arms**, Featherstone (page 372), Bridge House at the **Milecastle Inn** near Hadrian's Wall (page 328) and on the village green at Bardon Mill (page 366).

there are hundreds of pots for sale (plenty of good-value seconds here), and decorative items for the home and artworks in a small gift shop.

A little **heritage display** in the yard chronicles the history of the pottery with old newspaper cuttings, black-and-white photos and explanations of pot production from working the clay to firing.

¶ FOOD & DRINK

The Bardon Mill Village Store & Tearoom ☏ 07756 790108 ☉ Thu–Tue. Opposite the pottery is this warm and inviting community hub also popular with cyclists. They sell Ordnance Survey maps and basic supplies as well as traybakes, toasties, scones and hot drinks.

The Bowes Hotel ☏ 01434 344237 ☉ from 16.00 Wed–Sat & lunch Sun ♿. Old inn with modern furnishings (and a pool table) serving decent pub dinners and Sunday lunches to non-guests, as well as those staying in the upstairs B&B.

14 BELTINGHAM

Lovely Beltingham, a tiny place of half-a-dozen houses about a church and green a mile from Bardon Mill, is a hamlet of superlatives: home to the oldest yew tree and one of the only Perpendicular-style church in Northumberland. It also has the smallest village green in England (you could just about pitch a four-man tent on its circle of grass) and is the most picturesque hamlet in the county. At least I think so. In truth, I can't verify any of the above claims except the rare 15th-century church but the **yew tree** at the north end of the churchyard (the one whose torso is being pulled in by metal belts) is truly ancient. The church guide refers to estimates of it being 2,000 years old, though it is more likely to be about half that.

"Walking east you descend into the most beautiful wooded gorge in the whole of Northumberland, Allen Banks."

There is little to do here, few places to see and nowhere to eat or drink (unless two well-to-do ladies invite you in for coffee with the vicar) but you may want to pause by Georgian **Beltingham House** – one of the finest sandstone country houses in Northumberland. It was, incidentally, visited more than once by the late Queen Mother who popped in to see her relatives, the Bowes-Lyons.

A wooden lych gate marks the entrance to 15th-century **St Cuthbert's Church**. Some believe an earlier timber structure stood here and was visited by monks carrying St Cuthbert's body in the 10th century. Apart from the aforementioned yew trees, note the 7th-century Saxon cross in the churchyard.

There are two very pleasant **walks** from Beltingham. Heading west across farmland you come to **Willimoteswyke Castle** – an impressive, albeit derelict, 16th-century fortified manor house with 7ft-thick walls and an intact pele tower; walking east you descend into the most beautiful wooded gorge in the whole of Northumberland, **Allen Banks** (page 395). I did say this was a place of superlatives.

15 HALTWHISTLE

'Welcome to Haltwhistle – Centre of Britain.' Most visitors to this attractive working town in the Tyne Valley would never have guessed the geographical centre of Britain is so far north. As it happens, it's not. Well, at least if you believe the inhabitants of Dunsop Bridge in Lancashire or Allendale in the North Pennines, who also claim the title. It depends on how the centre is calculated, of course.

"Haltwhistle railway station is one of the most unchanged on the Newcastle–Carlisle line and retains its original buildings."

What is true is that this market town was, for 300 years, the centre of many clashes between the Scots and the English and warring Border clans, hence the large number of defensive **bastle houses** (page 235) along the High Street. In fact, Haltwhistle claims (quite accurately) to have more of these defensive buildings in and around its town than anywhere else in the North East. A good number are clustered about the marketplace and include the **Centre of Britain** building (also noted for its 15th-century pele tower).

Haltwhistle's **town centre** is almost solidly made of stone and is, in essence, one long, main thoroughfare with a park at the western end and the marketplace in the centre. A scattering of local shops, antique stores, two great butchers, a library (which operates as a **tourist information point**) and a few sandwich bars and tea rooms connect the two.

Haltwhistle **railway station** is one of the most unchanged on the Newcastle–Carlisle line and retains its original buildings, as well as the old water tank (a relic from the days of steam). Note the engineer's plates dated 1861 with their decorative seahorses. The signal box is an elegant building made of weatherboards above a brick base.

Behind the marketplace is the early 13th-century **Holy Cross Church**. Note the very old stone stoup supported on a column, which some believe could be Roman. Three lancet windows simply decorated with stained glass by William Morris & Co rise elegantly above the altar. On passing the pulpit, a memorial stone on the floor in Latin translates as:

> To God the greatest and the best
> After a short, difficult, useless life
> Here rests in the Lord
> Robert Tweddle
> Of Monkhazelton Durham
> Dies 1735. Aged 23

Continuing eastwards along Main Street, the shops peter out and domestic dwellings made of sandstone sit side by side with agreeable uniformity. Soon the noises of the town are replaced by the cheerful chatter of garden sparrows and jackdaws clucking on rooftops.

Mill Lane on the left leads to **Haltwhistle Burn**. A footpath hugs the tranquil waterway for 1½ miles upriver, passing a number of relics from the days when Haltwhistle was a prosperous industrial town in the 18th and 19th centuries, including a brickworks, a couple of mills, a drift mine and lime kilns. If you continue northwards, you will reach the Military Road and Hadrian's Wall.

Families may enjoy Haltwhistle's heated **outdoor swimming pool** (close to the town centre ✆ 01434 320727 ⏲ mid-Apr–early Sep daily) with giant inflatables and a slide.

🍴 FOOD & DRINK

Haltwhistle boasts two butchers including **Billy Bell's** ('fish, game and poultry') where you can also pick up really good sausages, local honey, smoked kippers from Craster and Seahouses, fruit and veg and Slack House Farm raw natural yoghurt (a most delicious live yoghurt produced a couple of miles away).

Black Bull Market Sq ✆ 01434 320463 ⏲ eve Thu–Sat, lunch Sat & Sun. For good pub food and a friendly welcome, I'd recommend this traditional old inn tucked behind the main street and reached by an old, cobbled cart track. Picture low beams studded with brassware, stone floors and working men relaxing at the bar after a day's toil. Food portions are generous; popular dishes include steak and ale pie, burgers, and sausage and mash (with meat from the butcher across the road).

Pillar Box Café Main St ✆ 01434 321780 ⊙ 09.30–14.00 Mon–Sat. A queue is always a good sign. In Haltwhistle, what caught my eye outside this fetching bright-red café (sit in or take-away) was watching two elderly ladies elbow their way to their favourite table – it was that busy. Among a delightfully unsophisticated menu of all-day breakfasts, toasties, sandwiches and burgers and chips, you can order a 'milky coffee' for £2 – something I haven't seen in a long while.

THE SOUTH TYNE VALLEY

Scenically, the northern reaches of the South Tyne Valley are typical of the wider Tyne Valley and Hexhamshire countryside: green pastures carved by dry-stone walls and hedgerows, parkland studded with mature oaks, broad-leaved woodland and the odd stone hamlet here and there; but the landscape steps up a gear quite quickly on heading south, and certainly by the time you reach **Lambley** the Pennine moors are looming tantalisingly close.

Alston, a remote, picturesque market town (just over the border in Cumbria and not described in this guide), is particularly popular with cyclists, railway aficionados and walkers.

* * *

THE SOUTH TYNE TRAIL BY BICYCLE OR ON FOOT: HALTWHISTLE TO ALSTON

❀ OS Explorer maps OL43 & 31; start: Haltwhistle train station; 13 miles; fairly easy, albeit a long route; cycle ride strenuous in a few places.

The mixed-use waymarked **South Tyne Trail** is an ideal way to discover the valley and some of the most scenic river, woodland and hill country in the North Pennines. For the most part it follows the railway path (signed as the **Pennine Cycleway NCN Route 68**) as far as Alston. Continuing south from Alston to Garrigill and on to the source of the Tyne (not described here but the route is easy to follow on the Pennine Way), walkers stay close to the riverside; cyclists take a quiet hilly lane via Leadgate. For this route, walkers (and cyclists, space permitting) can make the return journey from Alston as far as Slaggyford on the delightful South Tynedale Railway (page 374). Walkers can also take the infrequent bus, Tynedale Links 681 (⊘ gonortheast.co.uk) from Alston to Birdoswald Roman Fort, which stops at Slaggyford & Haltwhistle but you'll have to time your walk carefully or be prepared to book a taxi (page 336) for the return if you miss the last bus.

1 From the Carlisle-bound platform at **Haltwhistle station**, a level walkway leads to a bridge over the River South Tyne restricted to cycles and those on foot (you can also reach this bridge from the B6322). Cross the river and turn left at the T-junction on to Plenmeller Road for 500yds to the A69. Take great care crossing the bypass, picking up Plenmeller Road again on the other side. In a couple of hundred yards on your right, you'll see the disused railway line – the South Tyne Trail/Pennine Cycleway.

Thickets of birch and oak and gentle countryside soon give way to more dramatic scenery as you follow the line south. After 2½ miles the cycleway crosses a lane at **Featherstone Rowfoot** (turning left here will lead you on a recommended detour to the **Wallace Arms**, page 372, a hundred yards up the road). Back on the cycleway, continue your journey south for another mile.

2 At **Thorneyhole Wood** car park you can take an alternative route via Lambley avoiding the viaduct (see note below) by turning right on the road. Otherwise, cross the road and pick up the railway line on the other side.

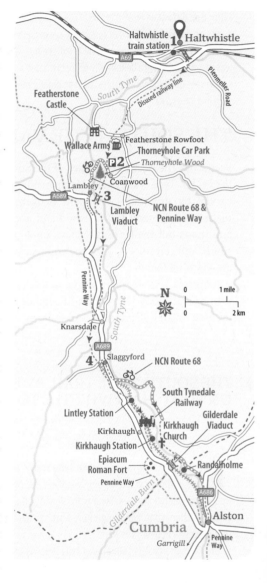

3 The wooded gorge of the South Tyne is most spectacularly viewed from the towering arches of **Lambley Viaduct**, a mile south of Thorneyhole Wood car park. On crossing the viaduct, you have to carry your bike down to the river and then haul it back up the other side via steps because sadly there is no access along the 100yd stretch of the old trackbed in front of the former train station (which is now in private hands). If you can't face carrying your bicycle, then you can follow the redirected road route signed just under a mile back at Thorneyhole Wood car park that passes above Lambley village (be prepared for a heck of a climb from river to moor level).

Once back on the railway line, the temperature drops as you enter the North Pennine moors proper, with heather covering the highest plateaux, and woods and fields descending to the river.

4 Four miles south of Lambley Viaduct is **Slaggyford**, with its quaint old railway buildings and platform and delightful **tea room** in an old railway carriage (page 375). You can catch the heritage train here to Alston if you don't want to walk the last leg of this route.

CYCLISTS head for the river via Slaggyford village, following the NCN Route 68 signs along quiet country lanes for the last five miles to Alston. This is wonderful cycling: quiet with some challenging ascents and descents, and glorious river and countryside scenery: pastures divided by dry-stone walls, old farm buildings, an unusual church at **Kirkhaugh** (page 372) and farmers rounding up sheep with Border collies.

WALKERS continue due south at Slaggyford station, following the **South Tynedale Railway** (page 374) where heritage narrow-gauge steam engines puff by. There's a small **viaduct** between Kirkhaugh and Alston that spans **Gilderdale Burn**. Below is a secluded swimming pool. The route ends at the market town of **Alston**, with its painstakingly restored Victorian station, 4½ miles from Slaggyford.

16 FEATHERSTONE CASTLE & SURROUNDS

Few people know of Featherstone Castle and its elegant single-arch Georgian crossing and even fewer know that a prisoner of war camp once housed thousands of World War II German officers here by the banks of the River South Tyne.

Featherstone Castle is an imposing 13th-century embattled manor with turrets, a gatehouse and pele tower. There's no general access to the fortress but it appears quite impressively across parkland from the banks of the River South Tyne. Half a mile north is the curious, lopsided 18th-century **Featherstone Bridge** (♀ NY675619), set within a dreamy riverscape lined with mature trees. A footpath on the west side of the bridge leads to the waterside for a pleasant half-mile **walk** to a footbridge, with the river on your left. Return along the riverside road.

If you were to continue south on the **River Tyne Trail** (a mile beyond Featherstone Bridge) you'd amble straight through a **World War II**

POW camp – or 'Camp 18' as it was known. The ruinous red-brick buildings once housed several thousand German officers who lived in the secluded spot and worked in neighbouring farms. The camp even had its own theatre, orchestra, bakery and library and produced a newspaper: *Die Zeit am Tyne* ('The Time on the Tyne') for inmates.

To see all three historic sights on a **circular walk**, follow the River Tyne Trail from Featherstone Bridge to Lambley Viaduct (page 370) and return along the South Tyne Trail disused railway via the Wallace Arms (see below) at Rowfoot. This is a beautiful five-mile circuit with wonderful riverside views and a great pub on your way back.

⑪ FOOD & DRINK

Wallace Arms Rowfoot NE49 0JF ✆ 01434 298921 ⊙ variable but usually late afternoon Wed–Fri & from noon Sat & Sun 🐾. Only really known to locals, cyclists and long-distance walkers, this friendly watering hole several miles from the nearest town is a welcome sight. It's right on the South Tyne Trail (and Pennine Cycleway) and everyone inside is in a good mood because, just like you, they spotted the glow of a real fire and local ales on tap just when their legs were giving way. At times like these, it doesn't even matter that they don't serve food.

17 KIRKHAUGH CHURCH & AROUND

Unusually dedicated to the Holy Paraclete (in other words, the Holy Ghost), this secluded Victorian **church** with a distinctive needle-like spire (described by Alfred Wainwright as like 'an upside-down umbrella') stands in farmland by the River South Tyne and adjacent to a grand villa with shuttered windows. Apparently the rector was influenced by churches he'd seen in Germany's Black Forest. A stone cross in the churchyard dates to before the Norman invasion, reminding visitors of the Anglo-Saxon church that once stood here. Inside, a hammerbeam roof and the chairs instead of pews will catch your attention, as will the wood-burning stove, which shows just how cold it gets up here.

The surrounding **countryside** is extremely pretty: fields with mature trees leading to the river, a scattering of old farm buildings, 17th-century bastle houses and a pele tower at **Randalholm**. Quiet lanes

1 The South Tyne Trail passes through some beautiful countryside. **2** The South Tynedale Railway. **3** While there is no visitor access to Featherstone Castle, it appears quite impressively across parkland from the banks of the River South Tyne. **4** Lambley Viaduct. ▶

connect all these places that are within walking distance of Alston and can be incorporated into a circular jaunt via Epiacum (Whitley Castle) Roman Fort (see below).

18 EPIACUM (WHITLEY CASTLE) ROMAN FORT

♥ NY694486; 2 miles north of Alston off the A689 or reached from the Pennine Way & Isaac's Tea Trail

All that remains of Britain's highest-built Roman fort, which once housed a garrison of 500 men and was probably connected with lead and silver mining, are its impressive earthen ramparts and the faint outline of the foundations of barrack blocks (now turfed over). Roman altar stones, masonry from a bathhouse hypocaust and smaller finds have been recovered over the centuries, although no major excavation has ever taken place.

By road, the fort is reached off the A689 where there's a car park and café (see below). A signed path leads steeply uphill via a bastle house to meet the ramparts.

¶¶ FOOD & DRINK

Nook Farm Shop & Café Epiacum Roman Fort ✆ 07415 029398 ◷ daily ♿ 🐾. Wonderful hillside views and right by the car park and access trail to the Roman Fort. Lovely breakfasts, scones, cakes and lunches (jackets, quiche, sandwiches and great burgers made with own farm beef). Also a farm shop stocked with pantry items.

19 SOUTH TYNEDALE RAILWAY

Alston CA9 3JB ✆ 01434 338214 (office), 01434 382828 (talking timetable) ⏿ south-tynedale-railway.org.uk ◷ Easter–Oct usually weekends & bank holidays and some weekdays; trains run three times daily (check website for operating days at other times of the year such as at Christmas); bikes allowed space permitting ♿ 🐾

Steam trains trundle through the wooded South Tyne Valley for five miles from **Alston to Slaggyford** and back, stopping at Kirkhaugh and Lintley stations and offering glimpses of moorland scenery and crossing the Tyne Viaduct. A one-way journey takes around 35 minutes but you might want to hop off at **Kirkhaugh Station** and wander up to Epiacum (Whitley Castle) Roman Fort (see above) or down to the river.

Originally a branch of the Newcastle–Carlisle railway, the Alston to Haltwhistle line opened in 1852 and closed in the 1970s. A decade later it reopened under the care of the local railway preservation society who replaced the trackbeds and then restored the station buildings, allowing the first narrow-gauge steam engines to enter passenger service in 1983.

Alston station preserves most of its original architecture and fixtures, including its original signal box (still in operation), level crossing and ticket office. There's a café here while you wait for your train (see below). **Slaggyford station** holds similar heritage appeal and operates a little café in an old railway carriage (see below).

To the rear of Alston's restored train station in an old goods shed is a quirky museum dedicated to transport heritage. Filling every space inside **The Hub Museum** (Station Yd, Alston CA9 3HN ✆ 01434 381609 ☉ 11.00–16.00 Sat & Sun ♿) are vintage motorbikes and a few cars, as well as a large collection of bicycles showcasing, in a roundabout way, the evolution of this most enduring form of transport from the penny-farthing to a 1972 Raleigh Chopper. A mass of memorabilia hangs from the walls and ceilings: model aeroplanes, black-and-white photographs, road signs and vintage advertisements.

🍴 FOOD & DRINK

There are plenty of places to eat and drink in the picturesque Cumbrian market town of Alston (not covered by this guide) with restaurants and pubs dotted about the old streets. I've listed a couple I particularly like but also keep in mind the two cafés operating at either end of the South Tynedale Railway. At Alston, **The Crossing Café** (✆ 07751 596469 ☉ Fri–Sun) is a busy station café trading in everyday light lunches, coffees, ices, cakes etc. At Slaggyford is **The Buffet Car** (✆ 07810 540510 ☉ from 10.30 on days when trains are running), a welcome sight for cyclists and walkers on the South Tyne Trail, offering carriage dining at the old station (serving hot and cold drinks, traybakes and snacks).

Cumberland Inn Townfoot, Alston ✆ 01434 381875 ☉ daily 🐾. Agreeable, proper old pub, a five-minute walk from Alston station, with a fire, countryside views from the beer garden, simple meals and a fantastic range of ciders and cask ales from local breweries.
Saddlers Bakery 3 West View, Alston ✆ 07494 129845 ☉ Tue–Sat. Make sure you come early as this chic, popular bistro gets busy and the food sells out. Hearty breakfasts, delicious bowls of soup, pies made fresh the same day, stottie sandwiches, quiche, cakes and scones.

HEXHAMSHIRE

To the south of Hexham lies the sparsely populated countryside of **Hexhamshire** – once a county in the 12th century but now part of

Northumberland and known locally as 'The Shire'. The view for miles around is of lush farmland criss-crossed by hedgerows and dry-stone walls, broad sweeps of heather blazing the tops of distant moors, shallow burns flowing merrily through wooded valleys, and stone cottages and farmsteads. **Juniper**, **Whitley Mill**, **Whitley Chapel** and **Newbiggin** are some of the hamlets and villages you might wander through. Exploration on foot is recommended, perhaps along the enchanting **West Dipton Burn**, **Devil's Water** (see below), **Rowley Burn** or through **Letah Wood** (see opposite). Here I've described a couple of walks that take in the lovely pastoral scenery in and around Hexhamshire.

"The view for miles around is of lush farmland criss-crossed by hedgerows and dry-stone walls."

20 DEVIL'S WATER & DILSTON PHYSIC GARDEN

Under the shade of pine, beech, rowan and birch trees the visitor saunters along the winding pathway, by banks covered with the trailing flowers ... Crossing a narrow plank, he proceeds to the right, along a rustic pathway, through a tangled copse, perfumed by the honey-suckle and wild rose, until he reaches the haughs already seen from the heights above. Here he seems to stand in the arena of a vast amphitheatre, with tiers on tiers of foliage sloping upwards from the river's edge.

W W Tomlinson, *Comprehensive Guide to Northumberland*, 1888

A few miles east of Hexham, the wooded slopes rising from **Devil's Water** (a name derived from the 12th-century settlement, Dyvelston) are as scenic today as when travel writer Tomlinson wrote the above account in 1888, and many of the same plants, trees and foliage observed then still colour Dilston's woods and meadows.

Wild swimmers will find several inviting **bathing pools**, including at **Swallowship Gorge** (a couple of miles west of Dilston and only accessible by footpath; ♀ NY958623), and at the confluence of Rowley Burn and Devil's Water, a mile east of Juniper (♀ NY947587).

If travelling along the B6306 from Hexham, slow down on crossing Devil's Water by **Linnels Bridge** (♀ NY955616; two miles south of the town) where you may want to take out your camera. The fabulous Victorian house seen from the crossing was one of the first to be lit by electricity in the world, and once caught the eye of Pennine writer Alfred Wainwright, who had this to say: 'I hung over the bridge and

DILSTON CASTLE & THE JACOBITE REBELLION

Dilston Castle 1½ miles south of Corbridge, NE45 5RJ, in the private grounds of Cambian Dilston College, signed off the B6307. Group visits by appointment only ⌀ northumbrianjacobites.org.uk

Looming high above the wooded slopes of Devil's Water stand the 15th-century ruins of Dilston Castle and its 17th-century chapel and gatehouse. The secluded setting is fitting for the romantic and tragic tale of the legendary third Earl of Derwentwater, James Radcliffe.

Dilston was the ancestral home of the powerful Radcliffes for 200 years, but its links to the family and the last Earl of Derwentwater were extinguished in the years following the Jacobite Rebellion of 1715.

The earl's life was cut short for his leading role in the rising against George I. He was just 26 and newly married. The Jacobite army had been initially successful in many towns in Northumberland, but when they proceeded south through Lancashire they were defeated at Preston. The earl was imprisoned in the Tower of London and later executed.

yearned for that house so much that I am afraid I became oblivious to all else. I saw at last the house of my dreams.'

From the eye-catching bridge (a plaque dates it to 1581 though it was rebuilt in the late 17th century) the view of the boulder-strewn river, house and 18th-century **water mill** is wonderfully picturesque.

Gardeners and those interested in the medicinal use of plants may enjoy the **Dilston Physic Garden** (NE45 5QZ ⌀ 07879 533875 ☉ May–Oct Wed–Sun; Nov–Apr Fri–Sun ⚑ 🐾), a two-acre site between Hexham and Corbridge. Created by a neuroscientist at Newcastle University researching the healing properties of plants, the gardens offer visitors a tranquil space to wander with winding paths taking in the profusion of scents and colour produced by some 800 plants with healing properties.

Events (see ⌀ dilstonphysicgarden.com) run in the Herbology House (a timber hut in the gardens) include tuition on using plants to boost health, perfume making, botanical first aid, and, for children, potion making, a witches den, croquet and explorer trails.

21 DIPTON MILL & LETAH WOOD

♀ NY944608; Newbiggin (2 miles south of Hexham)

This is a beautiful mixed woodland, cared for by The Woodland Trust, and what is thought to be Northumberland's last wild **native daffodil**

wood. It's not big – around 14 hectares – but parts are ancient and it's a very rewarding place for a stroll owing to the abundance of woodland flora and birds. Among the beech, oak and soaring Douglas firs and Scots pines, you could even glimpse a red squirrel. Wild garlic is conspicuous in spring, along with wood sorrel, lesser celandine and, of course, daffodils (particularly on the south-facing slopes). A **walk** through these woods can be combined with a visit to the pub at Dipton Mill (page 360).

* * *

A WOODLAND WALK IN HEXHAMSHIRE: DIPTON MILL & LETAH WOOD

❄ OS Explorer map OL43; start: Dipton Mill Inn, Dipton Mill Rd (a couple of miles south of Hexham), NE46 1YA (B6306) ♀ NY929610; 2 miles; easy

A wander through Letah's daffodil woods is the highlight on this short family trail from a very old pub and brewery nestled in Hexhamshire countryside.

1 With your back to **Dipton Mill Inn**, cross the river over the road bridge and continue for 100yds to Dipton Mill Cottage. Turn right, following the privacy fence line and the sound of the cheerful **West Dipton Burn**, which you'll

soon meet. At the next field gate, take the footpath to the right. Ignore the log bridge and continue ahead.

2 Below **Hole Cottage** ('Hole House' on OS maps), cross the burn at a white iron bridge and turn immediately left through a gate, now with the burn on your left. After passing through a gate at the end of the field, you part company with the river on a bend and follow instead a track steeply uphill to buildings and a stile. Catch your breath while taking in the view below of birch and conifer woodland.

◀ **1** The Dukesfield Arches are the only surviving structures connected to a mill built to smelt lead ore. **2** The Dilston Physic Garden is home to some 800 varieties of plants with healing properties. **3** Devil's Water. **4** Rare native daffodils in Letah Wood.

3 Turning left on to Hill Road for a couple of hundred yards, descending steps on your right lead into enchanting **Letah Wood** (page 377), with its profusion of native daffodils in March and April. At the woodland floor, veer left, enjoying only the sound of birdsong and Letah Burn trickling over stones as you wander through the trees towards **Newbiggin**.

4 Exit the woods by a wicket gate and turn left on to **Hill Road** for three-quarters of a mile (continuing past the entrance to Letah Wood).

5 At a crossroads, take the bridleway on your right back to the pub car park.

* * *

22 WHITLEY MILL & WHITLEY CHAPEL

Elevated on a bank above Rowley Burn is the charming stone hamlet of **Whitley Mill**. I can't think of any compelling reasons to visit this little idyll by a ford and footbridge, unless a paddle and short stroll along a happy waterway on a warm day appeals. There are some very pleasant gentle **walks** around here, including a four-mile circuit via Mollersteads to the sleepy hamlet of **Juniper**; continue along Rowley Burn to Pethfoot Bridge where you begin the return leg by tracing Devil's Water to Whitely Chapel via the Dukesfield Arches (see below).

"The churchyard is rather lovely on a spring day: full of the melodic songs of thrushes, and the bleating of nearby lambs."

St Helen's Church in the village of **Whitley Chapel** stands on a raised hump above the streets. The churchyard is rather lovely on a spring day: full of the melodic songs of thrushes, and the bleating of nearby lambs. St Helen's dates to the mid 18th century though it was altered somewhat a century later. Near the church door is the grave of Thomas Dixon, who died aged 33 and has the following inscription: 'All you that come my Grave to see/ As I am so must you be/Make no delay repent in time/For I was taken in my prime.' An old hearse house and a fish weathervane may also catch your eye.

Dukesfield Arches & Hall

♥ NY943581; 1 mile east of Whitley Chapel; accessed from the B6306

Two hundred years ago, this tranquil leafy valley along the banks of Devil's Water throbbed with the sound of mill machinery, ponies, carts and men toiling to convert lead ore mined in the North Pennines into bars of lead. Relics of this long-dead industry are found all over

Hexhamshire and the North Pennines – as well as here, 200 yards or so from where the road to Juniper and Whitley Chapel crosses Devil's Water.

A woodland path leads from a small parking area to two huge brick and stone arches known as the **Dukesfield Arches,** the only surviving structures connected to a mill built to smelt lead ore. The arches supported horizontal flues that carried poisonous fumes away from the mill to chimneys (the bases of which are still visible on the bank above the arches). Lengths of iron, known as 'pigs', were then transported to Blaydon on the River Tyne.

If you follow the stony uphill track by the arches for 20 minutes or so, you'll emerge out of woodland by **Dukesfield Hall** – a highly picturesque farm that time forgot. The oldest parts date to the 1700s including the detached building with a dovecote and stone slate roof that once housed drovers overnight upstairs and their pack horses downstairs.

To extend this **walk** into a longer four-mile countryside loop, equip yourself with OS Explorer map OL43 and follow a fairly obvious route via Steel Hall Farm and then along a beautiful stretch of Devil's Water before entering open countryside for the return to Dukesfield Arches. It's a varied and scenic route with many natural and historical points of interest along the way.

23 SLALEY

A single row of cottages, a pub, church and shop comprise the tranquil hillside village of Slaley on the edge of its namesake forest, where blackbirds seem to be perpetually in song and neighbours chat over garden walls. Many road users are on their way to **Slaley Hall** – a modern golf and spa hotel built around an Edwardian pile.

St Mary the Virgin is at first glance a small and fairly unremarkable 19th-century village church; but there are a few architectural features worthy of note: the pulpit designed by Ralph Hedley (a well-known Victorian artist from the North East), a wonderful World War I memorial window dedicated to five fallen soldiers, and a very old headstone in the porch. Believed to be the oldest outdoor gravestone in Northumberland, you can just about make out a few letters of the name 'Richard Teasdale', a 'gentleman' who died in 1635.

At the **Slaley Show** (second Saturday in August; western end of Slaley village), expect all the usual dog and sheep competitions, as well as flower and craft displays and games for children.

INTO THE NORTH PENNINES

It's mining that's responsible for the pitted fells, terraces of stone cottages, Methodist chapels, schools and reading rooms; the way the meadows rising out of the valleys are boxed into 'allotments' where miner-farmers toiled to support their families in lean times; the smelt mill flues, mine entrances and chimneys; the railway lines, workshops, blacksmiths and mine agents' houses. Relics from the 18th- and 19th-century lead-mining and quarrying industries lie scattered in every hamlet and on every hillside in the North Pennine valleys, and occasionally the rich minerals in this **UNESCO Global Geopark** reveal themselves above ground; but to the casual visitor, with the exception of the odd striking chimney, lime kiln and water wheel, it is far from obvious that this was once the biggest lead-mining region in the world.

For the most part, however, the **North Pennines National Landscape** – the second largest in the UK, covering 770 square miles and spanning four counties – is characterised by wooded gorges, heather moors and flower-filled upland meadows. If there is one corner of Northumberland that gets forgotten about – this is it.

24 DERWENT RESERVOIR

Derwent Waterside Park Visitor Centre, DH8 9TT ✆ 0345 1550236 ♿ 🐾

The River Derwent's journey from the Pennine moors to the Tyne is halted by the two-mile-long Derwent Reservoir – one of the largest reservoirs in the North East, straddling the Northumberland–Durham border, and a popular recreation area with local families, anglers and boat-owners. A **visitor centre**, café and shop selling snacks and knick-knacks for children operates from the north side of the dam, about a mile northeast of Edmundbyers, reached from the B6278. This is the main hub, with a large playground, but there are a number of other quieter picnic and parking sites around the water with less infrastructure.

A four-mile mixed-use **path** curls halfway around the lake between the visitor centre and Pow Hill Country Park via the dam wall, gaining views of sailing dinghies, wildfowl in the shallows, and the surrounding upland meadows and fellsides sloping to meet the water's edge. The surfaced paths are largely wheelchair and pushchair accessible, though they can be a little muddy and bumpy in places. Picnic tables on grassy areas overlook the water close to all parking areas.

Two of the busiest spots are the **Pow Hill Country Park** and the area around the visitor centre at **Derwent Waterside Park** which are very popular on sunny weekends and during the school holidays when there are queues to buy ice creams and food. A quieter area with picnic tables and toilets but no café is **Millshield** on the north banks of the water, not far from the sailing club.

¶¶ FOOD & DRINK

Pick up coffees, ice creams, sandwiches and snacks at the main visitor centre at **Derwent Waterside Park** (DH8 9TT ✆ 01207 255250 ◷ daily 🐾) on the north side of the dam, but for a proper sit-down meal and good plates of food, consider the **Derwent Arms** at Edmundbyers, 1½ miles south of the visitor centre.

25 BLANCHLAND

🏠 **Lord Crewe Arms**

Hunkered in a hollow by the wooded River Derwent and seemingly unchanged for several hundred years, Blanchland is the most historically alluring village in the Derwent Valley. On summer's evenings, the sandstone houses and little humpback bridge spanning the Durham–Northumberland border are soaked in ochre sunshine, providing one of the most intact 18th- and 19th-century vistas you will find anywhere in England. But, for me, Blanchland is at its most timeless in winter when the smell of coal wafts through the village, luring ramblers off surrounding fells and towards the yellow glow from the Lord Crewe Arms.

Blanchland almost certainly gets its name from the French white-robed Premonstratensian Canons who established an abbey here in 1165 (hence the white letterbox in the village). According to folklore, during the turbulent centuries of cross-border fighting, the monastery almost evaded plundering by the Scots, who had lost their way on the fells in heavy fog. Unfortunately, the untimely ringing of the bells announcing it was safe to emerge from hiding revealed the abbey's whereabouts to the invaders. Blanchland later suffered under Henry VIII following the Dissolution of the Monasteries and the abbey closed in 1539. Over 170 years passed before it eventually came into the ownership of Lord Crewe, Bishop of Durham.

Almost every building in the village grew around the **abbey** in the centuries following the Reformation and particularly in the 18th century. The outer court became the **village square** with cottages around three of its sides and the monastic church became the parish church. **The Lord Crewe Arms**, once the Abbot's lodge, kitchen and guesthouses, was remodelled into a family home, also in the 18th century, but much original stonework survives in the building's complicated arrangement of rooms. It's now an expensive hotel, restaurant and bar, so you can navigate its stairways and corridors to inspect its nooks, quirks and very old masonry. The rear beer garden was once the cloisters and retains its original quadrangle layout.

St Mary's Church, hidden by trees just beyond the embattled gatehouse, is hugely atmospheric, built out of the ruined abbey with a soaring archway and lancet windows of the Early English style; the rest was reconstructed in the 18th century. A stained-glass panel high above the altar shows a white-robed monk, the folds of his cloak just visible.

Blanchland is a wonderful setting for a snail's-pace wander and those with a nose for anything of antiquity will find much to catch the eye, from the striking **gatehouse** with its arched passageway (15th century but, again, altered in the mid 18th century), the **pump house** (or pant) commemorating Queen Victoria's Diamond Jubilee opposite the post office, to more prosaic buildings: the intact run of Victorian privies, sheds and coal holes at the back of Shildon Road, and the cart shed, pigsties and farm buildings nestled by the banks of the Derwent.

Once you've explored the centre and admired the stone square of cottages, visited the church, gift shop, tea rooms and fetching post-office-cum-village shop (note the **white letterbox** built into the window – a rare 'Ludlow' design), you might consider a stroll down to the river (see opposite) or up the lane north out of the village for half a mile to the ruins of a lead mine. **Shildon lead-mining engine house** dates to the early 1800s and once housed a steam-powered pump that drew water out of a nearby mine. Continue ahead for a longer and more strenuous circular **walk** via Pennypie House and then west over grouse moors (Burntshieldhaugh Fell), following the old packhorse track, the Carriers' Way. The obvious return is via Birkside Fell, Newbiggin Fell, Newbiggin Hall and Baybridge, with its old chapel, before returning to Blanchland by the side of the Derwent. You'll need OS Explorer map 307 for this six-mile route.

The annual Blanchland & Hunstanworth **agricultural show** (⟨⟩ blanchlandshow.co.uk) is held over the August Bank Holiday, bringing together local communities and the best farm animals and produce in the region for some good traditional fun.

* * *

BLANCHLAND RIVERSIDE STROLL

✳ OS Explorer map 307; start: by the humpback bridge on the village side of the River Derwent ♀ NY966503; 1¼ miles; easy

Though muddy in places, this is a straightforward riverside trail through gentle wooded countryside that makes for a pleasant evening wander if you're staying in Blanchland. There's a lovely bathing pool with a shingle bank for children to play on not far after leaving the village.

By the old stone bridge and with your back to the village, turn right following a grassy track to the **River Derwent**, past a little playground and then over a wooden bridge. Keep the Derwent on your left, following a well-trodden path upstream through trees. A waterfall trickles down the opposite side of the gorge to meet the river, where dippers and grey wagtails are a familiar sight. Pass through a couple of gates and walk the length of the boardwalk until you reach a road.

Turn left at the road, crossing a bridge over the Derwent (turning right here, incidentally, would take you back to Blanchland via farmland to the north, above the village, with plenty of views of the stone houses and surrounding countryside). Now on the south side of the Derwent, you'll see the entrance to **woodland** on your left. Follow the trail through dark conifers and then broad-leaved trees, re-entering the village by the humpbacked bridge.

* * *

SPECIAL STAYS

Lord Crewe Arms Blanchland ✆ 01434 677100 ⊘ lordcrewearmsblanchland.co.uk. Nestled beneath swelling Pennine hills in the centre of this picture-perfect 18th-century village, the Lord Crewe hides a number of top-end rooms in the main inn as well as over the road in former miners' cottages. They are all decorated to a high standard with tartan bed throws and tasteful fabrics and artwork depicting rural scenes. The Lord Crewe began life in the 12th century as a guesthouse associated with the abbey, for which the village is famed. Masonry several centuries old survives in many corners and includes a medieval vaulted crypt, which now functions as the hotel's bar. **Dining** at the Lord Crewe is a treat – from breakfast to evening meals and everything in between (lunches, afternoon tea, light bar bites and Sunday roasts). Evening dinners are served in the stripped-back Bishop's Dining Room upstairs. Dishes are fancily described on the menu but are essentially upscaled

THE ALLEN VALLEYS

The rivers East and West Allen run off the central Pennine moors and flow north through farmland and woodland until they converge not far from Haydon Bridge, forming the River Allen. **Cupola Bridge** – a magnificent trio of arches built in 1778 – spans the confluence of the Allens and marks the head of **Allen Banks** (one of the region's oldest and most enchanting woodlands (page 395).

Travelling upriver into the heart of the North Pennines – and the southern reaches of Northumberland – the scenery takes on an increasingly wilder look where meadows become rough grasslands and ramshackle barns replace cottages. Snow markers line the sides of the highest roads and a ski-tow appears above Allenheads.

On high slopes, evidence of lead mining is glimpsed here and there, and many buildings associated with the industry are found in the likes of **Allenheads**. You might well spot the odd bastle house and defensive tower, evidence that farmers and landowners in the late medieval period once feared the appearance of Border Reivers riding over the hills to steal livestock – and worse.

variations on fish and chips, and meat and veg with some vegetarian options. Look out for grouse and venison from local moors, Durham rare breed pork and salmon (smoked on-site).

¶¶ FOOD & DRINK

If you can't get a lunch reservation at the Lord Crewe Arms (booking ahead strongly recommended) but would like more of a substantial meal than what they offer at White Monk's tea room, consider the short drive or cycle ride to Edmundbyers where you have more chance of an on-spec table at The Derwent Arms.

White Monk Refectory & Tea Room Blanchland ✆ 01434 675044 ⊙ Tue–Sun ♿ 🐾.
Relaxed café housed in Blanchland's old school and catering well for a passing lunch crowd, and walkers looking for take-away sandwiches – of which they have a wide, made-to-order selection. Also on the menu are jackets, quiche, soup, scones and traditional-recipe cakes.

26 ALLENHEADS

A sense of order pervades the buildings at Allenheads with its neat rows of miners' houses, workshops and office buildings, many of which were constructed under the instruction of Victorian engineer and mine agent,

1 Derwent Reservoir. 2 The Lord Crewe Arms, Blanchland – once the Abbot's lodge, kitchen and guesthouses. 3 Ski-Allenheads is volunteer run. 4 A row of miners' houses and workshops in Allenheads. ▶

MIKE HORROCKS/SKI-ALLENHEADS

STEPHEN DOREY CREATIVE/A

Thomas Sopwith, who was fixated with rules, punctuality and self-improvement – and presumably profit, this being the most important lead-mining area in Britain at one time. Today, the village centre, which is reached off the B6295 by an easily overlooked slip road, is full of old-world character and seems to hide away in a wooded hollow (inhabited by red squirrels).

Allenheads' **Heritage Centre** (NE47 9HN ☺ daylight hours) is a good starting point for an introduction to the village, its mining and farming heritage and community life in the 19th century, and includes a recreated blacksmith's and restored Victorian hydraulic engine once operational in the mine.

In addition to serving food and drink, the friendly **Hemmel Café** (page 389) also showcases the works of some talented local knitters and potters in its little gift shop. **The Allenheads Inn** stands prominently at the other end of the village, catching the eye with its vintage bicycles, road signs and mine 'tubs' (wagons) in the beer garden. Built in 1770, it was the former home of the Beaumont family – one of the biggest mine owners, producing a quarter of all England's lead – but now opens its doors to weekend cyclists on the Coast-to-Coast route and anyone on the hunt for a pint of real ale.

Those interested in the **lead-mining heritage** of the area should take a stroll to the old mine yard in the large car park on the other side of the road from the inn to see an excellent example of some bouseteems and a few other historic buildings connected to the industry.

Interpretation panels dotted around the village bring various aspects of Allenheads' industrial past to life. A few buildings worth pointing out include the long, single-storey **mine offices** opposite the slip lane to the village centre, and the old **school** on the hillside. Built by Sopwith in 1849, he could spy on pupils from his office using a telescope; any pupil caught arriving just a few seconds late would be reprimanded. Note too, on the other side of the road from the offices, the cobbled **horse track** sloping into an old mine entrance.

A couple of hundred yards north from the rear of the Allendale Inn, the lane passes a working **farm** dating to the early 1800s with a courtyard of quite some size. Cart sheds, byres, stables and haylofts face inwards to some slabs in the centre that mark where a central pool was once used for washing mine horses. You can see the courtyard from the road but there is no public access.

SNOW FUN

Possible snow tomorrow
Ski-Allenheads's newsfeed, November 2024

Don't expect Alpine runs and a fashionable après-ski scene, but fun is guaranteed on Ski-Allenheads' (⌀ ski-allenheads.co.uk), two 100yd beginner/intermediate slopes operated by rope tows above **Allenheads**. It's volunteer run and you'll need to be a member (easy to join online) to use the tows and hire equipment (a bargain at £5). Membership costs from £25 for the whole season. Do check the snow forecast before setting off as snow cover is very unpredictable.

More experienced skiers and boarders should try the blue runs at **Yad Moss** (⌀ yadmoss.co.uk) in Alston or the **Weardale Ski Club** (⌀ skiweardale.com) near Daddry Shield with more challenging routes and longer ski runs.

🍴 FOOD & DRINK

The Allenheads Inn Allenheads ✆ 01434 685200 ⊙ 16.00–22.00 Mon–Fri (closed Mon & Tue in winter), 14.00–22.00 Sat & Sun 🐾. An old-fashioned 300-year-old free house with a log fire, and outdoor tables that catch the evening sun. Local beers draw in a local crowd on Friday evenings, and jolly Coast-to-Coast cyclists at the weekend. Meals are now only served to guests in the simple B&B rooms upstairs.

Hemmal Café & Farm Shop Allenheads ✆ 01434 685568 ⊙ Thu–Tue 🐾. Popular café and gift shop in a converted cow barn attracting cyclists and day-trippers on fine days when tables in the sheltered courtyard get snapped up. When the weather turns, warm yourself by the log burner inside. The breakfast menu includes all the usual full-English items and a hot veggie and vegan option. Lunches are mainly cold, with a few hot plates including burgers; cakes are delicious and made locally. Free Wi-Fi is helpful in this mobile-signal dead zone, and there's a little play area nearby.

27 ALLENDALE

A tangle of streets at the heart of Allendale reveals the town's medieval origins but most of the buildings date to the 19th century. Squeezed among them are a scattering of 18th-century houses, a couple of Methodist chapels, a reading room, an old pharmacy with heritage features including vintage bottles in the window, a village hall, an original Co-operative food store, a post office, and a handful of venerable inns. Many buildings still have their original lettering and frontages. One fetching detail worth mentioning is the **sundial** on the south aisle wall of **St Cuthbert's Church**. Inscribed on the face are the co-ordinates '54 50' to reflect the (much-debated) claim that Allendale stands at the centre of Britain.

The **Allendale Forge Studios** (Market Pl ✐ 01434 683975 ◷ Wed–Mon ♿) is an artists' co-operative on the site of an old blacksmiths where accomplished craftsmen and women produce and display their works: jewellery, knitted clothes, photography, handmade cosmetics, artworks and so on. Plenty of low-priced gifts here alongside a café serving breakfasts and lunches.

Round the corner from the Forge Studios in the marketplace is one of the quirkiest and certainly the most unexpected museum to find in the Pennines: **The Museum of Classic Sci-Fi** (Osborne House ◷ Mon & Fri–Sun). Collector, schoolteacher and sci-fi obsessive Neil Cole transformed the 300-year-old cellar of a Georgian townhouse into a Tardis-like retirement home for over 200 sci-fi costumes and props featured in television and films over the last 50-odd years. *Doctor Who* is best represented, alongside the likes of *Planet of the Apes*, the Marvel films, *Star Trek* and *Star Wars*. Visitors travel from many corners to delight in the restored costumes and accompanying video recordings.

On heading north out of Allendale, just before the B6295 crosses the River East Allen, a turning on your right leads into the **Allen Mill** heritage park (NE47 9EA). Once a centre for lead processing in the 17th century, the complex of low-rise buildings houses a couple of places to eat and shop, with a **sculpture trail** being developed around the wider historic site where an old smelt mill once operated. The well-known **Allendale Brewery** is based here, as well as the studio of local nature and travel portrait artist, **Carol Davison**. **Coffee & Kuriosities** (✐ 01434 671601 ◷ Thu–Sun ♿ 🐾) is a café and gift shop run by a marvellous cake baker and her wood-craftsman partner who makes hand-turned gifts.

ALLENDALE BA'AL FESTIVAL

New Year's Eve in Allendale is a spectacle of fire, light, ceremony and drunkenness that begins long before local men dressed in costume called 'Guisers' (a hereditary position) parade in a circuit around the town centre with flaming tar barrels on their heads, and ends in a raucous celebration in the streets and pubs. The procession, thought to have Pagan origins, is timed so that the men return to the centre and tip their barrels into the huge bonfire in the marketplace, setting it alight on the stroke of midnight.

SCENIC ROAD: ALLENDALE TO CARRSHIELD

Traversing the high moors between the East and West Allen valleys is a memorable journey by road or across country following Isaac's Tea Trail (page 397) or the old packhorse route, the Carriers' Way. There are a few routes that take motorists and cyclists high up on to the Pennine moors where snow posts line the verges and the views extend for many miles, including **Allendale to Coalcleugh** and this route from **Allendale to Carrshield**.

On rising out of Allendale, a blanket of heather and windswept cotton grasses dominate the plateau of **Dryburn Moor**, with uninterrupted views all around. It's pretty desolate, which is this landscape's greatest appeal, but the moors are not featureless or without wildlife. The skylark can always be relied upon up here and if you pull over, you may hear the plaintive 'pu-pee-oo' cry of the golden plover. Two prominent lead-mining chimneys punctuate the skyline 2½ miles southwest of Allendale (♀ NY807537) and below them, a raised turf mound shoots across the landscape – one of the old 'horizontal chimneys' or smelting mill flues so prevalent in these parts.

⅋⅋ FOOD & DRINK

For inexpensive sandwiches, scones or a bowl of soup, there are three perfectly fine places to choose from in the marketplace, including the **Allendale Forge Studios** (page 390) for breakfasts and lunches. **The Lion House** (Market Place ✆ 01434 683225 ☉ daily 🐾) offers a few decent local beers and roasts on Sunday, or you might want to take a trip into the surrounding countryside to one of two good pubs: **The Crown** (see below) or the **Carts Bog Inn** (page 394).

The Crown Catton NE47 9QS ✆ 07872 975213 ☉ from 16.00 Thu–Sun (closed Sun in winter) ♿. The view is a huge draw for those looking for a country pub lunch in the Allendale area, particularly on sunny days when you can sit in the garden looking out over fields and the heather-topped Pennine moors. Local ales and a changing pop-up menu: from fish and chips to Indian street food. Folk music nights and various community events.
Jill's Catton NE47 9LT ✆ 07957 571885 ☉ Fri–Sun 🐾. Quite wonderfully situated on a hillside with expansive views of Allendale's countryside is this timber hut run by a fantastic cook who makes everything on the menu from scratch: coleslaw to cakes; pies to pastries. Her gooseberry tart is delicious. Sit outside and watch lapwings tumbling across the surrounding farmland.

28 LANGLEY CASTLE & SURROUNDS

Places of interest around Langley, not far from Hexham, must be hunted out – some more than others. Langley Castle is signposted off the A686,

but finding the old lead smelt mill, flue, and one of the most complete 19th-century collieries in England (see below), requires a bit of detective work with an OS Explorer map

One of the most impressive defensive tower houses in Northumberland, **Langley Castle** (NE47 5LU ✆ 01434 688888) is immediately impressive, with embattled turrets on each corner of a central block, and much wow factor. Though restored in the 19th century, much of what you see is the original 1350 building with 7ft-thick walls, huge fireplaces, a chapel and some of the best-preserved medieval garderobes you will find anywhere.

Now an upmarket hotel and popular wedding venue in landscaped grounds inhabited by resident peacocks, the owners have gone to town with plush pseudo-medieval furnishings (red fabrics, tapestries and dark wooden furniture) to reflect the castle's medieval origins. Non-guests can dine here or take afternoon tea (page 394).

Like many manmade pools in the North Pennines, **Langley Reservoir** was built to power the now demolished smelt mills, but you can walk up to a surviving **chimney** by taking the B6305 away from the reservoir in the direction of Hexham. You can't miss it at the top of the hill, but you might overlook its **flue** – a 'horizontal chimney' that runs across the fields for nearly a mile (now cut by the B6305), connecting the

"Langley Castle is immediately impressive, with embattled turrets on each corner of a central block."

mill to the vertical chimney. Like those elsewhere in the Pennines, it was designed to release harmful lead and silver vapours and particles away from human habitation and farmland. The grassy mound can be seen from the road (♀ NY838611) and the tunnel opening is visible from old Langley Station. **The Garden Station** (Langley NE47 5LA ☉ daily unless closed for private functions), as it is now known, is a wonderfully lush place for a wander among the profusion of plants lining the platform and disused railway line. Weekend tabletop sales are sometimes held inside the fetching old waiting room.

Most remarkable of all the industrial buildings and structures remaining in this area is the early 19th-century **Stublick Colliery**

◀ **1** While Langley Castle was restored in the 19th century, much of what you will see is the original 1350 building. **2** Allendale's Museum of Classic Sci-Fi. **3** New Year's Eve in Allendale at the Ba'al Festival.

BLACK GOLD

Evidence of lead mining in the North Pennines appears from medieval times, though it's very likely the Romans also mined here. Boom time came in the mid 18th century and lasted for over a century but the industry crashed in the 1870s when cheaper markets for lead opened on the continent. At its peak in the 1860s, the North Pennines produced a quarter of Britain's lead.

The two big lead-mining companies operating in the North Pennines (W B Lead in the Allendales and Weardale, and the London Lead Company in Teesdale and Alston area) had a profound impact on the character of settlements through their promotion of obedience, discipline and education, which is partly why you see so many chapels, schools, reading rooms and mine agents' houses in Pennine villages. Allenheads and Nenthead are good examples.

Miners received paltry recompense for the lead ore they dug and for their reduced life expectancy due to breathing in dangerous dust, so it became commonplace in the 18th and 19th centuries for them to supplement their income by farming. Small houses and enclosed fields, known as 'allotments', are still extant on some North Pennine hillsides.

(500yds north of the B6295/B6304 junction), considered one of the best examples of its type in the region, which once extracted coal to power the smelt mills. It retains its engine houses and chimneys and, though there's no public access to the derelict site, you can view the group of buildings from the road.

¶¶ FOOD & DRINK

Carts Bog Inn Langley NE47 5NW ✆ 01434 684338 ☺ lunch & evening meals Wed–Sat, lunch Sun ♿ through the back door 🐾 bar only. Make sure you come on an empty stomach – the dishes are filling and portions generous, especially their signature dish: the Bog Pie filled with beef, mushrooms and bacon. A traditional 18th-century coaching inn, the Carts Bog is a welcome sight in remote countryside. Much of the food is sourced from the area, with local beef, game from the Northumbrian hills and fish from North Shields. While the inn now has new owners, the menu remains more or less the same: chicken stuffed with haggis; salmon; lamb; scampi; and of course the famously good Bog Pie. Local ales.

Langley Castle Langley, near Hexham NE47 5LU ✆ 01434 688888. Intimate evening tables in a medieval tower house, for which you must book ahead and expect to pay a fair whack for a three-course dining 'experience' in the plush Josephine Restaurant (all gold and reds in keeping with the medieval décor, oil paintings, heavy quilted drapes, candlesticks on white linen tablecloths and so on). To start, you could choose the pigeon breast with baked celeriac and black pudding; for your main course, something from the grill or venison with mushrooms and a blackberry sauce.

Lighter lunches (hot sandwiches, soups, fish goujons, burgers) are served in more casual surroundings but scones and afternoon teas (book in advance) are enjoyed in the medieval-styled drawing room (log fires, tapestries, exposed stone walls, chandeliers) for those wanting to pop in and savour the period building.

29 ALLEN BANKS & STAWARD GORGE

South of the River Tyne, between Haydon Bridge & Bardon Mill ♀ NY798640. Allen Banks is easily reached by road from the A69 (look out for the brown signpost which directs road users to a designated car park) or travel on foot from Bardon Mill railway station in under an hour (1½ miles) via Beltingham; National Trust

Under the boughs of oak trees and around boulders and shingle banks where herons stand by the river's edge and dippers dive from rocks into the water, the River Allen flows lazily through a steep-sided wooded gorge on its way to the Tyne.

In spring, the familiar tunes of woodland birds are occasionally interrupted by a more unusual song: the rhythmic notes of a pied flycatcher or the coin-spinning song of a wood warbler, both birds newly returned from Africa and infrequently heard elsewhere in Northumberland. In wood clearings look out for **wild pansies** – this area is well known for them – and, in the conifer trees, red squirrels.

"In spring, the familiar tunes of woodland birds are occasionally interrupted by a more unusual song: the rhythmic notes of a pied flycatcher."

Allen Banks is a precious broad-leaved woodland – ancient in places – and utterly enchanting: visit on a balmy summer's evening when swifts are gliding above the canopy and the first bats have emerged to catch insects by the river, and you'll see what I mean; glimpsing an otter on an evening like this would not be unheard of.

A number of the footpaths, river crossings and summerhouses were installed over a 35-year period from around the 1830s by the estate owner at the time, Susan Davidson, who also planted many of the mature beech trees you see on the banksides. This was her 'wilderness garden' and it remains wonderfully rampant and romantic to this day.

Footpaths are well-trodden and easy to navigate, particularly the popular 1½-mile riverside trail to **Plankey Mill** (OS Explorer map OL43 might come in handy) via **Briarwood Banks**, a precious semi-natural

SS

SS

SANDRA STANDBRIDGE/S

DAVE HEAD/S

ISAAC'S TEA TRAIL

This little-known 37-mile circular trail (marked on OS Explorer maps) from Allendale takes in some of the best moorland and valley scenery in the North Pennines, encompassing the East and West Allen valleys and a stretch of the Pennine Way along the South Tyne.

The circuit follows in the footsteps of **Isaac Holden**, a devout Methodist and philanthropist who travelled the Pennines in the mid 19th century selling tea and raising money for good causes. Most walkers set foot from **Allendale** in a southerly direction following the River East Allen upstream before hiking out over heather moorland to **Nenthead** and then on to **Alston**. From here, the trail swings north on the Pennine Way before breaking out across high ground and dipping into the West Allen valley at **Ninebanks**. The last eight miles or so from Ninebanks to Allendale is a walker's delight: across meadows and along the verdant River East Allen with its many overhanging trees. It's on this final three-mile leg that you will also pass **Keenley Chapel** (♀ NY803567), one of the oldest Methodist chapels in the world, dating to 1750 – soon after John Wesley preached here under a sycamore tree. It was largely rebuilt in the late 19th century and remains delightfully remote.

woodland managed by the Northumberland Wildlife Trust. Extending this route to **Staward Gorge** (a steep climb through the wooded valley, but the views over the canopy from the pele tower at the top are worth the effort) and back to the car park would make for a round trip of 5½ miles. At the time of writing, some paths were closed due to storm damage. Check online at ᛩ nationaltrust.org.uk/allenbanks for the latest on path closures.

30 WHITFIELD, NINEBANKS & THE WEST ALLEN VALLEY

The quiet sheep-grazed meadows and steep wooded slopes of the **West Allen Valley** are sparsely populated – and very beautiful in summer. Miles of riverside walking are made possible by lacing together Isaac's Tea Trail (see above) with some other minor paths that connect the two Allen rivers.

Whitfield is scattered about a bit with a pub, a surprisingly grand Victorian church, a fist of houses and a shop-cum-café. If you turn uphill

◄ **1** The remains of a smelting flue on Dryburn Moor. **2** You may spot the day-flying short-eared owl over the North Pennine moors. **3 & 4** Look for pied flycatchers at Staward Gorge.

by Whitfield Village Pantry, you'll reach a primary school opposite a tiny 18th-century **church** high above the lapwing-populated valley.

One conspicuous building in the hamlet of **Ninebanks** stands out from the 18th-century miners' houses and farm buildings: a defensive **pele tower** dating to the times of the Border Reiver conflicts in the 16th century. The **church**, half a mile south, is notable for its stone hearse house (which once housed the village's horse-drawn funeral cart), built in the 19th century with money raised by local philanthropist and tea peddler, Isaac Holden (page 397).

¶¶ FOOD & DRINK

Whitfield Village Pantry Whitfield NE47 8HA ℰ 01434 345709 ☉ variable so phone to check but usually mornings Mon & Sun, 08.00–16.00 Tue–Sat ♿. Pleasant little café and community hub serving breakfasts, sandwiches, jackets, soups, cakes and scones. You can also pick up the papers and basic food cupboard items.

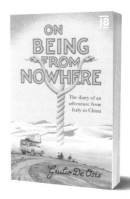

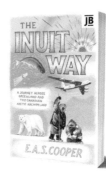

INDEX

Entries in **bold** refer to major entries; those in *italics* indicate maps.

bridges
Berwick-upon-Tweed
145, **153**
Chantry Footbridge,
Morpeth 274
Coquet 214
Cupola Bridge 386
Featherstone Bridge 371
High Level Bridge,
Newcastle 29, **32**
Linnels Bridge 376
Lion Bridge, Alnwick 16,
79, **82**
medieval 77, 93, 175, 214
Millennium Bridge,
Newcastle–Gateshead
31–2
North Tyne 268, 309
railway 55, 334, 338 *see
also* High Level Bridge
Roman 309
Royal Border Bridge,
Berwick 153
South Tyne 364, 371
Swing Bridge, Newcastle
29, 32
Till 164, 175
Tweed 153, 157, 162
Twizel Bridge 16, 164
Tyne **32**, 338, 348
Union Chain Bridge 157
Wallington's Palladian
bridge 291
Wansbeck 274, 291
Warkworth Old Bridge 93
Weetwood Bridge 175
Brigantium Roman Fort 237
Brinkburn Priory **211–14**
Brizlee Tower, Alnwick 84
Brocolitia Roman Fort *see*
Carrawbrough Roman Fort
Bronze Age sites 165, 174,
203, 229–30
Brough Law hillfort 204–5
Brown, Lancelot 'Capability'
81, 84, 248, 252, **289**, 291
Budle Bay 126, **130**
bus travel 18, 333–4 *see also*
getting around
Byker **42**, 47
Byrness 236
Bywell 346

C
Cambo 289, **291–2**
Cambois Bay 70
camping 116, 139, 156, 244,
252–3, 256, 259, 305 *see
also* wild camping
Carey Burn Linn 191

Carlisle Park, Morpeth 272,
274–5
Carrawbrough Roman
Fort 310
Carter Bar **235**
castles
Alnwick **80–2**, 84, 236
Aydon 16, **353–4**
Bamburgh 65, **125–6**
Belsay 284–6
Berwick 153
Bothal 279
Bywell 346
Chillingham 176–80
Chipchase 270
Dilston 377
Dunstanburgh **107–8**,
114–15
Edlingham **209**, 216
Elsdon motte & bailey 240
Etal 165–8
Featherstone 371
Ford 171–2
Harbottle 223–4
Haughton 270
Kielder 259
Langley 393
Lindisfarne 133, **136–7**
Mitford 277
Morpeth 275
Newcastle (Keep) **34**, 47
Norham 15, **161**
Prudhoe 341–3
Simonburn 269
Thirlwall 324
Twizel 164
Tynemouth 56
Warkworth 93–4
Willimoteswyke 367
Catcleugh Reservoir 235
cetaceans 12, 112, 119, **124**
Chain Bridge Honey Farm
158
Charlton 252
Chatton 174–6
Chattonpark Hill **175–6**, 218
Cheese Farm 283
Cherryburn 343–4
Chesterholm Roman
Milestone 318
Chesters Roman Fort 307–9
Cheswick Sands 67, **142**
Cheviot, The 189, 196–7,
200–2
Cheviot goats 193, **195**
Cheviot Hills 189–207,
226–34
Cheviot valleys
Breamish (Ingram)
203–7, 216

Cheviot valleys *continued…*
College 192, **193–6**
Happy 202–3
Harthope 200–3
Upper Coquetdale 219–34
Chew Green Roman camp
233, **237**
Chillingham Castle and Park
176–80
Chipchase Castle 270
Chollerton 270–2
churches 165, 189
All Saints, Newcastle 32, 35
All Saints, Rothbury 214
All Saints, Ryal 294
Biddlestone Catholic
Chapel, Alwinton 220
Brinkburn Priory 211–14
Christ Church, Hepple 221
fortified 165
Gibside Chapel 51
Hexham Abbey 356–9
Holy Cross, Haltwhistle 368
Holy Paraclete, Kirkhaugh
371, **372**
Holy Trinity, Berwick-
upon-Tweed 149
Holy Trinity, Cambo 291
Holy Trinity, Embleton 108
Holy Trinity, Matfen 294
Holy Trinity, Old Bewick
165, **181**
Holy Trinity, Whitfield
397–8
Keenley Methodist
Chapel, Allendale 397
Ladykirk 160
Our Lady, Seaton Delaval
Hall 69–70
St Aidan's, Bamburgh 129
St Aidan's, Fourstones 363
St Aidan's, Thorneyburn
249–51
St Andrew's, Bothal 279
St Andrew's, Bywell 346
St Andrew's, Corbridge
165, **348–9**
St Andrew's, Heddon-on-
the-Wall 306
St Andrew's, Newcastle 35
St Anne's, Ancroft 165
St Bartholomew's,
Newbiggin-by-the-
Sea 71
St Bartholomew's,
Whittingham 208
St Cuthbert's, Allendale
389–90
St Cuthbert's, Bellingham
165, **244–5**

churches *continued…*
St Cuthbert's, Beltingham
366–7
St Cuthbert's, Corsenside
165
St Cuthbert's, Elsdon 165,
241–2
St Cuthbert's, Norham 160
St Cuthbert's Chapel,
Farne Islands 124
St Ebba's, Beadnell
116–18
St Francis of Assisi,
Byrness 236
St Giles's, Chollerton 270
St Gregory's, Kirknewton
192
St Helen's, Whitley Chapel
380
St John the Baptist,
Edlingham 165, **209**
St Lawrence's, Warkworth
92
St Mark's, Ninebanks 398
St Mary and St Michael's,
Doddington 174
St Mary Magdalene,
Mitford 277
St Mary Magdalene,
Whalton 287
St Mary the Virgin, Slaley
381
St Mary's, Belford 132
St Mary's, Blanchland 384
St Mary's, Lindisfarne 135
St Mary's, Morpeth 275
St Mary's, Newton-by-
the-Sea 110
St Mary's, Ovingham
340–1
St Mary's, Ponteland
165, **281**
St Mary's, Stamfordham
296
St Mary's Catholic
Cathedral, Newcastle 35
St Mary's Chapel, Etal 167
St Maurice, Eglingham
181
St Michael and All Angels,
Alwinton 226
St Michael and All Angels,
Ford 165, **171**
St Michael and All Angels,
Ingram 207
St Michael's, Alnwick 83–4
St Mungo's, Simonburn
269
St Nicholas's Cathedral,
Newcastle 35

THE BRADT STORY

In the beginning

It all began in 1974 on an Amazon river barge. During an 18-month trip through South America, two adventurous young backpackers – Hilary Bradt and her then husband, George – decided to write about the hiking trails they had discovered through the Andes. *Backpacking Along Ancient Ways in Peru and Bolivia* included the very first descriptions of the Inca Trail. It was the start of a colourful journey to becoming one of the best-loved travel publishers in the world; you can read the full story on our website (**bradtguides. com/ourstory**).

Getting there first

Hilary quickly gained a reputation for being a true travel pioneer, and in the 1980s she started to focus on guides to places overlooked by other publishers. The Bradt Guides list became a roll call of guidebook 'firsts'. We published the first guide to Madagascar, followed by Mauritius, Czechoslovakia and Vietnam. The 1990s saw the beginning of our extensive coverage of Africa: Tanzania, Uganda, South Africa, and Eritrea. Later, post-conflict guides became a feature: Rwanda, Mozambique, Angola, and Sierra Leone, as well as the first standalone guides to the Baltic States following the fall of the Iron Curtain, and the first post-war guides to Bosnia, Kosovo and Albania.

Comprehensive – and with a conscience

Today, we are the world's largest independently owned travel publisher, with more than 200 titles. However, our ethos remains unchanged. Hilary is still keenly involved, and **we still get there first**: two-thirds of Bradt guides have no direct competition.

But we don't just get there first. Our guides are also known for being **more comprehensive** than any other series. We avoid templates and tick-lists. Each guide is a one-of-a-kind expression of an expert author's interests, knowledge and enthusiasm for telling it how it really is.

And a commitment to wildlife, conservation and respect for local communities has always been at the heart of our books. Bradt Guides was **championing sustainable travel** before any other guidebook publisher. We even have a series dedicated to Slow Travel in the UK, award-winning books that explore the country with a passion and depth you'll find nowhere else.

Thank you!

We can only do what we do because of the support of readers like you – people who value less-obvious experiences, less-visited places and a more thoughtful approach to travel. Those who, like us, take travel seriously.

Bradt GUIDES
TRAVEL TAKEN SERIOUSLY